292
QR

THE COMPLETE
ENCYCLOPEDIA OF
GREEK
MYTHOLOGY

THE COMPLETE ENCYCLOPEDIA OF

GREEK MYTHOLOGY

The world of the Greek gods and heroes
in words and pictures

GUUS HOUTZAGER

REBO PUBLISHERS

© 2003 Rebo International b. v., The Netherlands

Text: Guus Houtzager
Production: TextCase, Groningen, The Netherlands
Illustrations: Janneke Maas
Photographs: Allard Pierson Museum, Artis Planotarium, Artmaster/Cinemaster,
Fokke van Balen, Museum Duijmano van Beuningen, Kitty Coert, Dordrechts Museum,
Renate Hagenouw, Guus Houtzager, Kunsthandel Mieke Zilverberg,
Munt and Pennigkabinet
Redaction: Lieneke Ipema, Renate Hagenouw (for TextCase)
Cover design: Minkowsky Graphics, Enkhuizen, The Netherlands
Layout: Studio Imago, Amersfoort, The Netherlands

ISBN 90 366 15011

Contents

Introduction

Greek Mythology Through the Ages

Despite almost twenty centuries of Christianity, the gods and heroes of ancient Greece and Rome are far from forgotten. The ruins of the temples where they were once revered still attract millions of tourists annually, their representations are considered to be priceless works art, and the ancient tales about them remain as popular as ever. Greek mythology, the whole range of stories about the world of the Greek gods, is therefore an incomparable cultural treasure trove, a fascinating monument of human imagery and story-telling.

Myths are stories about the gods that were probably originally developed in order to explain natural phenomena and incomprehensible events on earth (such as life and death, or the workings of fate). In early cultures, in which no trace of scientific knowledge existed, people needed to explain the fact that, due to some secret force, crops emerged from the soil regularly every year. This force was personified as a god or goddess. With the passage of time, new properties were attributed to the forces that caused the natural phenomena to occur, and more stories and legends became associated with them. In this way, mythologies and mythological systems emerged, many of which were highly complex and intricate.

The ruins of ancient buildings are major attractions that have fascinated visitors since the Renaissance period. Oil painting by Pietro Capelli, 17th–18th century.

Greek mythology is one of the greatest cultural treasures known to man. In this 18th-century oil painting by Arnold Houbraken, Athena, who was also the goddess of arts and crafts, visits Apollo and the Muses, the protectresses of the Arts.

In contrast to the mythologies of many other cultures, Greek mythology is noticeably light-hearted and cheerful, and this has certainly done much to ensure its enduring popularity. Not that the more sinister sides of existence were neglected by the ancient Greeks. The major gods were certainly not seen by them as lacking in grim aspects. In the case of life after death, the Greeks had fewer illusions than most other nations but an ominous

The stories of Greek mythology are often characterized by a certain graceful elegance. Here, a boy is shown climbing onto a sea monster. Painting on an Athenian vase, 6th century BCE

A glimpse of the night sky was sufficient to remind the ancient Greeks of their mythical world. Many signs of the zodiac signs are still referred to by the names of characters in Greek mythology. Ancient ceiling paintings depict signs of the zodiac.

Artemis, the virginal goddess of the hunt and of unspoiled nature, had a sweet as well as fierce side to her character. Her arrows could bring death and destruction. Statue from Antalya, Turkey.

Mythology was inextricably linked with the religion of ancient Greece. Offering scene, painted on an Athenian vessel, 5th century BCE

The ancient gods were omnipresent and were even depicted on currency. Roman silver coin (denarius) dated 61 BCE showing Ceres (Demeter) the goddess of agriculture.

Landscape on Crete. Crete was viewed as the cradle of Greek civilization.

Triumphal arch of the Roman emperor Constantine the Great. Constantine recognized Christianity in the 4th century CE as the official religion of the Roman Empire.

expectation about an inevitable end to the world and to all creation, such as can be found in Germanic mythology or the myths of the natives of Central America , was absent from them.

This does not mean that a constant representation of all the gods and heroes existed throughout Antiquity. Given the length of this time period this would have been impossible. What is normally referred to as "Greek culture" existed around 2000 BCE on the island of Crete. When the Roman Empire finally fell in 476 CE this culture came to an end and a new period in western history—the Dark Ages—began followed, in around 1000 CE, by the Middle Ages. The traditional Greco-Roman culture, along with its religion and mythology, were well past their prime by the fifth century of the common era. Around a century earlier, Christianity had been adopted as the official religion of the Roman and the early Christians were anything but tolerant of the old "heathen" world view. Their one God rapidly replaced and superseded the many ancient gods, who led a kind of shadowy underground existence in the Middle Ages and were only rediscovered centuries later.

Even in its heyday, Greco-Roman mythol-

ogy was not a static set of beliefs in which fixed, dogmatic ideas existed about the gods. The representation of the gods and their

The conquest of Alexander the Great resulted in the spread of Greek culture throughout the Middle East. Head of Alexander on a gold coin (stater) from Amphipolis, 4th century BCE

The Pantheon in Rome, one of the oldest buildings of the Western world still remaining intact. The Pantheon was built in the 2nd century CE as a temple to all the Roman gods, hence the name, meaning "All the gods."

worship altered and developed rapidly. The importance of some gods increased and that of others decreased. There were also large regional differences. Some gods were worshiped fanatically in certain areas, but were seen as insignificant in others. In this respect, it is important to realize that "ancient Greece" covered a much greater area than modern Greece. The Greek world, which in ancient times never formed a single political unit but was composed of many city-states and small empires, also included the western part of Asia Minor (present-day Turkey) and the islands off its shores, as well as Sicily and Southern Italy, which were colonized in the eighth and seventh centuries BCE by Greek seafarers and traders. When the Greek world suddenly expanded in the fourth century BCE, into the vast Macedonian Empire created the conqueror Alexander the Great, Greek culture and mythology became a very successful "export." In the entire Middle East and Mediterranean region, the Greek gods merged with the ancient local gods, so that Greek mythology itself was also "enriched" with eastern features.

The Romans, who later incorporated the Greek world into their gigantic empire, looked up to Greek civilization, which they already knew at close quarters from the colonies in Southern Italy, known as Magna Græcia. Not only did well-to-do Romans begin to speak Greek with each other, but even Greek mythology was adopted by the Romans. Ancient Roman and Italian gods (Italian refers to the Italian peninsula in ancient times) were therefore "identified with" comparable Greek gods—the same fusion that took place

From the Renaissance onward, artists returned to mythological themes. This river-god that decorates one of the Quattro Fontane on the Quirinale in Rome dates from the late 16th century.

Remains of ancient buildings have contributed to our knowledge of mythology. Ruins of a temple dedicated to the goddess Hera in the Valle dei Templi on Sicily.

throughout the Mediterranean world. Most of the gods retained their Roman names but, for instance, Jupiter, the ancient Roman god of heaven and the elements was identified with the supreme Greek god Zeus, Venus, the Roman goddess of love was identified with her Greek counterpart Aphrodite, and so on. The myths about the Greek gods were now also linked to the Roman gods, while the existing myths and traditions connected with them continued to flourish. In this way, mythology remained a vital and lively concern, that was continuously refashioned and reinvented in everyday life, as well as in the work of painters, sculptors, poets, and writers.

Thanks to these all these great artists, mythology was brought back to life again from the Renaissance period onward, when Christianity was beginning to lose its grip on Western thought. Painters such as Raphael and Michelangelo went down to view underground remains of ancient Roman palaces and discovered frescoes of unimaginable beauty, that were to greatly influence their own work. In the libraries of ancient monasteries, classical texts were researched by authors. The original manuscripts had not always been well cared for and often needed diligent reconstruction. Knowledge of Latin, the language

of the ancient Romans, was well maintained in the Middle Ages, mainly due to the fact that it was the official language of the church, but the knowledge of ancient Greek had to be thoroughly "revived" by humanists such as the Dutch scholar, Erasmus. Anyone from the time of the Renaissance onward who has taken an interest in mythology is, compared with the ancient Greeks and Romans, like someone at an advanced age who tries to learn a foreign language from a book. Mythology is no longer fed automatically to the people of the modern world, they have acquired their knowledge of it from the carefully reprinted works of the ancient writers and from painted vases, sculptures, frescoes, and other material remains of the ancient world.

Amazingly enough, Greek mythology has been more than just rediscovered and reconstructed. While the accompanying religious worship is no longer practiced, having been replaced by the monotheistic religions, this has not prevented later generations from seeking inspiration from the ancient myths and building on this foundation. Ever since the Italian poet, Dante Alighieri, one of the founders of the Renaissance, in his major poetic work, *The Divine Comedy*, allowed himself to be guided through the fires of hell by

The myth of the hunter Actaeon, who accidentally caught a glimpse of the virgin goddess Artemis and her nymphs bathing naked and was punished in a terrible manner for doing so, was more than just an erotic horror story. Oil painting by Andreas Goetting, 17th century.

the Roman poet Virgil, a great many painters, writers, and composers have allowed themselves to be influenced by classical mythology. The great Athenian dramas about Œdipus, the Theban king who murdered his father and married his mother, became a model for numerous writings on the same theme, from the father of psychiatry, Sigmund Freud, to the playwright Stephen Berkoff .

The myth of Orpheus, the musician of genius whose playing conjured his dead love, Eurydice, back to the land of the living, has inspired many composers, including Glück and Meyerbeer. Artists not only admired the works of their great forebears from the age of Antiquity, but also read the classics. Thus, over the past five hundred years a great many mythological tales retold by the Roman poet Ovid have been "illustrated" by the Old Masters, while no less an artist than Pablo Picasso was obsessed with the myth of the Minotaur, the savage beast, half-man, half-bull, that lived in the Labyrinth on the island of Crete.

The great attraction of the Greek myths lies, to a great extent, in their universal application to human behavior. Many myths at first appear fantastical, comical, absurd, or even ridiculous, but on closer examination they seem to contain a deeper wisdom or hidden meaning.

Take the story of Actæon, the unlucky hunter who accidentally came upon Artemis,

A "powerful mother goddess" was originally worshiped on Crete. These women may have been the priestesses of this goddess. Painting from the palace at Knossos

13

According to the ancient Greeks, the summit of mount Olympus, frequently shrouded in mist, was the home of the twelve Olympic gods.

The supreme Greek god Zeus was god of the heavens. He could produce thunderbolts, cloud cover, rain, hail and snow. Bronze statue from Egypt, Roman period, early modern era.

the virginal goddess of nature, while she was bathing, and was transformed by her into a deer, to be torn to pieces by his own hunting-dogs. This seems at first glance to be little more than a rather nasty fairytale with an erotic flavor. Yet when considering the story on a deeper level, the myth can be seen as a comment on the relationship between man and nature. When man treats unspoiled nature disrespectfully, nature will take its revenge. This is one possible message that can be gleaned from the story.

Many of the ancient myths are almost certainly conceived in this way. the story of Actæon and Artemis was probably part of the ritual connected with the hunt. It is interesting to note, in this respect, that in a totally separate culture—that of the Mayas of Central America—similar myths and rituals existed that are reminiscent of the myth of Actæon. The purpose of these hunting rituals was to appease the gods of the forest, from whom something which they own is being "snatched" during the hunt.

Much more could be written about the similarities between myths of different cultures, but there is no room to dwell on this subject. Let us now consider the general concept that the ancient Greeks and Romans shared about the world of their gods.

The Representation of the World of the Greek Gods

It has been shown in the preceding paragraphs that the period known loosely as "Ancient Greece and Rome" lasted for a very long time. The era was, furthermore, far from being static and experienced many far-reaching developments, including in the areas of religion and mythology.

Exactly what was considered as religion and myth in early Greek culture can no longer be established with certainty. Written sources of the period are lacking, but everything points to the theory that, as in many other prehistoric cultures, a supreme mother goddess was worshiped. It seems that on Crete, the cradle of Greek civilization, a primitive earth-mother was worshiped, who was responsible for the fertility of the crops and the earth. On Crete, a kind of cult of the bull must also have existed, as indicated by countless images, as well the Greek myths about Crete, that evolved much later, in which bulls play a major role. In Asia Minor, (present day Turkey) both the mother goddess and the bull have been worshiped. Later conquerors, who came from the north in the second millennium before Christ, probably worshiped heavenly gods. After a period of time, these new gods forced the mother goddess and the other earth and fertility gods into second place.

Much of this theory is based on speculation, but what is certain is that in Greek mythology known to us from written sources, of which the earliest examples date from around 800 BCE, the heavenly gods occupy the place of honor. The supreme Greek god was called Zeus (Jupiter by the Romans). He was also the god of thunder, lightning, and all other heavenly phenomena. According to the most representations, he could take on human form and lived in a palace on Olympus, a mountain 9700 feet high, in the border region between Thessalonika and Macedonia. From its centuries old snow-capped peak, often covered by clouds, Zeus looked down upon the earth and human beings, and when he found it necessary he intervened in earthly affairs, by sending bolts of lightning, for example, to strike those people who disobeyed his rules. Zeus was surrounded by a ring of eleven other "Olympic" gods (as well as some immortal servants). They also looked like humans, were members of his family, and "managed" certain natural phenomena or abstract concepts. These gods had subjected themselves to Zeus, but did not truly recognize his authority, and frequently opposed it, until Zeus brought

As well as the gods themselves, many supernatural beings of a lower level appeared in Greek mythology, among them satyrs. Head of a satyr in pottery from Sicily, 5th century BCE.

order to their activities once again. There were also various minor gods of the earth and sea , who were subservient to the inhabitants of Olympus.

The most important gods besides Zeus were his brothers, Poseidon (the Roman Neptune) and Hades, who ruled respectively over water

The Olympic gods, who lived with Zeus on Olympus, resting beside a nymphaeum. Oil painting by Maerten van Heemskerck, 16th century.

Each river in Greek mythology is personified by a separate god. This statue of the river god of the Nile dating from the 4th century CE has graced the Piazza del Campidoglio in Rome since the 16th century.

and the underworld. They were the peers of Zeus, yet they accepted him as the supreme god. The Greeks envisaged the world as a flat disk, covered by the lands of which they were aware. They knew of the existence of India, Northern Europe, and the northern part of Africa, but America, China, and Japan were still beyond their horizon. This world disk was surrounded by a ring of water, the world sea or Ocean, named for the god Oceanus, who reigned over it. The sky rested on this flat world, presented as a dome-shaped firmament. Across this firmament, carried by the

The famous demigod from Greek mythology was Heracles, a son of the supreme god Zeus and the mortal woman Alcmene. This sarcophagus from Antalya (Turkey) depicts various scenes from the life of Heracles.

giant Atlas, the sun-god Helios traveled every day on his fiery sun-chariot. He departed every morning from the eastern side of the Ocean and reaching the western side in the evening, and journeying back at night by boat to the east again.

Under the world disk lay the dark underworld, the empire of the god Hades. This empire of the dead was inhabited by the shades or shadows of dead inhabitants of the earth. They did not experience pain or sorrow, but the Greco-roman underworld was no heavenly hereafter, either. The shadows were a kind of gray apparition, without consciousness or memory of their earthly existence. The deepest part of the underworld, the Tartarus, was a sort of hell, in which those who had committed grave sins against the gods and their laws suffered terrible, eternal punishment.

The gods themselves were immortal. Furthermore, they were blessed with eternal youth. Disease and physical disability were unknown to them. They ate a delicious, supernatural divine food called ambrosia, and drank nectar, a special divine drink. They were not, however, immune to pain and other physical discomforts for there were many stories about gods who suffered (minor) injuries. A brief treatment with ambrosia generally cured them of their ills.

The Olympic gods and goddesses, according to the general mythological vision of the world, while immortal, were not, apparently, eternal. The best known Greek tale of creation tells how, from a kind of primitive space called Chaos, Gaia, the earth-mother, was created. From her union with Uranus, god of the sky, twelve children resulted. These were the Titans, gigantic and somewhat primitive gods. The youngest of the Titans, Cronos, dethroned his father and took command of the universe. In order to avoid the same fate as Uranus, he killed the children born out of his union with his wife Rhea immediately after their birth, out of concern for their future. However, through Rhea's guile, Zeus, their youngest son, was spared and he disposed of his father later, after a long battle against Cronos and the other Titans (the "Battle of the Titans"). Thus began the world order as it existed in Greek mythology.

Besides the many gods, discussed in more detail in the encyclopedia section, there were many other kinds of supernatural and immortal beings, including river gods, nymphs, satyrs, centaurs, giants, and strange monsters. Sometimes these were "minor" gods, only worshiped in a particular locality; sometimes they were spirits from the natural world, who were connected to a particular tree, mountain, stream, or other location. If they played a part in important myths, they will be further discussed in the encyclopedia section.

On this relief carved from a stone wall in Arsameia (Turkey), a king is depicted shaking hands with the demigod Heracles. By using such examples, royalty suggested that they originated from the gods or that they ruled with a divine mandate.

There was yet another important category of beings, whose status lay somewhere between that of the gods and mortals. These were the demigods or heroes. As their name implies, they had one divine and one human parent. Thanks to their origins, they displayed certain supernatural powers, such as

Stone heads of gods and heroes at the archaeological site Nemrut Dagh in Turkey. Archaeological findings indicate that some mythological stories are (partially) based on historical fact.

incredible strength, great courage, or tremendous stamina. Despite this they were mortal, generally adding a tragic dimension to their lives. These demigods were the leading figures in many famous myths. The important demigods, such as Heracles (the Roman Hercules, who eventually attained immortality), Theseus, Perseus, and Achilles, were the subject of countless stories, sometimes with regional variations. Sovereigns identified with these demigods or claimed to be descended from them, and many cities boasted that they had been founded by a demigod.

Some heroes could not lay claim to divine origins, but were afforded the special protection of one or more gods. Odysseus, for instance, was one of the most famous figures from the whole panoply of Greek mythology, despite being an "ordinary" human. Without the constant support of the goddess Athena, however, he would never have succeeded in his adventures.

Mythology and Historical Fact

Myths and mythological stories do not have the same logic as real life. Not only is supernatural intervention on the part of the gods and all kinds of fairytale elements part of the fabric of the story, but the chronology frequently clashes with actual timespan. Some heroes lived to an incredibly great age, or were involved in events which, according to other stories, should have taken place long before their birth. The attentive reader will often be confronted with these kinds of inconsistencies. They are inherent in the mythical way of thinking, which does not depend on history and the chronological record of events, and often resulted from the fusion of traditions from various regions and cultures.

Many stories from Greek mythology are not mere fables completely divorced from reality. For instance, for a long time it was assumed that the Trojan war described by the poet Homer and other authors of antiquity was a complete fabrication, not based on actual occurrences. However, when, in the late nineteenth century, the German adventurer and amateur archaeologist, Heinrich Schliemann, excavated the exact spot described by Homer, he came upon the remains of an ancient city from ancient times—in fact, of several cities, which rose layer by layer from the ruins of each other. One of these cities was clearly

The Egyptian goddess Hathor depicted on the wall of a temple in Philae. The Greek historian and world traveler, Herodotus, was very interested in the connection between Greek and Egyptian gods.

seen to have been destroyed by a terrible fire identifying it as "Homer's Troy." The infamous battle, according to the proud discoverer, must have been fought there. The dating of the remains of this city more or less conformed to the chronology known to the ancients, according to whom the Trojan war took place around 1200 BCE. Had "the real Troy" been found? After around a hundred years of academic research this question is still the subject of heated debate among scholars and researchers, and a definitive conclusion has yet to be reached.

Later authors, such as Herodotus of Halicarnassus, who lived in the fifth century BCE, the first historian and travel writer of the western world, were supplemented by personal observations, stories from third parties, conjectures on the part of the author, and myths. Herodotus had a remarkably sober, critical attitude and used his powers of observation shrewdly during his long journeys through what, at that time, was uncharted territory. The origins of the Greek gods interested him and he devoted much consideration to the subject of the resemblances between Greek and Egyptian gods.

Written Sources

The two authors mentioned above are among to the few sources available on which to build a knowledge of Greek mythology. Homer, the poet with whom Greek—and therefore western —literary history begins, is one of the most important sources of information. Although there is some dispute as to whether the work attributed to him was, in fact, written by one man, very little is known about him and it is not even certain that he existed. It is assumed that Homer originated from Asia Minor (present day western Turkey) and that he lived in the first half of the eighth century before the common era. A tradition persists that Homer was blind, but the incredibly vivid visual descriptions in his work seem to belie this. In addition to the minor works that may not have actually been written by him, two of his narrative epic poems have survived—the *Iliad* and the *Odyssey*.

The *Iliad* describes an episode from the last year of the ten-year siege of the city of Troy. The great Greek hero, Achilles, refuses to continue to be involved in the battle, due to a conflict with his commander-in-chief, Agamemnon. Soon after his close friend Patroclus, who tries to help the beleaguered Greeks, is killed by Hector, the Trojan, Achilles once more springs into action. He kills Hector and defiles the body, by laying it in the dust before Patroclus' funerary bier. Eventually, he is prepared to hand over the body of Hector to the latter's aging father, King Priam of Troy.

The *Odyssey* is less grim in atmosphere and theme. It describes the endless voyage home of Odysseus, the shrewd Greek hero who originally developed the stratagem by which Troy was defeated (Odysseus had an enormous wooden horse built in which Greek warriors were hidden. When the other Greeks pretended to have given up their siege of Troy, the Trojans brought the horse into the city). Odysseus spends ten years trying to reach his island home of Ithaca. On the way, he encounters angry gods, sea-monsters, one-eyed giants, crafty sorceresses, and many other obstacles. He eventually reaches the island and defeats the profiteers (suitors") who have encamped in his palace in their attempt to marry his faithful spouse Penelope.

These epic poems, were regarded as unsurpassed literary masterpieces in ancient Greek and Roman times and still retain this status to the present day. They are also treasure troves of mythology. Homer provides detailed descriptions of the gods, whom he introduces as human beings with supernatural powers. They watch the human world from Mount Olympus (a bit like watching the traffic down below

The poet Homer was the founder of Greek—and thus of all western—literature. He was not only a great writer, but an important source of knowledge about prevailing beliefs of the time. This is an imaginary depiction of Homer on the Goethe monument in the park of the Villa Borghese, Rome.

from an "eye in the sky" as far as the modern reader is concerned), sometimes interfering in events and always having their own favorites and enemies among humans. The Homeric image of the gods was a major factor in defining the manner in which they were represented by all the authors who succeeded him—and thus also in the way in which we think of them.

The poet Hesiod was a contemporary of Homer. In his considerably shorter narrative poems, the *Theogony* and *Works and Days*, Hesiod imparted much mythological knowledge, though this sometimes conflicts with the vision of Homer. Hesiod told of the existence of the gods and the creation of the world and human beings. He is a much less skilled narrator than Homer and his style is sometimes obscure, but our knowledge of the Greek tales of creation, the Clash of the Titans, and related themes can all be attributed to him.

The three great Athenian tragedians, Æschylus, Sophocles, and Euripides, lived in the sixth and and fifth centuries BCE and between them wrote a large number of plays, of which many are still being performed. All their tragedies are reworkings of mythological material, and certain general human themes are examined deeply in an intelligent and penetrative manner. For our detailed knowledge of the terrible myth of the Theban king Œdipus and the aftermath of the murder of Agamem-

non, the Greek commander-in-chief in Troy, we mainly have these authors to thank.

Virgil, who lived in the first century BCE, was the Roman equivalent of Homer. He composed the *Æneid* in response to the example of the *Iliad* and the *Odyssey* The *Æneid* was an impressive heroic poem in Latin about the Trojan hero Æneas, who managed to escape from burning Troy with a group of faithful followers, reaching Italy after many wanderings, including a visit to the North African city of Carthage (now in modern Tunisia), where he had a fateful love affair with Queen Dido. In Italy, Æneas founded his own empire on the Italian peninsula, after a raging battle with local rulers.

Virgil's epic had major political implications because the first Roman emperors claimed to be descended from Æneas, calling upon Virgil's story as the proof, and thus attempted to provide their dominion with mythical, divine foundations.

The work of Virgil's contemporary, Ovid, is of a very different character nature. His light-hearted, playful, and kaleidoscopic narrative poem *Metamorphoses* contains numerous myths that merge into the transformation (metamorphosis) of the loading figure. The thought behind this is the old philosophical adage that nothing in this world remains the same, everything that exists is in a constant state of flux. Among the stories told by Ovid is that of King Midas, who was given donkey's ears by the god Apollo for his poor musical taste, Phæthon, who was killed in an accident while driving the chariot that belonged to his father, the sun god Helios, and from Hermaphrodite, who with her water-nymph, Daphne, fused into an androgynous nymph. Daphne was, in turn, changed into a laurel bush. Ovid described these events in his imaginative, virtuoso, and frequently witty verses.

Needless to say, there were many more writers and poets in ancient times who told mythical tales and adapted their material from the prevailing mythology. It is simply not possible within the confines of this book to deal with all of these authors—this is after all is an encyclopedia of mythology and not a history of Greek and Roman literature.

The encyclopedia section of the book contains many amusing quotations from the works of these and other classical authors. They serve to illustrate the stories in words, providing an even better impression of the manner in which people experienced mythology in ancient times. If the quotations whet your appetite and leave you curious to know more, you can then consult the bibliography to find the titles of the works quoted.

About the Encyclopedia Section

In the encyclopedia section of this book you will come across the names of many gods and heroes from Greek mythology, and in a few exceptional cases, Roman mythology. These are used as the basis for the names of the entries. The name of each entry is used as a reference point for discussing the role of the protagonist in classical mythology.

Due to the complex nature of Greek mythology, in which the stories of all manner of characters are often intricately interwoven, often in a very bizarre way, and with numerous variations, particular myths and episodes tend to recur frequently, even if from different perspectives. Thus, the adventures of the Argonauts is dealt with under the entry "Argonauts," although it also appears under the entries "Jason" and "Medea." In both of the latter cases, the emphasis is naturally on the role of those figures in the history of the Argonauts and on their remaining vicissitudes.

In the case of less important figures, only a cross-reference (see...) is provided, whether

as a separate entry, or with the text of another catchword. The Roman names of the important gods and goddesses are also included as catchwords with a similar reference.

Unless otherwise stated, the names under which the entries appear are all Greek names. The most common spelling of these names in the Latin alphabet is used for them, but since Greek has its own alphabet, Greek words may be transliterated into English in several different ways. So do not be surprised to encounter the name Œdipus spelled as Oidipous or that of Phædra as Phedra, or even Fedra, in another book. There is no right or wrong way of spelling Greek words in Latin characters, only a preference for a certain transliteration method to make it easier to reproduce the pronunciation or writing.

Men and women bringing an offering to an altar, accompanied by the god of wine Dionysus, known to the Romans as Bacchus. In the encyclopedia section, this god is listed under his Greek name. Painting on a vase from Apulia, Italy, ca. 330 BCE.

ANCIENT ROME

ETRURIA

ADRIATIC SEA

ROME
OSTIA   ALBA LONGA
LAVINIUM   ITALY

△VESUVIUS
POMPEII

TYRRHENIAN SEA

ÆTNA△
SICILY

SYRACUSE

CARTHAGE

AFRICA

ANCIENT GREECE

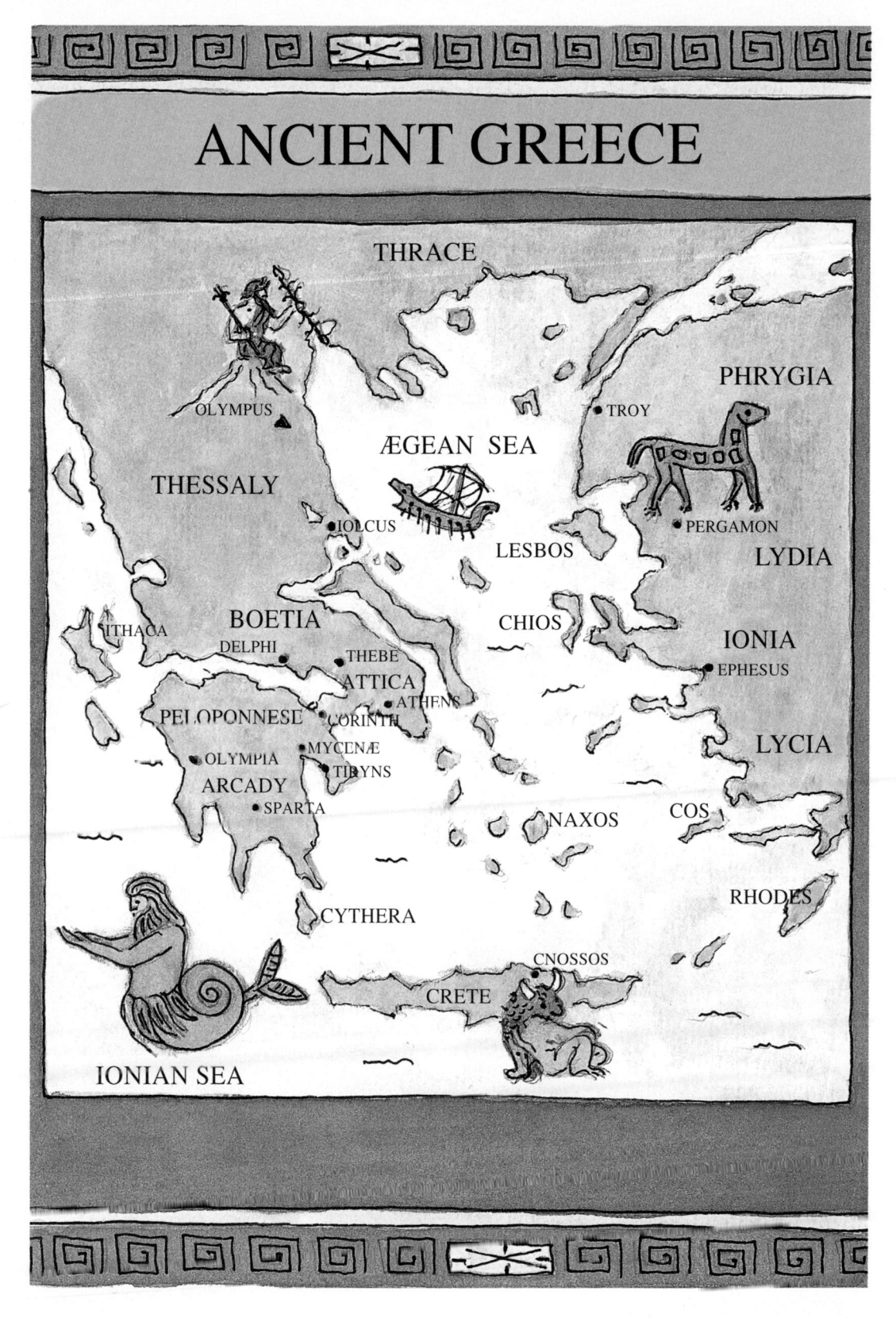

THRACE

OLYMPUS

PHRYGIA

TROY

ÆGEAN SEA

THESSALY

IOLCUS

PERGAMON

LESBOS

LYDIA

CHIOS

ITHACA

BOETIA

DELPHI

THEBE

IONIA

EPHESUS

ATTICA

ATHENS

PELOPONNESE

CORINTH

LYCIA

OLYMPIA

MYCENÆ

TIRYNS

ARCADY

SPARTA

NAXOS

COS

RHODES

CYTHERA

CNOSSOS

CRETE

IONIAN SEA

Greek Mythology Entries

Achilles

Achilles, son of the goddess Thetis and the mortal Peleus, was one of the great heroes of Greek mythology. Of all those who fought in the battle of Troy he was the most formidable. Achilles' role in the war was a decisive factor in the final Greek victory, but it was not granted to him to witness the fall of Troy. In spite of all his superhuman qualities, Achilles was, in fact, mortal. His death was specifically foretold, and unlike a figure such as Heracles (Hercules) (*q.v.*), there was no deification waiting for him, but a hopeless life as a shade in the underworld. The extremely strong, cruel, arrogant, and stunningly good-looking Achilles thus became the prototype for all those who were required to pay for living a fast-paced, illustrious, and dangerous life. Such a life always resulting in an early death, as shown such examples as the Macedonian conqueror, Alexander the Great, himself a great admirer of Achilles, to twentieth-century heroes including James Dean, Jimi Hendrix, Ayrton Senna, and Barry Sheen.

Initially, both Zeus and Poseidon courted the charming Thetis, daughter of the sea-god Nereus, but because according to an old

The demigod Achilles was the most formidable hero who fought in the Trojan War. He killed many adversaries but knew that he himself did not have long to live.

prediction Thetis' son would surpass his father (*see* **Prometheus**), she became the wife of Peleus, King of Phithia in Thessaly. At their magnificent wedding celebration, the seeds of the Trojan war were sown when Eris, the goddess of discord, threw a golden apple down among the guests. It was meant for the most beautiful goddess, Hera, but Athene, Aphrodite, and Hera quarreled among themselves as to who deserved the apple, and so Paris, the Trojan crown prince, was finally asked to judge between them—with disastrous results (*see* **Aphrodite**, **Helen**, **Paris**, *and* **Thetis**).

Thetis knew that her son would grow up to become an outstanding hero, but she also knew that it was almost certain he would not live to a ripe old age. Careful and loving as she was, she did her very best to avert his fate, by dipping the young Achilles in the waters of the underworld's River Styx in order to make him immortal. She almost succeeded in her aim, but when she immersed her little boy in the water, she held him by one heel, and this part of his body remained mortal. In the end it was his "Achilles heel" that proved fatal to the hero. According to another interpretation, Thetis tried to make the young Achilles immortal, to his father shock and horror, by laying him in the hearth fire at night and rubbing him daily with divine ambrosia.

Achilles was brought up by the wise centaur Chiron, who instructed various heroes. Among other things, Achilles received intensive training from Charon in sprinting, something that was to benefit him greatly later in battle. One of his regular epithets in Homer's heroic poem *The Iliad* is the "fleet-footed."

Because Thetis knew that Achilles ran a great risk of dying in battle, she sent him to the court of King Lycomedes on the island of Scyros, where he had to spend his days disguised as a girl. Yet even this did not prevent him from fathering a son, Neoptolemus, with Lycomedes' daughter, Deidamiate.

Achilles' stay in this sheltered place did not last long. When the Greeks wanted to sail to Troy to bring back the abducted Helen, Artemis refused to provide the necessary wind unless the Greek commander, King Agamemnon of Mycenæ, offered his

In the hope that she could make her son invulnerable, Thetis baptized Achilles in the waters of the river Styx. She almost succeeded in her attempt, though not completely, because Achilles retained a vulnerable heel. Oil painting by Peter Paul Rubens, 17th century.

daughter, Iphigenia, to her. Agamemnon enticed Iphigenia to the fleet's harbor at Aulis, with the promise of marriage to Achilles Achilles' arrival had to be arranged by the cunning hero, Odysseus, who did so with enthusiasm. He concealed some weapons among the jewels in the women's quarters of Lycomedes' palace. Odysseus then arranged for an alarm signal to be sounded on the trumpets, at which point a "maiden" (the disguised Achilles) made straight for the arms instead of the jewels...

In Troy, Achilles immediately confirmed his reputation as an unbeatable and ruthless warrior. The Trojans quaked with fear whenever he rode out in his battle chariot with his

Chiron was the wise and amiable Centaur, who acted as Achilles' tutor, helping the hero to fulfill his spiritual and physical potential. Fragment from a terra-cotta dish dating from the 2nd or 3rd century CE

charioteer, Automedon. The chariot was drawn by the immortal horses, Xanthus and Balius, that could speak with human voices (*see* **Xanthus and Balius**). Even before the start of the actual siege of the city, Achilles killed Cycnus, one of the sons of Poseidon. Cycnus was immune to ordinary weapons, so Achilles strangled him with the chinstrap of his own helmet.

Troilus, one of the sons of the Trojan Queen Hecabe and the god Apollo, was killed by Achilles who lay in wait for him in an ambush, as Troilus was escorting a number of Trojan women, including Polyxena, to fetch water outside one of the gates of the city. This deed was by no means a brave act on the part of Achilles, however.

During the ten-year-long siege of Troy, the Greeks carried out raids for miles around and plundered the various smaller towns surrounding the city-state. Achilles played a leading role in these attacks. During one of these predatory raids, he kidnapped the beautiful Briseis, whom he made into his mistress. The Greek commander-in-chief, Agamemnon, who benefited from a substantial share of the spoils of war taken by Achilles, had also taken a mistress. Chryseis suited him better than his wife, Clytemnestra, whom he had left at home, but Chryseis was the daughter of an important priest of Apollo, and in

Due to a trick played by Odysseus (right), Achilles—dressed as a girl—reaches for the weapons. The daughters of king Lycomedes watch in fear. Oil painting by Peter Paul Rubens, 17th century.

The Trojan Prince Troilus (right) was killed by Achilles (left) in an ambush. Illustration on a bronze mirror from Praeneste, 4th century BCE.

order to avoid the wrath of the god, Agamemnon was forced to send Chryseis back to her father. Achilles was one of those who had strongly urged him to do this and Agamemnon then claimed Briseis for himself. As commander-in-chief, he could not bear anyone else to benefit from greater sexual favors than he did.

Achilles reluctantly gave up Briseis, but he refused to have any more to do with the battle. His pride had been injured, and the hero even asked his mother Thetis to implore Zeus to make the fortunes of war turn in favor of the Trojans. And that is what happened. The siege of Troy lasted ten years, the besieging Greeks becoming more and more hardpressed. The Trojans marched out against the Greek camp on the beach, but Achilles refused to join battle. When the Trojans threatened to set fire to the Greek ships, however, he permitted his comrade-in-arms and best friend Patroclus to become involved in the confusion of battle. Patroclus dressed himself in Achilles' armor and immediately achieved spectacular successes, since the Trojans took him for Achilles which made them all take to their heels. But even though Patroclus may have looked like Achilles, he wasn't Achilles. The Trojan crown prince Hector killed him and robbed the corpse of Achilles' armor (*see* **Patroclus**).

Achilles was extremely upset when he heard that his greatest friend had been killed. Even his divine mother, who visited him in his tent, was unable to console him. Achilles merely wanted revenge on Hector and when Thetis warned him that it had been foretold that he would die shortly after Hector's death, Achilles replied, "I would die here and now, since I could not save my comrade. He has fallen far from home, and in his hour of need, my hand was not there to help him." (*Iliad*, XVIII, 98–100) Thetis realized that she could not restrain her son, so she called on Hephæstos, who wrought some splendid new armor for Achilles.

Dressed in this suit of armor, the hero mounted his battle chariot and rode onto the battlefield, where he caused a bloodbath among the Trojans. He chased Hector three times around the city walls, then killed him, and dragged his naked body behind his chariot. He flung Patroclus' body to the ground from where it was lying-in-state and dragged it through the dirt each day. Only after a considerable time was Thetis able to mollify him and persuade him to relinquish Hector's body to his father Priam. Priam, guided by Hermes, the messenger of the gods, and bringing an "immeasurable" ransom with him, personally

The youthful Macedonian conqueror, Alexander the Great, illustrated here on his beloved horse Bucephalus, regarded Achilles as his great role-model. Fragment from the "Alexander Sarcophagus," 2nd century BCE.

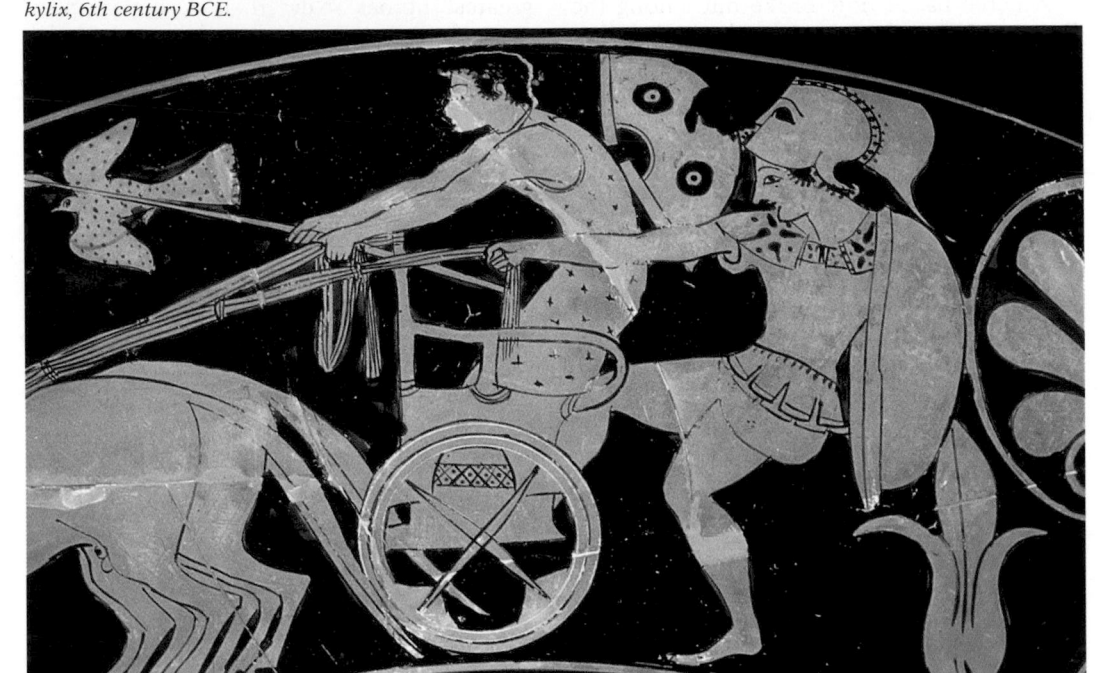

came to pay his last respects at Achilles' tent. The younger man was moved by the sorrow of the older man, handed over the body of his son to him, and told him that he was able to bury Hector in peace in a suitable resting place. This history, from Achilles' resentment at the loss of Briseis to the return of the body of Hector and his burial, is comprehensively and impressively described in *The Iliad*.

Shortly before his own death, Achilles was involved in the battle against an army of Amazons, who came to help the Trojans. He felled their queen, Penthesileia, with his spear, but fell in love with her when he saw her dead body no longer clad in her armor.

Not very much later, Achilles himself was struck by an arrow from the bow of Paris, who was anything but a great or brave fighter. Paris' arrow was also guided by the god Apollo. Apollo did not like Achilles very much and made sure that the arrow struck him in the only vulnerable part of his body, his heel.

Achilles was mourned for seventeen days by Thetis and the other daughters of Nereus. Even the muses came to sing a song of lamentation at his funeral pyre. After his cremation, his ashes were placed in a golden urn wrought by Hephæstos and laid in the same

This sarcophagus, carved with spectacular reliefs of war and hunting scenes, was incorrectly identified as the last resting place of Achilles' admirer, Alexander the Great. 'The "Alexander sarcophagus," 2nd century BCE.

grave in which Patroclus was buried beside the sea.

A fierce battle now broke out among the Greeks as to who should inherit Achilles' valuable armor. Ajax, who had recovered Achilles' body from the battlefield, claimed it, but it fell to Odysseus. Ajax then committed suicide, and Odysseus subsequently presented the armor to Achilles' son, Neoptolemus, who came to strengthen the ranks of the Greeks in the closing phase of the Trojan War.

This same Odysseus later met with Achilles' shade in the underworld, a scene described by Homer in *The Odyssey*. Achilles turned out to have completely changed his ideas and no longer had the "live fast, die young" mentality. "Do not console me on my death, King Odysseus," he confided to his visitor from the world of the living. "I would rather be a paid servant in a poor man's house and be above ground, than king of kings among the dead." (*Odyssey*, XI, 488–491).

According to another account, the shade of Achilles, who shortly before the departure of the Greeks from Troy had claimed Priam's daughter Polyxena for himself (*see* **Polyxena**), survived together with Patroclus on the island of Leuce, a paradise-like area of the underworld that was reserved only for the greatest heroes. Nevertheless, the supposition seems justified that the hero would also have gladly relinquished his existence as a shade for a simple life in the full light of the world of the living.

Actæon

Actæon was the son of Aristæus and Autonoe and grandson of Cadmus, founder of the city of Thebes. Thanks to the instruction he received from his father or the centaur Chiron, he was an excellent hunter. Maybe he was too good, since Artemis was annoyed by his boasting. She did not like the idea either that he planned to marry his aunt Semele. According to another account, during a pause in a hunting party, Actæon accidentally witnessed the chaste Artemis bathing, surrounded by her nymphs. In order to prevent Actæon spreading the news that he had seen her naked, she changed him into a stag. In this form, Actæon was shortly thereafter torn to pieces by his own hounds.

The hunter, Actæon, unintentionally interrupted the chaste goddess Artemis and her nymphs while they were bathing. The consequences for him were terrible. Painting of the school of Titian, 17th century.

Adonis

Adonis was actually an Asiatic (possibly a Phœnician) god who had been given a place in Greek mythology. His worship was very closely connected with that of Aphrodite.

In Greek mythology Adonis was supposed to be the son of the Cinyras, king of Cyprus, and his daughter Myrrha of Smyrna. Because Myrrha did not worship Aphrodite, the goddess of love, Aphrodite, with sufficient devotion, the goddess punished her by causing her to fall in love with her father. With the help of her wet-nurse, Myrrha succeeded in sharing a bed several times with Cinyras without him realizing to whom she was making love. When Cinyras finally discovered that he had been committing incest, he drew his sword in

The goddess of love Aphrodite. Adonis' beauty was irresistible to her, so much so that she became the "victim" of the sort of love with which she normally afflicted others. Statue carved in bone, Egypt, Roman period.

bewilderment, but Myrrha, who was by then pregnant, was able to escape and was turned into a myrtle tree by the gods. Eventually, the myrtle tree split open and Adonis was born into the world, who was outstanding even as a baby, because of his extraordinary beauty. Aphrodite was not pleased with this at all. She hid the young Adonis in a chest and brought him to Persephone, the goddess of the underworld. Once Persephone had glanced into the chest, she was won over, and brought up the charming child in her own palace, refusing to return him to the goddess of love.

Zeus had to take a hand in the matter. The supreme god decided that the extremely handsome youth was to spend a third of each year with Aphrodite, a third of the year with Persephone, and the remaining third would be his alone. According to another interpretation, the muse Calliope acted as judge in the dispute, and she ruled that Adonis had to spend six months of the year with each goddess.

In any case, Aphrodite fell completely under the spell of Adonis' good looks. The goddess of love was herself hopelessly in love—with a mortal. Her happiness was short-lived, however. She had been afraid of this and warned Adonis, in no uncertain terms, that he must be careful when hunting and should better devote his powers to more useful pursuits. However, the reckless young man disregarded her advice, and during a

To the great sadness of Aphrodite, Adonis was killed during a hunt by an aggressive wild boar—possibly the jealous war-god Ares. Wild boar hunt, oil painting by Abraham Hondius, 17th century.

hunting party he was attacked by a wild boar. Whether it was the offended Persephone who had persuaded Aphrodite's jealous lover, Ares, the god of war, to take on the form of the boar for this purpose was not clear, but the attack by the animal was nonetheless fatal. Inconsolable, Aphrodite caused a blood-red anemone to sprout from each drop of Adonis' blood.

According to some versions of the myth, Zeus allowed Adonis to be brought to life in spring and summer, so that he could spend this time with Aphrodite.

Adonis, whose name is still used today to describe male beauty, was, in fact, a god of vegetation. His legend, just like that of Persephone, is linked to the changing of the seasons, in which nature dies only to come to life again (see **Demeter** *and* **Persephone**).

Ægeus

Ægeus was the oldest (according to some versions, the adopted) son of Padion, King of Athens, and father of the great hero, Theseus. Ægeus received sole dominion over Athens, although he had promised to share the rule of the city-state with his two brothers.

After two marriages, Ægeus still had no children. When he consulted the oracle at Delphi about this, he received an ambiguous reply. Only once he was back in Athens, so

Ægeus made a deal with his son Theseus that, if he would return unscathed from Crete, he would fly a white sail on his ship. But Theseus forgot to lower the black sail...

The remains of holy places in Delphi dedicated to Apollo. Here can be found the famous oracle which was often consulted in Ancient times by, amongst others, the Athenian king Ægeus.

he was told, should he open his wineskin. Confused, he repeated the mysterious words to his friend King Pittheus of Troizen. Pittheus, who knew that the oracle had also prophesied the birth of a great hero, immediately saw a connection that he could use to his own advantage. He got Ægeus drunk and let him sleep with his daughter Æthra, so that the future hero would be his own descendant. But when Ægeus realized what had happened, he placed a sword and a pair of sandals under a large boulder. He then told Æthra that only if her son would subsequently appear in Athens with the sword and the sandals, he would recognize him as his son.

Once back in Athens Ægeus married the sorceress Medea, who had sought refuge with him after her marriage to Jason had come to a disastrous and bloody end (see **The Argonauts** *and* **Medea**). Medea presented Ægeus with a son, Medus.

When much later, Theseus, Æthra's son resulting from her liaison with Ægeus came to Athens, having built up a tremendous reputation as a hero in the meantime, Medea immediately realized who he was. But she had the interests of her own son, Medus, in mind, and did not inform Ægeus of Theseus' identity. She led him to believe that Theseus was not to be trusted and laced the guest's wine with a deadly poison. But at the moment that Theseus was about to drink from his goblet, Ægeus recognized the insignia on Theseus' sword and knocked the goblet out of his hand.

Medea fled from Athens and Ægeus organized great banquets in the honor of his newfound son. Theseus, in turn, assisted his father in his fight against the Pallantidoo, the fifty sons of Ægeus' brother Pallas, who were disputing Ægeus' dominion over Athens, and defeated them.

Other difficulties arose because Androgeus, son of Minos, the powerful king of Crete, was killed by the Athenians (according to some accounts he was the victim of a dangerous bull let loose by Heracles, which ravaged the area of Marathon—*see* **Heracles** *and* **Theseus**). Minos attacked the Athenians, but could not defeat them by military means. However, starvation, earthquakes, and epidemics did bring the Athenians to their knees. On the advice of the oracle at Delphi Ægeus accepted Minos' peace conditions, that included that once every nine years seven Athenian youths and seven Athenian maidens must be offered to the Minotaur, a half-man half-bull (*see* **Minos**), in the labyrinth designed by the brilliant master builder Dædalus.

With the help of Minos' daughter Ariadne, Theseus finally killed the Minotaur and released the city from its hideous obligation (*see* **Ariadne** *and* **Theseus**). But on his return journey to Athens, Theseus forgot the agreement that he had made with his father before he set out. If everything had gone well, he was supposed to hoist a white sail on his ship. But Theseus, saddened because he had had to leave his beloved Ariadne behind on the island of Naxos (or delighted because he

Æneas was one of the few men who managed to escape from burning Troy. He did so even though he had to carry his elderly father, Anchises, on his shoulders.

was almost home again), left the black sail hanging from the mast. Ægeus saw Theseus' ship approaching in the distance with the black sail and in an attack of despair threw himself from a high rock into the waves. Ever since then, the sea in which the unfortunate Athenian king lost his life has been known as the Ægean Sea.

The Mausoleum of Augustus, the first Roman emperor, at Mars' Field in Rome. Augustus demonstrated his power and alleged mythical origins by presenting himself as a descendant of Æneas.

Æneas

Æneas was the son of Aphrodite (Venus) and the mortal Anchises. Æneas' role in Greek mythology is fairly modest, but for the Romans his significance was immeasurable. After the destruction of his city, Troy, by the Greeks, Æneas traveled to Italy where he founded a kingdom from which Rome later emerged. It was to Æneas that the great Roman poet Virgil dedicated his famous epic poem, the *Ænead*, inspired by the writings of Homer.

Æneas' father, Anchises, was a descendant of the Trojan king Tros, after whom the city of Troy in Asia Minor was named, and was therefore a member of the Trojan royal family. Anchises was unable to participate in the Trojan War because when the war broke out he was too old, and besides Zeus had made him partially lame because he had once boasted of his relationship with Aphrodite, from which Æneas was born.

During the Trojan War, Æneas was, after Hector, the greatest hero on the Trojan side yet he was not the equal of the strongest of the Greek heroes. Diomedes would have killed him with no difficulty at all, had his mother Aphrodite and the god Apollo not intervened together and removed Æneas from the battlefield. There was a certain amount of friction between Hector and Æneas, and also between Æneas and Hector's father, the Trojan king Priam. Æneas was married to Priam's daughter Creusa and they had a son, Ascanius.

Unlike most of the Trojans, Æneas was able to escape from Troy after the Greeks had managed to conquer the city thanks to their ruse of sending in the wooden horse. Various versions exist of the exact circumstances of his flight. The most important, which was also recorded by Virgil, claims that Æneas escaped from the burning city with the aged Anchises on his back, leading Ascanius by the hand. Before this he had vainly tried to save Cassandra from the clutches of the Greeks and witnessed how Priam had been killed and the royal palace of Troy overrun. Creusa vanished without trace during the flight, but her shade predicted a successful future for Æneas in the west.

After Æneas had taken over the leadership of the Trojan survivors at the foot of Mount Ida, and had organized the building of ships, there began the long and difficult voyage westward, which brought Æneas and his companions in adversity to Crete, among other places, on the basis of a misunderstood pronouncement by the oracle. It was then clearly foretold to Æneas, in a dream, that he must sail to Hesperia, the "evening land." A storm sent him off course, however, to the Strophades, where the Trojans were plagued

The site of the ruined city of Troy as it looks today. It is from here that Æneas and his companions fled the burning city, after it had been conquered by the Greeks.

by the Harpies (q.v.), winged monsters with the face of old crones, and one of the Harpies made dire predictions about the rest of the journey.

After this Æneas landed in Epirus, where his fellow countryman, the prophet Helenus, who in the meantime had married Hector's widow Andromache, instructed him to sail to Sicily and prophesied that he would be the founder of a great nation. On the west coast of Sicily, at a sanctuary dedicated to Æneas' mother Venus, Anchises passed away and was laid in his final resting-place.

Hera (=Juno) was still ill-disposed toward the Trojans and Æneas, and intervened to cause a storm to break, so that Æneas' fleet was diverted to North Africa instead of Italy. Here, on the southern shores of the Mediterranean, the young queen Dido was preoccupied with founding of the city of Carthage. Even though Æneas had vowed never to remarry, there sprang up an intense love between him and Dido, which was sealed during a hunting-party, when a storm broke and the lovers had to shelter from the rain in a cave. The relationship between Dido and Æneas is one of the best-known love stories of Antiquity, and countless writers, poets, painters, and composers have been inspired by it.

The love story came to a tragic end, because Æneas realized that he could not follow his heart, but was bound to obey the divine commands to found a new realm. Hermes (Mercury), the messenger of the gods, again visited Æneas, on behalf of Zeus (=Jupiter) to remind him of his duty. Æneas obeyed and departed, and Dido killed herself with a sword that Æneas had given her as a present. For their descendants, this sad episode was to have even greater consequences, in that it was the origin of the great enmity that existed between Carthage and Rome and which in the second and third centuries BCE was to lead to three wars, resulting in the destruction of Carthage.

Æneas returned to Sicily, remaining there for some time, to hold games in honor of the deceased Anchises and to found a city for the Trojan women and the elderly who had become tired of the continual traveling. He then sailed away to the Italian mainland. At Cumæ, Æneas descended into the underworld, where he met the shade of his father,

Æneas' ship strayed off course during a heavy storm and ended up on the coast of what is now Tunisia. This painting by the 17th century painter Frederik van Valkenborch depicts a romantic image of the shipwreck.

Two Roman field-marshals shake hands. Æneas was a great role-model for the soldiers of the Roman empire. Oil painting by Peter Paul Rubens, 17th century.

In Italy Æneas, Ascanius, and the other Trojans had to endure a bitter and protracted battle against the local populations. Roman relief illustrating battle.

mother. In the end, a duel between Æneas and Turnus became the deciding factor. Æneas defeated Turnus and wanted to offer him mercy, but when he saw that Turnus was wearing the belt of the dead Pallas as a war trophy, he killed him on the spot.

Once peace had been restored, Æneas married Lavinia. From this point on the

The Ponte Fabricio was built in 62 BCE and is the oldest existing bridge over the Tiber in Rome. Not far from here, Æneas' descendants, Romulus and Remus, founded their city in 753 BCE

who gave him advice and once more confirmed that he would lay the foundations of a great empire.

Æneas continued in a northerly direction. He sailed up the river Tiber and landed in the region of Latium (present-day Lazio), which was then ruled by King Latinus. His grown-up daughter, Lavinia, was promised to Turnus, the king of the Rutulians, but an oracle indicated that it would be better if Lavinia were to marry a foreigner. Accordingly, Latinus gave Lavinia's hand to Æneas. Following this, Hera sent Alecto, one of the Furies, the goddesses of revenge, to incite Latinus' wife Amata and her former betrothed, Turnus, against Æneas. Turnus acquired allies among other peoples from the surrounding areas, and Æneas did the same, getting the Etruscans to side with him. In addition, his mother, Aphrodite, arranged for new armor to be wrought for him by her husband Hephæstos (=Vulcan).

There followed a very long battle, in which Æneas' young son, Ascanius, also took an active part. Many were killed, including Pallas, the son of Æneas' important ally, Evander. At one point, Æneas himself was wounded in the hand, but he was cured by his

Trojans and the Latins lived in peace together and the Trojans adopted the language and customs of the local population. Æneas founded the city of Lavinium, named for his new wife. Later, Ascanius (who was also called Iulus—which is also why the "Juliuses," Caesar and Augustus, attributed their ancestry to him) founded the city of Alba Longa, which grew into the capital city of the area. Centuries later, Romulus, the son of Ares (=Mars) and the Princess Rhea Silvia who came from Alba Longa, was to found the city of Rome on the Palatine hills, overlooking the Tiber.

While Virgil in his *Ænead* allowed himself to be strongly inspired by Homer and included so many references and allusions to the *Iliad* and the *Odyssey* that his epic poem almost seems to "mirror" the epic by Homer, the atmosphere of the *Ænead* is completely different to the Homeric works. Æneas also has a totally different character from the impulsive Greek heroes, such as Achilles and Odysseus, with their zest for "life in the fast lane," Æneas is often referred to as "the pious Æneas" by Virgil, and indeed he is a god-fearing, disciplined figure who, with his strong sense of duty and obedience, has the typical sober Roman that is so diametrically opposed to that of the Greek heroes.

Agamemnon

Agamemnon was the son of the Mycenæan king Atreus and his wife Anaxibia. After Atreus was murdered, Agamemnon and his brother Menelaus, with the help of the Spartan king Tyndareos, took over the throne of Mycenae and Menelaus later succeeded Tyndareos as king of Sparta. Each brother married a daughter of Tyndareos, Agamemnon married Clytemnestra and Menelaus married the ravishingly beautiful Helen. Agamemnon and Clytemnestra had three daughters, Iphigenia, Electra, and Chrysothemis, and one son, Orestes.

When Helen was kidnapped by the Trojan prince Paris, causing the Greeks to declare war on Troy, Agamemnon became the commander-in-chief of the Greek army that consisted of representatives from the many Greek kingdoms. In his determination to defend Menelaus' damaged honor, Agamemnon went to extremes. When the Greek fleet was unable to sail from Aulis to Troy because Artemis, whom Agamemnon had once insulted, refused to provide a suitable wind, he was prepared to offer his daughter Iphigenia to the goddess as a human sacrifice. While not all sources agree that this offer was actually made and, according to some, Iphigenia was

The Ponte Fabricio was built in 62 BCE and is the oldest existing bridge over the Tiber in Rome. Not far from here, Æneas' descendants, Romulus and Remus, founded their city in 753 BCE

As supreme commander of the Greek forces, Agamemnon led a large fleet of ships to Troy. Mosaic showing ships from the Roman port city of Ostia, 1st-4th century CE.

spared and became a priestess of Artemis in Tauris. Whatever story is accepted, the episode is indicative of Agamemnon's unscrupulous character (*see* **Iphigenia**).

In Homer's *Iliad*, Agamemnon is depicted as a brave but also cold, arrogant, and

Achilles (the young man, right) became furious with his supreme commander, Agamemnon (on the throne), who had taken his mistress, Briseis, away from him. The goddess, Athena (above), unsuccessfully tries to calm the emotions. Oil painting by Peter Paul Rubens, 17th century.

stubborn leader, who often allows himself to be guided by his own whims and desires, and was not prepared to take the others into account, treating his fellow rulers as vassals. Homer mentions that Agamemnon sailed to Troy with one hundred ships and that he possessed an ivory scepter made by Hephæstos.

Agamemnon made a dangerous move when he claimed Achilles' mistress Briseis for his own, after he had had to give his own slave, Chryseis, whom he had captured in battle, back to her father Chryses, a priest of Apollo. Achilles, who did not like his haughty commander-in-chief very much anyway, became bitterly resentful, and refused to fight any longer. The Greeks, who up until then had had the upper hand in the Trojan War, now found themselves in a really tight corner. In one attack, the Trojans advanced quite a long way and threatened to set fire to the Greek ships. Achilles' comrade in battle, Patroclus, wearing Achilles' armor, was barely able to prevent this disaster.

Agamemnon had made very few friends at home, and this became clear after his return from Troy. His wife, Clytemnestra, had not been able to forgive him for the offering of Iphigenia as a sacrifice and had taken Ægisthus, one of the murderers of Agamemnon's father, as her lover. According to the account by Homer, who described how

37

Lance and shield belonging to the mighty Ajax.

Lance and shield belonging to the mighty Ajax.

Ajax

Homer's *Iliad* contains two heroes named Ajax, both of whom fought on the side of the Greeks. The most important of the two, also known as "the greater Ajax," was a son of Telamon of Salamis. After Achilles, he was the most formidable Greek hero in the Trojan War. He is described as a silent, brave but forthright man.

Ajax performed many heroic deeds in the battle, almost succeeding in killing the great Trojan hero, Hector, in a duel. He often went to the aid of his wounded comrades-in-arms. He once rescued Odysseus who had been wounded in a fight against superior numbers of Trojans. When Achilles' closest friend, Patroclus, was killed by Hector, Ajax covered the body with his huge shield. And when, later, the great Achilles fell to an arrow fired by Paris, it was Ajax who carried the dead hero and his arms from the battlefield.

This last action was to lead directly to his death, because the Greek heroes fought among themselves over the issue of who could lay claim to Achilles' expensive armor,

Odysseus met Agamemnon's shade in the underworld, Agamemnon was invited by Ægisthus to a banquet and was there treacherously murdered by Ægisthus and Clytemnestra, together with a large number of his comrades-in-arms and the Trojan princess Cassandra, whom he had taken as part of the spoils of war. According to the tragedian Æschylus, Clytemnestra and Ægisthus set upon Agamemnon while he was taking a bath in his own palace, and killed him with blows from a hatchet.

The feared Ajax killed and wounded many Trojan fighters with his lance. This image of a wounded fighter is depicted on an Athenian kylix of the 6th century BCE.

The city walls of Troy in their current state. Ajax often fought before these walls, but no longer played a part when the city was conquered.

The goddess Athena. Ajax the Lesser experienced her unreconcilable enmity after he raped the Trojan princess Cassandra in front of Athena's altar, and overturned the the statue of the goddess. His misdeeds sealed his fate.

that had been made personally by the god Hephæstos. Odysseus was the winner. Ajax felt so hard done by after this decision that he planned a nocturnal attack on his own comrades. The goddess Athene struck him with madness, however, and instead of his hated competitors Ajax only killed a flock of sheep. He came to his senses the next day, but the disgrace became too much for him and he fell on his sword. While other accounts of Ajax's end exist, this version, elaborated on by the tragedian Sophocles in his drama *Ajax*, is the most accepted one.

The other Ajax who appears in *The Iliad*, the "lesser Ajax," was the son of Oileus. He excelled in running and his skill in throwing the javelin. Unlike his great namesake, he was a haughty man, who bore a particular grudge against Athene. After the fall of Troy, he brought down the wrath of the goddess upon himself by dragging the Trojan princess Cassandra, out of the sanctuary of Athene where she had sought protection, and raping her, Although Ajax had committed this

horrifying and blasphemous deed, and also dashed the statue of the goddess to the ground. The other Greeks did not punish him for this, although Odysseus—a special protegé of Athene—wanted to do so. The deeply offended Athene, who had continually supported the Greeks during the Trojan War with all her powers, now asked her father Zeus to strike the Greeks on their journey home with a savage storm. This was done, and Athene herself caused Ajax's ship to sink with a bolt of lightning. Ajax was able to survive by swimming away, but Poseidon caused him to drown..

The name Ajax, in spite of the misdeeds committed by the lesser Ajax, has remained connected with power, bravery, and nobility. At least, it must be assumed that when they named the famous Amsterdam football club "Ajax," were thinking of the 'greater" Ajax and not the "lesser."

Alcestis

Alcestis was the daughter of King Pelias of Thessaly. Pelias required her future husband to be a man who was capable of harnessing a lion and a boar to the wedding chariot. King Admetus of Pherae succeeded in this, thanks to the help of Apollo. The god granted Admetus this favor in return for Admetus doing a year of penance. Admetus forgot to perform

Thanks to the courageous actions of the brave hero Heracles, Alcestis was saved from the underworld just in time. Here Heracles is portrayed on a gold stater coin of Macedonian origin.

the necessary sacrifice to Artemis, the goddess of the hunt, in gratitude for the wedding. Out of revenge, she filled the marital bedchamber with snakes, a sign that Admetus had not long to live. Thereupon, Apollo deceived the Fates and made them promise that Admetus could live, as long as someone else died in his place. Alcestis indicated that she was prepared to offer herself up on behalf of her husband. Persephone, the wife of the god of the underworld, Hades, was so impressed that she allowed Alcestis to return to the world of the living.

According to another version of the myth, the hero Heracles, who happened to be a guest at Admetus' palace, brought Alcestis back from the underworld. The Athenian tragedian Euripides, based his drama *Alcestis* on this variation.

Alcmene

Alcmene was the daughter of Electryon—a son of the hero Perseus—and the mother of Heracles, the greatest of all the Greek heroes. She became the wife of Amphitryon, the king of Tiryns in the Peloponnese but demanded that he first avenge the murders of her brothers before she would let him share her bed. In performing this act of revenge, Amphitryon

The supreme Greek supreme god Zeus pursued—and conquered—many mortal women, including Alcmene. On this vase painting, Zeus chases after one of his victims. Athenian amphora, ca. 475 BCE.

Alcmene's famous son, Heracles, is portrayed here as a young, still beardless man. The lion-skin thrown over his left arm shows that he has already killed his first lion. Small Sabellic bronze statue, 4th century BCE.

had to contend with many setbacks, including the accidental killing of his father-in-law. This resulted in his being banished with Alcmene to the city of Thebes. After he had finally slain the murderers, he was told to his amazement that his wife had already slept with him the previous night. Amphitryon learned from the seer, Tiresias, what had really happened. In fact, the supreme god, Zeus, had taken on the appearance of Amphitryon and had sought out Alcmene, the most sensual and most beautiful earthly woman he could find, to father a mortal who was to perform great deeds. When the time came, their son would aid the gods in their battle against the Giants.

Alcmene became pregnant with twins, Heracles, the son of Zeus, and Iphicles, the son of Amphitryon. During Alcmene's pregnancy, the careless Zeus made it widely known that an extraordinary mortal fathered by himself was to be born into the world. Zeus' jealous wife, Hera, asked the goddess of childbirth, Eiliethyia, to frustrate the delivery but Alcmene and her sons were saved by a

trick of one of Alcmene's maidservants. Hera then placed two gigantic snakes in Heracles' cradle, but the little hero strangled the creatures with his bare hands.

Zeus prevented Hera from making further attempts to kill Heracles and also placed Alcmene under his protection. When Amphitryon wanted to burn her to death because she had been unfaithful to him, Zeus sent down a sudden downpour that put out the pyre.

After Amphitryon's death, Alcmene married the Cretan Rhadamanthus (according to another version, she had to flee to Attica because she was threatened by Eurystheus, the tormentor of her son Heracles). When she finally died of old age, Zeus caused her body to be brought to the Elysian Fields by Hermes. There she led a happy and eternal life at the side of Rhadamanthus, who acted as one of the judges of the souls of the departed (*see* **Heracles**).

Amalthea

Amalthea was a nymph who owned a goat or herself had the form of a goat. She lived on Mount Dicte or Mount Ida on the island of Crete, and she- or her goat— suckled the supreme god Zeus in a cave after his mother Rhea had entrusted him to her care as a baby. According to some versions of the myth Zeus was fed with the contents of a broken off

goat's horn, that contained inexhaustible supplies of nectar, the drink of the gods, and ambrosia, the food of the gods. This was the proverbial cornucopæa, the "horn of plenty."

The Amazons

The Amazons were a savage female warrior race, the offspring of a relationship between Ares the god of war and the naiad (water-nymph) Harmonia. They inhabited an area to

The Amazons, female warriors, were outstanding horsewomen and archers.

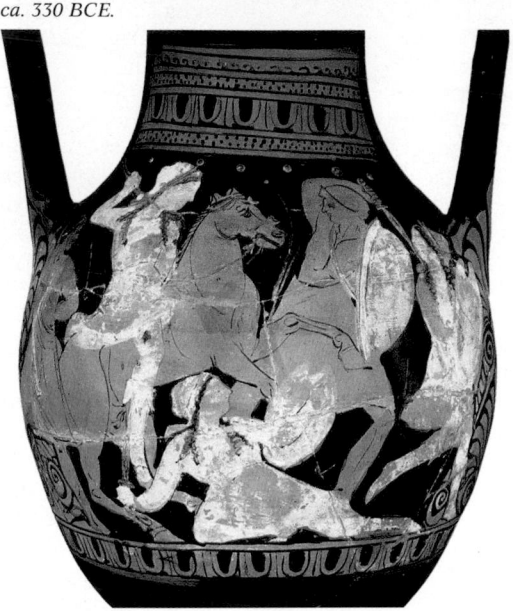

the east of the Black Sea. The Greek name "amazon" (without one breast) was possibly connected to the fact that they had one of their breasts cut off in order to be more easily able to draw an arrow through a bow. In addition to their forefather Ares, the Amazons also worshiped the Artemis, the virginal goddess of the hunt. The Greeks believed that the Amazons sometimes had relations with

A large number of Amazons perished in the battle which ensued after Hera had turned the subjects of queen Hippolyte against the hero, Heracles. An Amazon wounded by a lance, fragment of a vase painting from Tarente, 4th century BCE.

men of another tribe. They then raised any girls born of the union and killed the boys. Their queen, Lysippe, established their matriarchal society, in which the women became the warriors and went to war, while those men who were allowed to survive were deliberately turned into semi-invalids only had to do household chores.

The Amazons were tough but excellent warriors, who excelled with the bow and arrow. Under their successive queens Marpesia, Lampado, and Hippo they conquered a considerable area of western Asia. Even Troy was once conquered by them. During the Trojan War, the Amazons fought on the side of the Trojans against the Greeks. The great Greek hero, Achilles, killed their queen, Penthesileia, and then fell under the spell of her charms when he viewed her dead body.

One of the twelve labors that Heracles had to perform was to steal the girdle of the Amazon queen, Hippolyta. Hippolyta felt herself attracted to Heracles and would have gladly given up the girdle to him voluntarily, but in spite of this, the episode came to a tragic end, because Heracles killed Hippolyta and several more Amazons.

During a military expedition, the hero, Theseus, kidnapped the Amazon queen, Antiope, who fell in love with him according to some accounts. The other Amazons pursued Theseus and fought a fierce battle against him on Athenian territory. In the end, Theseus triumphed. From the relationship between Theseus and Antiope (or Hippolyta, according to some accounts) a son was born who was called Hippolytus. According to other accounts, Theseus did not travel alone to the country of the Amazons, but accompanied Heracles when he went to try and obtain Hippolyta's girdle.

Amor, *see* Eros

Andromache

Andromache, the daughter of Eetion, the king of Asia Minor, was the wife of Hector, the greatest and bravest of the Trojan heroes. Hector and Andromache had one son, Astyanax. Andromache's seven brothers, as well as her father, Eetion, were killed by the Greek hero, Achilles, as was her husband Hector. Achilles was bent on bloodshed

In a moving passage in *The Iliad,* Homer describes how Hector, who knows that the Trojans will eventually come off worst, takes leave of his wife and his young son before the battle. At this, little Astyanax is frightened by the plume waving on Hector's helmet. No less impressive are the lines in which Andromache hears that her beloved husband has fallen in battle. She laments for Hector and her son who has become fatherless: "Even though he (Astyanax) escape the horrors of this woeful war with the Greeks, yet shall his life henceforth be one of labor and sorrow. Other will seize his lands. The day that robs a child of his parents severs him from his own kind. His head is bowed, his cheeks are wet with tears." (*Iliad*, Book XXII, lines 486-491).

However, such a future was not to be, for after the fall of Troy, Astyanax was dashed from the city walls. As part of the spoils of war, Andromache herself was captured and taken to Greece by Neoptolemus, the son of Achilles. The son showed the same violent temper as his father, by killing the aged Trojan King Priam at the altar of the temple of Zeus. Andromache gave Neoptolemus a son (three sons according to some accounts) and had to suffer the hatred of his barren Greek wife, Hermione. She and her father, Menelaus, even tried to kill Andromache—an act that was prevented by Neoptolemus' ageing grandfather, Peleus.

because only shortly before this, his closest friend, Patroclus, clad in Achilles' armor, had been killed by Hector.

Later, Andromache married the prophet Helenus who, like her, had been taken from

Ruins of the city of Pergamon, where Andromache may have spent the final years of her life.

Andromeda was chained to a rock beside the sea, as prey for the monster sent by the sea god Poseidon.

Troy by Neoptolemus. She spent her years with him in Pergamon, a new city in Asia Minor that was named for Pergamos, the fortress of the destroyed Troy. According to a different version, Pergamus, the son of Helenus and Andromache, founded this city.

As a defenseless, loving wife who became the victim of a ruthless war, Andromache has remained a mythological figure of very human proportions whose fate has, unfortunately, lost little in topicality. In addition to Homer, she also features in Euripides' harrowing anti-war drama *The Trojan Women*, that tells the sad tale of Andromache and her fate as the concubine of Neoptolemus, as well as the attempts by Hermione to eliminate her (*see* **Hector** *and* **Neoptolemus**).

Andromeda

Andromeda was the daughter of Cassiopea and the Ethiopian king Cepheus. When Cassiopea boasted that Andromeda's beauty exceeded that of the Nereids, the sea-nymphs, the latter complained to the sea-god Poseidon. Indignant about such arrogance, he sent a sea monster to destroy the empire of

Andromeda was placed in the universe as a star constellation. This illustration from an old stellar atlas shows how the mythological figure could be "seen" in the star constellation.

Andromeda's boastful mother, Cassiopeia, also lived on as a stellar constellation. This illustration does not show that she adorned the sky upside-down.

Cepheus. An oracle suggested that further disaster could be averted by offering Andromeda—who was innocent of her mother's boasting—to the sea monster, so she was chained to a rock beside the sea. It was there the hero, Perseus, found her when he flew by on his winged shoes.

Perseus carried with him the head of the gorgon Medusa, whom he had recently defeated (*see* **Gorgons** *and* **Perseus**). He instantly fell in love with Andromeda and, having ascertained that she was free to marry, went into battle against the sea-monster. To the great relief of Cepheus and Cassiopea, Perseus was able to kill the monster with the special saber that he had received as a gift from the god, Hermes. With the help of the head of Medusa—that could turn living creatures into stone with its glare—he subsequently turned the seaweed into coral.

Of course, after this, the hero was allowed to marry the beautiful princess. Unfortunately, the wedding turned into a bloodbath. As it happened, Cepheus had already promised his daughter to his brother Phineus, who would not forgive the broken promise. Perseus won the fight, with the help of the head of Medusa because he turned Phineus and his supporters to stone. Eventually, Perseus and Andromeda established themselves as king and queen of the city of Tiryns in Argos.

After their death, Athena placed them both together as a constellation in the sky. Cassiopea became a constellation, as well, but as punishment for her arrogance she was placed upside down in the firmament.

Antigone

Antigone was the daughter of the Theban King Œdipus and his wife and mother Jocasta. Sophocles, the Athenian tragedian and playwright, tells her story in his dramas *Œdipus Rex* and *Antigone*.

When Œdipus became aware of the fact that he had unintentionally killed his father and married his mother, he put out his eyes. He was then banned from Thebes. Jocasta hanged herself (*see* **Œdipus**). Œdipus' uncle Creon became the regent over Thebes but later Antigone's brothers, Eteocles and Polynices, seized the throne from him. Meanwhile Antigone accompanied Œdipus while he wandered through Greece as a blind penitent. In the end, King Theseus of Athens granted Œdipus asylum and protection. The

Correct burial of the dead was a holy duty for ancient Greeks. Antigone would have loved to treat her brothers like this deceased woman, who was wept-for by those close to her. Exhibit on black Athenian stoneware from ca. 525 BCE

chastened penitent found peace of mind at last and could die in peace. Before that happened, however, his second daughter Ismene arrived with the message that Eteocles had driven out Polynices in order to become absolute ruler over Thebes. He had the support of Creon, who even brought his army to Athens in order to capture Antigone and Ismene. Creon abandoned this intention after the intervention of Theseus and both sisters voluntarily returned to Thebes.

Meanwhile, the ousted Polynices, who had gone into battle with six supporters against his hometown, had died there in a duel with Eteocles, who also perished. Creon once again ascended the throne. He had Eteocles buried with royal honors but left the body of Polynices unburied outside the town —the most humiliating experience that could befall a Greek citizen. Creon forbade everyone specifically, under penalty of death, to bury Polynices. Antigone defied the ban and symbolically sprinkled three handfuls of soil over Polynices. Creon had her arrested and sentenced her to death, but in order to prevent himself being guilty of causing the death of a close relative, he ordered for her to be walled up alive in a cave with a store of food and drink.

Shortly thereafter, the blind prophet, Tiresias, urged Creon to bury Polynices and to release Antigone. Creon, frightened by Tiresias' words, followed his advice but when Antigone's cave was broken open, she was found to have hanged herself. Creon's son Hæmon, Antigone's betrothed, who had unsuccessfully pleaded for her life with his father, cursed Creon and committed suicide (as did Creon's wife).

Several versions of this myth exist. In all of them, the role of Antigone as a woman who shows great moral courage in a family tragedy, is the central feature. The powerful fascination of this theme, that was developed so brilliantly by Sophocles in the play he wrote ca. 440 BCE, has never diminished. Sophocles' drama been interpreted in many different ways, and the modern French playwright Jean Anouilh (1910-1987) wrote his own version of *Antigone*, a drama which is widely performed and much read.

Aphrodite (Roman=*Venus*)

Aphrodite, the Greek goddess of love and beauty, was one of the twelve gods and goddesses who lived on Mount Olympus with

Aphrodite forms the handle of this Athenian mirror dating from the 5th century BCE She is accompanied by flying swans and doves, her permanent companions.

the supreme deity Zeus. Venus, the Roman goddess of love, is her equivalent.

Aphrodite brought beauty and love to the world, especially erotic love, since she did not particularly stimulate conjugal fidelity. On occasion, she ran foul of Hera (Juno) who acted specifically as guardian of the marital bond. Aphrodite was described as a perfect, seductive young woman with an irresistibly sweet smile. Her entourage included the Three Graces and her son Eros (Cupid), the little winged god of love, equipped with bow and arrow. In later depictions, Aphrodite is often accompanied by several of these little baby gods (*see* **Eros**).

The worship of Aphrodite started in the Middle East where similar goddesses, such as Astarte (Ashtoreth), the Phoenician goddess of fertility, whose Mesopotamian equivalent is the goddess Ishtar, had been worshiped since ancient times. The cult reached Greece via the islands of Cythera and Cyprus. According to legend, Aphrodite was born on one of these islands. It so happened that the

Aphrodite, the goddess of love, was allegedly born from the sea foam and first set foot on land in Cythera or Cyprus. The dove was dedicated to her.

frivolously inclined Aphrodite—like her father—was often unfaithful to her husband. Homer describes how Aphrodite deceived Hephæstos with the physically far more attractive war god Ares. But the sun-god Helios, who had seen them together in an intimate embrace, informed Hephæstos. In a blind fury, the deceived husband forged a net as fine as gossamer that was almost invisible and fixed it over his bed. Subsequently, he let it be known that he was going on a journey and Ares immediately visited the house of Hephæstos. But as soon as the two hot-blooded lovers landed up in bed, the net fell on top of them, so that they couldn't move and were pinned to the bed. The aggrieved Hephæstos returned home and invited the other gods to witness the scene, and they found it hilarious to observe the disgraced, adulterous couple. Yet the messenger-god Hermes admitted frankly on this occasion: "Even if three times as many ropes were to tie me and even if all of you gods and goddesses were watching, I would love to sleep with the golden Aphrodite!" (*The Odyssey*, book VIII, line 340-342). In the end, the sea-god, Poseidon ensured that Hephæstos and Aphrodite again became reconciled with each other.

Ares conceived several children by Aphrodite. They were Deimos and Phobos ("fright" and "fear"), Harmonia (the wife of Cadmus), and Eros, although it was also said

Like their mother, the swans, Aphrodite's sons and helpers, possessed the power to make people fall in love. These swans are pulling Aphrodite's chariot (her arm is just visible, left). Decorated vase, 5th century BCE.

titan Cronos had cut off the genitals of his father, Uranus, god of the heavens and first ruler over the universe, and threw them into the sea (*see* **Cronos**). A foam developed on the water from which Aphrodite emerged (the Greek word *afros* means "foam"). She walked ashore as a fully-grown young woman on Cyprus or Cythera. One of Aphrodite's fixed epithets was therefore "the Cypriot" or "the Cytherian," and on occasion she was called "the surfacing one".

According to the version favored by Homer, Aphrodite was the daughter of the supreme deity Zeus and the earth goddess Dione who was worshiped in Dodona in Ætolia. Aphrodite's' husband on Olympus was, of all people, Hephæstos (Vulcan) the deformed, crippled craftsman god. The

of Eros that he had conceived himself at a much earlier date.

As Hermes' words, quoted above, indicate, Ares was not the only one who desired Aphrodite. Either Hermes himself or the god of wine and vegetation Dionysus (Bacchus) made her pregnant through the fertility god Priapus, who was equipped with an enormous phallus. Hermaphrodite, a nymph who was both male and female, was born out of the relationship between Hermes and Aphrodite (see **Hermaphrodites**).

Only one mortal was also lucky enough to be allowed to make love to Aphrodite. His name was Anchises, and he was the father of Æneas, the Trojan hero who laid the foundations for the future city of Rome. Aphrodite herself fell for the beauty of the handsome youth, Adonis, but the love affair ended sadly when Adonis was killed by a wild boar while out hunting.

Aphrodite not only fell in love herself, she also had the ability to inflame others—gods and mortals—with passion. The only beings who were able to resist her gift were the virtuous and virginal goddesses Athena, Artemis, and Hestia. According to Homer, Aphrodite possessed a "love-belt embroidered with fur" that she lent out on occasion

The goddess Athena, and the owl dedicated to her, form the head and tail of this 5th century Athenian coin. Aphrodite and Athena were occasionally rivals and they competed in the contest known as the Judgment of Paris that lead to the Trojan War.

to Hera when she wanted Zeus to lose his head over her...

Sometimes, however, Aphrodite's whims had terrible consequences. She was, to a large extent, responsible for starting the Trojan War.

It all began so innocently when, during the wedding between the mortal Peleus and the sea-goddess Thetis, the goddess of strife Eris—who had not been invited—threw a golden apple among the wedding guests, that bore the inscription "for the most beautiful one." Hera, Athena, and Aphrodite were each of the opinion that this apple must be meant for them. Zeus ruled, therefore, that Paris, the handsome son of the Trojan King Priam, had to decide which of the three goddesses was the most beautiful.

All three tried to influence Paris' judgment. Hera promised him power, Athena promised him success in battle, and Aphrodite promised him the most beautiful woman in the world. Obviously Paris didn't have to think long about this. So Aphrodite therefore won this, the first beauty pageant, and you could say there was no context. It was just a pity that Helen, the most beautiful woman in the world, was already spoken for. She was the wife of king Menelaus of Sparta. Thanks to Aphrodite's assistance, however, Helena was instantly smitten by Paris and eloped with him to Troy. Menelaus, his powerful brother Agamemnon, and many other Greek rulers equipped a fleet in order to get her back. They sailed to Troy and finally destroyed the city after a bitter ten- year siege.

Many others fell victim—voluntarily or involuntarily—to Aphrodite's powers. Thus

Aphrodite (right) is probably honored in this wall painting from the Villa of Mysteries in Pompeii (1st century BCE). In addtion to her charms, Aphrodite had a less appealing dark side.

Remains of a temple dedicated to Aphrodite in modern Turkey. Aphrodite (Venus) was one of the most popular and honored of the gods and goddesses, throughout the Greco-Roman period.

Apollo, god of light and of the arts, playing the lyre. Apollo was an important god with many facets.

Queen Dido of Carthage fell in love with Aphrodite's son Æneas, with disastrous consequences for herself.

Aphrodite was easily offended and punished others because they had slighted her or had held her in contempt. For instance, she let Pasiphæa, the wife of the Cretan king Minos, become pregnant by a bull and brought the terrifying Minotaur into the world. The women of Lemnos, who had neglected to worship her, were given such an unpleasant body odor by her that their men abandoned them. The offended wives murdered all the husbands. The muse, Clio, who had made fun of Aphrodite and her love for the mortal Adonis, was punished by falling in love with a mortal herself. The muse, Calliope, who according to some had acted as referee in the conflict over Adonis between Aphrodite and Persephone, had to suffer when her son, Orpheus, was killed by savage Mæneads who had conceived a great passion for him. Poor princess Psyche, who was so stunningly beautiful that the people forgot to worship Aphrodite and who unintentionally even conquered Eros' heart, witnessed the blackest and most unattractive aspects of Aphrodite's character (*see* **Psyche**).

The goddess of love herself was, although immortal, not entirely invulnerable. When she tried to rescue her heavily wounded son Æneas from the battlefield on one occasion during the Trojan War, the Greek hero Diomedes wounded her in the arm with his lance so that she screamed in pain. The altogether more powerful Athena literally felled her to the ground when she came to the rescue of her lover Ares.

Apollo

Apollo, also called Phœbus Apollo, was one of the most important Greek gods. He belonged to the twelve gods who lived on Mount Olympus together with the supreme deity Zeus. Apollo, the son of Zeus and Leto, was—amongst other things—the god of the art of fortune-telling, the arts (specifically music), and archery. He was also a god of light connected with the sun (Phœbus or *foibos* means "shining"). He spread infectious diseases with his arrows, yet he was also able to cure illness, which is why he was also called "the one who strikes from afar." This dual nature was also reflected in the fact that he was the guardian deity of the shepherds while at the same time being identified with their archenemy, the wolf.

Apollo came from Lycia, located in what is now southwestern Turkey. By around 1000 BCE, Phœbus Apollo was already worshiped as one of the major Greek gods.

Artemis, wrapped warrior-like in lion-skin, was the twin sister of Apollo. Just like him, she was an exceptional archer—here she holds her bow in her left hand. Artemis Bendis from Tarente, 4th century BCE

killing the divine snake, he was allowed to establish his famous oracle in her former place of residence. The oracle of Delphi (connected with the sanctuaries of Apollo) that according to the Greeks was situated near the "navel" formed by Python's grave (or the center of the world) maintained a formidable

A vast area of Delphi, containing various buildings, was dedicated to Apollo. These are the ruins of the gymnasium that was part of the complex.

Dolphin on a small vase. The dolphin was dedicated to Apollo, and was used as the figurehead on the ship of his high priest, when he sailed around Greece.

Leto brought Apollo and his twin sister, Artemis, goddess of the hunt, into the world on the island of Delos, where she felt safe from the wrath of Zeus' jealous wife, Hera (*see* **Leto**). Apollo grew into an adult very quickly and traveled to the Delphi on the Greek mainland where the giant female snake Python lived in a crack in the ground. Python was the daughter of the earth goddess, Gaia. Earlier she had crossed Leto and had tried to prevent the birth of Apollo and Artemis. Apollo killed the monster with (according to the poet Ovid) "a thousand arrows." Although he had to do penance for the sin of

reputation throughout ancient times. It not only existed in mythology but also in reality, and was consulted by countless people. Answers to difficult questions were given by the clairvoyant–priestess, the Pythia (the word "python" was still part of her name). She sat on a three-legged stool placed over the crack in the ground in which the giant snake once lay and from there predictions were whispered to her by the one and only Apollo. This "oracle language" was usually obscure and was capable of interpretation in a number of different, a fact that greatly contributed to the reputation of the oracle for infallibility. According to modern thinking, the Pythia was probably overcome by poisonous fumes emanating from the depths, confusing her thoughts and turning her speech into gibberish. Her words would be treasured and interpreted into a "usable" prediction.

The Pythian Games were introduced in Delphi after the killing of Python. They began with music contents and later included sporting events. According to legend, the first priests of Delphi came from Crete, when Apollo (in the shape of a dolphin) led their ship to the harbor of Delphi.

After killing Python, Apollo felled many more with his arrows . He and his sister Artemis killed the giant Tityus because he tried to rape their mother. This act was different from killing Python because it was approved by Zeus. Tityus was subjected to perpetual torture in the Tartarus, the most "hellish" part of the underworld.

Niobe also became a victim of the revenge of Apollo and Artemis. She was the wife of the Amphion, King of Thebes, and had seven sons and seven daughters. She boasted that she was far more fertile than Leto, and even thought it totally unnecessary to make sacrifices to the goddess. Niobe suffered a terrible punishment for her arrogance. Apollo shot Niobe's seven sons dead with his arrows, while Artemis took care of her daughters. When only Niobe's youngest daughter, Chloris, was left alive and clasped her mother's dress in agony, Niobe begged them to spare her, but her plea was in vain. The youngest daughter was also hit by an arrow (although according to one version she remained alive, see **Chloris**). Niobe herself turned to stone from grief (see **Niobe**).

Apollo had to do penance for his acts of violence by placing himself in the service of a mortal. During this slave labor, he built the city walls of Troy (amongst other things)

Bronze Eros from the 2nd century BCE. Eros and Apollo came into conflict, when Apollo belittled Eros' accomplishments as an archer. Eros shot the boastful god with a love-arrow, causing him to have a burning desire for the nymph, Daphne.

along with the sea-god Poseidon (according to a different version, he undertook this work for payment but the Trojan king Laomedon refused to honor the debt).

During the Trojan War, Apollo was the most fanatical and feared divine supporter of the Trojans. He caused an epidemic of the Plague among the Greeks when they kidnaped the daughter of a priest of Apollo. According to some, Apollo was responsible for the death of Achilles, the greatest Greek hero of the Trojan War. Achilles lost his life because one of Paris' arrows hit him in the only vulnerable part of his body, his heel. It would have been Apollo, however, who would have ensured that the mediocre archer Paris would hit the target. Apollo granted prophetic gifts to the two children of the Trojan king Priam, Helenus and Cassandra. But because Cassandra rejected Apollo as a lover, she was not allowed to take much pleasure in her gift of clairvoyance because Apollo ensured that her predictions—although always accurate—were never believed.

Asclepius, the god of medicine, was a son of Apollo, who occasionally spread contagious diseases with his arrows. Bronze statue from Roman times.

Apollo contemplates while playing his lyrenear a temple graced with a golden statue of the god. Apollo was an outstanding and sensitive musician, but took vengeance on those who criticized his talent, as King Midas could bear witness. Illustration on a krater from Tarente, 4th century BCE.

The Temple of Apollo in the Roman city of Pompeii, with Vesuvius, the volcano that destroyed the city, in the background. The Romans honored Apollo as an example of Greek civilization.

Cassandra was not the woman to reject Apollo's advances, the nymph, Daphne, also spurned him. Eros, who had been offended by Apollo, took revenge by letting the mighty deity fall in love with Daphne. In desperation, she fled from the voluptuous god. When he was close to catching her, she begged to be released from the body that had aroused his desire and was changed into a laurel bush (*see* **Daphne**). Apollo was more successful with the boys. His relationship with the handsome Hyacinth resulted in tragedy, however, when Apollo accidentally killed his friend with a discus (*see* **Hyacinthus**).

Yet Apollo managed to produce some offspring, and the son he conceived by the princess Coronis, Asclepius, became the god of medicine. Not that Asclepius was brought into the world in a wholly conventional manner. Since Coronis was disloyal to Apollo, Artemis killed her. Apollo himself or Hermes took the as-yet- unborn Asclepius from Coronis' dead body as it lay on the stake.

One important aspect of Apollo that was of overwhelming importance was his gift for art and music. In his capacity as an artistic god, he was the leader of the nine muses, the tutelary deities of the arts and sciences. Apollo himself invented the kithara, the Greek instrument that is acknowledged of as the predecessor of the lute and the guitar, but his favorite instrument, with which he was most often depicted, was the harp. Apollo did not develop this instrument. The youthful Hermes gave it to him as compensation for stealing some cattle from Apollo (*see* **Hermes**). Apollo also played the flute, and with some distinction. The satyr Marsyas, who thought that he could play better and was so arrogant as to challenge the god to a flute contest, suffered a humiliating defeat and was subsequently skinned alive by Apollo. The Phrygian king Midas also experienced Apollo's somewhat over-sensitive reaction with regard

The war-god Ares was fearsome and savage, but not particularly intelligent.

The goddess Aphrodite (Venus). The seductive goddess of love, wife of the disfigured blacksmith Hephæstos, had an extra-marital affair with the warlike Ares. Stoneware statue from the 1st century CE.

to appreciation of his music. After he first heard the god Pan play on his reed-pipe and then heard Apollo give a virtuoso performance on the harp, he disagreed with the other listeners who preferred Apollo's performance to that of Pan. This so irritated Apollo that he gave Midas donkey's ears.

As Apollo gave the oracles their predictions, he also inspired poets, singers, and musicians who played his beloved instruments. The thoroughly Greek Apollo also inspired the Romans who admired and imitated Greek civilization. The first Roman emperor, Augustus, dedicated a temple to Apollo in 28 BCE on the Palatine Hill, in the heart of Rome. Augustus wanted to indicate by this that , as ruler of the Roman Empire, he was spreading civilization across the world

Ares (Roman=*Mars*)

Ares, son of the supreme deity Zeus and his wife Hera, was the Greek god of war. He was one of the twelve Olympian gods who, lived with Zeus on Mount Olympus. Unlike from the strategically gifted, intelligent Athena who also often occupied herself with warfare, Ares was a hooligan, a violent and aggressive figure who contributed little to humanity. Once, his father Zeus told him bluntly that he hated him most of all Olympian gods and that the only reason why he was tolerated in his presence was that he was his and Hera's son.

Ares did not marry but conducted

Ares (right) met his match at the Battle of Troy, in the form of the much more intelligent Athena (left). Oil painting by Peter Paul Rubens, 17th century.

many extramarital affairs. The most famous is his relationship with Aphrodite, the goddess of love and beauty, by whom he conceived Harmonia (the wife of Cadmus) and the twin sons, Deimos ("fright") and Phobos ("fear"). There is a well-known story about Aphrodite's husband Hephæstos who became aware of her adultery and made an invisible net that he fixed above his bed. When Ares and Aphrodite fell on the bed, they became entangled in this net, after which Hephæstos humiliated them by showing them to the other gods (*see* **Aphrodite**).

Ares was worshiped in the Greek city-state of Sparta where everything connected with warfare was held in high regard. Nor was he neglected in Athens,the city of culture. The hill on which the highest Athenian court of law was located was called the Areopagus, the "Hill of Ares." According to a certain myth, a son of the sea-god Poseidon had once raped the mortal woman, Alcippe, there. Ares had beaten the criminal to death and was tried on the spot—and acquitted—by a council of the gods. This is why the hill was named for him.

Ares supported the Trojans in the Trojan War but his performance on the battlefield was far from impressive. The mortal Diomedes wounded him and was put to flight, and he also tasted defeat in a direct confrontation with Athena. The great hero Heracles once also managed to wound Ares.

Mars, the Roman god of war who was on a par with Ares, was of much greater significance for the Romans, because he was the father of Romulus and Remus, the founders of the city of Rome. In fact, he was partly responsible for the enormous success of the Romans who were able to establish their world empire, thanks to their perfectly organized armies and their focus on military might. The Romans dedicated the Campus Martius, the Field of Mars, in the heart of their city to him. The month of March is also named for Mars.

The Argonauts

The Argonauts ("navigators of the Argo") were a group of heroes who sailed to the land of Colchis on the *Argo*, a ship commanded by Jason in order to obtain the Golden Fleece, the coat of a supernatural ram. The history of the eventful journey of the Argonauts can be considered as one of the oldest adventure stories in western literature. Many classical authors, including the Hellenistic poet Apollonius of Rhodes and the Roman poet Ovid, described the expedition of the fifty fearless heroes to distant Colchis.

The prelude to the journey of the Argonauts was the flight of Phrixus and Helle, two royal children, from Bœotia. Seated on the back of a flying ram with a golden fleece they

The Argo had the most outstanding heros of Greece as crew members. This relief of a ship was carved in the 8th century BCE in Anatolia. The Argonauts sailed along the northern coast of Anatolia.

On the ship Argo, the Argonauts sailed to the distant land of Colchis, east of the Black Sea. The Argo may have looked similar to this modern replica of an Athenian trireme.

tried to escape from their stepmother Ino. Along the way, Helle fell off the ram and drowned in the sea that is still named for her—the Hellespont. Phrixus was able to reach Colchis (located to the east of the Black Sea) and stayed there at the court of King Æetes. The golden fleece of the ram was hung up in a holy forest that was dedicated to Ares and guarded by a dragon that never slept.

Later, Jason, son of Æson, was instructed by his uncle Pelias to go and get this Golden Fleece. Pelias' intentions were far from honorable. At the expense of Jason's father, he had seized the throne of Iolcus, a city-state in Magnesia, part of Thessaly. Jason's mother pretended that the baby Jason was dead but secretly had him raised by the centaur Chiron, an excellent teacher who had in the past taken several great heroes under his wing (*see* **Chiron**). Meanwhile, the evil Pelias was told by the oracle at Delphi that danger was looming in the shape of a descendant of Æson who only wore one sandal. When Jason returned to Iolcus as a young gentleman, his patron Hera ensured that, when crossing a river, he lost one sandal, so that he arrived at

The Dioscuri, Castor and Polydeuces, were among the heroes who accompanied Jason. Polydeuces' talents as a boxer were useful to the Argonauts. This is a statue of one of the Dioscuri at the Capitol in Rome.

the court of Pelias with one bare foot. Pelias immediately realized what had happened and promised the throne of Iolcus to Jason, but only if he got him the Golden Fleece. The fact was that this was an impossible task and Pelias was sure that Jason would not survive the mission.

The oracle at Delphi, however, judged Jason's chances favorably. That is why he had Argus ("the swift") build the *Argo*. The goddess Athena added a beam to the prow of the Argo made from a branch of a talking oak tree from the holy forest of Zeus in Dodona. Jason gathered fifty heroes to accompany him on the perilous journey. Each of the Argonauts were excellent men. They included the Dioscurians, Castor and Polydeuces, Peleus (husband of the goddess Thetis and father of Achilles), Theseus, the great hero of Athens, the famous singer and musician Orpheus, Zetes and Calais (the sons of Boreas, the north wind), the helmsman Tiphys, the shipbuilder Argus, Admetus of Pherae, and even Heracles, the greatest of all Greek heroes.

The courageous sailors braved many adventures. The Argonauts conceived offspring after Aphrodite had lifted her curse on the island of Lemnos, where the women developed a terrible body odor thanks to Aphrodite and subsequently killed their menfolk for spurning them.

Heracles left the *Argo* after he had saved the ship from a number of belligerent six-armed earth giants. Captivated by the beauty of his shield-bearer, Hylas, who had been

Hylas, a handsome young man was abducted by water-nymphs in Bithynia. This water-nymph guards a pond in the Villa Borghese in Rome.

monsters. Phineus was, however, freed from them and as a token of gratitude, gave the Argonauts valuable advice for the future.

The Argonauts encountered the Symplegades near the Bosphorus, the entrance to the Black Sea (called Pontos Euxeinos or "hospitable sea" by the Greeks—a classic euphemism!) The Symplegades were two rocks that continuously opened and closed. Fortunately Phineus had given them the

To conquer the Golden Fleece, Jason first had to yoke a team of fire-breathing oxen to a plow. Rhyton (drinking-cup) in the form of an ox-head from Tarente, 4th century BCE.

kidnaped by water nymphs, he stayed behind in Bithynia. He then had to return to Greece in order to complete his Twelve Labors (*see* **Heracles**).

King Amycus of the Bebrycians had a nasty habit of challenging all his visitors to a boxing-match with him that invariably ended in death. Anyone who did not accept the challenge would be thrown into the sea from a high cliff. Polydeuces, one of the two Dioscurians, was an excellent boxer, however, killed the king during their boxing-match. The subjects of Amycus turned out to be no match for the other Argonauts.

The next port of call of the *Argo* was Salmydessus, the capital of the Thracian kingdom of Thynia. The local king, Phineus, who was blind and could predict the future, was being persecuted by the Harpies (*see* **Harpies**). These monstrous beings, half bird, half-woman, robbed him of his food and soiled his table with their dung. The winged heroes, Calais and Zetes, drove the Harpies away but were ordered by Zeus not to kill the

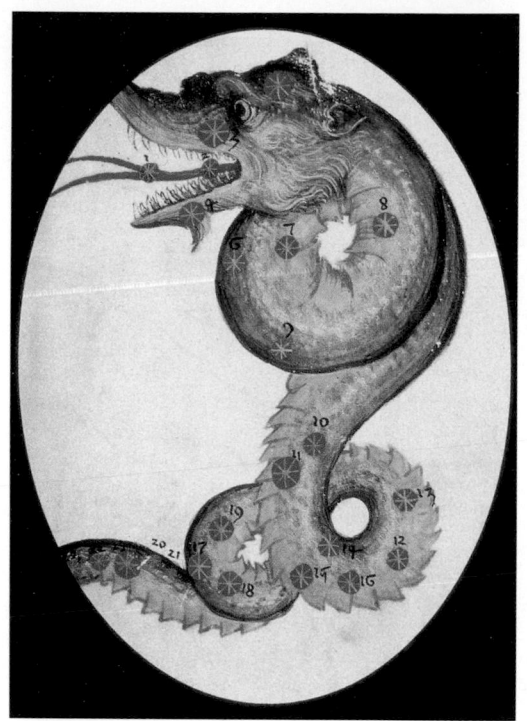

advice of letting a pigeon fly through the gap first. The bird just made it, although it lost some tail-feathers. Whatever a pigeon could do, the exceedingly strong rowers on board of the *Argo* could do as well. The ship passed through the dangerous rocks safely, although it lost a piece of its stern. After the passage of the *Argo* no other ship was ever again obstructed when passing through the Symplegades or Dark Rocks.

After some minor adventures, Jason and his traveling companions reached in the capital city of Colchis, where Jason asked king Æetes if he could be permitted to take the Golden Fleece away with him. The king consented but stipulated that Jason had to hitch up two fire-breathing bulls with steel noses and bronze hooves to a plow. He then had to plow a plot of land, sow dragon's teeth in the soil, and conquer the heavily armed men who would spring from these infernal seeds. Æetes thought that this was an impossible task but he did not foresee that his daughter, Medea, a gifted sorceress, would fall head-over heels in love with the foreign hero. Medea gave Jason a magic ointment that made him immune from the flaming breath of

the bulls and advised him to throw a heavy stone between the warriors who emerged from the dragon's teeth so that they would start fighting amongst themselves. Everything went according to Medea's plans and Jason was able to collect the Golden Fleece from the sacred wood. Conquering the dragon that guarded the sacred wood did not pose an insurmountable problem because Medea had

given Jason magic herbs that immediately caused the monster to fall into a deep sleep.

Æetes furiously pursued the Argonauts who had taken Medea on board and had left Colchis immediately. After this, Medea killed her little brother, Apsyrtus, and cut his body into pieces, which she threw into the sea. Æetes could not leave his son unburied and recovered his remains so the Argonauts managed to escape and sailed back to Iolcus.

According to another version it was the (adult) Apsyrtus who instigated the pursuit on the instructions of his father. Jason negotiated with him and agreed that he could keep the Golden Fleece but only on condition that Medea would return to Colchis with Apsyrtus. Medea was furious with Jason who maintained that he had intended to deceive Apsyrtus. Jason and Medea subsequently murdered Apsyrtus treacherously. Zeus was so disgusted with this atrocity that, communicating through the speaking beam of the prow of the *Argo*, ordered Jason and Medea to do penance for their sins, with Medea's aunt, the sorceress, Circe.

Circe lived on the island of Ææa off the west coast of Italy. Circe exonerated Jason and Medea of their sins, but she realized the seriousness of their crime, she foresaw a diffi-

The coast off the island of Crete. From here, the frightening bronze man Talos threw huge rocks at the Argo.

cult future ahead for them, and begged them to leave her house.

Pelias accepted the Golden Fleece but he had no intention of abdicating. Even this depraved character was no match for Medea's crafty schemes. Shortly after the arrival of the *Argo*, Medea succeeded, with the help of her sorcery, in rejuvenating Jason's old and seriously weakened father, Æson. Pelias' daughters came to know about this and wanted the same to be done for their father. Medea was very willing to demonstrate how to go about it. She cut up an old ram and cooked the mutton in a pot with plenty of magical herbs. The animal jumped out of the pot as a young spring lamb. Pelias' daughters then killed their father and cooked him— but unfortunately for them Medea had omitted to add the required herbs.

After this act of revenge, Jason did not become king of Iolcus but left for Corinth with Medea, where both their sons were born. At a certain moment, Jason decided to divorce Medea and to take Glauce, the daughter of the Corinthian king, as his wife. Medea's response was devastating. She had her sons deliver a beautiful wedding dress, which was treated with sorcery. Glauce caught fire when she put on the dress and the future bride and her father, who tried to rescue her, were killed in the flames. Medea then killed both their sons in order to hurt Jason even more. She escaped to Athens in a float carried by flying dragons. There she sought refuge with King Ægeus whom she later married (*see* **Ægeus** *and* **Medea**).

Jason remained behind in Corinth, a broken man. He could often be found beside his old ship where, in a somber mood, he reflected on his glorious past adventures. The *Argo* itself only fared marginally better than its former captain. One day a piece of rotten wood fell off the ship and killed Jason (*see* **Jason** *and* **Medea**).

Ariadne

Ariadne was the daughter of King Minos of Crete and his wife, Pasiphae. When the hero of Athens, Theseus, came to Minos, accompanying the seven boys and seven girls who had to be sacrificed every nine years by the city of Athens to the carnivorous Minotaur (who patrolled in the Labyrinth near Minos' palace) Ariadne fell in love with him.

Theseus promised to marry Ariadne if he

succeeded in killing the Minotaur and returning alive. Ariadne consulted the artist Dædalus (the architect of the Labyrinth) and thought up a scheme. When Theseus entered the Labyrinth she gave him a long cord that was fixed to the entrance. Theseus killed the Minotaur and found his way back out of the complicated maze, thanks to Ariadne's rope. After this Theseus and Ariadne escaped from Crete but for some obscure reason, Theseus abandoned Ariadne on the island of Naxos. One possibility is that he had to give her up to the god of wine, Dionysus, but it was also possible that Dionysus took it upon himself to look after the abandoned Ariadne. According to the most accepted version, she became the bride of the god, and in her honor, he threw her diadem high in the air and ever since it can be admired at night as the Northern Crown constellation (*see* **Dædalus**, **Minos**, *the* **Minotaur** *and* **Theseus**).

Homer produced a completely different version of events. He lets his hero Odysseus recount that during his short visit to the underworld he saw Ariadne amongst the shades. Artemis had her killed on Naxos on the instructions of Dionysus.

Arion

Arion came from Methymna on the island of Lesbos and was a famous singer and lyre-player. He spent a large part of his life at the

The thread that Ariadne gave to the hero, Theseus, to enable him to find his way out of the Labyrinth.

court of Periander, the tyrant of Corinth (an historical figure who ruled between 625–585 BCE). At one point, Arion successfully toured Italy and Sicily. He wanted to sail back to Corinth, and for safety reasons, he took a ship with an entirely Corinthian crew. This was a miscalculation, because the seafarers robbed him of his earnings and were about to throw him overboard. Arion begged them to let him live and asked as a last request if he could sing a song on the afterdeck of the ship. The sailors didn't object

Part of the Palace of King Minos at Cnossos on Crete. The mythical Labyrinth, inhabited by the Minotaur may have been part of this giant complex.

and after singing a beautiful aria dedicated to Apollo, Arion jumped overboard. After the ship had sailed on for some time, a dolphin came to the rescue of the singer. The

The marriage of the wine-god Dionysus and the heavily-veiled Ariadne. Dionysus married Ariadne on the island of Naxos. Painting on an Athenian kylix of the 6th century BCE.

came by and took Arion on its back, putting

The famous singer, Arion, was saved by a dolphin after the crew of the ship on which was traveling, robbed him and threw him overboard. Decoration on an octagonal dish of the 4th century CE.

him ashore in the Peloponnese. Arion travelled to Corinth and told his story to Periander who listened in disbelief. But when the sailors subsequently told Periander that they had left Arion in Italy, the singer suddenly appeared and the seafarers were shown up for

According to the Greeks, the Northern Crown star constellation (Corona Borealis, left) was Ariadne's diadem, thrown into the firmament by her newly-wed husband, Dionysus.

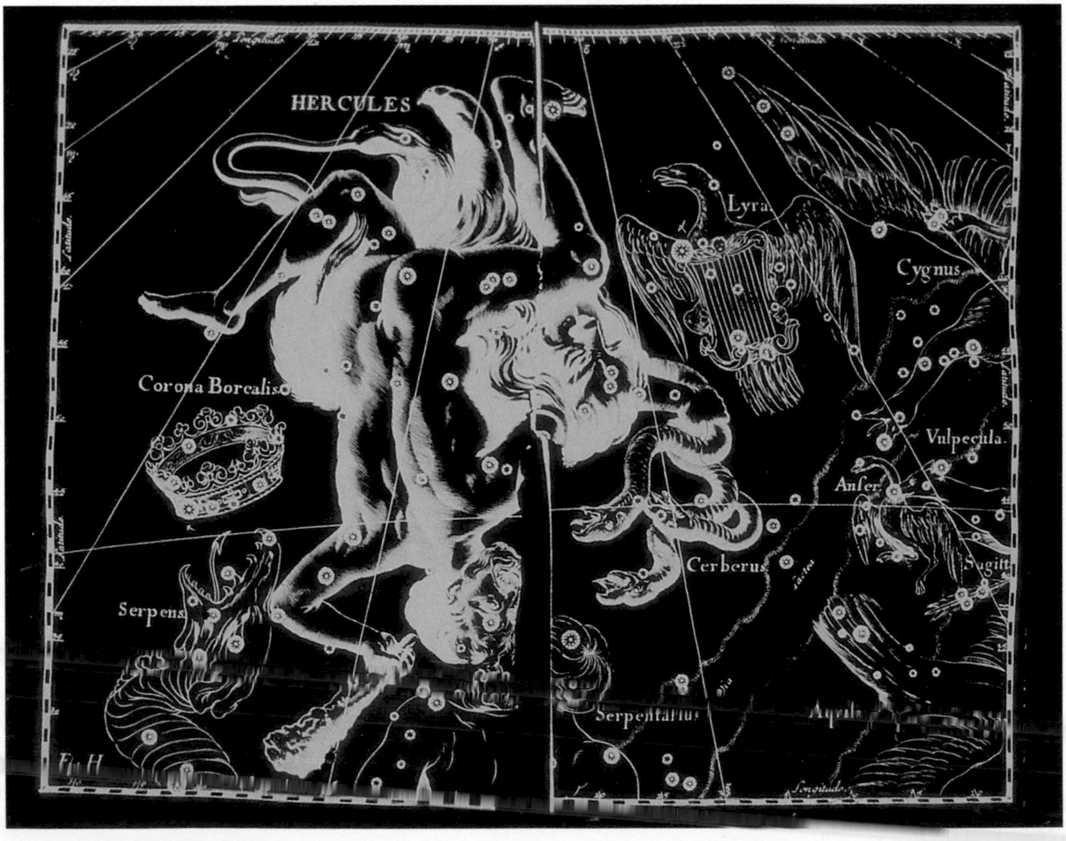

the liars that they were.

Artemis (Roman=*Diana*)

Artemis, the daughter of the supreme deity Zeus and Leto, was one of the twelve Olympians who dwelt with Zeus on Mount Olympus. She was Apollo's twin sister and the goddess of the hunt and the countryside. Although Artemis is mostly depicted as a virginal goddess who had an expressed loathing of sexuality, she originally was probably a less prudish mother-goddess who was worshiped in Ephesus (in what is now western Turkey).

Artemis' brother Apollo killed people by spreading contagious diseases although at the same time was the god of medicine. In the same way, Artemis was goddess of the hunt as well as the patron of wild animals (the poet Homer called her "mistress of the animals.") Like Apollo, Artemis was very skilled with the bow and arrow. Apollo preferred to kill men with his arrows, but Artemis would strike at women who had done wrong. In this

Head of Artemis. The goddess of the chase was sometimes wrapped in a lion skin. The head of the animal forms a hood on her head. Antefix from Tarente, 4th century BCE.

The goddess of hunting and nature, Artemis, was as experienced in handling the bow and arrow, as her twin brother Apollo.

way Apollo killed the sons of Niobe, who bragged about the fact that she was more fertile than Leto (the mother of Apollo and Artemis), but her daughters were killed by Artemis (see **Apollo** *and* **Niobe**).

The giant Tityus, who had raped Leto, also became the victim of a collective act of revenge by the divine twins. After they killed him his body was banished to the Tartarus, in

Hades, where he was subjected to perpetual torture. Due to the murderous and sinister aspects of her character, Artemis was put on a par with the frightening Hecate, the goddess of sorcery and magic. Artemis could, indeed, be very scary. King Admetus of Pherae, who had not properly worshiped her, found his bedroom full of snakes after his wedding (see **Alcestis**). The mighty Mycenæan king, Agamemnon, had to sacrifice his daughter Iphigenia to the goddess after he had once insulted her (see **Agamemnon** *and* **Iphigenia**). Artemis' dark side expressed itself literally in the fact that she was associated with the moon goddess, Selene; her twin brother Apollo (the "shining one") was associated with the sun.

Artemis was no match for Zeus' wife Hera who was bore a grudge against all the children that Zeus had conceived by other women. Homer describes how Hera once cursed and swore at Artemis (who supported the Trojans in the Trojan War) and hit her over the head with her own bow. The otherwise tough Artemis burst into tears and crawled sobbing to the lap of her father Zeus.

Artemis, despite of her principled virginity, was not insensitive to male physical beauty. This emerges from the tale of the great Bœotian hunter, Orion. Artemis fell for his charms and invited him to go hunting with her. According to one version, Orion subsequently slept with Eos, the goddess of dawn, and the jealous Artemis then killed him. Another

Artemis seen drying herself after bathing. The hunter Actæon suffered the consequences of seeing Artemis naked—even though it was not deliberate. Oil painting by Peter Paul Rubens, 17th century.

Artemis discovers that Callisto, a victim of the erotic escapades of her father Zeus, is pregnant. Artemis demanded that her followers remain virgins. Oil painting by Adriaan van der Werff, 17th–18th century.

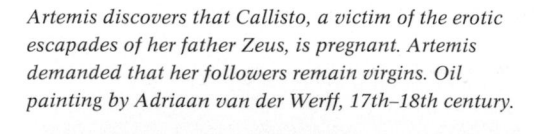

Ascanius

version says that Apollo was jealous of the relationship between his twin sister and the handsome tyrant. He cunningly persuaded Artemis to unwittingly kill Orion (who was swimming in the sea without her knowing) from a great distance with an arrow shot (*see* **Orion**).

Actæon discovered that Artemis usually stood by her principles. He was the accidental witness to a scene of Artemis undressing and bathing with her nymphs. The goddess changed him into a deer, which caused him to be torn to death by his own pack of hounds (*see* **Actæon**).

Callisto, one of Artemis' attendants, lost her virginity when Zeus raped her. While bathing, Artemis discovered that Callisto was pregnant, and immediately expelled her from her circle. Hera who was jealous because Callisto had aroused passion in Zeus subsequently turned her into a bear. Later, Zeus placed Callisto in the sky as the Great Bear constellation, but Hera still demanded the last word, and ensured that this constellation could not set in the sea (*see* **Callisto**).

Ascanius was the son of the Trojan hero Æneas and his first wife, Creusa. According to Roman mythology, Ascanius founded the city of Alba Longa, thirty-three years after a group of Trojan fugitives under the leadership of his father arrived in Italy (*see* **Æneas**). His second name was Iulus (originally Ilus, derived from Ilium, the Greek name for Troy) and because of that the Iulii or Julieranians (the family of Julius Caesar and the Emperor Augustus) maintained that they were descended from Æneas and Ascanius.

The Roman historian, Livy, maintained that Ascanius' mother was not Creusa but Lavinia, the Latin princess whose marriage to Æneas sealed the peace between the Trojans and the Latins. Æneas founded Lavinium in order to honor her. According to this version, Ascanius became king of Lavinium after Æneas' death and founded Alba Longa. Several generations later, his descendants, the brothers Romulus and Remus, founded the city of Rome.

The statue of the Roman supreme commander and statesman, Julius Caesar, dominates the Roman Forum. Caesar and his family members claimed to be descended from Ascanius and Æneas.

to their ability to "rejuvenate" by shedding their skin every year.

Asclepius was married to Epione and had two sons, who fought in the Trojan War and nursed their wounded fellow combatants. Curiously enough, Asclepius, although a god and a healer, was not immortal, and his ability to resurrect others from the dead proved to be his undoing. The supreme deity Zeus struck him dow with a thunderbolt as a punishment for his presumption.

Apollo eventually placed his son in the sky as the constellation of Ophiucus, the snake-bearer, who bestrides the sky between Sagitarius and Scorpio.

Asclepius was delivered by caesarean section from the dead body of his mother, Coronis. Painted dish by Francesco Urbini and Giorgio Andreoli, 16th century.

Asclepius (Roman= *Æsculapius*)

Asclepius was the Greek god of medicine, the son of the great Apollo and the nymph Coronis. Apollo's twin sister, Artemis, killed Coronis before she could give birth to Asclepius because she had been unfaithful to Apollo, but Asclepius was removed from his mother's dead body by his father or Hermes. The centaur, Chiron, who had educated many of the gods and heroes, raised him and taught him the arts and medicine. As a son of Apollo—who himself also possessed therapeutic powers—Asclepius already had the natural gift of healing.

Asclepius was worshiped in Epidaurus in the Peloponnese. The island of Cos also had an important Asclepium, a sanctuary of the god visited by pilgrims to find a cure for their illnesses. In Asclepius' medicine, the snake that was dedicated to him played an important role. In depictions, this snake often wriggles around his staff, and the staff of Asclepius remains the international medical symbol, even today. The power of healing attributed to snakes could possibly be related

Ruins of the large Asclepium on the island of Cos. This Asclepium, containing a well that spurts out sulfurous water, was a type of health spa.

This small temple, with its Ionic columns is dedicated to Asclepius. It was built in the 18th century in the grounds of the Villa Borghese in Rome. A statue of the god stands inside the temple.

Antique illustration of the Snake Holder star constellation. After his death, the mortal god Asclepius was set in the universe, by his father Apollo, as the Snake Holder.

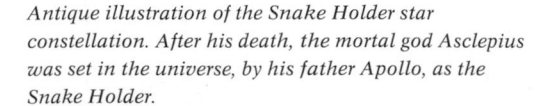

This small temple, with its Ionic columns is dedicated to Asclepius. It was built in the 18th century in the grounds of the Villa Borghese in Rome. A statue of the god stands inside the temple.

Antique illustration of the Snake Holder star constellation. After his death, the mortal god Asclepius was set in the universe, by his father Apollo, as the Snake Holder.

Atalanta

There are two different versions of the myth of the great huntress, Atalanta. In the first version, she was the daughter of Iasus of Arcadia; in the second version her father was the Bœotian Schœneus. In both cases, her mother was called Clymene.

Atalanta was abandoned as a child on a mountainside because her father would have liked to have had a son. A she-bear took care of her and suckled her, after which hunters raised her further. Due to this very unusual

Stoneware rooster of the 6th century BCE. When the Athenian philosopher, Socrates, was condemned death by being forced to drink from a poisoned chalice, he asked his followers to offer a rooster to Asclepius so that his soul would finally be freed from the prison of his body.

childhood, Atalanta became very unfeminine and was only interested in typical male pursuits. She was strong and able-bodied, as two centaurs soon found out when they tried to rape her and were killed by her arrows. Atalanta was even conscripted as an Argonaut (*see* **the Argonauts**) but their leader, Jason, did not approve of having a woman on board of his ship.

When the area surrounding the city of Calydon was ravaged by an evil wild boar that had been sent by Artemis, Atalanta joined the hunting party that set out to kill the monster. She was one of the few who succeeded in hitting the animal with her arrow. This caused some of her companions to make spiteful and jealous remarks and this led to fatally reckless behavior on their part. Eventually, Meleager, who had his eye on Atalanta, killed the boar. When slaughtering the boar, he let her share in the kill, something else that the other hunters didn't like, so Meleager killed two of them.

Atalanta did her best to avoid marriage. She demanded from her father that whoever wanted to marry her had to defeat her in a race, but anyone who lost against her had to be killed on the spot. Because of Atalanta's extreme beauty, many men accepted the challenge, but all marriage candidates lost against

her fleetness of foot, although they ran naked and Atalanta ran fully dressed. With the help of the goddess of love. Aphrodite, Milanion

(in the Arcadian version) or Hippomenes (in the Bœotic version) eventually managed to stay ahead of Atalanta, thanks to Aphrodite's ruse of giving the young man three golden apples which he dropped on the concourse at different spots during the race. Curious about these unusual fruits, Atalanta (who had already fallen in love with the young man and could not bear the thought that he would die) stopped in order to pick them up. In this way Milanion/Hippomenes won the race and also Atalanta as his wife. He failed to show the goddess of love any gratitude, however, and even dared to make love to Atalanta in the temple of the goddess Cybele, which was very inappropriate. The offended Aphrodite therefore turned Milanion/ Hippomenes and Atalanta into lions. This punishment was even crueler because in Antiquity, it was believed that lions did not mate with each other but with panthers.

Athena (Roman=*Minerva*)

Athena or Pallas Athene was one of the twelve Olympic gods who lived on Mount Olympus together with the supreme deity Zeus. She was one of the most important Greek goddesses and had many aspects to her characteristic. She was the goddess of war but also the goddess of wisdom and science, and the patron of various occupations.

Athena also had a special affinity for cities, and especially Athens, where she was worshiped in many temples as the pre-eminent tutelary deity.

The wisdom and versatility of the virginal Athena were a direct consequence of her remarkable birth. Zeus once conceived a child by the Oceanide Metis ("wisdom" or

Athena came into this world in a unique manner, being born out of the head of her father, Zeus.

"thought") who, according to some versions of the story, was his first wife. After the

goddess of the earth, Gaia, and the god of the heavens, Uranus, predicted to Zeus that the god who would be born of Metis' next pregnancy who would be superior to him, he devoured every part of the frightened Uranus. Some time later, Zeus got a thumping headache. Hephæstos, the craftsman amongst the gods, came to the rescue and with his tools he split open the skull of his father from which Athena (fully-grown and in full battledress) jumped out. So Athena could rightly be called a daddy's girl who in many ways took after her almighty father.

The owl and the olive branch on this Attic coin were characteristic symbols of Athena, the guardian goddess of Athens and Attica.

Athena's considerable valor was her most striking feature. The tall, slender goddess wore a helmet most of the time and was armed with a spear. She wore the *ægis* (the "goatskin") given to her by her father over her shoulders. It was decorated with tassels and the head of the gorgon, Medusa. This terrifying face, whose glare could turn people to stone, also adorned her shield (*see* **The Gorgons**). An owl, the creature that symbolized her wisdom, often accompanied Athena. The poet Homer called her "the owlish one" which seems to support the theory that the goddess was once worshiped in the form of an owl. Athena's little owl is also depicted on coins minted in the city of Athens.

Athena's special ties with Athens were established after she competed with the sea-god Poseidon for possession of the province of Attica, in which Athens was located. The sea-god used his trident to create a well that rose from the Acropolis but Athena caused an olive-tree to grow on the same spot. The gods and goddesses who acted as referees thought this to be a more valuable gift. So the local inhabitants choose Athena to be their patron goddess and named their city for her. The most important temples built on the Acropolis, the Erechtheum and the Parthenon—literary "the house of virgins" because of Athena's virginal status—were dedicated to her. The Parthenon contained a magnificent, 40-foot-high statue of the goddess made by the great sculptor Phidias. Her robes were of pure gold. The holy olive-tree offered to the city by Athena had a place of honor within the temple complex on the Acropolis. The tree

The warrior-like goddess Athena, in full weapon attire. Detail from an oil painting by Arnold Houbraken, 18th century.

Athena dressed in helmet and robe. The heavenly "goatskin," is draped over her shoulders, and on her hand there perches the owl, the creature that symbolizes her wisdom. Small bronze statue from the 1st century BCE.

Like Artemis, the tall and slim Athena was a virgin out of conviction. Nevertheless she had a preference for strong, extremely manly heros. Small stoneware statue from Tarente, 3rd century BCE

miraculously began to grow again after the Persians had destroyed the acropolis in 480 BCE. Even today, a living olive-tree grows just outside the temple.

According to another story from the mythical early history of the city, Athene wanted Hephæstos to make love to her as compensation for the fact that he had helped to bring her into the world, but at the last moment, Athena escaped his embrace and Hephæstos' sperm ejected onto the floor. From it sprouted Erichthonius whom Athena entrusted to the daughters of Cecrops, one of the first kings of Athens, but this had terrible consequences (see **Cecrops**). Erichthonius was later made king of the city.

Athena, in contrast with the goddess Artemis, was not shy and retiring, and did not want to live in the woods and mountains, away from mankind. In fact, she intervened actively in the lives of humans, and there are countless myths and stories about her activities in this respect. Few of the gods were more actively involved in the Trojan War, in which she was an indefatigable helper of the Greeks. She encouraged them to wage war in the first place, protected them, came to their rescue, and would sometimes fight alongside them. Her half-brother, Ares, the god of war, who supported the Trojans, was no match for her, but that is not surprising because Ares was the god of headstrong, ill-advised battle while Athena embodied the well-considered art of warfare. Her support of the Greeks was not unlimited and unconditional, however. When the youthful Ajax raped Cassandra, daughter of the Trojan king, on her altar after the fall of Troy while at the same time knocking over her statue, she stopped supporting the Greeks. It ended badly for Ajax (see **Ajax**) and only Odysseus remained in Athena's favor. But then Odysseus was a man after Athena's heart, a hero who did not use brute force but rather his intelligence

Other heroes who were supported by Athena in their superhuman tasks were Heracles (who had much to thank her for), Jason, Bellerophon, and Perseus. Perseus killed the gorgon, Medusa, with Athena's help. Medusa had insulted Athena and was turned by her into a hideous creature, so repulsive that anyone who saw her was instantly turned to stone. Perseus hacked off the head of Medusa and offered it to his guardian who affixed it to her *ægis* and depicted it on her shield.

Orestes was the son of Agamemnon and Clytemnestra, who killed his mother to

In this illustration—which points to her role as guardian goddess of art and industry—Athena/Minerva is in the unfamiliar company of four putti. Oil painting by Jacob de Wit, 18th century.

revenge the murder of his father by her (see **Orestes** *and* **Agamemnon**). For this reason, he was pursued by the Erinyans, and with Athena's help, obtained asylum in Athens. The goddess ensured that he would be tried on the Areopagus and cast her deciding vote in his favor. In this way, she stood at the cradle of the Athens' tradition of the fair administration of justice by means of a jury. Another Athenian tradition was that of granting asylum to political and other refugees. In mythology, the embattled King Œdipus also benefited from this custom.

Minerva, the Roman goddess of the arts, industry, science, and wisdom, was worshiped throughout Italy. Originally, she was probably an Etruscan goddess. At an early period, she was equated with Athena and although at first she lacked Athena's warlike streak, the Romans later depicted her in battledress. Like Athena, Minerva became a goddess of war as well as wisdom. Roma, goddess of the city of Rome, was depicted as having her appearance

Atlas

The Titan, Atlas, was the son of Iapetus and the nymph Clymene. After the Titans had been conquered by Zeus and his brothers, Atlas was not imprisoned with the rest of them in the hellish Underworld. Zeus inflicted a special punishment upon him by making him carry the arch of heaven on his shoulders. Atlas performed this demanding task in the remotest western corner of the world (as it was then known then to the Greeks), not far from the Straits of Gibraltar.

The Titan Atlas was not imprisoned in the underworld, like the other Titans but as an alternative punishment, he had to carry the heavens upon his shoulders.

The great hero Heracles visited Atlas as one of this Twelve Labors, he had to collect the golden apples from the Hesperides. The earth-goddess, Gaia, had given these apples to Hera when Hera married Zeus. Hera had given them to the Hesperides, the daughters of Atlas, for safekeeping. The apples were stored in a beautiful garden, where they were guarded by the dragon, Ladon.

Atlas put a proposition to his visitor. In order to save Heracles the trouble of fighting the dragon, he would go fetch the apples himself. Heracles would only have to carry the arch of heaven for a short while. Fortunately, Heracles was strong enough for the task and Atlas went into the garden. When he returned with the apples, he suggested that he would be delighted to deliver them himself to Heracles' principal, Eurystheus, and the hero

Atlas bearing the heavens on his back, showing Zeus enthroned as the supreme god, ruling over the star constellations of the zodiac.

could continue to perform his task in the meantime. Heracles pretended to agree with this arrangement, but asked Atlas to carry the arch for a short time, so that he could put a

The head of the gorgon Medusa (unusually beautiful in this representation), was used by the hero Perseus to turn Atlas into stone, thereby forming the Atlas mountains. Stoneware head of Medusa from Tarente, 5th century BCE.

cushion on his painful shoulder. Atlas readily agreed with this request, Heracles escaped with the apples, and Atlas has groaned ever since under his terrible burden.

The poet Ovid describes how the hero Perseus (like Heracles, another son of Zeus) visited Atlas. Perseus asked if he could stay the night with Atlas. Atlas refused, recalling that an oracle had once predicted that a son of Zeus would come and rob the apples from his daughters (this probably referred to Heracles). Atlas threatened Perseus who subsequently used the head of Medusa (*see the* **Gorgons** *and* **Perseus**) to turn Atlas into a stone mountain, the Atlas Mountains of Morocco. The problem with this version of the story is that Perseus apparently visited Atlas before Heracles, yet Heracles still saw Atlas as a Titan rather than as a mountain.

Atreus

Atreus was one of the sons of Pelops and Hippodamia. He was king of the powerful city of Mycenæ and father of Agamemnon, the Greek commander-in-chief of the Trojans during the Trojan War, and Menelaus. The family of Pelops and Atreus suffered terribly from the spell that Myrtilus, a son of the god Hermes, cast on Pelops who had betrayed him and lethally wounded him (*see* **Pelops**). This led to a gruesome cycle of bloody revenge and murder, which finally ended after Atreus' grandson Orestes was brought to trial in Athens (*see* **Agamemnon** *and* **Orestes**).

As a descendant of Pelops, Atreus suffered the consequences of which Myrtilus, a son of the god Hermes, had spoken. Bronze Hermes from Etruria, 5th century BCE.

Atreus and his brother, Thyestes, killed their half-brother Chrysippus and were exiled by Pelops from his kingdom, Pisa, in Elis. Consequently, his wife Ærope, who had fallen in love with her brother-in-law

Entrance to the so-called Treasury of Atreus in Mycene, the city described by the poet Homer as "the gold-laden Mycene."

Thyestes, and helped him become the king of the city of Midea by a trick, betrayed Atreus. Thanks to help from Hermes, Atreus was able to once again outsmart Thyestes through trickery and recover his kingdom. He exiled his brother, but regretted this "light" punishment when he discovered the manner in which Ærope and Thyestes had tricked him. Consequently, Atreus killed Thyestes' three sons and invited his brother for a "reconciliatory banquet."

During the meal he served Thyestes the meat of the bodies of his own children. When Thyestes had finished eating, Atreus showed him the hands and feet of his sons and told him what he had just eaten. Later, Thyestes conceived another son by his own daughter, whom the oracle predicted would revenge the atrocity Atreus had committed. Through a miraculous set of circumstances this son, Ægisthus, was educated in Atreus' house. After Atreus' sons, Agamemnon and Menelaus, had captured Thyestes, Ægisthus realized what had happened to his family and how he had been brought into this world. As a result, he killed Atreus.

Later, Ægisthus became the lover of Clytemnestra, Agamemnon's wife. Clytemnestra and Ægisthus killed Agamemnon and were, in their turn, killed by Agamemnon's son, Orestes. Only after Orestes had been convicted of the murder in Athens, was the curse that had rested on the family finally ended.

Attis

Attis, son of the river-nymph Nana, was raised by a goat. Attis was a handsome young shepherd who was loved intensely by the Phrygian mother-goddess, Cybele. When Attis wanted to marry one of the daughters of King Midas, Cybele was seized with a terrible jealousy. She brought Attis to a state of ecstasy and in a trance, he robbed himself of his manhood. According to one version of the myth, he did not survive this act and the inconsolable Cybele turned him into a pine-tree. She introduced a yearly ritual of mourning for him and declared that in honor of his memory all of her priests had to be eunuchs. According to another version, Attis was killed by Cybele's father and was later resurrected by her. His grave was worshiped near Pessinus, in Phrygia.

In another version of the story by the

The handsome young shepherd Attis, lies sleeping on a rock, with a goat at his feet. Stoneware statue from the Hellenic period.

Roman poet, Catullus, assumed that Attis survived his self-inflicted castration and was forced to become a priest of Cybele. He described how Attis was overtaken by feelings of regret because he had become a "she" and had to live in the Phrygian forest as Cybele's slave. "No longer sleeping, no longer held by turbulent madness, Attis turned his mind to those things which he had done to himself and calmly now, clearly, he saw where he was and what he was lacking; struck with horror, he ran back to the windblown fringe of the ocean and stood there in tears..." (Catullus, *Collected Verses*, 63) After Attis had made this confession, Cybele sent a lion to Attis to chase him ("her") back into the forest.

The myth and adoration of Attis has much in common with the story and worship of Adonis (*see* **Adonis** and **Cybele**).

Bacchus *see* Dionysus

Balius *see* Xanthus and Balius

Bellerophon

The hero Bellerophon rides Pegasus, the flying horse that he tamed.

The hero, Bellerophon, was a son of the Corinthian king Glaucus and a grandson of Sisyphus, one of those who was most severely punished in the underworld. Bellerophon succeeded in taming the winged horse, Pegasus, considered an impossible task. Pegasus had been created from the blood that flowed from the body of the gorgon Medusa when the hero Perseus cut off her with his sword

Pegasus, the flying horse, illustrated on a Corinthian silver coin of the 4th century BCE.

(see **Gorgons**, **Pegasus** and **Perseus**). Pegasus shied away from humans, but Bellerophon broke him in with the help of a bridle given to him by Athena.

Bellerophon was exiled from Corinth because he had killed the tyrant Bellerus. Afterward, he changed his original name, Hipponous, into Bellerophon, meaning "killer of Bellerus".

Bellerophon found asylum with King Proteus of Argos, but the king's wife, Sthenebœa, fell in love with him. Bellerophon did not respond to her advances, so she wrongly accused him of sexual harassment. Proteus believed his wife's story, but did not dare murder his guest. So he sent Bellerophon to his father-in-law, Iobates, in Lycia, carrying a sealed letter in which he asked Iobates to take the life of his daughter's abuser. Iobates also did not dare to kill Bellerophon, but gave him a life-threatening task. The hero had to kill the Chimæra, a gruesome monster with the head and body of a lion, a tail in the form of a snake, and a goat's head on its back. From his winged horse, Bellerophon killed the Chimæra with his arrows, after which the shocked Iobates let him fight the neighboring tribes, including the Amazons. Bellerophon won successive victories in these battles. As a last resort, Iobates had Bellerophon ambushed by his own bodyguard, but even this ploy did not succeed. Finally, Iobates told Bellerophon what was written in his son-in-law's letter and accepted Bellerophon's version of events.

According to a lost tragedy by the Athenian playwright Euripides, Bellerophon later took revenge on Sthenebœa. He invited her

The Chimæra, a creature with the head and torso of a lion, a tail in the form of a snake, and the head of a goat on her back. Bellerophon had to slay this monster. Silver coin of the 4th century BCE.

Pegasus as a star constellation, illustration from an ancient astronomical text.

Pegasus as a star constellation, illustration from an ancient astronomical text.

for a ride on Pegasus and threw her off the horse as it flew at a great height.

In the end, Bellerophon became the victim of his own pride. After all the heroic deeds he had performed, he considered that he was no longer inferior to the gods and decided to fly on Pegasus' back to their halls on Mount Olympus. Zeus was so angered by this act of presumption that he sent a hornet to sting Pegasus. The flying horse bucked and threw his rider off. Bellerophon survived the fall, but was crippled for the rest of his life, and died a lonely and broken man.

Boreas

Boreas was the god of the north wind, the son of Eos, goddess of daybreak, and the Titan Astræus. He lived in Thrace, north of the Ægean Sea. Boreas was quite different in nature to Zephyrus, the mild west wind, and was notorious for his terrible storms. He is depicted as a figure with two faces and enormous wings.

Boreas once kidnapped Orithyia, daughter of the Athenian king, Erechtheus. As she danced on the banks of the River Ilissus, he covered her with a cloud and spirited her away to Thrace. She bore him two daughters and two sons, Calais and Zetes, the winged heroes who joined Jason and the Argonauts to sail to distant Colchis. During the journey, Calais and Zetes released King Phineus from persecution by the Harpies (*see* **Argonauts**).

A special bond existed between Boreas and the city of Athens, and annual festivities were held there in his honor. The fact that the north wind sometimes sided with the Athenians became clear during the sea-battle of Artemisium in 480 BCE, when Boreas caused terrible damage to the attacking Persian fleet who were routed by the Greeks, despite their superior numbers.

On the advice of Athena, Cadmus sows the dragon's teeth—from which would sprout heavily-armed warriors—close to where the city of Thebes would be founded.

Boreas, god of the wild and stormy North Wind, abducts Orithyia, daughter of the Athenian king.

Cadmus

Cadmus was the son of Agenor, king of the Phoenician city of Tyre. He was the brother of Princess Europa and the founder of the city of Thebes.

The supreme deity, Zeus had a passionate desire for Europa. He turned himself into a white bull and kidnaped her, taking her to Crete, where he had three sons by her, Minos, Rhadamanthys, and Sarpedon (*see* **Europa**). Cadmus and his brothers had to go search their sister. If they failed, they would no longer be welcome at Agenor's court.

Cadmus was accompanied by his mother, but she died in Thrace, whereupon he consulted the oracle at Delphi. It advised him to look for a cow with a crescent-shaped mark on her flank. At the place where this animal rested, Cadmus was to found a city. Cadmus bought a cow that fitted the description from King Pelagon of Phocis and on the spot where the animal dropped down from exhaustion, near the River Asopus, he decided to found his city, Thebes (meaning "cow's rest," but initially named Cadmæa, after himself). But when Cadmus wanted to offer the cow to Athena as a thanksgiving sacrifice, and ordered some men to get water, a dragon killed them. Cadmus killed the dragon, that had been sent down by Ares, the god of war, and scattered half of the

Athena (left) hands a stone to Cadmus. He had to throw the stone among the heavily armed warriors, who sprouted from the dragon's teeth that he had sown. Athenian amphora dating from ca. 440 BCE.

monster's teeth around him, on the advice of Athena. From these teeth heavenly-armed men sprouted, who started fighting amongst themselves after Cadmus had thrown a stone among them. Five of them survived the battle. Together with Cadmus they built Cadmæa and would later be considered the progenitors of the most important Theban families.

Because Cadmus had killed the dragon sent by Ares, he had to atone for his sins for eight years. When he had accomplished this penance, Athena crowned him king of his city and Zeus offered him Harmonia, daughter of Ares and the goddess of love, Aphrodite, for a wife. Because Harmonia was descended from the gods, the wedding was attended by almost the entire pantheon, something that was really exceptional. The only mortal who ever shared this honor was the hero, Peleus, when he married the goddess Thetis.

The wedding guests brought wonderful gifts with them. Aphrodite gave her daughter a necklace wrought by Hephæstos, which gave the wearer irresistible beauty, Athena gave her a gorgeous wedding gown, Hermes offered a lyre, and Demeter, grain.

Even though Cadmus and Harmonia had a happy marriage and ruled their city well, all sorts of misfortunes struck their children. Their daughter, Autonoe, saw her son Actæon being transformed into a deer and ripped to pieces by his own hunting-dogs after he had accidentally come across Artemis bathing (*see* **Actæon**). The jealous Hero drove Ino insane and made her throw herself from a high cliff into the sea, along with her youngest son, (*see* **Ino**). Semele was impregnated by the god of wine Dionysus, who had been created by Zeus, and was burned by the brilliance of Zeus because she desired to see the supreme deity in his true form (*see* **Dionysus**). Finally, Agave, a Mænead, ripped her own son to pieces in a state of ecstasy (*see* **Dionysus**). Polydorus, the only son of Cadmus and Harmonia, was spared from immediate misery, but his descendants were struck by terrible misfortune. Polydorus' grandson, Laius, was murdered by his son Œdipus, who in turn married his own mother Jocasta (*see* **Antigone, Laius,** *and* **Œdipus**).

In his old age, Cadmus abdicated in favor of his grandson, Pentheus. After Pentheus' terrible death, Cadmus and Harmonia left their city on the advice of Zeus. They traveled to Illyria and were later changed into benign snakes by Ares. Ultimately, Zeus brought them to Elysium, the islands of the blessed, in the westernmost point of the underworld.

Panoramic view of the landscape around the ruined city of Troy. Calchas, the seer of the Greek army, based his predictions on the flight of birds over the area.

Calchas

Calchas, the son of Thestor, was attached to the Greek army as a seer in the Trojan War. He predicted the future by the flight of birds, but was also able to perfectly interpret other premonitions. Before the Greek fleet left from Aulis, the Greeks saw a snake devour a sparrow with its brood of eight young, and then turn to stone. Calchas concluded from this that the war would last nine full years and would end during the tenth year—a prediction that came true. Once more, in Aulis, when a favorable wind failed to materialize so the fleet could not leave the harbor, he declared that Iphigenia, daughter of Agamemnon, the Greek commander-in-chief, had to be sacrificed to the goddess Artemis (*see* **Agamemnon** *and* **Iphigenia**). When the war was in its tenth year, Calchas concluded that the wrath of Apollo, who had caused an outbreak of the Plague among the Greeks with his arrows, would only be appeased if the kidnapped daughter of the priest of Apollo, Chryses, were returned to her father.

Calchas died shortly after the fall of Troy, in the manner that had been prophesied since his youth. He was defeated in a clairvoyance contest with Mopsus, grandson of the famous seer, Tiresias (*see* **Tiresias**), and died of shame. According to one version of this story, Mopsus predicted when Calchas was planting vines that he would never drink wine from them. Some time later, Calchas invited his colleague to come and taste the first wine from his vines. On that occasion, Mopsus once again made the same prediction, to which Calchas burst out in raucous laughter. The laughter turned into hysteria, causing him to die.

Decorative image of the Great Bear star constellation, from a medieval astronomy text. Zeus placed the unfortunate Callisto in the universe, as the Great Bear.

Artemis is utterly enraged when she discovers that Callisto is pregnant. She drives the miserable girl from her presence,. Callisto is shown here, supported by two friends. Oil painting by Peter Paul Rubens, 17th century.

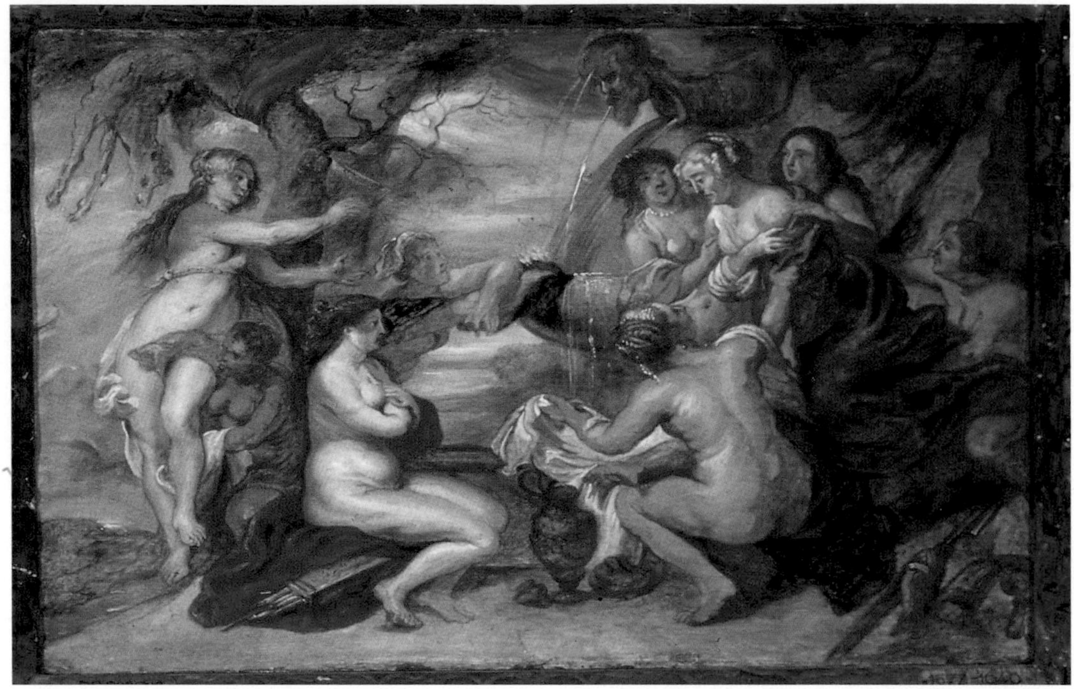

Callisto

Callisto, daughter of the King of Arcady, Lycaon, was part of the retinue of Artemis, the virgin goddess of hunting and wild nature. The girls and nymphs of the goddess' entourage had to swear to remain virgins forever. The supreme deity, Zeus, fell in love with the athletic, Callisto, however, and one afternoon, when she was resting in the forest, he took the form of Artemis, talked with her and kissed her, "uncontrollably, like a girl would never kiss." (Ovid). He then raped her. When Artemis was bathing nine months later with her friends, Callisto was seen to be heavily pregnant. Artemis was outraged and cast out the girl from her retinue.

Callisto had a son, Arcas. Hera, who was already jealous because Zeus had impregnated Callisto—refusing to accept that this had happened against Callisto's will—was enraged and turned the unfortunate young mother into a bear. Years later, when Arcas was out hunting, he came face to face with his mother, and shot her with an arrow. Zeus put Callisto in the sky as a sign of the zodiac, Ursa Major, the Great Bear (or Big Dipper). Arcas accompanied her in the firmament as Ursa Minor, the Little Bear (or Little Dipper). The jealous Hera had the last word, however.

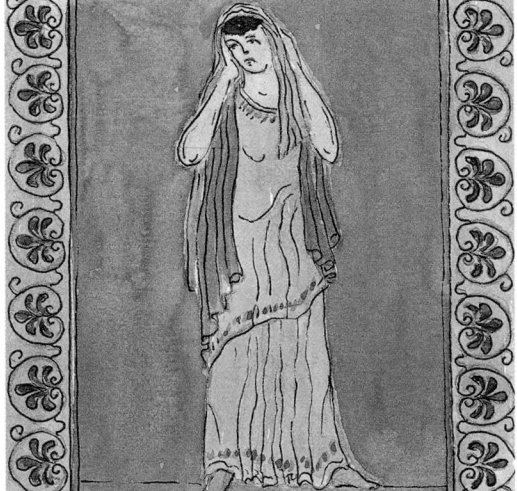

Cassandra, the daughter of the Trojan king, was horribly punished by the offended god Apollo. He gave her the gift of clairvoyance but also ensured that nobody took her predictions seriously.

She ensured that the constellation could never dip into the sea and was doomed to revolve around the pole star forever (*see* **Artemis**).

Cassandra

Cassandra was the daughter of the Trojan king Priam and his wife Hecuba. She was considered the most beautiful of Priam's daughters. According to the poet Homer, her beauty rivaled that of the goddess of love Aphrodite.

It should come as no surprise that the powerful god Apollo fell in love with her. While he was courting her, he taught her how to predict the future. Ultimately, Cassandra rejected the god's advances, upsetting him so much that he cunningly punished Cassandra. He condemned her to a life of making true predictions that were not believed by anyone.

Because Cassandra went in strange state of ecstasy when she had her moments of clairvoyance, people thought she was crazy. She predicted that Troy would be struck by great misfortune after her brother Paris had kidnapped Helena. This prophecy was rejected, as was her warning not to bring into the city the wooden horse that had been left outside the walls by the Greeks .

After the conquest of Troy, Cassandra was raped near the sanctuary of the goddess Athena by Ajax, the son of Oileus. Ajax and the other Greek warriors were severely punished for this act (see **Ajax** and **Athena**).

Eventually, Cassandra became a slave of Agamemnon, the Greek commander-in-chief.

This sculpture clearly shows the misery of the unhappy Cassandra. Fragment of a relief from Tarente, 3rd century BCE.

His wife, Clytemnestra, and her lover Ægisthus murdered Agamemnon and Cassandra. Before she was stabbed to death, she managed to predict the terrible consequences that Clytemnestra's crime would have on her and her descendants (see **Agamemnon** *and* **Orestes**).

The figure of Cassandra is emotionally portrayed in two famous Athenian tragedies: Æschylus' *Agamemnon* and Euripides' *The Trojan Women*.

Castor and Polydeuces *see* The Dioscures

Cecrops

Cecrops was a creature who emerged from the earth. He had the body of a human and the tail of a snake, and was the first king of Attica and Athens. His wife, Aglauros, gave him three daughters and one son, though the son died young, and the daughters, Herse, Pandrosos, and Aglauros, also met with misfortune. The goddess Athena asked them to to guard a basket in which the little Erichthonius was hidden. Erichthonius had been born from the depths of the Attic earth, when Hephæstos attempted to rape Athena, and his seed has fallen in the ground (see **Athena**). Athena forbade Cecrops' daughters to look into the basket, but Aglauros could not control her curiosity and opened it. Next to the

The daughters of Cecrops open the basket entrusted to them by Athena. Therein is hidden little Erichthonius, wo reaches out to them in happiness. But the girls also see something else, that brings them to a state of hysterical panic. Oil painting by Moses van Uyttenbroeck, 17th century.

baby, the girls saw a monstrous snake, that so terrified Herse and Pandrosus that threw themselves off the Athenian Acropolis in a state of shock. Erichthonius, who according to some versions, had the lower body of a snake, just like Cecrops, later became king of Athens.

When Athena and Poseidon held a competition for the possession of Attica, Cecrops was one of the panel of referees. The goddess made an olive-tree come to life on the Acropolis and was pronounced victorious over Poseidon, who had produced a spring of brackish water on the same spot (*see* **Athena**). Cecrops founded a courthouse on the Athenian Areopagus (the hill of Ares) that had originally been the site of the trial of the war-god Ares, who had killed his daughter's rapist in that same place. The courthouse was used in historic, non-mythical Athens. Another important contribution by Cecrops was his decision to end human sacrifice.

Centaurs were wild and clumsy creatures with the head and torso of a human, and the body of a horse. They were usually destructive and dangerous.

The Centaurs

The centaurs were creatures with the head and torso of a human, but the body of a horse. They were descendants of Ixion, the first human, who murdered one of his family members. Ixion conceived Centaurus, the first centaur, near a cloud that the supreme deity, Zeus, had given the form of his wife Hera (*see* **Ixion**).

This aggressive Centaur is on the verge of throwing a stone at someone's head. The skin of a panther is thrown over his left arm. Image on an Athenian scyphos (drinking cup) from ca. 450 BCE.

The centaurs lived in the forests around Mount Pelion in Thessaly and were considered to be uncivilized brutes. They were in conflict with the neighboring people, the Lapithae, because during the wedding of the King of the Lapithae, Pirithous, they had tried to steal the bride and other Lapithae women. The battle that ensued took the lives of many of the centaurs. The heroes Theseus and Nestor fought in this battle and Nestor, who lived to a very great age, told many epic stories about it.

On this Italian vase, dating from the 3rd century BCE, two Centaurs flank a winged head of Medusa. Nike, the goddess of victory. tops the vase.

Chiron was a most unusual centaur, a kind and cultivated personality who was the educator and teacher of many of the gods and heroes (see **Chiron**).

The greatest of all the Greek heroes, Heracles, had some violent confrontations with the centaurs. Once, when he was a guest of centaur, Pholys, and was out hunting for the boar, Erymanthische, the hero complained that he wasn't being served any wine, even though a carafe of wine was present. Pholus pointed out that the god of wine, Dionysus, wanted this wine served to all the centaurs. The carafe was opened and the other centaurs, who had smelled the aroma of the wine, flocked in. A fight broke out, in which Heracles killed several centaurs with his poisoned arrows. His host, Pholus, also died, and an arrow that had pierced another centaur accidentally hit the immortal Chiron. Chiron suffered such severe pains from this wound that he finally renounced his immortality.

The centaur, Nessus, would eventually take revenge on Heracles. Much later, after a failed attempt to rape Heracles' wife, Deianeira, and lethally wounded by the hero's arrow, he thought of a cunning plan. He whispered to Deianeira that he had an effective remedy should Heracles would ever lose interest in her. He instructed her to collect some of the blood that flowed from his wound and, whenever she doubted Heracles' marital fidelity, she should smear it on his clothes. After this he would never betray her again. Without Heracles' knowledge, Deianeira filled a flask with Nessus' blood, which she carefully stored.

Years later, in a mood of uncertainty and jealousy, Deianeira followed Nessus' advice. The consequences were disastrous. Heracles' clothes, covered in Nessus' poisoned blood, caused horrible burns and the hero died suffering from hellish pains (see **Heracles**).

Cerberus

Cerberus was a monstrous dog, who acted as the underworld's guard dog (see **Hades**). Cerberus was conceived by the monsters, Typhon and Echidna, and was believed to be the brother of the Hydra and the Chimæra, creatures that were just as terrifying as he was (see **Heracles** and **Bellerophon**) Cerberus had three heads, although according to some sources, there were potentially many more. He had the tail of a snake and on his back,

Cerberus, the fearsome three-headed guard-dog of the underworld, being carried off by the hero Heracles (left, partly visible). Fragment of a black-painted Athenian terra-cotta vase by the "Theseus painter," 6th century BCE.

there was a kind of mane of snake heads. His breath and saliva were extremely poisonous, and just like the gorgon, Medusa, a glance from Cerberus could turn people to stone.

Hades, god of the underworld, kept his guard-dog mainly to prevent the shades from escaping his realm. Cerberus also had to prevent the living from entering the underworld. One of the Twelve Labors of Heracles was to drag Cerberus out of the underworld. Hades consented, provided that Heracles refrained from using weapons. Heracles captured the hellish dog with his bare hands, took him to his patron Eurystheus, and then returned him to the underworld.

Ceres *see* Demeter

The Charities (Roman= The Graces)

The Charities, who are better known under their Roman name, the *Graces*, were the daughters of the supreme deity Zeus by Eurynome, a daughter of Oceanus and Tethys. According to the most frequent version, the three Charities were named Aglaia, Euphrosyne, and Thalia. These fairly minor goddesses were part of the retinue of Aphrodite, goddess of love and beauty. They were themselves goddesses of beauty, who embodied everything that was beautiful, lovely, and charming. They offered physical beauty to humans who were chosen by them.

The three Charites or Graces, played a modest role in mythology but embodied everything that was beautiful, lovely, and appealing.

The Charites were followers of the goddess of love, Aphrodite, and were at least her equal where beauty was concerned. Bronze statue of Aphrodite, Hellenic period.

In Homer's *Iliad*, reference is made to a Charity who was named Pasithea. Hypnos, the god of sleep, longs for her "all days of my life." Hera, jealous as usual, promises to offer her to Hypnos as a bride if he is willing to put Zeus into a deep sleep.

Charon

Charon was the son of Erebus ("darkness") and Nyx ("night"). He acted as the ferryman, rowing the shades of the dead across the underworld river, the Styx, in his boat so they could enter into Hades' realm of the spirits. Charon was a grumpy, unpleasant old man

In ancient Greece, the dead were buried with a coin—an obolus—between their lips, in order to pay the ferryman Charon, who would take them across the River Styx to the kingdom of death. Silver obolus from Arados, 4th century BCE.

who charged his customers one obol (a coin), for the crossing. The Greeks maintained the ritual of burying their dead with an obol between their lips.

Charybdis
see Odysseus *and* Scylla

Chimæra

The Chimæra was a fire spitting monster that combined three animals in her body. She had a lion's head, and behind it—half-way down her back a goat's head, and finally a tail with a snake's head. The Chimæra roamed

The Chæmera was a composite monster, consisting of parts from three different animals. She was eventually killed by the hero Bellerophon.

through Lycia in southwestern Asia Minor (now Turkey). The hero Bellerophon, who rode the winged horse Pegasus, managed to kill the Chimæra (*see* **Bellerophon**).

The wise and mild-mannered Chiron had a very different character to the other Centaurs. He became a tutor to a number of great heroes. One of his pupils was Achilles, who was allowed to ride on his back and thus learned to ride a horse. Oil painting by Peter Paul Rubens, 17th century.

Chiron

Chiron was an exceptional Centaur (*see* **Centaurs**), a creature with the torso of a human and the body of a horse. He was unlike the rest of his kind, who were descended from Ixion, because he was the son of Cronos and Philera. He received his Centaur form because Cronos made love to the nymph Philyra in the form of a horse, so as to ally the suspicions of his wife, Rhea.

While the other Centaurs were crude brutes, the immortal Chiron distinguished himself by his very civilized, friendly, intelligent, and wise character. He was very musical and was famous for his extensive knowledge of medicine. The heroes in Homer's *Iliad* were full of praise for the herb treatments for war wounds that he invented. The great god, Apollo, who was a personal friend, trusted him with the education of his son Asclepius, the god of medicine, which the Centaur considered a great honor. Thanks to Apollo, Chiron also became a capable archer. Asclepius wasn't the only pupil Chiron had. The talented, patient Centaur also instructed Jason, Actæon, Achilles, and others.

Chiron lived in a cave on Mount Pelion in Thessaly. He was married to Chariclo and had one daughter. Chiron's grandson, Peleus,

Chiron was set in the universe by Zeus, as the star constellation Centaur. This medieval illustration shows clearly how to recognize the arrow-shooting Centaur.

received valuable support from Chiron, among others, when Peleus wanted to court the pretty sea goddess Thetis (it was from the relationship between Peleus and Thetis that great hero Achilles was born).

Unfortunately, the gentle Centaur suffered a cruel and extremely painful end. Heracles, while visiting the Centaur, Pholus, got into a fight with some other Centaurs over a carafe of wine. Chiron was accidentally struck by one of Heracles' poisoned arrows (see **Heracles**). Chiron suffered such severe pains that he eventually gave away his immortality as a gift to Prometheus. After Chiron's death, Zeus placed him in the firmament as the constellation of the Centaur.

The formidable magician Circe lived in a palace on a small island off the Italian coast. Unexpected guests ran the risks of her magic. This is how she turned the hero Odysseus' men into pigs.

Romans adorned themselves with flowers and their behavior was elated and exuberant.

Circe

Circe, a daughter of the sun god Helios and the sea nymph Perse, was a sister of Æetes, King of Colchis, and aunt of the infamous sorceress, Medea. Circe herself was also a powerful sorceress. She lived on the island of Ææa, which was probably located off the Italian coast, not far from what is now Naples. Harmless wolves and lions roamed around her palace, a direct consequence of her specialty of turning humans into animals.

Circe's speciality as a sorceress was to turn people into animals. Many harmless wolves and lions—victims of her experiments—swarmed around her palace. Illustration of a small bronze lion from Corinth.

Chloris, the appealing goddess of flowers and the personification of spring, was the excuse for enjoyable Roman spring festivities.

Chloris (Roman=Flora)

Greek mythology has two figures with the name of Chloris. The first was the youngest daughter of Niobe, the mother who had insulted the goddess Leto and for this was forced to watch as her children were killed by arrows from Apollo and Artemis. According to some sources, Chloris survived this terrible act of revenge (*see* **Apollo** *and* **Niobe**).

The second Chloris was given a more pleasant role, she was the goddess of spring and flowers. She was not very well-known in the Greek pantheon, but the Romans honored her under the name of Flora. Every year, at the end of April, people celebrated the Floralia festivities in her honor. During these festivities, which lasted for six days, the

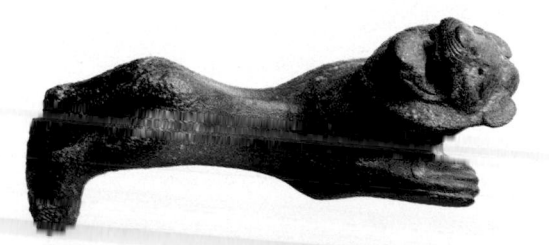

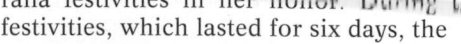

Circe changed the members of Odysseus' crew into pigs when they visited Æææa on their eventful homeward journey from Troy. They retained human consciousness in their new form but were locked in a shed. Odysseus had been given a special herb from the god, Hermes, that made him immune to Circe's magical powers, and when Odysseus threatened Circe with his sword, all of his men were changed back into human form. After this, Odysseus shared the bed of the attractive sorceress for one year. He and his men lived on the island in luxury and abundance, but eventually, Odysseus had to move on, and although Circe would have preferred to hold onto him, she instructed him on how to perform his next dangerous mission, a visit to the underworld (*see* **Odysseus**).

Jason and Medea also visited Circe's island, according to one of the versions of the story of the Argonauts. They came to Circe to do penance for their sins, the gruesome murder of Medea's brother Apsyrtus (*see the* **Argonauts**). How evil and dangerous Circe could be can be seen by the fate of the poor nymph Scylla. The jealous sorceress turned her into a hideous sea-monster, who guarded the Straits of Sicily, with the whirlpool, Charybdis, making them extremely dangerous (*see* **Scylla**).

Creon

Creon was the son of Menœccus and a descendant of the armed men who sprang from the dragon teeth sown by Cadmus, founder of the city Thebes.

Creon was the brother of Jocasta, wife of King Laius of Thebes. When Laius was murdered outside his city (by his son Œdipus, who had been abandoned as a baby and did

During the regency of Creon, the city of Thebes was ravaged by the Sphinx, a monster that killed everyone who could not solve her riddles. These boys are fleeing from the Sphinx. Athenian vase painting, ca. 550 BCE.

not recognize his own father), Creon became regent. Meanwhile, a monster, the Sphinx (*see* **Sphinx**) plagued the area and killed any passers-by who were unable to solve the riddle she presented to them. Creon offered the throne and Jocasta's hand in marriage to anyone who would outsmart the Sphinx. Œdipus solved the riddle, became king of Thebes, married Jocasta and conceived children with her. Only years later, when Thebes was struck by an epidemic of the Plague, did the seer Tiresias reveal that Jocasta was actually Œdipus' mother and that he had killed Laius, his own father. The bewildered Œdipus put out his eyes and was exiled from Thebes. Jocasta hanged herself and Creon became regent once again.

Œdipus' sons, Eteocles and Polynices, then ruled, but quarreled with each other. Creon took Eteocles' side. After the brothers killed each other in a duel, and Creon once again ruled Thebes, he gave Eteocles a proper burial. Polynices, however, had to remain unburied outside the city wall—an unspeakable disgrace among the Greeks. Eteocles' sister Antigone, who earlier had stood by her tormented father, could not resign herself to the situation. Despite of Creon's explicit ban, she scattered earth over Polynices' body, to symbolically bury him. Creon was afraid to sentence Antigone to death and had her bricked in alive in a cave. The seer, Tiresias, pointed out to Creon that he had to bury the dead and free the living from their tombs, if he wanted to continue to see the light of day. Consequently, Creon followed Tiresias' advice, but by the time the cave was broken open, Antigone had already hanged herself. Creon's son, Hæmon, Antigone's betrothed, who had unsuccessfully pleaded with his father on her behalf, cursed Creon and committed suicide. Creon's wife also took her own life. Creon himself remained alive and acted as regent for the youngest son of Eteocles (*see* **Antigone** *and* **Œdipus**).

Much earlier, Amphitryon, Alcmene's husband, paid for his sins, staying with Creon in Thebes, because he had accidentally killed his father-in-law. Consequently, the hero Heracles was born in Thebes, conceived by Zeus and Alcmene. Heracles would later marry Creon's daughter Megara, whom he murdered in a fit of insanity caused by Hera (*see* **Heracles**). Creon was eventually killed by Lycus, who invaded Thebes. In another version, Lycus was killed by the Athenian hero, Theseus, with whom he had been in conflict previously when Theseus had offered asylum to Œdipus.

There are many different versions of Creon's story, which are alluded to in the great Athenian tragedies. There was another Creon in Greek mythology, a King of Corinth who extended hospitality to Jason and Medea after they had fled from Jason's home in Iolcus. This Creon met his death after he offered Jason his daughter Glauce in marriage. The jealous Medea offered her a bewitched wedding dress, which engulfed Glauce in flames when she put it on. Creon died trying to save his daughter from the conflagration (*see the* **Argonauts** *and* **Medea**).

Cronos (Roman=Saturn)

The Titan, Cronos, was a son of the god of heaven, Uranus, and Gaia, the earth goddess. Uranus behaved cruelly toward Gaia and their children, the Titans, the hundred-armed giants, and the Cyclopes. He held the Cyclopes prisoner in their mother's body, in other words, deep inside the earth, and prevented them from seeing the light. Gaia suffered severe pains as a result. With the help of a sickle given to him by his mother, Cronos cut off his father's manhood, and he gained control of the universe. He married his sister, Rhea, but soon turned into a tyrant as terrible as his father. He again imprisoned the Cyclopes and devoured his own children immediately after their birth, because it had been predicted that one of his sons would dethrone him. Hestia, Demeter, Hera, Hades,

and Poseidon subsequently suffered this fate. When Rhea gave birth to their youngest son, Zeus, she handed Cronos a rock wrapped in blankets instead of the baby. Zeus was secretly raised on Crete by the nymph (or goat) Amalthea (*see* **Amalthea**). When Zeus became an adult, he forced Cronos to vomit up his brothers and sisters, probably with the help of the Oceanide, Metis (the personification of wisdom and intelligence).

There was a power struggle, in which Zeus and his brothers defeated Cronos and the other Titans. The decisive factor in the proverbial "Titanic struggle" was the support that Zeus received from the hundred-armed giants whom he had freed from the Tartarus. The Cyclopes, who were also freed, gratefully created Zeus' thunderbolts, Poseidon's trident, and Hades' helmet, which could make him invisible. After their defeat, Cronos and the other Titans were thrown into the Tartarus. Only the Titan Atlas received a different punishment. He was forced to carry the canopy of heaven on his shoulders (*see* **Atlas**). From then on, Zeus and his brothers ruled the universe. Zeus ruled over heaven, Poseidon over the waters, and Hades over the underworld.

The Romans equated Cronos with their god of agriculture, Saturn. The Saturnalia, the feast in his honor, was one of the happiest events in old Rome (*see* **Saturn**).

Remains of the Temple of Saturn in the Roman Forum in Rome. Unlike the Greek god Cronos, with whom he was equated, Saturn was honored by the Romans as the god of agriculture,.

After the battle of the Titans, the Olympian gods had to fight another battle against giants. who were sons of the earth-goddess Gaia. The battle of the Giants is often confused with the battle of the Titans. Mosaic from the Villa del Casale, Sicily, 3rd-4th century CE.

Cupid *see* Eros

Cybele

Cybele was originally a Phrygian goddess. The Greeks mostly equated her with the Mother of Gods, the mother of Zeus, and other important gods. Her cult probably derived from the ancient worship of a great mother or goddess of fertility, just like Demeter's, the goddess of agriculture.

According to a Phrygian myth, Zeus had once, when he was sleeping on Mount Didymus in Phrygia (what is now central Turkey) released his seed onto the ground. A hermaphroditic creature was born who was castrated by the gods. This is how the goddess Cybele was created. From her severed genitalia there grew an almond tree. The fruit of this tree landed in the womb of the nymph Nana. Consequently, she became pregnant and had a son, whom she abandoned after his birth. The boy, Attis, was raised by a goat and grew into a beautiful young man. Cybele fell madly in love with him. When he started to make wedding plans to marry another woman she became so jealous that she forced him

A worn statue of the earth and fertility goddess Cybele, flanked by two lions, in a temple at Phrygia in what is now Turkey. The worship of the goddess Cybele, who was not Greek, began in this region.

castrate himself (*see* **Attis**). There are many versions of the myth of Cybcle and Attis, all of which have themes of death and resurrection. According to some versions, Attis did not survive his self-mutilation and was turned into a pine-tree. According to other versions, he was buried in Pessinus and resurrected by Cybele. Still other versions claim that he lived on as a eunuch and priest of Cybele.

In Rome, Cybele grew to be an important and popular goddess. During a disastrous phase of the Second Punic War that was disastrous for the Romans (218-201 BC), her cult was introduced into Rome because, according to some prophecies from the Sibyline Books (some kind of oracular utterances), Rome could only be victorious if the "Great Mother" was worshiped in the city.

The lion, the strongest animal in nature, was dedicated to Cybele. The goddess was depicted many times as a lioness in a carriage pulled by lions. The poet Ovid described her "on her lion chariot riding across heaven." Her progress was accompanied by the "sounding of cymbal music and sounds from a buxus flute." Loud rituals and processions also characterized Cybele's worship in Rome.

Cybele, who was worshiped extensively in Rome from the 3rd century BCE, sits here upon a throne as the great mother goddess, with a cymbal in her hand and a lion cub in her lap. The lion was dedicated to her. Marble statue from Athens, 4th century BCE.

During the festivities, her priests, the Galli, first buried a pine-tree, which symbolized Attis. A few days later, they pierced the flesh of their arms in an ecstatic mood and sprinkled the goddess' altar with their blood. On the last day, Attis' resurrection was celebrated and Cybele's statue was carried around in a procession and later ritually cleansed.

The Cyclopes

The Cyclopes were giants who had only one eye, in the middle of their foreheads. The first

The Cyclopes—evil, one-eyed giants—described by Homer, lived as primitive sheep-breeders on a remote island, probably Sicily.

Cyclopes were sons of the god of heaven, Uranus, and the goddess of earth, Gaia. They were pushed back into their mother's body (the earth) because Uranus was afraid that his own sons would depose him as ruler of the universe. After the Titan Cronos had dethroned his father Uranus, they were briefly set free, but were soon imprisoned in Tartarus, the most desolate part of the underworld. Cronos' son Zeus, later the supreme deity, freed them forever. Zeus and his brothers needed their support in their battle for control of the universe, known as the Titanic battle, against Cronos and the other Titans. Thanks partially to the Cyclopes, Zeus and his brothers were victorious. The Cyclopes, grateful for their release, forged lightning bolts for Zeus, a trident for Poseidon, and for Hades, god of the underworld, a helmet that could make him invisible. The image of the

Cyclopes as skillful technicians, who assisted Hephæstos, craftsman of the gods, lasted throughout Antiquity. The Roman poet, Horace, who lived during the first century BCE referred to "the powerful forges of the Cyclopes," which would have been located in the volcano Mount Ætna. According to another great Roman poet, Virgil, it was deep inside Mount Ætna that the Cyclopes forged the armor for the hero, Æneas. The walls of the Greek cities of Tiryns and Mycenæ were also said to have been built by Cyclopes.

Homer presents a very different picture of the Cyclops in his *Odyssey*. On his wearisome return home from Troy, Odysseus landed on an island inhabited by the Cyclopes—probably Sicily. These Cyclopes were "an over-confident people who knew no laws, did not plant or plow, but relied on the gods' favor." These giants had no technical ingenuity; they were primitive shepherds and inhospitable bandits. The Cyclops, Polyphemus, a son of the sea-god Poseidon, ate six of Odysseus' friends and held the hero and his men captive in a cave, with the aim of devouring them. But Odysseus, who told Polyphemus that his name was "Nobody," got the Cyclops drunk and put out his only eye

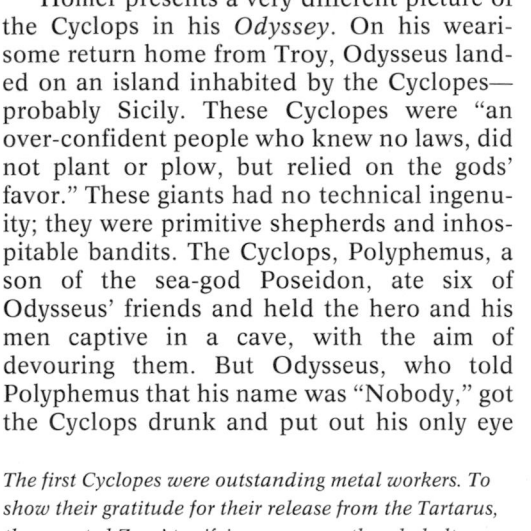

The first Cyclopes were outstanding metal workers. To show their gratitude for their release from the Tartarus, they created Zeus' terrifying weapons, thunderbolts. Bronze hand with thunderbolt, Roman period.

The so-called Ear of Dionysius, a cave on Sicily. The cave of the Cyclops Polyphemus, in which Odysseus and his men suffered many anxious hours, probably looked just like this.

Odysseus (center, with drinking bowl) offers wine to the man-eating Cyclops, Polyphemus (portrayed here with three eyes instead of one!), with the intention of making him drunk. The sheep that helped Odysseus and his men escape from Polyphemus' cave are visible in the foreground. Mosaic from the Villa del Casale, Sicily, 3rd-4th century CE.

with a burning brand. When the other Cyclopes heard the screaming of the blinded Polyphemus, he let them know that "Nobody" had outsmarted him. The other Cyclopes thought that Polyphemus had gone crazy and Odysseus and his men were able to escape from the cave by hanging from the bellies of Polyphemus' sheep (*see* **Odysseus** *and* **Polyphemus**).

Homer's evil, cannibalistic Cyclopes seem to have been the models for the dangerous giants that have since then populated countless fairytales and children's books, from the Brothers Grimm to Roald Dahl.

Dædalus

Dædalus was a brilliant Athenian inventor, technician, architect, and artist. There were many different versions of his lineage, but he was probably a member of the royal family of the city of his birth. The great Athenian philosopher, Socrates (469-399 BCE), even claimed to be one of Dædalus' descendants.

Dædalus' nephew, Talos (or Perdix), who was also his apprentice, appeared to be smarter and handier than his master. Inspired by a fish with a jagged fin on its back, he invented the saw. He also made the first compass and the first potter's wheel. Dædalus was so jealous of this that he pushed Perdix from the Acropolis, but Athena saved the boy by turning him into a partridge.

The Athenian Dædalus was a universally gifted artist and technician. The decorations in the Palace of Cnossos on Crete are of extraordinary quality and according to legend, were designed by him. Wall painting from Cnossos, reconstruction based on originals from the second millennium BCE.

Dædalus was exiled from Athens for his crime. He settled on Crete, where he created various works of art for King Minos. For Minos' wife, Pasiphae, he built a hollow wooden cow disguise that allowed the beautiful white bull she had fallen in love with to impregnate her. This bizarre relationship resulted in the creation of the dangerous Minotaur, a human with the head of a bull (*see* **Minos**, **Minotaur,** *and* **Pasiphae**).

Minos was so embarrassed by this offspring that he made Dædalus construct the Labyrinth, a gigantic underground maze of tunnels and chambers, with only one entrance and exit. The Minotaur was let loose in this place, where he lived off human flesh. The Athenians, who now owed taxes to the Cretans (*see* ***Ægeus, Ariadne,*** *and* ***Theseus***), had to sacrifice seven boys and girls to Minos every nine years.

The Athenian hero, Theseus, eventually killed the Minotaur, with the help of Minos' daughter Ariadne. Because Dædalus had helped Ariadne, Minos locked Dædalus and his young son, Icarus, up in the Labyrinth. Dædalus knew better than anyone that it was virtually impossible to escape from Minos' clutches. As a last resort, he made two pairs of wings from feathers and beeswax, one for Icarus and one for himself. Before taking off, he warned Icarus not to fly too low and

especially not to fly too high. The wings worked well. The inventor and his son took off like birds in the sky and left Crete far behind them. Soon they passed the islands of Delos, and Paros and Samos came into sight. Even though Dædalus was keeping a close eye on his son, Icarus became over-confident. In spite of Dædalus' warning, he ascended to great heights. He came too close to the sun and the wax on his wings melted—exactly as

The flying Dædalus (above) witnesses his over-confident son Icarus (above, left), crashing down because the wax on his wings was melted by the sun. Oil painting, in the style of Paul Bril, 16th-17th century.

The vast size and complexity of the Palace of Cnossos, adds weight to the myth about the Labyrinth being built by Dædalus.

his father had predicted. Icarus crashed into the sea and drowned, after which his grieving father buried him on the island that has since then borne his name, Icaria.

Dædalus found refuge in the court of the Sicilian king Cocalus. Minos was able to find him there by means of a smart trick. As Minos had suspected, Dædalus was the only person who knew the solution to the question of how to move a string through a shell of very complex shape, (a kind of triton's horn). Dædalus made a hole in the shell and attached the string to an ant, which crept through the hole. Cocalus, however, did not want to give up his valued guest to the Cretan king. Only after Minos had laid siege to his city, Camicus, was Cocalus prepared to make concessions. He invited Minos to a banquet to seal their peace treaty. Before dinner, Minos was offered a bath, during which he was tended by Cocalus' daughters. Dædalus however, had constructed special pipes to the bath that would carry scalding water to it, and this proved fatal to Minos.

Dædalus probably died on Sicily. In Antiquity, many important buildings, works of art, and tools were attributed to him. He supposedly invented the mast, the sail, glue, the ax, and the plumb line. He also supposedly created special wooden statues, that had moveable eyes and limbs, and were even able to walk. According to some, he even constructed the Egyptian pyramids. Dædalus' figure began to resemble that of the legendary deified Egyptian architect, Imhotep, who constructed the first pyramid, the step pyramid, at Sakkara, for the Pharaoh Djoser, and was responsible for many inventions.

Danæ

Danæ was the daughter of Acrisius, King of Argos. Because an oracle had predicted that Danæ's son would kill Acrisius, he locked her up in a bronze tower. There, the supreme deity, Zeus, visited her in the form of a golden rainbow, and this is how the hero Perseus was conceived. Acrisius sealed his daughter and grandson into a box and threw them into the ocean, but instead of drowning they were washed ashore on the island of Seriphos, where the fisherman, Dictys, saved them and offered them hospitality. Later, his brother, the local king, Polydectes, (who wanted Danæ for himself), sent Perseus on a mission to retrieve the head of the gorgon, Medusa, a

Danæ's son, Perseus, was ordered by King Polydectes to deliver him the head of the gorgon Medusa—a seemingly impossible assignment. Running gorgon, stone statue from Greece.

task that he hoped and assumed would be impossible (*see* **Perseus**). Perseus returned one year later, after experiencing many adventures. Luckily, he was just in time to rescue Danæ and Dictys, who had been put in a tight spot by Polydectes. He showed the king Medusa's head, which was so terrible a sight that everyone who saw it turned immediately into stone. Polydectes and his followers were no exception to this rule.

Danæ accompanied Perseus and his bride, Andromeda, to Argos, where Perseus accidentally killed Danæ's father, Acrisius, with a discus (the oracle, as always in mythology, had been right). According to the Roman poet Virgil, Danæ eventually came to Italy, and Turnus, the great opponent of Æneas, was her grandson (*see* **Æneas**).

The Danaids

The Danaides were the fifty daughters of the North African king Danaus. After a conflict with his brother, Danaus fled with his daughters to Argos, in Greece. Ægyptus' fifty sons came after them, however, to claim Danaus' daughters as their brides. Danaus consented, but gave his daughters daggers so they could kill their husbands on their wedding night.

The Danaids, the fifty daughters of king Danaus, were punished in the underworld for their unspeakable crimes. They had to continuously fill bottomless jars with water.

Daphne

Daphne was a daughter of the Thessalian river god Peneius. Just like Artemis, she was a virgin goddess of hunting and nature. In the

There was no possibility of Daphne escaping the god Apollo, who desired her with a vengeance. So the desperate nymph changed herself into a laurel bush.

All the girls did their father's bidding, with one exception. Danaus' eldest daughter, Hypermnestra, loved her husband, Lynceus, and ensured that he escaped unharmed. The Roman poet Horace wrote of the terrible wedding night: "They were evil, what more could they have done? They were evil, could use the pitiless steel, killing their husbands. Only one, out of so many, was worthy of her marriage flame, to her faithless father a glorious traitor. All the ages will honor this virgin." (*Odes and Epodes*, III, 11)

Hypermnestra was imprisoned by her father and put on trial, but she was released after Aphrodite intervened. The other forty-nine Danaids were purified in a ritual at the command of Zeus by Hermes and Athena and remarried men from Argos, who initially showed little interest in having them as their wives. Danaus, however, offered them handsome wedding presents and organized track and field competitions, of which the winners were allowed the pick of his daughters.

After their death, the Danaids still had to be punished for their terrible crime. They were sent to the Tartarus, the most desolate part of the underworld. There they had to pour water into bottomless pitchers for all eternity (*see* **Hades**).

most famous story about her, she was desired against her will by the great god Apollo.

The direct cause for this was that Apollo had insulted Eros, the god of love. Apollo, who liked to boast of how well he could handle a bow and arrow, thought Eros was a rather poor archer. Eros took revenge on Apollo by piercing him straight in the heart with a gold-tipped arrow, causing him to fall hopelessly in love with Daphne. Eros also hit Daphne, but in this case, the arrow was tipped with lead, which made her even more averse to love than she was already. Apollo, completely out of his mind, began the pursuit of his loved one by calling out to her: "I implore you, nymph, daughter of Peneus, do not run away! Though I pursue you, I am no enemy. Stay sweet nymph! You flee as the lamb flees the wolf, or the deer the lion, as doves on fluttering wings fly from an eagle, as all creatures flee their foes! But it is love that drives me to follow you…" (Ovid, *Metamorphoses*, I). Daphne could not escape Apollo. In the end, she desperately begged her father to free her from the body that had aroused Apollo's desire and he turned her into a laurel bush.

In revenge, Eros, who was offended because Apollo had insulted him by calling him a worthless archer, shot the god with a love-arrow, so that he would fall madly in love with Daphne. Stoneware Eros from Egypt, 1st century CE.

Decorative painting from the House of the Vettii in Pompeii, based on the myth of Apollo and Daphne. Painted in the fourth Pompeian style.

Daphnis

Daphnis was a Sicilian shepherd, though it was said that the god Hermes might have been his father. Daphnis grew up surrounded by the forest nymphs in the mountains of Sicily. He was considered to be the founder of pastoral poetry (the genre of poetry in which the beauty of nature is praised and shepherds and shepherdesses play the leading role). Daphnis was a protegé of Apollo, Artemis, and Pan, who offered him his flute.

According to the poet Ovid, Daphnis was the victim of a dramatic love story, being turned to stone by the actions of a nymph who had become jealous of a woman to whom Daphnis had made love. There are several versions of the story about Daphnis and his love affairs with nymphs and mortal women. The poet Virgil dedicated a poem to the death of Daphnis. In it, Daphnis is presented as a Dionysus-like figure, who had his chariot pulled by tigers, and taught people how to make the *thyrsus (see* **Dionysus***)*. In the poem, humans, animals, nymphs, and gods mourned Daphnis' death, but their mourning was short-lived, because very soon afterward the shepherd was deified.

In the 3rd or 4th century CE, the Greek writer Longus wrote a shepherd novel about two foundlings, Daphnis and Chloe, who were raised by foster-parents. They fell in love with each other, married, and lived a long and happy life in a bucolic setting. Since then, Daphnis and Chloe are considered the epitome of the perfect shepherd couple.

The arid Sicilian landscape, where the shepherd Daphnis lived among the nymphs. Daphnis was considered to have laid the foundations of pastoral poetry.

Demeter (Roman=*Ceres*)

Demeter with a cornucopæa, a "horn of plenty," from which stalks of wheat are overflowing. Demeter, a sister of Zeus, was the goddess of agriculture and cultivation.

Demeter was one of the twelve Olympian gods and goddesses who lived in Mount Olympus, with the supreme deity Zeus. She was a daughter of Cronos and Rhea, and a sister of Zeus, Poseidon, Hades, Hera, and Hestia. As goddess of the earth, agriculture, and grain, Demeter was one of the most important Greek goddesses. She should also be considered as one of the variants of the

The 'primary mother' or great mother-goddess had been honoured since the Old Stone-Age in Europe and the Mediterranean world. The statue of this goddess, flanked by lions, was found in Turkey and dates to the 6th or 7th millennium BCE

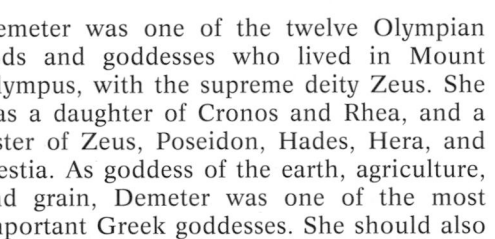

great Mother Goddess who has been worshiped since the earliest days of mankind. Prehistoric statues from the Early Stone Age show that around 20,000 BCE fertility and a mother goddess were worshiped in Europe and the Middle East.

Demeter is also related to the Egyptian goddess Isis, the Phœnician goddess Astarte (Ashtoreth), and the Mesopotamian goddess Ishtar. In Greek mythology, several goddesses have characteristics of a "primitive goddess," in addition to Demeter, Aphrodite especially, and to a lesser extent Artemis and Athena. The Phrygian Cybele, who was later worshiped in Rome as the "Great Mother," also belongs on this list. Aspects of the cult of the mother goddess persist in the worship of the Virgin Mary, mother of Jesus Christ.

The worship of Demeter involved themes of death, growth, and resurrection, and had the characteristics of a mystery cult. In Eleusis, about fifteen miles from Athens, the Eleusinian Mysteries were performed each year in September or October. The participants walked in procession from Athens to Eleusis, where they were initiated into the secret rituals, that probably bore similarities to primitive harvest rites and made reference to death and resurrection. During the Mysteries, the story of Demeter and her daughter Persephone was probably enacted. This was

Portrait of a woman with two torches. Male and female participants in the Eleusian Mysteries walked in procession from Athens to Eleusis. At their destination, secret rites were performed relating to the myth of Demeter and Persephone. Small Greek vase, 5th century BCE.

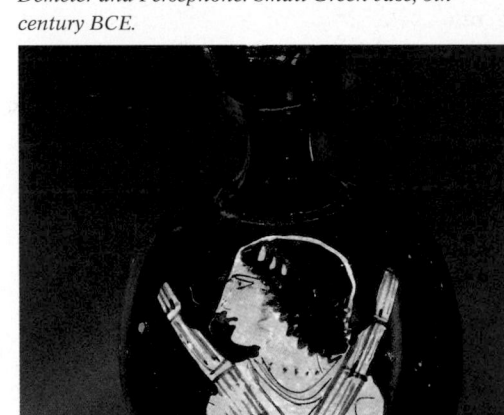

the most important myth of Demeter.

Persephone was Demeter's only daughter, and was conceived by Zeus. Without Demeter's knowledge, Zeus promised her as a bride to his uncle, Hades, ruler of the underworld. As a result, Hades did not handle the situation very sensitively. While the young Persephone was on Sicily picking flowers in the forest with her friends, the daughters of Oceanus, or the river-god Achelous, who, according to some, turned into Sirens (*see* **Sirens**), the dark god of death suddenly appeared in his chariot, drawn by black horses, and carried Persephone off. The girl dropped her freshly picked flowers and called out for her mother, fearing for her life, but nothing could be done. Hades had kidnaped her and carried her off to his realm, the underworld.

When Demeter realized that her beloved daughter had disappeared, she immediately set out to search for her. Nine long days she wandered without food or drink in her search for Persephone. At some point, she met Hecate, who had heard Persephone's cries of fear. Hecate brought Demeter to the sun-god Helios, who could see everything that happened on earth from his sun-chariot. He told the goddess that Persephone had ended up in the underworld (though according to the poet Ovid, Demeter received this news from the nymph Arethusa).

Demeter was so shocked that she brought down drought and hunger throughout the world. She did not return to the halls of the gods on Mount Olympus, but wandered the earth, dazed with sadness. While she was sitting dejectedly near a spring in Eleusis, having taken the form of an old woman, the daughters of King Celeus and Queen Metaneira came to fetch water. They took Demeter home with them because she had told them she was a Cretan child-nurse who had been kidnapped by robbers. There she was allowed to care for the newborn prince, Demophon. Demeter decided to make the baby immortal. During the day, she smeared him with ambrosia, and at night she put him in the fireplace. Metaneira surprised her in this act and Demeter revealed her true identity. She ordered Celeus and Metaneira to found a sanctuary for her in Eleusis, which later became the location at which the Eleusinian Mysteries were performed.

Demeter stayed for one year in her new temple, avoiding contact with the other gods. Meanwhile, nothing would grow and the

Demeter's sadness after the abduction of her daughter to the kingdom of death, had terrible consequences. The crops shriveled, and Zeus was compelled to intervene. Demeter, stoneware statue from Tarente, 4th century BCE.

earth was completely barren. Zeus realized that something had to be done, so he sent his messenger, Iris, to Demeter to reason with her. But Demeter only wanted one thing—she wanted her daughter back. Although Zeus swore to her that there was hardly a better candidate for a husband than Hades, his only brother, who rivaled him in status, Demeter remained adamant. Nothing could be done but to bring Persephone back from the underworld, and Hermes, the messenger god was sent to fetch her. There was a hitch, however. According to an old ordinance of fate, a person could only leave the underworld if he or she had not eaten anything there. Hades knew this provision and had made Persephone eat the seeds of a pomegranate (according to Ovid, Persephone picked the fruit herself on a walk through Hades' garden). Persephone initially denied that she had eaten anything, but Ascaphalus, the son of a nymph, had witnessed it and informed the gods.

Eventually, Zeus determined that Persephone was to be allowed to stay with her mother for part of the year and with Hades for the other part of the year. When she was with her mother, the grain grew and ripened, and when she was with Hades the earth was scorched and barren. The beginning of Perse-

Demeter 's task was to spread grain cultivation throughout the world. In olden times, grain was considered as an essential foodstuff and a valuable gift from the gods. Coin (nomos) from Metapontum, 6th century BCE.

Deucalion, the Greek equivalent of the biblical Noah, built a boat on the advice of his father, the wise Titan Prometheus, in order to survive the floods produced by the gods. Silver coin (obolus) from Arados, 4th century BCE.

phone's "above the ground" period was associated with the Fall and lasted until the beginning of summer, from the time of sowing the grain until it was harvested. The time she spent underground fell during the sweltering, dry Mediterranean summer months, when the fields were barren and scorched. Later, it was assumed that Persephone stayed with Hades during the winter (when nature "rests"), and with Demeter in the spring and summer (when nature "grows.") This is how the myth of Demeter, Hades, and Persephone explained the changing seasons.

After Demeter had found her daughter again, she ordered Eleusis, who was originally from Triptolemus (according to some, he was the same Prince Demophon whom Demeter had nursed), to spread agriculture and grain harvesting throughout the world. The story of Demeter thus symbolizes the change in human civilization from a hunter–gatherer culture to a settled agricultural life (*see* **Hades** and **Persephone**).

Deucalion

Deucalion, the Noah of Greek mythology, was the son of Prometheus and Pronoia and husband of Pyrrha, daughter of Epimetheus and Pandora. Mankind was still in a relatively primitive moral state. in his time, which explains why the Arcadian king Lycaon

offered Zeus, who came to check if he was indeed as godless as was claimed, a stew made from human flesh. Zeus turned him into a wolf and furthermore decided to destroy mankind by means of a flood.

Only Deucalion and Pyrrha were allowed to survive this disaster. On the advice of Deucalion's father, Prometheus, they built a boat in which they weathered the rains for nine full days. Eventually, their boat came to a rest on the slopes of Mount Parnassus.

When Deucalion and Pyrrha realized they were the only surviving humans, lonely and desperate, they begged the goddess Themis, whose shrine had not washed away, to tell them how to prevent the final destruction of mankind. She ordered them to wear veils, loosen their clothing, and throw their mother's bones over their shoulders. At first, Deucalion and Pyrrha refused to obey, as they refused to desecrate the remains of the dead. Then Deucalion realized that "mother" meant mother earth and "bones" meant rocks and did as Themis had instructed.

From the stones that Deucalion cast over his shoulder, men sprang up, and from the stones thrown by Pyrrha, women sprang up. Thus, the new human race was created and mankind's continued existence was guaranteed. Helenus, the son of Deucalion and Pyrrha, held a special position among these new humans, as the progenitor of the Hellenes, or Greeks.

Dido

Dido, sitting on her funeral pyre, ends her life after Æneas decides not to marry her but to instead to carry out his divine duties.

Dido, the legendary first queen of the Northern African city of Carthage, was the daughter of Mutto, King of the Phœnician city of Tyre. Her significance in mythology is mainly due to her tragic love affair with the Trojan

When Dido and her supporters established themselves in North Africa, the creatures living there included wild ostriches and donkeys, Tunisian mosaic, Roman era.

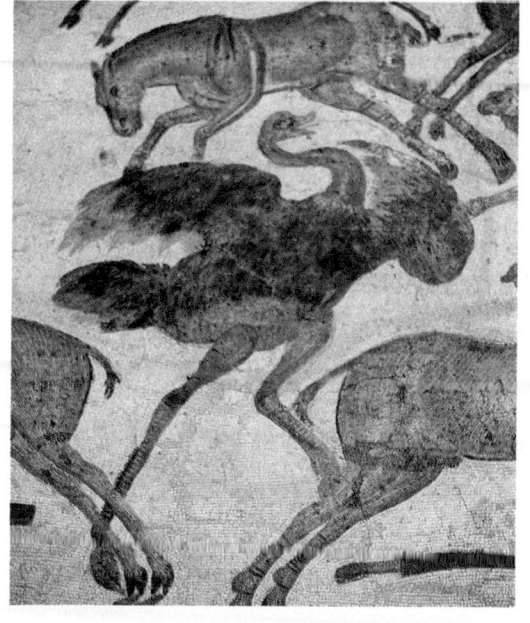

hero, Æneas, who after escaping from Troy spent some time with her in north Africa.

Dido had to flee her native city after her husband was killed by her brother, Pygmalion. With her sister, Anna, and a group of trustworthy companions she landed on the shores of North Africa, in what is now Tunisia.

Iarbas, a local king, was prepared to sell her a piece of land, but size of the land was to be no larger than the skin of a bull. Cunning Dido therefore cut a bull skin into narrow strips and with them demarcated the location for the city she wished to establish—Carthage.

While Carthage was under construction, Æneas landed at the new city. His ship had been blown off course when a storm blew up on the Italian coast. A passionate love affair quickly flared up between himself and Dido. When, during a hunting party, a heavy storm broke, the lovers sought refuge in a cave, where Dido gave herself to Æneas. Understandably, she expected that he would become her new husband. Æneas felt the same, but the gods reminded him that his

The area of Carthage was later colonized by the Romans who thought of themselves as descendants of Æneas' Trojans. This monumental amphitheater is located at El Djem in modern Tunisia.

destiny lay in Italy, and the foundation of a new kingdom. Æneas, a god-fearing and obedient hero, left her.

Dido, deeply offended and dishonored, ascended a funeral pyre and stabbed herself with a sword that she had received as a present from Æneas.

During the first and second century BCE, various wars were fought between Æneas' descendants the Romans, and Dido's people, the Carthaginians. The dramatic love story of Dido and Æneas was recorded by the Roman poet, Virgil. Many artists were also subsequently inspired by this story (*see* **Æneas**).

Diomedes

There are two characters called Diomedes in Greek mythology. The first was a son of Ares, the war god, who kept four man-eating horses, that at one time had to be caught by Heracles, as one of the Twelve Labors imposed upon him (*see* **Heracles, Eighth Labor**).

The second Diomedes was the son of Tydeus and Deipyle. He was king of Argos and one of the most fearsome Greek heroes in the Trojan War. Battle was in Diomedes' blood. His father, an ally of Œdipus' son Polynices (*see* **Creon** *and* **Œdipus**), had fallen in battle before the city of Thebes. Later, Diomedes himself, along with the other sons of the "seven" who had besieged Thebes, concentrated their forces against the city. These sons, known as the Epigones, performed

much better in battle than had their fathers. The Thebans had to flee their city and the city walls were demolished.

Later, Diomedes was one of the Greek monarchs who sought the hand of the beautiful Helen. Like all her other suitors, he swore that he would provide Menelaus, who was chosen to be her husband, with assistance should he ever get into difficulties because of Helen (*see* **Menelaus**). Diomedes kept his promise and traveled to Troy with a large fleet of troop-ships. During the ten-year siege of the city, He showed himself to be a great hero, surpassed only by Achilles and "the great" Ajax. However, according to Helenus, the clairvoyant son of the Trojan King Priam, the extremely belligerent Diomedes was "the strongest of all Greeks,"who caused him even more anxiety than Achilles. Diomedes often collaborated with the crafty Odysseus, who seemed to him to be a perfect comrade-at-arms. Like Odysseus, Diomedes was a particular favorite of the goddess Athena. She ensured that he killed many Trojans—including the prominent archer Pandarus— in the tenth year of the war. Diomedes also severely wounded the hero Æneas and was not overawed by the gods who fought alongside the Trojans on their side. He outfaced Apollo,

Diomedes, son of the war god Ares, kept four man-eating horses. The hero Heracles fed him to these animals, who were themselves later devoured by predators. Greek vase painting.

Diomedes was a fiery warrior, who was not even afraid of the gods. Here he is wounding Aphrodite, goddess of love, in the arm.

wounded and drove away none other than Ares the god of war, and with his lance, managed to wound the goddess of love, Aphrodite —not exactly a warlike individual—fairly badly in the arm.

With his friend Odysseus, Diomedes would go out every night to reconnoiter far outside of the Greek camp. The Trojan, Dolon, was killed on one of these forays, as was King Rheses, a Thracian ally of the Trojans, and twelve of his men. Previously, Lycier Glaucus, fighting on the Trojan side, fared better, when he and Diomedes discovered that their grandfathers—Æneus and the hero Bellerophon—had been very good friends. So they decided not to fight each other, but instead to exchange weapons. This provided Diomedes with fabulous golden armor, worth more than ten times as much as his own bronze weapons.

Diomedes accomplished many more heroic deeds, both with and without the aid of Odysseus. Together they stole the Palladium, a statue of Athena, from Troy, as it was necessary for victory for the Greeks. He also accompanied Odysseus to Lemnos to fetch the archer Philoctetes (*see* **Odysseus**).

After the Trojan War, Diomedes returned home safely, but he later was forced by Aphrodite to renounce the throne of Argus, because she had not forgotten that he had wounded her. He then settled in southern Italy, where he founded the city of Argyripa or Arpi. On the way there, many of his comrades were changed into water-fowl by Aphrodite because they provoked the goddess. Diomedes felt that there was little to be gained by allying himself with Æneas' opponents in Italy, as they wanted to drive out the Trojan ancestor of future Romans from "their" territory. He thought he had annoyed Aphrodite enough already and therefore preferred to make peace with her son Æneas.

Dionysus (Roman=Bacchus)

Dionysus, son of Zeus and Semele, is famous as the god of wine,,especially in the guise of Bacchus, but his significance in Greek mythology is much wider. As the god of vegetation and ecstasy, Dionysus was one of the most important in the Greek pantheon, especially during the Hellenistic period (325–30 BCE).

Dionysus was originally worshiped in Thrace and Phrygia, where he probably performed a similar function to Demeter, goddess of agriculture. It was not until relatively late that he permeated the Greek culture of the time. In the work of the poet Homer, who lived in approximately 800 BCE, he was still a minor god, but later he was worshiped more enthusiastically. His mainly female disciples, the Mænads ("mad ones") or bacchantes (q.v.), were renowned for the zealotry of their devotions.They indulged in frenzied gyrations, got into states of ecstatic intoxication, dressed in deer skins, wandered around with torches and *thyrus* staffs (staffs on which a pine cone was placed and which were wrapped in ribbons and vine and ivy tendrils), and sometimes even devoured live animals.

Dionysus was begotten by Zeus with

The birth of Dionysus from Zeus' thigh. Zeus rescued his unborn son from the body of his mother, Semele, and implanted him in his own thigh.

Dionysus on horseback, in the company of a panther. Predators were included to the wine god's permanent retinue. Athenian painted vase of the 5th century BCE.

Dionysus with three Mænads. Each holds a thyrus staff in her hand. Fragment of a painting on a vase from Tarente, 4th century BCE.

Semele, a daughter of Cadmus, founder of the city of Thebes. Zeus made love to her in human form, but after being tricked by jealous Hera, Semele asked the supreme god to show himself to her in his true form. Zeus knew what the consequences of this would be if he granted her wish, but could not refuse her. When Semele beheld him in all his brilliant splendor, she was scorched by his radiance (*see* **Semele**). Zeus was hardly able to save Dionysus from her womb in time. He made a gash in his thigh and placed the tiny god inside. And so Dionysus was born of his

The triumphal procession of Bacchus (the Latin name of Dionysus). Oil painting by Peter Paul Rubens, 17th century.

father some time later, after which Semele's sister Ino took pity on him (*see* **Ino**).

Dionysus was raised by nymphs and later by Silenus, an old, bald, stout man who often rode a donkey or who, because of his state of inebriation, had to be supported by satyrs. Although he was often under the influence of drink, Silenus possessed great wisdom and gifts of prophecy. When Dionysus was fully grown, Silenus remained part of the god's extended retinue, which consisted of nymphs, satyrs, and Mænads.

Satyrs were depicted with hooves and horns, and Dionysus himself also had an animalistic appearance for a time. When Hera made life particularly dangerous for him, Zeus or Hermes changed the young god into a goat, and put him into the safekeeping of the nymphs on Mount Nysa. According to some versions, it was on this mountain that Dionysus discovered the secret of wine and viticulture, which he would later spread all

The birth of Dionysus, image in relief from Nysa, modern day Turkey. According to myth, the mountain of Nysa is where Dionysus is supposed to have discovered the secret of making wine.

Dionysus" guardian Silenus being taken away drunk. Silenus was almost always intoxicated, but this did not affect his wisdom. Image in relief from Nysa.

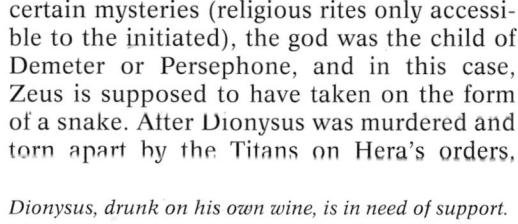

Zeus is supposed to have given his heart to Semele to eat, after which he was born again and the story of Zeus and Semele began. One of Dionysus' epithets was "twice-born"—a name that can also be explained by the fact that he first originated in Semele and then sprouted from Zeus' thigh.

As a newcomer among the gods, Dionysus was not accepted by everyone. Not only did Hera hate him, others also doubted his divine status. Lycurgus, King of the Edones, attempted to kill Dionysus, but the sea goddess Thetis took pity on him and Lycurgus was smitten with blindness. Pentheus, king of Thebes, Dionysus' birthplace, refused to recognize his divinity. Dionysus then came to Thebes, in the guise of a handsome young man, accompanied by a retinue of Mænads, and Pentheus had him thrown into prison. But Dionysus' chains fell from him and the doors of his cell flew open. The god told Pentheus that the Mænads and Theban women, who had been enchanted by him, were going to perform spectacular orgies on Mount Cithæron. Pentheus' curiosity was aroused. He was told that to be able to witness these excesses he would have to disguise himself as a woman. Pentheus watched the erotic display from a tree until he was discovered by the Mænads. In their ecstatic state they saw the king as a lion, and under the leadership of his mother Agave, a fanatical Mænad, they dragged him from the tree and

over the world.

There are other versions of the birth of Dionysus birth and his early youth. According to these versions, which played a role in certain mysteries (religious rites only accessible to the initiated), the god was the child of Demeter or Persephone, and in this case, Zeus is supposed to have taken on the form of a snake. After Dionysus was murdered and torn apart by the Titans on Hera's orders,

Head of a menacing satyr. Satyrs could be agressive and were inclined to sexual misconduct. Terra-cotta mask, 4th century BCE.

Dionysus, drunk on his own wine, is in need of support. Mosaic from Antolia, Turkey.

tore him to pieces. Agave later returned to her senses, buried her son, and with her parents, Cadmus and Harmonia, went into exile.

This story conveys something of the fear and aversion felt among many aristocratic Greeks, worshippers of the old gods of Olympus, for the new god with his crazed disciples. In various cities and locations, stories circulated of people, who, because of their fanatical worship of Dionysus became insane and lapsed into dangerous rages. This also happened to the daughters of king Midas.

Dionysus gave wine to humanity, but this gift met with a mixed reaction. According to an Athenian myth, he instructed the humble Icarius and his daughter Erigone in viticulture. But when Icarius' neighbors became drunk on the wine, they feared that they had been poisoned and killed Icarius. Erigone committed suicide when she discovered what had happened to her father. As a result, Dionysus struck the Athenians with madness, and many Athenian women hanged themselves, just like Erigone. When the Athenians later realized the injustice they had committed, they established a festival in which they hung pictures from trees in honor of Icarius and Erigone.

In Ætolia, Dionysus was well received. King Œneus (whose name is almost the same as the Greek word for wine, *oinos*) even

The satyrs in this painting are busy pressing wine. Wine pitcher from Athens, 5th–6th century BCE.

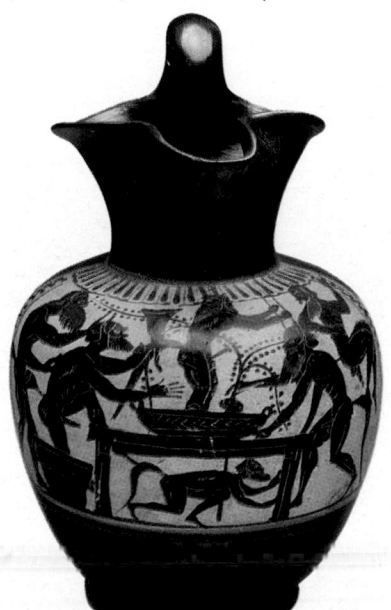

Dionysus on board a ship being guided by dolphins. Clusters of grapes are growing from the mast. Painting on a Greek dish.

offered him his wife, Althæa. From their union, Heracles' future wife, Deianeira, was born. The grateful Dionysus rewarded Œneus with the gift of viticulture.

Dionysus' married Ariadne, the daughter of the Cretan king Minos, who before marrying the god had helped the hero Theseus to kill the Minotaur. According to some versions, Ariadne was abandoned on the island of Naxos by Theseus, with whom she had fled from Crete, and Dionysus took pity on her. In other versions, Dionysus claimed her as his bride, and Theseus was forced to accept a lonely and sad return journey to Athens (*see* **Ariadne** *and* **Theseus**).

Gradually, the cult of Dionysus spread throughout the Greek world and beyond it, but the god's Phrygian dress and exuberant behavior retained a certain "foreign" touch. During winter months in Athens, various Dionysus festivals were celebrated, of which the major and minor Dionysia were most famous. The Anthesteria, celebrated in February, was a flower festival during which the first new wine was consumed and Dionysus brought into the city in a ship's cart (*carrus navalis*, in Latin). This laid the foundations for the future Christian pre-Lenten carnival, in which elements of the Mænadic frenzy were retained.

During the great Dionysian festivals, celebrated in March, comedies, tragedies, and satyr games were performed in the theater of Dionysus at the foot of the Acropolis. The tragedy (the Greek word *tragoidia* originally meant "buck or goat song") developed from songs and dances performed by farmers in goat costume. Thus, the worship of Dionysus

Dionysus riding on a panther's back with a thyrus staff in his hand. Mosaic floor, Pella.

Greek tragedy developed from rituals which formed a part of the worship of Dionysus. Actor from Alexandria, earthenware statuette, 3rd century BCE.

gave birth to a literary genre that is read and performed not only in its original form, but also in a modernized form that is still popular today. New tragedies are still being created by playwrights.

With his emphasis on intoxication and ecstasy, Dionysus represented a particular aspect of Greek civilization. It was in strong contrast to the intellectualism personified by the sensible, controlled, and artistic god, Apollo. Dionysus was also worshiped in Delphi, the center of the Apollo cult . In winter, when Apollo left to dwell with a tribe that lived in the frozen North, the Dionysian revels were celebrated. In the spring, Apollo returned and Dionysus "died," only to be reborn again later in the year.

Orphism, in which Orpheus was associated

The orchestra of the Greek amphitheatre in Syracuse, Sicily. Once upon a time, a statue of Dionysus stood here.

with Dionysus, was an offshoot of the worship of Dionysus that developed into a theological refinement of the cult that emerged in Greece around the sixth century BCE. At first, adherents of the cult were persecuted by

the Dyonisian priests, but eventually Orphism merged into the Dyonisian cult (*see* **Orpheus**).

As a savior figure who rose from the dead and promised eternal life, Bacchus, the Roman god of wine, was frequently depicted on sarcophagi during the Roman Empire. When Christianity supplanted the old gods, the figure of the wine-god was sometimes simply replaced by another victor over death—Jesus Christ. Many other later "satanic" rituals, in which participants reach a state of ecstasy through the use of alcohol and other drugs and Satan shows himself to his witches, are similar to the Dionysian or Bacchanalian rites, during which the god moved among his disciples in the form of a goat.

The Dioscuri

The Dioscuri—literally "sons of Zeus," better known as "the heavenly twins"—were Castor and Polydeuces. The latter is better known under his Roman name, Pollux. These twin brothers were the sons of Leda, the wife of King Tyndareos of Sparta. Their sisters were called Helen and Clytemnestra. Although the poet Homer assumed that all four of Leda's children were mere mortals, a later tradition claimed that Polydeuces and Helen were begotten by Zeus when the supreme god visited Leda in the form of a swan (*see* **Leda**). Castor and Clytemnestra, on the other hand, were fathered by Tyndareos. Polydeuces and Helen were therefore immortal, but Castor and Clytemnestra were mortal. Yet another tradition claimed that Leda laid three eggs after her encounter with the swan, from which both her mortal and immortal children

The Dioscuri Castor and Polydeuces were usually presented as twin brothers. However, they were most likely not twins, certainly not identical. Polydeuces was considered to be a son of Zeus, Castor a son of Tyndareos.

Ruined temple of Castor and Pollux in the Forum in Rome. At the Forum, the Dioscuri are said to have proclaimed the definitive defeat by the Romans of the Etruscan King Tarquin the Proud.

were hatched.

The Dioscuri, who were patrons of seafarers, were particularly honored in their birthplace, Sparta, and in Rome, both cities having a distinctly warlike tradition. The Romans believed that these inseparable heroes had

Leda with an agressive swan, in reality the supreme god Zeus, who by her begat the beautiful Helen and the hero Polydeuces. Athenian earthenware statuette from ca. 440 BCE.

assisted their armies in the war against the Etruscan King, Tarquin the Proud, in historic times. It was said that they were seen in the Roman Forum, where they proclaimed Roman victory. This is why a temple was dedicated to them in the Forum. The Dioscuri were also the patrons of Roman nobility.

As young men, the Dioscuri, along with many other heroes, took part in the Argonauts' quest, under the leadership of Jason (*see* **The Argonauts**). Castor, an excellent horseman, did not play a particularly distinguished role in the quest, but Polydeuces, an outstanding boxer, used his pugilistic skills against the obnoxious king Amycus, who forced his guests to box against him.

When the Athenian hero, Theseus, abducted the very young Helen, she was rescued by her brothers. Consequently, Castor and Polydeuces appointed a rival of Theseus as King of Athens. Another story about the Dioscuri concerns their own abduction of their cousins Phoebe and Hilaria, who became their wives. The two girls had already been promised to two of the Dioscuri's cousins but when these cousins, together with Castor and Polydeuces, stole a cow in Arcadia, a serious dispute broke out over the division of the

spoils. Both cousins were killed in the battle that broke out, and Castor was fatally wounded. Zeus then granted Polydeuces' request to divide the gift of immortality between the two brothers and from then on, the two brothers alternated their days between Olympus with their divine father and the underworld.

Eventually the twins were placed in the sky as the constellation of Gemini.

Echo *see* Narcissus

Electra

Electra was a daughter of the Mycenæan king Agamemnon and his wife, Clytemnestra, and the sister of Iphigenia, Chrysothemis, and

Eventually, the Dioscuri received a place in the firmament as the astrological sign Gemini, the twins.

Orestes. Her name means "amber" in Greek, or possibly "spark" (*elektron*), as static electricity can be generated by rubbing amber.

Agamemnon, who had fought in the Trojan War as commander-in-chief of the Greeks, was murdered by his wife, Clytemnestra, and her lover, Ægisthus, after his return from the war (*see* **Agamemnon**). The murderers also wanted to kill Agamemnon's young heir, Orestes, but Electra enabled him to escape to Phocis (according to another version Orestes had already been brought to Phocis previously).

Electra remained in Mycenæ and when

Electra and her younger brother, Orestes. Electra took care of Orestes after his return from Phocis. Together, they devised the plans for revenge on their mother Clytemnestra and her lover Ægisthus.

Orestes later returned there with his cousin and close friend Pylades, she advised him how to take revenge on Clytemnestra and Ægisthus, as they stood beside their father's grave. Electra was then also present during the act of revenge.

The story of Electra is one that inspired many Greek playwrights, including Sophocles (496–406 BCE) who wrote the tragedy *Electra*, and Euripides (480–406 BCE) who also wrote a tragedy entitled Electra, in which he gave events another twist. In Euripides' play, Electra marries a farmer with whom, because of the difference in their backgrounds, she cannot not have children. Together, they plan to avenge her father's murder. After Orestes' return from Phocis, Electra's plans for Ægisthus to be killed first on a nearby farm, and then Clytemnestra is to die in Electra's house. After taking her revenge, Electra is haunted by remorse, while Orestes—in essence not as guilty as Electra—is pursued by the Erinyes, the goddesses of revenge. The *Orestes*, a dramatic trilogy by the earliest great Athenian tragedian, Æschylus (525–426 BCE) deals with the entire murder and revenge cycle of Agamemnon's family is described, up to and including the trial of Orestes in Athens (*see* **Agamemnon, Atreus, the Erinyes,** *and* **Orestes**).

The story of Electra also inspired the American playwright Eugene O'Neill who wrote *Morning Becomes Electra* in 1930, as

Electra suffered one family tragedy after another. Her father killed her older sister on the altar, her mother murdered her father, and Electra took revenge on her mother. Women grieving over a corpse lying on a bier, fragment of an Athenian vase, 6th century BCE.

an illustration of the complexity of family life. The play was made into a movie.

Endymion

Endymion, the son of Æthlius and Calyce, was king of Elis in the Peloponnese. Selene, the moon goddess, later equated with Artemis, was smitten with an intense love for Endymion. Every night, she descended from the heavens to make love to the handsome young king. As a result of this union, she bore fifty daughters. Selene could not bear the thought that some day Endymion would die and ensured that he could sleep forever in a cave in Caries. According to another version, Zeus permitted Endymion to sleep forever so that he would never age.

Eos (Roman=*Aurora*)

Zeus is supposed to have granted Endymion eternal sleep, so that he would remain free from physical deterioration and decline. Zeus on a bronze coin from Alexandria, 3rd century BCE.

Eos was a daughter of Titans, Hyperion and Theia, and a sister of the sun-god Helios and the moon-goddess Selene. The winged Eos was the goddess of the dawn. Each morning, after awakening, she would rise out of the waters of Oceanus to bring light to the world. Before sunrise, she rode across the sky on a chariot pulled by the horses Phæton ("the shining one") and Lampos ("the bright one.") Her brother, Helios, the sun-god, enjoyed a higher status, and therefore drove a four-in-

hand. The poet, Homer, described the goddess of dawn with such expressive epithets such as "rose-fingered," "she who shines before mortals" and "she who sits on the golden throne."

Eos frequently fell in love with handsome mortals, but her love affairs usually ended unhappily. This was because Aphrodite, goddess of love, bore a grudge against her. Eos, as it happened, once had once tried to seduce Aphrodite's own lover, Ares, the god of war.

Tithonus, the handsome son of the Trojan King Laomedon, became Eos' husband. Eos

Eos traversed the early morning sky in a chariot drawn by shining horses. Bronze horse, 5th century BCE.

asked Zeus to grant him the gift of immortality, but forgot to also ask for eternal youth for him. As a result, the unlucky Tithonus, was afflicted by terrible aging. He dehydrated so much that he came to resemble a cricket. Eos shut him in his bedroom and herself got up as early as possible in order not to have to look at him.

Eos' other conquests included the great hunters Cephalus and Orion. When Eos went with Orion to the island of Delos, which was sacred to Artemis, Artemis was so offended that she killed Orion, but he ended up as a star constellation in the sky.

The Erinyes (Roman=Furies)

The Erinyes were goddesses of revenge who had an insatiable need to avenge great injustices that gods and mortals—particularly close family members—committed against each other.

The Erinyes are said to have sprouted from the blood of Uranus that was spilled when this first ruler of the universe was castrated by his insurgent son, Cronos (see **Cronos**). In a sense, this deed was the first unspeakable injustice committed in creation. Uranus' blood landed on Gaia, mother earth, and it is there that the Erinyes germinated. They looked terrifying. Their faces were contorted into evil grimaces, they had snakes instead of hair, and held burning brands and whips in

The three Erinyes or Furies were terrifying goddesses of revenge who were universally feared. They were associated with blood feuds and mercilessly pursued murderers.

their hands. It is unclear how many Erinyes there were at first, but in later traditions it was assumed that there were three Erinyes or Furies: Alecto ("she who never stops,") Tisiphone ("she who wreaks murder,") and Megeara ("the envious one.")

The Erinyes can be seen as the personification of guilt created by some crimes not punishable by human laws. The murder of a family member was considered such a crime and as a result, Orestes, who had killed his mother Clytemnestra to avenge the murder of his father Agamemnon (*see* **Agamemnon**), had to deal with them. They pursued him merci less, unwilling to accept any concession and ignoring the extenuating circumstances that applied in Orestes' case. Not even in the temple of Apollo in Delphi would they leave him in peace. It was only after Orestes had been tried in the Areopagus in Athens, where Athena had founded a special court of law, that the Erinyes allow themselves to be placated. Orestes was obligated to do penance, and henceforth the Erinyes were to be honored in Athens—not under their old name, but as the Eumenides, the "well-disposed ones." This story symbolizes the transition from the blood feud, the primitive way of avenging injustice, to a rational administration of justice, that will end the vicious circle of crime and retribution although the blood feud, as a form of rough justice, exists in primitive societies to this day.

Eris

Eris, a daughter of Nyx the goddess of night, was the personification of dispute and discord. Her most famous appearance in mythology took place during the wedding of Peleus and Thetis, to which, as one of the minor gods, she was not invited. She was so

Eris, insulted because she was not invited to the wedding of Peleus and Thetis, threw the "apple of discord" among the guests. Detail of an oil painting from Ferdinanc Bol, 17th century.

One of the frightening Erinyes. It was usually assumed that there were three of these goddesses. Fragment of a vase painting from Tarente, 4th century BCE.

enraged that she threw a golden apple (the classic "apple of discord") among the guests, that bore the inscription: "for the loveliest." The vain goddesses Hera, Athena, and Aphrodite all thought that this apple was for them. The Trojan prince, Paris, was invited to become the judge of a divine beauty contest among the three goddesses, with terrible consequences (see **Aphrodite**, **Paris,** and **Thetis**). According to Homer, Eris was a sister of Ares, god of war. He described how she accompanied Ares on the battlefield: "Quarrel, first small, swells, and finally her head reaches the sky, but her feet traverse the earth. She also wandered through the armies and ignited hatred in all, greedy for the groans of the men." (*Iliad*, IV, reg. 442-445)

Eros (Roman=Cupid or Amor)

Eros was the god of erotic, physical love. Originally he was considered a primal force, which together with Gaia, mother earth, had been created from Chaos, the primal space. He brought into being the union of Uranus, the sky, and Gaia, the earth. According to some traditions, the primal force of Eros even created the earth, the sky, and the moon.

Later, Eros was no longer viewed as an abstract principle, but as a son of Aphrodite, goddess of love, and her lover Ares, god of war. He was now portrayed as a good-looking, athletic young man. Statues of him stood

Eros as a baby, lying in his cradle, a wreath around his neck. Earthenware statuette, Tarente, 3rd century CE.

in the gymnasia, in which young men exercised, so that he became the patron of erotic relationships between adult and younger men.

During the Hellenistic period (325–30 BCE) and subsequent Roman era, Eros was portrayed as a chubby winged baby who, armed with a bow and arrow, spied on humans whom he could shoot with his love-arrows. This was the classical Roman version of Cupid. A later tendency emerged to duplicate him, and subsequent portrayals often

Eros, the god of love, had different types of arrows at his disposal. Gold-tipped arrows served to make people fall hopelessly in love, lead-tipped arrows caused an aversion to the pursuer.

Eros, son of Aphrodite, goddess of love, depicted as an infant. Bronze statuette from the Roman period.

Putti, the darling, angelic figures seen on innumerable works of art, are in fact Eros figures or cupids. Four putti by Hermanus Numan, 18th century.

show groups of cherub-like Cupids with tiny wings, sometimes surrounding their mother Aphrodite (Venus).

Eros or Cupid was not only a favorite subject in the visual arts, he also featured in the work of great Roman poets, such as Virgil and Ovid. In Virgil, Cupid is responsible for the love affair between Dido and Æneas (*see* **Dido** *and* **Æneas**). In his story of Daphne and Apollo (*see* **Daphne**), Ovid describes how Eros had various types of arrows at his disposal. The gold-tipped arrows were for people whom he wanted to fall hopelessly in love but the lead-tipped arrows were those for whom he wished to make averse to love.

Eros himself fell deeply in love once, with Psyche, "the soul" (*see* **Psyche**).

Euridyce *see* Orpheus

Despite their tricks, the Eros were benevolent gods, with the best of intentions for humanity. Eros figures with ta cornucopœa (horn of plenty) on an octagonal earthenware dish, 3rd-4th century CE.

Europa

Europa, after whom a continent is named,

Europa, daughter of a Phœnician king, is approached by a beautiful, mild-mannered bull. In reality this animal was the supreme god Zeus, who had her in his sights.

was the daughter of the Phœnician king Agenor and his wife Telephassa. Her brother, Cadmus, founded the Greek city of Thebes.

The supreme god, Zeus, saw Europa playing with her friends on the beach one day, and immediately felt a great desire for her. He changed himself into a beautiful, snow-white bull and approached Europa in this form. The girl fell under the spell of the handsome, gentle, playful bull and after a while climbed onto its back. The bull then leaped into the sea and swam away. The terrified Europa watched the land disappear far behind her.

The bull emerged from the sea at Crete where Zeus revealed himself to the girl. They made love, probably in the cave in which Zeus himself had been raised by Amalthea (*see* **Amalthea**), and from their union three sons were born, Minos, Rhadamanthys, and Sarpedon. Zeus gave Europa a javelin that never missed its target, an unusual dog, and a bronze man, Talos, who roamed over the island and drove strangers away by pelting them with stones (according to another version, Talos was a gift from Hephæstos to Europa's son Minos). Europa later entered into marriage with the Cretan king Asterius, who named her son Minos as his successor.

After Europa climbed on his back, the bull sprang into the sea and swam from Phœnicia (present-day Lebanon) to the island of Crete. Earthenware statuette from Boeotia, 4th century BCE.

Old image of the astrological sign of taurus, the bull. Bulls played a significant role in Greek mythology, particularly in stories connected with Crete.

Agenor, Europa's father, was upset by the inexplicable disappearance of his daughter and sent his sons out to look for her. One of them, Cadmus, had numerous adventures during his quest. This is the Cadmus who founded the Greek city Thebes (*see* **Cadmus**).

Cave on Mount Dicte, Crete. Zeus who was raised in this cave by the goat-nymph, Amalthea, made love there to the charming Europa.

Eurus

Eurus was the east or southeast wind. He was the brother of Boreas, the north wind, Zephyrus, the west wind, and Notus, the south wind. He brought light on his swift steed, but could also bring violent storms and heavy rain.

Eurystheus *see* Heracles

Fates, the, *see* Moiræ

Faunus

Faunus, son of Picus and grandson of Saturn (=Cronos), was an Italian god of nature. In some versions, he was the father of Latinus, who ruled over Latium when the hero Æneas, the forefather of the Romans, arrived there (**see Æneas**). Faunus closely resembled the Greek god, Pan, with whom he was eventually equated. He served as patron of cattle and

Faunus, the Roman god of nature, was associated with the Greek god Pan. Faunus had gifts of prophecy and sometimes supported the Romans in battle.

The goddess Fortuna brought prosperity and good luck, but her actions were completely arbitrary. That is why she is blindfolded and holds a ball that could roll in any direction.

also possessed gifts of prophecy. After a battle against the Etruscans, Roman soldiers heard his voice emanating from a forest, and announcing that the Etruscans had lost one man more than had the Romans in the fight. Inspired by this, the Romans inflicted a crushing defeat on the Etruscans.

Numa Pompilius, the second king of Rome, once made Faunus and his father the forest god, Picus (usually depicted in the form of a woodpecker), drunk because he wanted to know what he had to do to summon Jupiter (the Roman equivalent of the supreme god Zeus) from heaven. Faunus and Picus reluctantly gave him the information.

In Roman poetry, Faunus usually performed the same role as the Greek god, Pan. The poet Horatio mentions a festival celebrated on December 5 in honor of this god of nature and asks him to bless his cattle in an ode dedicated to "Faunus, lover of the ethereal Nymphs." (*Odes and Epodes, III 18*) (*see* **Pan**).

Flora *see* Chloris

Fortuna

Fortuna was the Roman goddess of destiny, of good luck and misfortune. Although her role in mythology was is not very significant, she was particularly honored by the lower classes, because she could determine whether people would be successful in life, or suffer misfortune. Many Roman temples were sacred to her and she was often invoked. In Præneste (present-day Palestrina, which was about 30 miles east of Rome) there was a

Fortuna, the benefactress of (some) followers, with a cornucopœa (horn of plenty). Bronze statuette,

Gaia, the Earth-mother, gave birth to many monsters and other terrifying creatures. Her offspring included Typhon, who battled against Zeus, and Python, an enormous serpent who lived in the ground at Delphi and was killed by the god Apollo.

large Fortuna sanctuary, built in the second century BCE. People could consult the oracle, who was part of this sanctuary, and draw lots to determine their future. Fortuna was often represented blindfolded, to symbolize that she was acting indiscriminately. On many depictions, she has objects with her that point to her arbitrariness and capriciousness, such as a ball and a wheel (the proverbial "wheel of fortune.") Another of her attributes is her cornucopœa or "horn of plenty," symbolizing the riches she could bestow on people if she chose to do so.

Gaia (Roman=Terra)

Gaia, the earth-mother, was one of the first creatures created from Chaos, the primal space. Her offspring were Uranus, the sky, Pontus, the sea, and the mountains. Her son Uranus begat the Titans with her, including Cronos and Rhea, the parents of the later supreme god Zeus and his brothers and sisters. In addition, the Cyclopes and the hundred-armed giants were born from the union of Uranus and Gaia.

Uranus allowed Gaia to suffer terrible pain by preventing the Cyclopes and the hundred-armed giants (*see* **Gigantes**) from leaving their mother's body (in other words, the earth). Gaia then gave her son Cronos a sickle made of flint, with which he castrated Uranus. Cronos flung Uranus' sexual organs into the sea. They washed up on Cyprus or Cythera, and from the foam that drifted around the island, Aphrodite, the goddess of love, was born. Uranus' blood landed on Gaia and created the Erinyes (the goddesses of revenge), the Gigantes, and the Melissan nymphs.

Cronos won the dominion over the universe and made his sister, Rhea, his wife. Soon he revealed himself to be no less of a tyrant than his father (*see* **Cronos**). He locked the Cyclopes and the hundred-armed giants in Tartarus, the most inhospitable part of the underworld, and devoured his own children as soon as they were born. Only Zeus, his youngest son, was spared this fate. Gaia gave Rhea a rock wrapped up in cloth, and Cronos devoured this stone instead of the baby. Zeus was brought to safety on Crete and raised by Amalthea (*see* **Amalthea**). When he grew to manhood, Zeus forced Cronos to vomit up his brothers and sisters (Hades, Poseidon, Demeter, Hestia, and

Hera) and liberated the Cyclopes and hundred-armed giants. Then the ten-year long Titan wars broke out, during which Cronos and the other Titans finally tasted defeat at the hands of Zeus and his allies. After their humiliation, the Titans were imprisoned in the Tartarus. Gaia was deeply outraged at this and from a union with Tartarus, she gave birth to the dreadful monster Typhon, whom Zeus had to depose from the throne. Zeus knew how to defeat this monster but, according to some versions, the battle was long and hard (*see* **Typhon**).

At Gaia's suggestion, the Gigantes then began a revolt against the Olympian gods that became known as the War of the Gigantes. Gaia cultivated an herb in order to make the Gigantes immortal and invincible, but Zeus ordered Helios, the sun god, and Eos, the goddess of daybreak, to extinguish the light. The universe was plunged into darkness of which Zeus took advantage to track down the herb before his opponents could harvest it. Eventually, the gods, with the vital support of the hero Heracles, achieved victory after a

The stadium that formed part of the complex of Delphi dedicated to Apollo. According to certain myths, the sanctuary at Delphi was originally founded by Gaia, a goddess associated with fortune-telling and oracles.

grueling battle.

As goddess of the earth, Gaia was associated with fortune-telling and oracles. The oracles were often located at sites of unusual geological phenomena, such as volcanos or deep clefts in the ground from which sulfurous fumes emerged. This was the case with the sanctuary of Delphi, later dedicated to Apollo, was originally founded by Gaia.

The earth-serpent Python, killed at Delphi with a thousand arrows shot by the god Apollo (*see* **Apollo**), was a daughter of Gaia. That is why after killing this monster, Apollo had to do penance by establishing the Pythian games and appointing the Pythia, the high priestess of the Oracle that was henceforth sacred to him.

Along with Typhon and Python, Gaia brought many other monsters into the world. Some sea gods, including Nereus, were also her children.

The Gigantes, who were defeated by the gods in a fierce battle (the War of the Gigantes), were the sons of Gaia. This is the giant, Enceladus, who was eventually crushed by the goddess Athena under the island of Sicily. Mosaic from the Villa del Casale, Sicily, 3rd–4th century CE.

Ganymede

Ganymede was the son of Tros, founder of the city of Troy, or of Laomedon, father of Priam, king of Troy during the Trojan war, depending on the version of the story. He was an extraordinarily handsome young man. The supreme god, Zeus, who had an eye not only for feminine beauty but also sometimes for handsome young men, changed himself into an eagle and in this form abducted Ganymede. Zeus made love to the boy, granted him immortality and eternal youth, and

appointed him as cupbearer to the gods on Olympus. As compensation, Zeus gave Tros two fabulous immortal horses, and a golden

vine made by Hephæstos.

Ganymede was placed in the firmament as

the constellation of Aquarius, alongside the constellation of Aquila, the Eagle.

Gigantes, The

The Gigantes were abominable giants who sprouted from the blood of the god Uranus that landed on Gaia, Mother Earth, when Uranus was castrated by his son Cronos. When the Titans were created, the Erinyes, the goddesses of revenge, were created, and the Melissan nymphs were also created.

The Gigantes were not only huge and unimaginably strong, they also looked very frightening. They had long hair and rough beards, and their legs ended in snakes.

When, after the Titan war ended, Zeus, imprisoned the Titans in the Tartarus, the most inhospitable part of the underworld, Gaia was so incensed that she provoked her sons, the Gigantes, into revolt against Zeus and the other gods of Olympus (*see* **Gaia** *and* **Titans**). Zeus knew that the gods could defeat the Gigantes only with the help of an unusual mortal. With this in mind, he fathered the formidable hero Heracles by Alcmene (*see* **Heracles**). Gaia also made her preparations, cultivating an herb which granted immortality to the Gigantes and made them invincible. Zeus then ordered Helios, the sun god, Selene, the

This giant, probably Porphyrion, was pierced by an arrow shot by Heracles or Apollo during the War of the Gigantes, when the giants fought against the gods. Mosaic, Villa del Casale, Sicily, 3rd-4th century CE.

Desolate slope of the Mount Vesuvius in Southern Italy. The giant, Mimas, was buried under this volcano by the god Hephæstos.

Ornamental torsos of Gigantes, in an old Italian villa.

moon-goddess and Eos, the goddess of dawn, to extinguish their light. The universe was cast into perpetual darkness, and Zeus took advantage of the situation to search for the herb before his opponents could harvest it.

The War of the Gigantes took place at Pallene in Thrace. It broke out when the Gigantes hurled rocks and burning branches at the sky-gods. The most important Gigantes were Eurymedon, Alcyoneus, and Porphyrion. Alcyoneus was important as long as he had contact with his place of birth. That is why, after shooting him with his poisoned arrows, Zeus dragged him out of Pallene, after which he died. Zeus then arranged for, Porphyrion to conceive a sudden desire for Hera, Zeus' wife, but when he ripped away the goddess' clothing to rape her, Zeus struck him with one of his thunderbolts. Heracles then finished him off with arrows. Various gods performed great feats during the battle. Apollo shot the giant, Aphialtes, in the eyes with his arrows, the giant, Enceladus, was buried by Athena under the island of Sicily, and the giant, Pallas, was flayed alive by Athena. The giant, Mimas, was buried under Mount Vesuvius by Hephæstos, and Poseidon threw a part of the island of Cos over the

115

giant Polybotes, thus creating a new island called Nisyrus. Hermes, Artemis, Hecate, and the Moiræ also fought alongside the other gods. Eventually, after a ten-year battle, the gods were victorious.

The gorgons were three sisters who were so horrifically ugly that everyone who looked at them immediately turned to stone.

Glaucus, *see* Scylla

The Gorgons

The gorgons were the daughters of Phorcys and Ceto. They were called Sthenno, Euryale, and Medusa, and lived in the westernmost part of the world, on the coast of the Oceanus, the sea that encircled the world. They had gold wings, copper hands, enormous fangs, and snakes for hair. Their appearance was so horrible that anyone who looked at them immediately turned to stone, though according to some, only Medusa possessed this ability. In any case, Medusa was the only one of the three sisters who was mortal. She was killed by the hero Perseus, who had been given the seemingly impossible task of capturing her head (*see* **Perseus**). When Perseus beheaded her, the monster Chrysaor and the winged horse Pegasus (*see* **Bellerophon** *and* **Pegasus**) sprouted from her blood. At the time of her decapitation, Medusa was actually pregnant, because she had been raped by Poseidon, the sea-god. This was odd, given her deeply unattractive appearance, and therefore it was believed

According to the hero Perseus, who eventually beheaded her, the gorgon Medusa had once been a strikingly lovely woman with beautiful hair but she offended the goddess Athena, who left little of this beauty intact. Medusa on the handle of a southern Italian krater, terracotta, 4th century BCE.

In Perseus' hands, the snake-covered head of Medusa was a true weapon of destruction, with which whole enemy bands could be turned to stone. Athenian lid by Meidias.

that Medusa had once been beautiful.

The poet Ovid explained through Perseus

that she had been a deeply desirable beauty, particularly because of her lovely tresses. Poseidon raped her in the sanctuary of Athena, in front of the statue of the virgin goddess, who was so upset by this that she turned Medusa into a monstrous creature with snakes for hair. It was also thought that Athena had robbed Medusa of her beauty and enabled Perseus to behead her because Medusa had once boasted that she was more beautiful than Athena.

Perseus donated the head of Medusa to Athena, after using it as a weapon a number of times, with considerable success. The goddess put the hideous petrified head on her ægis, the divine "goatskin" that she wore over her shoulders.

Graces, *see* Charities

Griffin or Gryphon, The

The griffin or gryphon was a mythical animal that closely resembled the Sphinx (*see* **Sphinx**) and looked like a winged lion with an eagle's head. The griffin of gryphon, which had its origins in the ancient Middle East and was known in Egypt from early times, was associated by the Greeks with the god Apollo, who spent his winters with the Hyperboreans, a race believed to have lived in the far north of Europe. The Greeks also placed griffins or gryphons in the same area, where

The agressively carnivorous head of a griffin. Bronze ornament from a piece of n Etruscan furniture, 3rd century BCE.

according to them, they guarded large supplies of gold. The one-eyed Arimaspen is supposed to have robbed them of the treasure that they guarded.

The Romans did not associate the griffin or gryphon with Apollo, but with Nemesis, the goddess of revenge (*see* **Nemesis**). The mythical significance of the griffin or gryphon was not very great with both Greeks and Romans, but the creature was a favorite subject in art. Griffins or gryphons decorate the walls of the throne room of the palace of Cnossos on Crete, from ca. 1700 BCE. This is the palace that may have belonged to the semi-mythical King Minos, (*see* **Minos**). The griffin remained a popular motif in the visual arts throughout the Roman era and beyond.

With their winged, leonine bodies, griffins or gryphons closely resembled a sphinx. The griffin or gryphon was used as an ornament and symbol in many cultures, from the ancient Mesopotamian civilizations to modern western cultures (especially on coats of arms).

Hades, the dark ruler of the kingdom of the dead, with his scepter and cornucopœa (horn of plenty). Those who ended up in Hades' kingdom could never escape from it.

One of the many duties of the youthful god Hermes, messenger of the gods, was to guide the souls of the dead to the underworld. Etruscan head, earthenware, 5th century BCE.

Hades

Hades was the god of death who ruled over the kingdom of the dead. This somber, dark god was a son of the Titans, Cronos and Rhea, and just as his brothers Zeus and Poseidon respectively ruled over the sky and the seas, he ruled over the underworld, which was known as "Hades."

The Greek underworld was generally

The Greeks attached great value to a decent burial and held their dead in great honour. This man is offering a wreath at the grave of a loved one. Illustration on an oinochoe (wine jug), 4th century BC

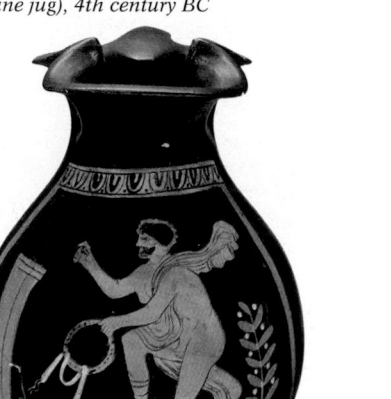

represented as a kingdom beneath the earth (according to some, the underworld was actually in the far west, at the edge of the world). After death, the souls of the dead led a boring and comfortless existence as shades or souls without bodies. After their death, they were brought to the frontier of the underworld by the messenger god, Hermes, in his capacity of Hermes Psychopompos ("guide of souls") (*see* **Hermes**).

After that, the forbidding ferryman Charon carried them in his ramshackle boat across the black waters of the Styx, the great river that separated the underworld from the land of the living. Charon performed this service only after receiving payment of a coin, an obolus. The dead who had not been buried with an obolus between their lips, as was proper, were doomed to remain roaming the earth without rest—an unenviable fate (*see* **Charon**).

Upon arrival, the dead were judged by three arbiters, Minos and Rhadamanthys, two former kings of Crete, and Æacus, a former king of Ægina. After this judgment, the great majority of the death stayed bodiless, bloodless, emotionless, and deprived of human consciousness in the gray asphodel meadows. After drinking water from the well of Lethe

One of those severely punished in the Tartarus was Ixion. He was chained to an eternally rotating wheel because he had been so insolent as to court Hera, wife of the supreme god Zeus. Relief carving from Turkey.

118

("oblivion"), they lost all memory of their earthly existence. Even though existence in the underworld was not torture, it was very tedious, as attested by Achilles, who declared to Odysseus, after paying a short visit to the underworld, that he would prefer to be "the day laborer of a poor master (...) than king over all the shades in the underworld."

For a number of the dead there were exceptions to the rule of being forced to live in Hades. Those who had distinguished themselves through extraordinary virtue or justice were allowed to live on in a type of paradise, the Elysium or the Elysian Fields. This was a privilege granted to very few. According to the poet Homer, Menelaus, the husband of Helen, was allowed to stay in the Elysian Fields after his death.

Tartarus, was a type of Hell, that was located in the deepest and darkest part of Hades. The Titans were confined to this abyss, as well as some of those who had committed heinous crimes. These included the giant, Tityus, who had assaulted Leto (see **Leto**), Tantalus, who had to suffer eternal hunger and thirst while all kinds of delicacies continually fell just out of his reach (for the "Tantalus torture,"see **Tantalus**), Sisyphus, who for eternity had to roll a boulder up a hill after which it immediately rolled back (the "Labor of Sisyphus,"see **Sisyphus**), Ixion, who was tied to an eternally revolving wheel (see **Ixion** and the **Danaides**, the fifty daughters of king Danaus, who were sentenced to forever to fill a bottomless barrel with water because all but one of them had murdered their husbands on their wedding night.

No escape from Hades was possible. Anyone who tried to get away fell prey to the terrible three-headed dog Cerberus (see **Cerberus**). Only a few mortals visited the underworld, and always because they had an exceptional task or mission to perform. As part of the Twelve Labors, Heracles had to fetch Cerberus and according to some he also rescued Alcestis (see **Heracles** and **Alcestis**). Orpheus went there to retrieve his dead lover, Eurydice (see **Orpheus**), and Odysseus, to consult the seer Tiresias (see **Odysseus** and **Tiresias**). Æneas went to confer with his father's shade (see **Æneas**) and Psyche to seize the unguent prepared by Hades' spouse Persephone, on the orders of Athena. Theseus and Prithous once attempted to retrieve Persephone from the underworld, but were tied to the chairs of oblivion by Hades.

Although the god Hades did not have the

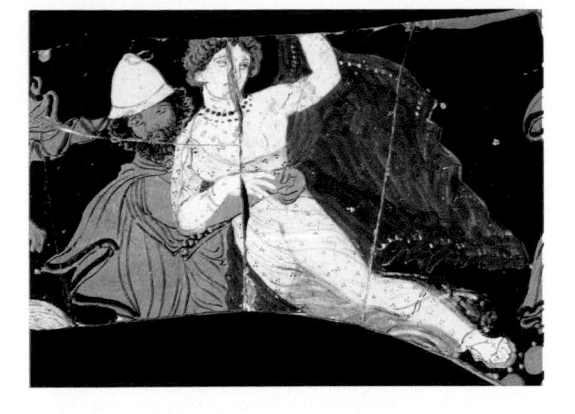

With the consent of his brother, the supreme god Zeus, Hades abducts his niece Persephone. Ultimately and for the remainder with her mother Demeter. Fragment from a painted vase, Tarente, 4th century BCE.

reputation of being a cruel or demonic figure, out of superstitious fear people dared not speak his name, which meant "the invisible one" (the Cyclopes had made a helmet for Hades which made him invisible). The Greeks preferred to call him Pluto, meaning "the rich one." This epithet referred to the many mineral resources to be found beneath the earth's surface. The Romans called him Dis, which meant the same. There were also many other euphemistic descriptions for the

Damaged image of Demeter in the middle of the Macedonian city of Philippi. Following the abduction of her daughter Demeter was inconsolable for a long time, with terrible consequences for the earth and humanity.

god of death, such as "the good counselor" and "the hospitable one."

Hades was married to the youthful Persephone, daughter of his brother Zeus and his sister Demeter, the goddess of grain and agriculture. Zeus had promised Hades Persephone as his wife, without Demeter's knowledge. When one day, the girl was picking flowers on Sicily, when dark Hades suddenly appeared in his chariot and carried her away with him. Persephone dropped her freshly picked flowers and, terrified, called out to her mother, but to no avail. Hades took her to his desolate kingdom.

Demeter was heartbroken and did everything she could to get her daughter back, but Hades was not prepared to concede. An ancient rule stated that anyone who ate anything in the underworld could never leave it. Hades had persuaded Persephone to consume some pomegranate seeds, so she was trapped there. Eventually, Zeus decided that Persephone could spend part of the year with her mother but she had to spend the rest of it in the underworld as Hades' wife. Through this myth, the Greeks explained the changing of the seasons. When Persephone was with her mother, Demeter was in good humor and the earth bloomed, but when Persephone was with Hades, Demeter was in mourning and nothing would grow. No children were born as a result of the union between Hades and Persephone (*see* **Demeter** *and* **Persephone**).

Harmonia, *see* Cadmus

Harpies, The

The harpies were monstrous flying creatures, half-bird and half-woman, with the heads and faces of girls. They were daughters of Thaumas and the sea-nymph Electra, and the sisters of Iris, a messenger of the gods. There were three of four harpies, whose names were Ællo, Okypete, Celæno, and Podarge. Podarge rode the extraordinary horses of the great hero, Achilles, through an alliance with Zephyrus.

The harpies, who were initially associated with the storm winds, had clawlike fingers that grasped anything on which they could lay their hands. Their most famous victim was the blind King of Thrace, Phineus, who suffered

Harpies were winged creatures with the faces of maidens. They had a malicious disposition and could mean a real nuisance to their victims. Painting of a harpy on an amphora from Etruria, 6th century BC.

constant hunger because the harpies stole his food from his table and fouled it with their excrement. The Argonauts visited Phineus and relieved him of his tormentors. Calais and Zetes, the winged sons of Boreas, the north wind, drove them away, but were not permitted to kill them (*see the* **Argonauts**). Thereafter, the harpies settled in a cave on Mount Dicte, on Crete.

Hecabe, *see* Priam

Hecate

Hecate was an earth and fertility goddess. She was also, however, a moon-goddess, who showed herself at night, and possessed distinctly morbid and gruesome attributes, so it is no wonder that Shakespeare made her the chief witch in his play, *Macbeth*, the witches urging him on to greater atrocities in his quest for power.

Hecate's origins in Greek mythology are unclear. According to most accepted versions she was a daughter of the Titans, Cœus and Phoebe. According to some sources, Zeus was her father, others claim it was Perses.

Demeter and Asteria were also cited as her mother. Hecate might have been a cousin of Artemis and Apollo, the children of Asteria's sister Leto, and she is sometimes even equated with Artemis. Furthermore, she displayed clear resemblance to Demeter, and to Demeter's daughter, Persephone.

Persephone, as co-ruler of the underworld, had a decidedly dark side, after all, just like Hecate.

Although Hecate initially counted as a benign goddess and Hesiod praised her copiously as a benefactress of humanity, she later became the sinister patroness of sorcerers and witches. Medea, the renowned sorceress (*see* **Medea** *and* **The Argonauts**) frequently invoked her, and Shakespeare made her the chief witch in his play *Macbeth*. Those who wished to meet Hecate or wanted to perform some magic rite for which her blessing was necessary, needed to go to a crossroads, or better still, a fork in the road, at night. The terrifying goddess would appear to them, accompanied by a frightening pack of barking, ghostly hounds. She had three faces, which were linked to the phases of the moon, and for this reason she was called Trivia by the Romans. Three-faced statuettes of her, that looked in three different directions, were often placed at forks in the road.

Hector

Hector was one of the sons of the Trojan king Priam and his wife Hecabe. He was married to Andromache and had one son, Astyanax. Hector was the greatest of the heroes who defended Troy during the Trojan War.

From Homer's heroic poem, *The Iliad*, Hector emerges as a noble, courageous and admirable figure. Hector despised his brother Paris, who by abducting Helen to Troy had provoked the Greeks to declare war. He even regarded Paris as a contemptible Casanova. He defended the city of Troy with great ardor, however, and led the Trojans into battle when the greatest Greek hero Achilles no longer wished to fight because of a conflict with his supreme commander Agamemnon (*see* **Achilles**). The Greeks were in a tight spot, as a result, so Achilles' close friend, Patroclus went into battle wearing Achilles' armor. He caused panic in the Trojan ranks, who thought that the fearsome Achilles had decided to re-enter the fray. This made Patroclus reckless, so he ventured far outside the Greek camp and was killed by the much stronger Hector.

Achilles was devastated by his friend's death and was keen to return to battle in order to avenge him. He made his peace with Agamemnon and furiously stormed on to the battlefield. All of the Trojans fled into the city, only Hector chose to stand up to Achilles. But Hector had absolutely no chance. Achilles chased him around the city three times, after which he quickly killed in him in short-lived single combat. Then Achilles tied Hector's corpse to the back of

Hector's last parting from his wife, Andromache, inspired the poet Homer to one of the most moving passages in his epic poem The Iliad. *Behind Hector and Andromache stands a wet nurse with the little Astyanax, their son, on her arm. Pencil drawing on paint wash by Ludwig von Schwanthaler, 19th century.*

The battle between Achilles and Hector. Although Hector was a strong and courageous warrior, he had no chance against Achilles. Achilles fought with greater fury because Hector had killed his bosom friend, Patroclus. Oil painting by Peter Paul Rubens, 17th century.

his chariot and dragged it along in a dishonorable manner. He flung it down by Patroclus' bier, and continued to drag it around, refusing to stop to let it be decently buried. Eventually, after invention of his mother, Thetis, Achilles was prepared to receive Hector's father Priam. The hero was affected by the old man's grief and gave him his son's corpse, so that it could be committed to the earth.

As already stated, Homer painted an impressive portrait of Hector. There is an especially poignant scene in which the hero bids farewell to his wife and son. After Andromache has begged her husband not to throw himself into the battle, and not make Astyanax an orphan and herself a widow, Hector replied: "Woman, all that I have very much at heart. But when I see the Trojans and their women in ragged clothes, I am ashamed to stay away from the battlefield like a coward. Likewise, my heart does not wish

it; because I have learned to be constantly brave and fight in the front lines." Hector is saying he realizes that Troy will soon be defeated, and what worries him most is what will happen to Andromache afterward: "... and your sorrow distresses [me] again, because you must miss the man who can resist the day of slavery. Should I be dead and should the soil of the burial mound cover me before I hear your cries for help when you are dragged away." (*The Iliad*, Book IV, lines 441–445 and 461–465. *See also* **Andromache**)

Helen's beauty was a direct result of her extraordinary origins. The supreme god Zeus begat her in the form of a swan from her mother Leda. Pen drawing from Leonardo da Vinci, 15th century.

Helen

Helen, the most beautiful woman of her time, was desired by all men. Therefore she was abducted twice in her life: by the Athenian hero Theseus at the age of twelve, and by the Trojan prince Paris when an adult. Here Helen's brothers, the Dioscuri, are abducting the daughters of king Leucippus. Picture on Athenian volutenkrater, 5th century BCE

Helen was daughter of the supreme god Zeus and Leda. She was the wife of King Menelaus of Sparta, but was abducted by the Trojan Paris. This was the cause of the Trojan War.

Helen was an extraordinarily beautiful woman. Aphrodite, the goddess of love, had promised her to Paris as a prize if he would chose the goddess as the winner in a beauty contest (*see* **Aphrodite**). Although Helen appears in Homer's work as a "normal" mortal, in most traditions she is considered immortal. This is because of her divine origins. Zeus had begotten her, along with Polydeuces, one of the Dioscuri, with her mother Leda, when in the form of a swan. Helen's sister, Clytemnestra, and her brother Castor were, according to this version, supposed to have been ordinary mortals, begotten by Leda's earthly husband Tyndareos (*see the* **Dioscuri** *and* **Leda**).

Helen grew up in Sparta, at the court of Tyndareos. When as young as twelve, she was abducted by the great Athenian hero Theseus, but her brothers, Castor and Polydeuces, freed her again. Later, all of Greece's most prominent bachelors beseeched her "illegitimate" father, Tyndareos, for her hand. Menelaus, a prosperous prince of Mycenæ,

eventually became the lucky man. He married Helen and succeeded Tyndareos as king of Sparta—his brother Agamemnon was already married to Helen's sister Clytemnestra. The other marriage suitors swore an oath that they would stand by Menelaus should he encounter difficulties because of Helen.

Initially, Menelaus and Helen had a happy marriage. They had a daughter named Hermione. Then Paris, son of the Trojan king, visited Sparta. Aphrodite put her special abilities into play and soon Helen fell for the visitor's charms. When Menelaus had to travel to Crete for his grandfather's burial, Paris saw his chance and departed for Troy with his willing human spoil and some of the contents of Menelaus' treasury. In Troy, he married Helen, but not to universal rejoicing. The courageous prince Hector, in particular, who did not think much of his insipid brother, Paris, the "ladies' man," was opposed to the marriage.

When Menelaus returned and discovered what had happened, he immediately informed his powerful brother, Agamemnon,

Helen married twice, first to Menelaus, who was chosen over many other suitors, later to Paris, who had carried her off from Menelaus' palace. Bride with cupids, painted lid, Athenian, 4th century BCE.

and the Greek monarchs who had sworn to support him. Together with Odysseus, Menelaus traveled to Troy to force the Trojans to hand over Helen, but in vain. Consequently, the Greeks raised a large army and set out for Troy. For ten years, they besieged the city, which eventually fell through a ruse devised by Odysseus (*see* **Odysseus**).

Throughout the war, Helen was cursed by both sides because of the trouble she had caused. She herself experienced the events with mixed feelings. In Priam's palace, she wove tapestries depicting scenes of the war and sometimes longed for Menelaus and her daughter, who she had abandoned. She called herself "a shameless creature" and felt that she should have ended her life rather than let herself be seduced by Paris.

By then, her love for Paris had long cooled down. When Aphrodite personally called upon Helen to take care of Paris after he had suffered a humiliating defeat in single combat with Menelaus, she began an argument with the goddess. Helen refused to share her bed with Paris any longer and Aphrodite threatened to set the Greeks and the Trojans against her: "Then a horrible fate awaits you!" Finally Helen went to Paris' bedroom, where she spoke to him reproachfully and contemptuously. Yet, this did not deter Paris from wanting to make love to her.

Much later, Paris was killed by an arrow shot by the Greek, Philoctetes. Helena thereupon became wife of his brother Deiphobus.

During the war, when Odysseus entered Troy disguised as a beggar, Helen was the only person who recognized him. She looked after him, did not betray him, and allowed him to kill various Trojans, because she really wanted to return to Greece and was very sorry that she had allowed herself to be duped by Aphrodite.

After the fall of Troy, Menelaus returned home after a long period of wandering. He had become reconciled with Helen and the couple lived peacefully together as if nothing had happened. When Telemachus, son of Odysseus, sought them in Sparta to obtain information about his father's fate, Helen was immediately struck by the strong resemblance between Telemachus and Odysseus. She herself was still beautiful, "similar to Artemis." She mixed a stimulating potion that she poured into the young man's wine and told him how she had helped his father during his secret mission in Troy. But as a result, Menelaus became aware of another side of her character. He remembered how, after the Trojans had brought the wooden horse into the city, Helen, in the company of her new husband, Deiphobus, had tried to provoke the Greek warriors inside the horse by calling their names and also imitating the voices of their wives.

In spite of this unpleasant anecdote, Menelaus and Helen lived long and happily thereafter.

A bizarre alternative version of Helen's vicissitudes emerges in Euripides' tragedy *Helen*. According to him, Paris never eloped with to Tory with the real Helen, but rather with a double or likeness of her. In the meantime, Helen herself remained in Egypt, where she was reunited with Menelaus when he arrived there from Troy on his journey home (Homer also mentions that Menelaus landed in Egypt, but with Helen at his side).

Independently of Euripides' strange version of her life story, Helen remains a mysterious, elusive figure. Although she was somewhat a victim of circumstances over which she had no control, she can be viewed as the first *femme fatale* in western tradition.

Helios (Roman=*Sol*)

Helios was the sun-god, the son of the Titan, Hyperion, and himself a Titan. In a fabulous

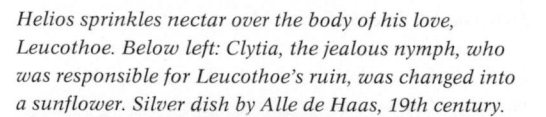

The sun god Helios made his daily journey from east to west across the sky in his golden chariot, drawn by four fire-spitting horses.

chariot made by the god Hephæstos of gold, silver, and precious stones, and drawn by four fire-spitting horses, Helios traversed the sky from east to west every day. At sunset, he descended into the Ocean which surrounded the world. Helios saw and heard everything in his chariot, which is why in Antiquity, oaths were sworn by him. Other gods sometimes benefited from Helios' knowledge. For example, when Demeter's daughter, Persephone, was abducted by Hades (*see* **Demeter**), and when Hephæstos' wife, Aphrodite, was unfaithful to him with Ares, the god of war (*see* **Aphrodite**), they consulted Helios to find out what had happened.

Aphrodite resented this interference so much that she made Helios fall hopelessly in love with the Persian princess, Leucothoe. Helios visited her every night in the form of her mother, while she was spinning. After he had revealed himself to her, he made love with her. The Oceanide Clytia, herself passionately in love with Helios, told Leucothoe's father what had occurred. The furious father buried his daughter alive, a punishment she did not survive. Helios still tried to save her by shining the sun's rays on her and sprinkling her with nectar, the drink of the gods, but in vain. Leucothoe's corpse evaporated and a bunch of incense herbs germinated on her grave. Clytia, the jealous nymph, languished away from envy and disappointment in love and changed into a sun flower, the plant that follows the sun.

The sun-god had many children by his wife, Perse. They included Pasiphæ (who became the wife of the Cretan King, Minos), the sorceress Circe, and Phæton. Helios was particularly revered on the island of Rhodes. In 290 BCE, a giant statue of him, known as the Colossus of Rhodes, was erected in the harbor of the city of Lindos, and was regarded as one of the Seven Wonders of the Ancient World. This statue that stood a hundred and forty feet high, bestriding the harbor, did not stay up for very long, however, because in 226 BCE it fell into the sea when an earthquake struck.

The most famous myth featuring Helios concerns his unfortunate son. This young man went to his father's palace because he wanted to know for sure whether Helios was, indeed, his father. After this was confirmed to him, Phæton got his father to allow him to take a trip in the sun chariot. But Phæton seemed unable to control the horses Pyrois, Eous, Æthon, and Phlegon, and flew so low that the earth was almost scorched. Zeus felt compelled to intervene and killed the awkward charioteer with a bolt of lightning (*see* **Phæton**).

Hephæstos (Roman=Vulcan)

Hephæstos, the crippled, deformed Greek god of craftsmanship, metallurgy and fire, was a son of Zeus and Hera. According to the poet Hesiod, Hephæstos was the child of Hera only, just as Athena was the child of

The crippled god, Hephæstos, was a brilliant smith and worker in precious metals. He excelled in all the applied arts and crafts related to manual skill and dexterity.

Hephæstos (left, seated) receives a visit from his wife, Aphrodite, who is accompanied by her clearly intimidated young son, Eros. Aphrodite was unfaithful to Hephæstos with the war god Ares. Engraving by Cornelis Bos, 16th century.

Zeus only. Hephæstos was one of the twelve gods who lived with Zeus on Mount Olympus. He was a very talented smith who made the most beautiful objects and creations for other gods and privileged mortals. He was particularly honored on the volcanic island Lemnos, where he is said to have had his forge. The Romans later believed that it was located in the heart of the volcanic Mount Ætna, on Sicily.

Hephæstos is said to have hammered at the anvil with the assistance of the Cyclopes. Hephæstos' special connection with Lemnos was created because Zeus had flung him from Olympus during a domestic quarrel with

On the Sicilian horizon, the volcanic Mount Ætna rises from behind Roman ruins. According to the Romans, Hephæstos/Vulcan had his forge in the heart of the volcano. The Greeks located his workshop on the volcanic island of Lemnos.

Hera, since he had spoken up for his mother. After a long flight through the air, he finally landed on Lemnos.

This was not the first time that Hephæstos had been ejected from Olympus. Previously, Hera had done the same, since she was ashamed of her deformed baby. Hephæstos then landed in the Ocean and was saved by the sea-gods Thetis and Eurynome. Under their care, he became adept at his craft and forged all kinds of jewelry. Hephæstos later took revenge on his mother by making her a golden armchair in which she was bound by invisible chains. It was not until Dionysus got him drunk that Hephæstos was prepared to release his mother. A reconciliation was arranged and the ugly smith received Aphrodite, the beautiful goddess of love, as his wife. She was later punished similarly to Hera, when Hephæstos discovered that she was being unfaithful to him with Ares, the god of war. He forged an invisible net just above his bed, in which the two adulterers became entangled. He then invited the other gods to come and look at them (*see* **Aphrodite**). On this occasion, the cuckolded husband was just as much a source of amusement as the humiliated Ares and Aphrodite.

Hephæstos often caused hilarity among the gods. Homer describes how the crippled god once took on the role of the cupbearer: "An irrepressible laugh burst out from the heavenly gods when they saw Hephæstos breathlessly hobbling through the room." (*The Iliad*, Book I, l. 599-600). Elsewhere in his epic poem, Homer describes the

Hera, wife of the supreme god Zeus, was the prototype of the domineering, jealous wife. The cuckoo on her staff is a reminder of the fact that Zeus proposed to her in the form of this bird.

magnificent handiwork of Hephæstos, including the palaces of the gods on Olympus and in his own home. At the request of Thetis, he forged a fabulous suit of armor for her son Achilles, after his old armor had been captured by Hector during the Trojan War. Homer's description of the activities of the "strong-armed artist" on his "skinny legs" scarcely matches the astonishing shield imaginatively decorated with tableaux that Hephæstos made for Achilles.

Hera (Roman=Juno)

Hera was the sister and wife of the supreme god Zeus. She was one of the twelve Olympian gods, who lived on Mount Olympus with Zeus. Hera was a daughter of Cronos and Rhea, and mother of Ares, the god of war, and of Hephæstos, god of metallurgy and the crafts (who according to the poet Hesiod was created without her husband's intervention), as well as of the goddesses Eileithyia and Hebe, patrons of birth and youth respectively.

Immediately after her birth, Hera was devoured by her father Cronos, who feared that his offspring would revolt against him. Hera's brothers and sisters also suffered this fate, except for Zeus, who through trickery was saved and eventually actively ended Cronos' rule (*see* **Cronos**).

As Zeus' consort, Hera was the most important of the goddesses. She was the queen of heaven and the patroness of marriage. In Athens, weddings were preferably held during the month of Gmelion, which was dedicated to Hera. The apple and the pomegranate, symbolic of the alliance of marriage, were Hera's sacred fruits.

Her name probably meant "ruler" and Hera did indeed have a domineering and proud character. In addition, she was extremely jealous, cruel, quarrelsome, and cunning. Her marriage to Zeus was characterized by constant tension and serious quarrels. Zeus was anything but a faithful husband, of course, and Hera never forgave him for his many dalliances with other goddesses, nymphs, and mortal women. The offspring of these relationships also had to pay for their father's infidelity. Thus, the great hero Heracles, born of a dalliance between

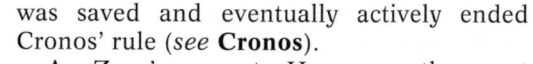

Sculpture of Hera in a regally relaxed pose at the Fountain of Power, one of the quattro fontane ("four fountains"), placed at a crossroads on the Quirinal in Rome in the late 16th century.

Hera, with two peacocks beside her, asks Argus (portrayed here as a human rather than a giant) to guard Io, who through Zeus' doing has been given the form of a cow. Oil painting by Aert Schouman, 18th century.

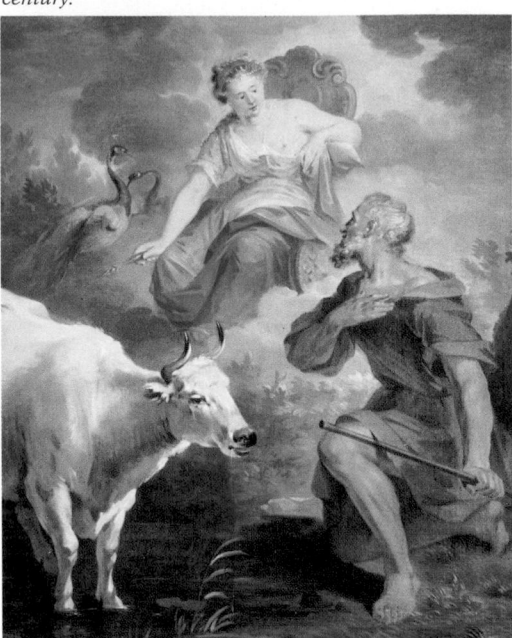

Zeus and Alcmene, was frustrated by Hera in the most infernal ways for all of his life (*see* **Heracles**). At a certain point, this became too much for Zeus. As punishment he hung his wife at the top of Mount Olympus by her wrists with anvils on her feet.

There are many stories of Hera's thirst for vengeance, from the tale of the unfortunate nymph Callisto who, because she was desired and raped by Zeus, was transformed into a bear by the jealous Hera, to the story of Semele, courted by Zeus in the form of a mortal. In this instance, Hera disguised herself as her nurse and whispered to her that she should ask Zeus to show himself in his true form. Semele was unable to tolerate the appearance of the shining supreme god, as Hera expected, and was scorched by his radiance (*see* **Dionysus** *and* **Semele**). Poor Io, whom Zeus had turned into a cow as a precaution, was placed by Hera under the guard of the hundred-eyed monster, Argus. On Zeus' orders, Argus was killed by Hermes, after which Hera had Io—still in the form of a cow—followed all over the world by a hornet (*see* **Io**). Later Hera placed Argus' eyes in the tail feathers of her sacred bird, the ostentatious peacock.

After Hermes kills the one hundred-eyed monster Argus, he presents the eyes to Hera, who places them in the tail feathers of her sacred peacock. Oil painting by Hendrick Goltzius, 17th century.

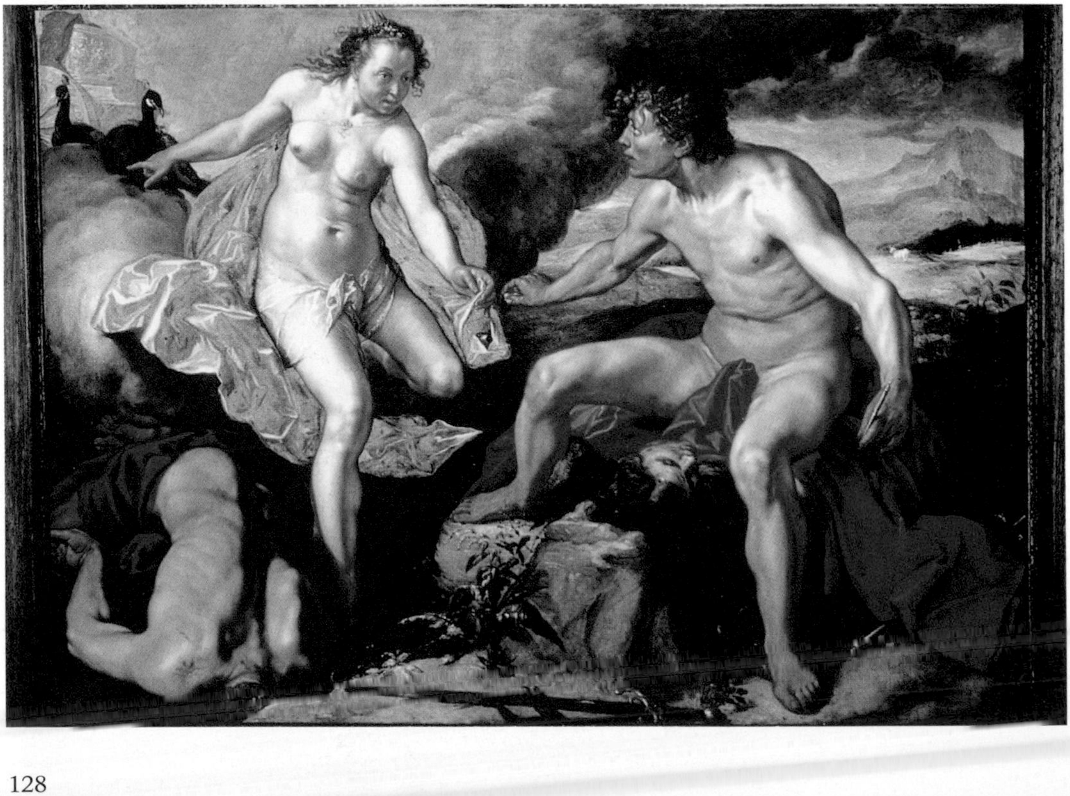

Despite Zeus' adventures, Hera herself did not develop the inclination to have affairs. She was a paragon of chastity, if not prudishness. Desiring her was even unwise. Ixion, who wanted to make love to her, was tricked by Zeus who sent down a cloud that looked exactly like Hera. After he had violated this cloud, he landed in Tartarus, where he suffered eternal torture.

The extent of Hera's aversion to sensuality was indicated when Zeus, in cheerful mood, claimed that women experienced more pleasure during sex than men. The seer Tiresias—who had spent some time as a woman—was consulted and agreed with Zeus. Because this answer displeased her, Hera smote him with blindness, after which Zeus gave him the gift of clairvoyance (*see* **Tiresias**).

Hera was worshiped in many parts of Greece. The inhabitants of Crete, Samos, Euboa, Naxos, and Argos all claimed that Zeus and Hera were married on their territory. Zeus is said to have sought shelter from a rainstorm he himself caused in the forest of Argos, by hiding under Hera's clothes, in the form of a cuckoo. He then proposed to her.

Hera was often actively involved in the lives of mortals—and not just her husband's mistresses. During the Trojan War, she was one of the most spirited supporters of the

Remains of a temple of Hera, dating from the 5th century BCE, in the Valley of the Temples, near Agrigentum, Sicily.

The Egyptian goddess Hathor was worshiped in the form of a cow or a woman with a cow's head, as may have been the case with Hera. In this wall relief of a temple in the Egyptian city of Thebes, she is depicted as a cow. In her later, human form, Hathor wore stylized horns on her headdress.

Greeks and did all she could to help them be victorious. Once, she even tricked Zeus in order to achieve her aims. Hera bore a grudge against the Trojans because the Trojan Paris had named Aphrodite, rather than her, as the most beautiful goddess in the beauty contest which was held after the "apple of discord" was found—the golden apple that Eris, the goddess of quarrels, had intended for the "loveliest" (*see* **Achilles, Aphrodite, Helen, Paris,** *and* **Thetis**). From time to time, Hera mingled actively in the turmoil of war, once even fighting against Artemis, who was on the Trojan side. (*see* **Artemis**)

Hera is usually depicted as a tall, majestic woman. However, Homer refers to her as "cow eyed," and this seems to indicate that in the distant past, Hera was worshiped in the form of a cow or a woman with a cow's head, like the Egyptian goddess, Hathor. The story of Io also indicates a connection between Hera, the cow, and Egypt (*see* **Io**). Hera's Roman counterpart, Juno, who is equated with her, is differentiated insofar as she bore Mars, the god of war (the Roman counterpart of Ares), without the involvement of a male, due to her anger at the birth of Minerva (=Athena) from the head of her husband Jupiter (=Zeus).

Heracles (Roman=Hercules)

Heracles, the son of Zeus and Alcmene, was the most awesome of all the heroes of Greek

The goddess Hera gently takes little Heracles to her breast. Her loving gesture would have painful consequences for her.

Heracles depicted as an unusually powerful man with a club in his hand and a lionskin over his shoulders. In Antiquity as well as in later periods, this was the customary pose of the greatest hero in Greek mythology. Oil painting by Peter Paul Rubens, 17th century.

mythology. The heavily muscled, extremely strong Heracles was an extraordinarily popular figure, about whom there were many stories and who was portrayed many times in art and literature. Heracles was a formidable archer and wrestler. Besides the bow, his favorite weapon was a club, which he preferred to cut himself from the wood of an olive tree. Heracles had a generous, noble nature, but was not without less attractive qualities. He sometimes became jealous and often extremely short-tempered. Certainly whenever he thought he was being dealt with unjustly he could suddenly explode into violent anger. Because of his unusual physical strength, the consequences of such rages were frequently terrible—not least for the hero himself who had to atone many times for murder or other violent deeds he had committed.

Heracles was the son of the supreme god Zeus and the mortal woman Alcmene, wife of Amphitryon (*see* **Alcmene**). When Amphitryon left the city of Thebes, where he and Alcmene were living at the time, to avenge the death of Alcmene's brother, Zeus took on his form and made love to Alcmene. This time, Zeus did not act purely out of lust, as during some of his other escapades. It was his specific intention to beget a son who could protect mortals and gods with his enormous strength. Heracles would later render invaluable service to the gods, by crushing the Gigantes' rebellion (*see* **The Gigantes**).

The begetting and birth of Heracles did not go down well with Zeus' wife, Hera. She was bitterly jealous and would frustrate the hero throughout his life. Their first meeting, arranged by Zeus and their daughter Athena, went off very badly. When Hera and Athena

Zeus begat Heracles because he required the support of a mortal hero in his conflict with the Gigantes, who rebelled against the Olympian gods. Several Gigantes received fatal wounds from Heracles' arrows. Mosaic from the Villa del Casale, Sicily, 3rd-4th century CE.

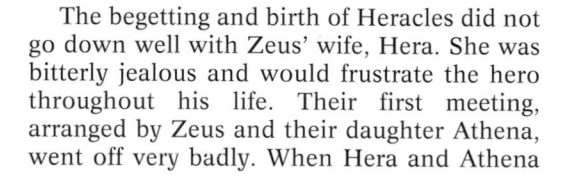

were walking outside of the city walls of Thebes, they saw a beautiful, strapping baby, but did not realize that this was Heracles. The little boy appealed to her so much that Hera put him to her breast to nurse. But Heracles sucked at her nipple with such force that Hera screamed in pain and angrily thrust the child away. Heracles' name, which literally means "glory of Hera," may be connected with this incident because Hera's milk could be considered as a glorious gift. Luckily for Heracles, not all gods were against him and he was later able to rely on the loyal support and protection of Athena.

When Heracles was eight months old, Hera made her first attempt to destroy him. After Alcmene had put him and his twin half-brother, Iphicles, down to sleep, Hera placed two huge snakes in the crib. They had orders to kill Heracles, but the result turned out differently. The little hero effortlessly strangled both the reptiles, one with his left fist, the other with his right.

Heracles received a thorough education from various excellent teachers. His earthly stepfather, Amphitryon, instructed him in charioteering, Castor, one of the two Dioscuri, instructed him in the use of the sword and in military science, and he received boxing lessons from the sons of Hermes. One of Heracles' teachers, Linus, however, became his first victim. Linus had to tutor Heracles in the playing of the lyre, a

skill that appealed little to the hero. When Linus boxed Heracles' ears for being disobedient, his pupil hit him with the lyre and killed him. For this wickedness, Amphitryon had Heracles herd cattle in the Cithæron Mountains. While he was there, at the age of eighteen, he killed a vicious lion which was ravaging his stepfather's herds and those of the neighboring King Thespius. During this period he produced offspring with Thespius' fifty daughters.

After the young Heracles had disposed of a number of dangerous enemies for the city of Thebes, the Theban King Creon gave him the hand of his daughter, Megara, and named him protector of the city. Nevertheless, the marriage was not blessed. The implacable Hera struck Heracles with insanity and in a fit of madness he killed several people, including six of his own children. After he had returned to his senses, Heracles advised the Oracle of Delphi that he had to make amends by going into the service of Eurystheus, King of the cities of Mycenæ and Tiryns on Argolis in the Peloponnese. Before his birth, Zeus had cherished a plan to allow Heracles to rule this territory, but Hera had been too quick for him and through a ruse had ensured that the land was given to her protégé, Eurystheus.

Eurystheus, a figure who was greatly inferior to Heracles, set him twelve seemingly impossible tasks. Only by successfully performing the Twelve Labors of Heracles, could the hero become a free man again.

As a penance Hercules had to perform twelve impossible tasks for Eurystheus, king of the cities of Mycenæ and Tiryns. The first task was to kill with his bare hands a monstrous lion that was terrorizing the neighborhood of Nemea. Black image on a colored background, Athenian kylix, 6th century BCE.

On this Roman sarcophagus from the 2nd century CE, the theme of the Twelve Labors of Heracles is shown in several tableaux. On the left, Heracles wrestles with the lion of Nemea.

1. The Lion of Nemea

Heracles wrestling with the Nemean lion. This animal was impervious to weapons. Pen drawing by Cosimu Tura, 15th century.

Nemea, an area located between Argos and Corinth, was being ravaged by a monstrous lion with a pelt that could not be wounded by metal, stone, or wooden weapons. After Heracles had tracked down the beast in the desolate area and unsuccessfully tried out his weapons on it, he finally decided to wrestle with the lion and strangle it with his bare hands. He brought the carcass to Mycenæ, giving Eurystheus a serious fright. Henceforth Heracles was not permitted to enter the city, but had to wait for Eurystheus' orders at the gates. While Eurystheus, with an eye to his own safety, had a large bronze jug made, Heracles skinned the lion. From this time forth, Hercules wore the invulnerable pelt as armor, with the head as a helmet. He is often pictured in this attire.

2. The Hydra of Lerna.

Heracles then received the instructions to kill the hydra of Lerna, a water serpent that lived in a swamp near Lerna, not far from Argos, in the Peloponnese. The hydra had nine heads, though according to some, it had even more. It was extremely poisonous, even its breath was fatal. With help from Athena, Heracles found the monster's lair, and energetically

Heracles wearing the skin of the Nemean lion over his head as a cap. Macedonian coin (tetradrachma), 4th century BCE.

Heracles in a life-or-death struggle with the hydra, the many-headed water snake from the swamps of Lerna. Relief on an earthenware vessel, Campania, 3rd century BCE.

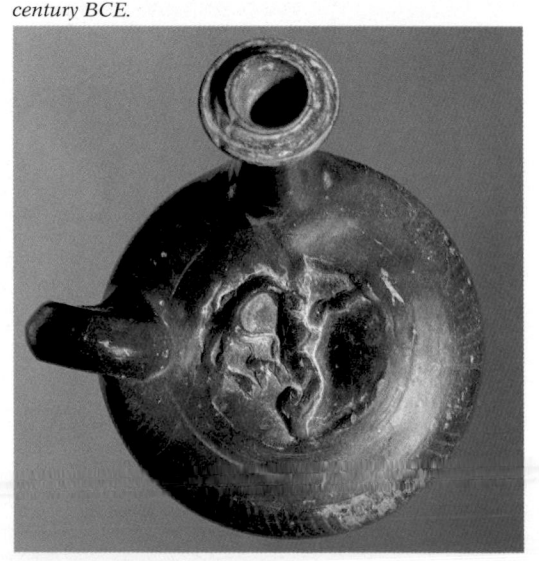

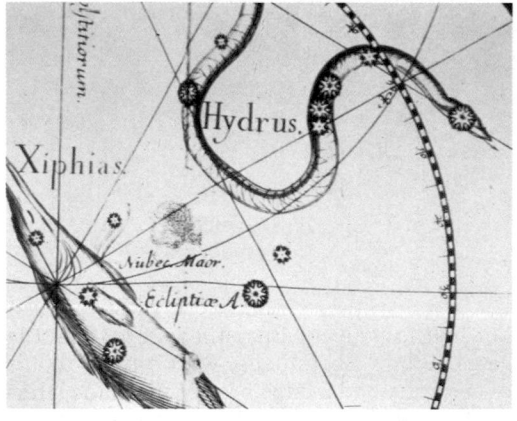

started to fight it. But every time he cut off one of the monster's heads, two or three heads immediately sprouted in its place. Meanwhile, Heracles was also under attack

Artemis, the goddess of the hunt and of unspoilt nature, reproaches Heracles for setting a trap in her sacred Ceryneian hind's territory, but forgave him when she realized that he was not acting on his own initiative. Roman bronze statuette, 1st century CE.

by a giant lobster or crab, sent by Hera to assist the hydra. The now cornered hero appealed to his cousin, Iolaos, who had accompanied him to Lerna as his driver. While Heracles was kicking the lobster to death, Iolaos set some trees on fire. With burning branches and trees he cauterized the hydra's wounds directly after Heracles cut off a head. Thus was the hydra killed. Before leaving the swamp, Heracles dipped his arrows into the water-serpent's poisonous blood, so that from then on, they would cause deadly and extremely painful injuries. The hydra and the lobster, who ended up helping him, were placed in the firmament by Athena as the constellations Hydra the Snake and Cancer the Crab.

Thanks to the help which Heracles had received from Iolaos, Eurystheus refused to count the killing of the hydra among Heracles' completed tasks. According to some sources, he originally charged Heracles to carry out ten tasks and imposed the last two deeds on him as a result of Heracles' alleged negligence.

3. The Ceryneian Hind

For his third deed, Heracles had to capture the hind sacred to Artemis, goddess of the hunt and nature, and bring it to Mycenæ alive. The animal had bronze hooves and golden antlers and had escaped from Artemis, after which it settled in the vicinity of the Ceryneian Hill, in the northern Peloponnese. Heracles pursued the swift hind for a year, from Arcadia to the Istrian peninsula at the northernmost point of the Adriatic Sea. Eventually, Heracles outwitted the creature, though without harming it in any way, after which he carried it on his shoulders to Mycenæ. To Artemis, who resented him capturing her sacred animal, he explained that he was acting on Eurystheus' orders, and the goddess forgave him.

4. The Erymanthian Boar

Again Heracles had to bring a live animal to Mycenæ. This time it was a wild boar, a fierce creature that was ravaging the area around Mount Erymanthus in northern Arcadia.

On the way to this place, Heracles enjoyed the hospitality of the centaur, Pholus (*see* **Centaurs**), but fell out with the other centaurs, who did not like Pholus pouring wine for Heracles from a jug that Dionysus had given to the centaurs. Many centaurs were

Heracles at the wine-cask of Pholus ,the centaur.
Pholus poured out wine for Heracles his guest, but the
other centaurs did not permit the hero to drink this
wine, which had been given to the centaurs by
Dionysus. A terrible fight ensued, in which many
centaurs lost their lives. Black-figured painting on
Athenian kylix, 6th–5th century BCE.

killed in battle by Heracles' poisoned arrows.
In the heat of battle, the old wise centaur Chiron was accidentally injured by one of Heracles' poisoned darts. Because Chiron was

Heracles drinks wine with the centaur Pholus. This
cheerful scene was soon disturbed by the furious
centaurs. Portrayal on a kylix in Athen, 6–5
century BCE.

immortal, the Hydra's poison was not lethal
to him, but he suffer agonizing pain, to Heracles' acute distress. This would later cause
him to give his immortality as a gift to
Prometheus (*see* **Chiron**).

Heracles caught the fearsome swine by
chasing it into a snowdrift and tying its legs.
When he produced the terrifying animal in
Mycenæ, Eurystheus, was so frightened that
he crawled away to hide in the specially made
bronze jug.

Frightened Eurystheus hides in his jug when Heracles
comes to deliver the Erymanthian wild boars.

After completing this task, Heracles joined
Jason and the Argonauts, who were going to
the distant land of Colchis in search of the
Golden Fleece (*see* **The Argonauts**).
Heracles probably played a significant role in
this expedition, but returned to Greece before
the ship the Argo arrived at Colchis.

5. *The Augean Stables*

Augeus, King of Elis in the Peloponnese and
son of Helios the sun-god, possessed more
and finer cattle than anyone else. The manure
produced by all of his beasts had not been
cleaned away for many years and the stench
had a pestilential effect in large parts of the
Peloponnese. Heracles was given the task by
Eurystheus of removing this problem from
the world forever. He had to clean out the
Augean stables in a single day. As compensation for this dirty and humiliating task, the
hero required to receive one tenth of Augeus'
herd. Instead of dragging buckets around,
Heracles decided on a radical approach. He

Picture of an angry bull on a coin. Silver coin (stater) from Thruium, 5th century BCE.

Heracles caught the wild bull that was ravaging the island Crete. This animal had previously produced the terrible Minotaur by mating with the Cretan Queen Pasiphæ. Man with bull, earthenware, Roman era.

Heracles hunts one of the Stymphalian birds in flight. For this deed, he uses a trap especially made for him by Hephæstos. Fragment of a painting on a Greek earthenware beaker, 5th–4th century BCE.

made holes in the stable walls and rerouted the Alpheus and Peneus rivers to run through them, so that the stalls were thoroughly washed clean. Nevertheless, Augeus refused to pay Heracles, with the excuse that he was acting on Eurystheus' orders. Eurystheus, in turn, refused to acknowledge the cleaning of the stables because Heracles was supposed to have been in Augeus' employment.

With his strong sense of justice, Heracles would, never forget the trick Augeus had played on him.

6. The Birds of Stymphalus

Heracles performed one more labor while in the Peloponnese. He drove away the dangerous, predatory birds that lived on the bank of Lake Stymphalus in lovely Arcadia. These birds, had feathers with metal tips that they used to attack humans, while their droppings contaminated the crops. Heracles chased the birds away, frightening them with a bronze rattle made for him by Hephæstos and given to him by Athena. With his arrows, he killed a large number of the birds that flew up in panic.

7. The Cretan Bull

Eurystheseus then sent Heracles to Crete, where a raging bull was terrorizing the island. This beautiful animal was, in fact, supposed to have been sacrificed to Poseidon by King Minos, but Minos did not have the heart to kill it. His wife, Pasiphæ, fell in love with the bull and had sexual intercourse with it, after which she became pregnant with the Minotaur. Heracles caught the bull, brought it alive to Mycenæ and Tiryns, and released it there. Later the bull terrorized the surroundings of Marathon, near the city of Athens, where it was eventually killed by Theseus (*see* **Minos**, **Pasiphæ**, *and* **Theseus**).

8. The Mares of Diomedes

In distant Thrace, Heracles had to seize the mares of King Diomedes. Diomedes was in the habit of feeding these horses with the flesh of his unsuspecting guests.

While traveling through Thessaly, Heracles visited his friend, King Admetus of Pheræ. He

Heracles in combat with the Amazons, who were incited against him by Hera. Painting on Athenian amphora, 6th century BCE.

soon discovered that the king's wife, Alcestis, (*see* **Alcestis**) had taken it upon herself to die in her husband's place. Heracles immediately intervened and wrested Alcestis from Thanatos, the god of death.

On arrival in Thrace, Heracles captured the horses and brought them on board his ship. When he was attacked by Diomedes and his men, he defeated them, after which he fed the cruel king to his own mares. Heracles tamed the animals and took them with him to Mycenæ, where he let them go. Later, the mares were devoured by wild animals not far from Mount Olympus.

9. The Girdle of Hippolyta, the Amazon.

Admete, daughter of Eurystheus, longed for a special gift. As a result, her father conceived with the idea of sending Heracles to fetch the girdle of Hippolyta, queen of the Amazons. The Amazons lived somewhere on the northern coast of Asia Minor (*see* **The Amazons**). Accompanied by Theseus and Telamon, as well as other companions, Heracles traveled to the northeast. He had many adventures along the way. For instance, he besieged the main city of the island of Paros, after the local monarch, a son of Minos of Crete, had had two of his men killed.

The warlike Hippolyta appeared to be not insensitive to the beauty of Heracles' muscular body. She immediately indicated her willingness to give Heracles the girdle, that had been given to her by Ares, the god of war. This was not to Hera's liking, however. So the goddess took the form of an Amazon and incited Hippolyta's rather volatile subjects against Heracles. When Heracles was

attacked by them, he mistakenly thought that Hippolyta had betrayed him. He killed her, stole her girdle and weapons, and then killed the Amazon leaders.

The return journey was also not without spectacular and violent adventures. That is how Heracles came to the aid of Laomedon, King of Troy who had to endure the attacks of a sea-monster sent after him by Poseidon because Laomedon had not paid the sea-god and Apollo for the construction of the walls of Troy. Heracles rescued Laomedon's daughter Hesione from the monster, and killed it with Athena's help. Laomedon, however, proved to disloyal to his daughter's rescuer and revoked his promise to give to Hercules the horses which had been given to him by Zeus.

Then, in Thrace, Heracles killed Sarpedon, brother of the local King Poltys. He also conquered the island of Thasos. After his return, Eurystheus placed Hippolyta's belt in the temple of Hera at Argos.

10. The Oxen of Geryon

His next labor brought Heracles even further from home, as far as the mythical island Erythea, that lay in the far west, past the Iberian peninsula. The oxen of Geryon, King of Tartessus, in Spain, grazed on this island. Geryon, who according to some versions was descended from the gorgon Medusa and according to others from the Titan, Oceanus, was a giant with three heads, three upper bodies, and six arms. Not surprisingly, he enjoyed a reputation for having extraordinary strength. His fine red cattle were tended by the cowherd, Eurytion, and the two-headed dog, Orthrus.

Heracles with the three-headed giant, Geryon. Some of Geryon's oxen are visible behind him. Heracles' sarcophagus, Antalya Museum of Archæology, Turkey.

Remains of a Heracles temple in Metapontum, southern Italy. During the many long journeys he had to undertake because of his labors, Heracles also traveled through Italy. According to legend, he founded the cities of Pompeii and Herculaneum.

A clean-shaven Heracles, leaning on his club, receives a branch with apples from one of the Hesperides. In the better-known version of the story, Atlas, the father of the Hesperides, fetched the apples for Heracles from his daughters' garden. Painting on an Athenian goblet (kelkkrater) by Pourtales, 4th century BCE.

On his long journey to the west, Heracles not only killed many vicious creatures, but on each side of the Straits of Gibraltar, he erected the Pillars of Hercules, still named for him. Later, irritated by the heat, Hercules aimed his bow at Helios the sun-god. The god, in good faith, put his cup-shaped golden boat at Heracles' disposal, enabling him to cross the ocean and reach Erythea. Once on the island, he killed the cowherd and his dog and loaded the cattle into the golden boat. Alarmed, Geryon set out in hot pursuit, but Heracles killed him with a single arrow that pierced all three of his bodies. According to some versions, Hera herself came to help Geryon, but was wounded by an arrow in her right breast.

Heracles' long return journey to the Peloponnese was anything but uneventful. He drove the herd over land through Italy, and even as far as Gaul (now known as France). His many attackers included the Ligurians, who were eliminated by Zeus by a shower of stones, and the three-headed shepherd Cacus. Cacus lived in a cave near where Rome would later stand and terrorized the area. One night, Cacus stole some of the finest cattle from Heracles' herd, but the hero followed him to his cave, effortlessly removed the huge boulder blocking the entrance, and just as effortlessly killed the dreadful Cacus. Together with the local king, Evander, who gave him a warm welcome, Heracles then built an altar dedicated to Zeus, thus helping to lay the foundations for his own worship in Rome. Heracles is said to have founded other cities, including Pompeii and Herculaneum (named for him), later on in his journey through Italy. Pompeii and Herculaneum are the cities that were buried under lava and ash when Mount Vesuvius erupted in which in 79 CE. They were not rediscovered until many centuries later.

On Sicily, Heracles had to compete against the wrestler and boxer, Eryx, who had taken possession of an escaped bull. In a single combat of three rounds, Heracles was able to defeat this aggressive figure, after which he killed him. The giant, Alcyoneus, said to have thought to frustrate Heracles, had to pay for his conduct when Heracles retaliated for the stone that Alcyoneus had thrown at him by clubbing him to death.

After Hera had broken up the herd near his home with the help of a hornet, Heracles finally arrived in Mycenæ. Eurystheus, surprised by the hero's return, sacrificed the cattle to Hera.

11. The Apples of the Hesperides

By now, Heracles had performed ten labors in just over eight years, but because Eurystheus felt that the death of the Hydra and the cleaning of the Augean stables had not followed the rules, he sent Heracles out again. Yet again, the hero had to travel to the edge of the known world. Eurystheus now required him to bring the golden apples of the

In order to discover the whereabouts of the garden of the Hesperides, Heracles had to wrestle with the sea-god, Nereus, who could assume countless different forms. Roman mosaic from Carthage, in present-day Tunisia.

During Heracles' stay in Egypt, the treacherous pharoah Busiris threatened to sacrifice him to Zeus. Busiris had to pay for his unlucky plan with death. This pharaoh sits on the lap of the goddess Hathor, the Egyptian counterpart of Heracles' archenemy, Hera

Hesperides (whose name means "maidens of the evening" or "daughters of the evening.") These were the daughters of the Titan, Atlas, who lived in the westernmost reaches of the world and bore the vault of the heavens on his shoulders (*see* **Atlas** *and* **The Hesperides**). The Hesperides lived near their father in a garden where, along with the hundred-headed dragon, Ladon, they guarded the golden apples that Hera had received from the earth goddess Gaia as a wedding gift.

Heracles did not know the location of the garden and wandered around for a long time before he was put on the right path. On the advice of two river-nymphs, he consulted the sea-god and soothsayer, Nereus, who could take on any form whenever he tried to escape an attacker. After succumbing to the pressure of Heracles' strong arms, during which he went through his entire repertoire of form changes, the sea-god finally surrendered and revealed to Heracles the location of the garden of the Hesperides.

Heracles eventually arrived at the garden after experiencing a number of other adventures. He landed in the Caucasus mountains, where he freed the Titan, Prometheus, who had been severely punished by Zeus for having first shot down the eagle which was continuously pecking at his liver (*see* **Prometheus**). In Libya, Heracles became involved in a wrestling match to the death with the giant, Antæus, a son of Gaia. As soon as Antæus touched the earth, his mother gave his new powers, so Heracles had to lift him high above the ground in order to be able to strangle him.

In Egypt, Heracles had to contend with the treacherous hospitality of King Busiris. The king had once asked the advice of a Greek soothsayer on how to combat the long-term drought that was causing famine in his land. The soothsayer, Phrasius, told him that the famine would end if Busiris sacrificed a stranger to Zeus every year. Busiris immediately followed this careful advice and had his priests put an end to Phrasius' life. Many unsuspecting guests suffered the same fate, until even Heracles ended up on the altar of Busiris' priests. But when the king raised his sacrificial ax to bring it down on the hero, the ax-head broke away and killed Busiris, his son, and all of the priests present.

When Heracles finally arrived at the garden of the Hesperides, he asked Atlas for help. Atlas was quite happy to fetch the apples, but only if Heracles would take the burden of the vaults of the heavens from him. Heracles agreed and took the heavens from Atlas, who, as good as his word, immediately stepped into his daughters' garden. He cheerfully brought the apples back to Heracles. He really liked not having the heavens on his neck, he declared. He wanted to offer further help to Heracles by making the difficult journey to Mycenæ and personally delivering the apples to Eurystheus. Heracles kept his head, however, and praised Atlas' initiative. Only, the heavens did not sit properly on his shoulders. He wished to put a cushion on his back, so would Atlas take the burden from him in the meantime? Atlas had no objection to this, whereupon Heracles gathered up the apples, warmly bid farewell to the poor giant, and traveled back to Mycenæ, where he presented the apples to his principal.

There is also another version of the story, in which Heracles himself fetched the apples from the garden, killing the dragon Ladon who was guarding them.

Eurystheus did not dare keep the sacred apples in his possession and returned them to Heracles, who dedicated them to Athena. The goddess ensured that they went back to their rightful owners.

12. The Capture of Cerberus

Heracles' final and most difficult labor even took him beyond the living world. Eurystheus made him go and fetch Hades' guard-dog, Cerberus, from the underworld. He did this in the hope of ridding himself of Heracles forever (see **Cerberus** and **Hades**). Before Heracles could begin this quest, he first attended the Eleusinian Mysteries, secret ceremonies in honor of Demeter and Persephone (see **Demeter**). Here, he was exonerated from blame for the slaughter of the centaurs, a necessary condition if he was to be allowed to enter the underworld.

Heracles began his descent into the underworld at Cape Tænarum, in the southernmost part of the Peloponnese. Athena accompanied him, as did Hermes, the permanent guide of the dead on their last journey. The ferryman, Charon, was frightened of Heracles

While in the underworld, the shades that Heracles saw included the horrific gorgon Medusa. Head of Medusa from Didyma in present-day Turkey.

and brought him across the river Styx to the underworld without protest, an act for which his master, Hades, would later punish him.

In the underworld, Heracles met many of the shades. These included Theseus—whose release from the kingdom of the dead he stipulated—the repulsive gorgon, Medusa, and Meleager, one of the Argonauts and killer of the Calydonian wild boar (see **Atalanta** *and* **the Moiræ**). Heracles was so impressed by the story of his death that he promised him he would marry his sister, Deianeira. Then Heracles performed more deeds in the underworld, but after slaughtering Hades' cattle to give to the shades so they could taste blood, Hades' wife, Persephone, requested him to restrain himself thereafter.

The forbidding Hades did not much like the thought of giving his dog to Heracles. According to some versions, he came to blows with the hero and had to have his injuries treated on Mount Olympus. In any case, with chilly reluctance, he permitted Heracles to take Cerberus if he could control the monster with his bare hands. Heracles did not need to be told twice. He grabbed the hellish hound by all three of its throats and squeezed them with such force that Cerberus ultimately allowed itself to be led away. The great Roman poet, Ovid, tells the following story of the journey of Heracles and Cerberus: "... stirred into furious anger, it filled the air with three times the barking and spread white flecks of foam over the green fields. They say that the foam congealed there and there, feeding on the rich ground, received harmful powers; and immediately, a poisonous plant sprouted on the rocky ground, and was called "aconite" by the farmers." (*Metamorphoses*, VII, 423-410).

Upon the arrival of Heracles and Cerberus in Mycenæ, Eurystheus crawled deeper than ever into his jug, shivering in fear. Reluctantly, he granted Heracles his freedom, after which the hero immediately took Cerberus back to the underworld.

Heracles' Life After Performing the Twelve Labors

Heracles had paid his dues, done penance, and was no longer forced to comply with the whims of the evil and cowardly Eurystheus. His earthly existence, however, was by no means over and he was to experience many more adventures.

Remains of a porticus (colonnade) and a wall in the gallery of the Athenians in Delphi. During a visit to the Oracle at Delphi, Heracles became so mad that the god Apollo himself had to intervene and got into a fight with the hero.

First of all, he divorced his wife Megara, and gave her to his loyal cousin, Iolaos. Then he took part in an archery tournament organized by Eurytus, King of Œschalia in Thessaly. As first prize, Eurytus had offered his daughter Iole, but although Heracles achieved victory, Eurytus did not wish to hand over Iole to him, given the tragic outcome of his first marriage. This sent Heracles into one of his terrifying attacks of rage (this time, not caused by Hera) and as a result, he smote Eurytus' son Iphitus with a rock. This was despite the fact that Iphitus admired Heracles and had taken his side.

Again, Heracles had to make amends. Not only did a king who was an ally of Eurytus refuse to assist him, even the Oracle of Delphi would not help. The Pythia, priestess of the Oracle, sent Heracles away, with the result that Heracles again flew into a rage, stole the priestess' stool, and threatened to destroy the Oracle. This infuriated the god Apollo, who entered into the fray. This was the start of a scuffle that lasted until Zeus himself intervened with his thunderbolt.

It was now decided that Heracles had to be sold into slavery. This is how he came to be owned by Queen Omphale of Lydia, in Asia Minor. According to some he was forced to dress in women's clothing, sit among Omphale's ladies and servants of the court, and occupy himself with weaving and spinning, then exclusively female tasks. As a joke, Omphale sometimes adorned herself with his lion skin, club, and bow. However, it is also claimed that Heracles helped her. He gave her a son and rid her of many of her enemies.

After Heracles had done enough penance in Omphales' service and had completely returned to his senses, Heracles settled a number of old scores with those who had dealt with him unjustly. He returned to Troy, which was still ruled by King Laomedon, the man who had not honored his word after Heracles had saved his daughter Hesione. Heracles besieged the city, which fell quickly, mainly because of actions of his comrade-in-arms Telamon, a brother of the hero, Peleus. Consequently, Heracles became so jealous of Telamon that Telamon felt it necessary to erect an altar in honor of "the triumphant Heracles." Laomedon and most of his sons were killed, and Hesione was given to Telamon as his wife. Laomedon's only surviving son, initially called Podarces but later Priam, was placed on the throne of Troy. The city flourished under Priam's long reign. Sadly Priam, when a very old man, also had to witness the definitive fall of Troy, after a ten-year siege by the Greeks (*see* **Priam**).

There now followed an adventure on the island of Cos, where Heracles landed as a result of a storm caused by Hera. Zeus was so incensed by this incident that he handcuffed his wife, weighed her ankles down with anvils, and chained her by the wrists to Mount Olympus. Heracles was not to be frustrated too much, because the gods needed him in the war against the Gigantes.

Heracles then turned on Augeus, King of Elis, who had broken his word to Heracles after his stables had been cleaned by him (the Fifth Labor). Because Augeus had the

Before he could claim Deianeira, Heracles had first to take part in a wrestling match against the river-god Achelous, whom he had insulted . Heracles defeated Achelous by breaking off one of his horns. Earthenware head of Achelous, 6th century BCE.

support of powerful allies, it took Heracles some time to deal with him. Eventually, he conquered Elis, killed Augeus, and proclaimed Augeus' son, Phyleus, as the new ruler of the kingdom. Then Heracles offered his thanks to his father Zeus and, according to some versions, established the Olympic Games.

Having settled scores with old enemies, Heracles remembered his promise to the shade of Meleager, that he would take his sister Deianeira as his wife. He traveled to Caledon in Ætolia, the western part of central Greece, where Deianeira lived as the daughter of the local king Œneus, although, in fact, her real father was Dionysus, the god of wine, who had repaid Œncus for the use of his wife with the gift of viticulture (the name Œneus is very similar to the Greek word for wine, *oinos*). Deianeira was not only very beautiful, she was also a strong, athletic woman, adept at charioteering and in the use of weapons. Heracles was, therefore, not the only suitor for her hand. His main rival was the river god, Achelous, whom Heracles insulted and challenged to a wrestling match. In this duel, Achelous, who normally had the form of a human with a bull's head, first transformed himself into a snake so that he could slip out of Heracles' iron grip, and then into a ferocious bull. It was not until Heracles broke off his right horn that he admitted defeat.

Heracles now entered into marriage with Deianeira, who gave him a son, Hyllus, and a daughter, Macaria. However, the family had

A superb wrestler, Heracles was especially revered in the songs sung at sporting events. This relief depicts a gymnasium, with Heracles in a place of honor in the center. Earthenware relief from Rome, 2nd century BCE.

to leave Calydon quickly because in a fit of rage Heracles killed a boy who had accidentally splashed him. Heracles set off eastward with his wife and children to Trachis. At the River Evenus, they encountered the centaur, Nessus, who offered to carry Deianeira across the water for a small fee. Heracles gratefully accepted the offer, but scarcely had Nessus taken his money when he took to his heels with Deianeiro and attempted to rape her. Deianeira screamed for help, Heracles grabbed his bow, and hit Nessus with one of his poisoned arrows. The centaur collapsed and as he lay dying, he whispered his last words to Deianeira. Should Heracles ever lose interest in her, he said, then there was an effective treatment for this. She had to collect some of the blood that streamed from his wounds and smear it on Heracles' clothes if she suspected him of adultery. After this, she could be assured that he would never again be unfaithful to her. Without Heracles' knowledge, Deianeira then filled a flask with Nessus' blood, and stored it carefully.

Upon arrival in Trachis, Heracles went to the aid of the local King Ceyx, and crushed his enemies. Some time later, he traveled to Thessaly where he fought out a duel with Cycnus, a son of Ares, god of war, who was killing and robbing pilgrims traveling to Delphi (this Cycnus is not to be confused with Cycnus, son of Poseidon, *see* **Poseidon**, or Cycnus, the friend of Phæton, *see* **Phæthos**). Cycnus was aided by his father, but when Heracles, assisted by Athena, wounded the war god, Zeus intervened by throwing a bolt of lightning between the fighters.

One of those by whom he had been unjustly treated, and whom Heracles had not yet been able to adequately punish was King Eurytus of Œschalia. The king had refused to grant Heracles the winner's prize, his daughter Iole, after he won the archery contest organized by Eurytus. Heracles left Trachis again, leaving Deianeira behind, and with an army of allies, became involved in a heavy battle in Œschalia against Eurytus and his men. Heracles killed Eurytus and all of his sons. Iole, tried to end her own life by throwing herself from the city walls, but she survived the fall because her skirts worked like a sort of parachute, and she fell into Heracles' hands. He slept with her, then sent her to Trachis with his prisoners-of-war. He also asked Deianeira to send him a clean tunic, because he wanted to make a sacrifice to Zeus at Cape Ceraneum in northwestern

Euboa. But when Deianeira, who by now was no longer young, saw the beautiful Iole, she was overcome with jealousy. Afraid that her husband had lost interest in her, she brought out the flask containing Nessus' blood and smeared it on Heracles' tunic, which she then gave to his adjutant.

Soon after, Heracles put on the tunic, and the poison from the Hydra, which had been mixed with Nessus' blood, began to do its work. Heracles felt a terrible burning pain on his skin. He tried to remove the tunic, but pieces of his skin came away with it. Covered in terrible burns, Heracles was brought back by ship to Trachis, where Deianeira, realizing she had been tricked by Nessus, committed suicide.

Heracles soon realized the cause of his intolerable pain and consulted the Oracle of Delphi, who advised him to have a funeral pyre built on Mount Œta in Thessaly. Heracles' son, Hyllus, prepared the funeral pyre and Heracles climbed onto it, but none dared light it. Only Philoctetes, son of Pœas, a shepherd who happened to be passing, was willing to do so. As payment, he was given Heracles' infallible bow and arrows.

As soon as the fire was lit and the flames reached Heracles' tormented body, a tremendous bolt of lightning came down, after which Heracles seemed to have disappeared.

Heracles' funeral pyre was erected by his son, Hyllus. This ruined gateway in the ancient city of Ephesus, is adorned with two Heraclides, or sons of Heracles.

His father, Zeus, had intervened and transported him to Olympus in a cloud, where he was granted immortality. Heracles finally made his peace with Hera and took the charming Hebe to be his partner for all eternity. It is remarkable that at the same time, according to the poet Homer, the shade of Heracles remained in the underworld, despite his immortality. The hero Odysseus, who had to obtain information in Hades' kingdom about the further progress of his difficult journey home, encountered Heracles there.

The now immortal Heracles came to earth one more time, when he and Hebe assisted Iolaos in defending Heracles' children against his old tormentor, Eurystheus. He is also supposed to have appeared in divine form to Philoctetes, to urge him to fight on the Greek side during the Trojan War. Heracles' bow would play a decisive role in this battle, since Philoctetes used the bow to kill the Trojan prince, Paris, instigator of the war.

The popular hero-cum-god Heracles was honored throughout the Greek world and beyond. In Rome, he was known by the name, Hercules, and he was also equated with the western Semitic god Melqart, worshiped in Phœnicia and Carthage. Heracles features frequently in classical literature. The great Athenian tragedians dedicated some of their plays to him. Euripides wrote the dramas *Alcestis* (a relatively light tragedy about the salvation of Alcestis, in which Heracles is portrayed as a courageous but somewhat coarse figure), *The Heraclides* (about the battle of Heracles' children against

Portrait of the Phœnician god Melqart on a coin. Melqart is equated with Heracles. Silver coin, (tetradrachma) from Tyre, 1st century BCE

This huge head of Heracles from Nemrut Dag in eastern Turkey shows just how widespread the worship of the hero was. Nemrut Dag, 1st century BCE.

King Mithridates I Kallinikos of the small kingdom Commagene in Asia Minor attempted to increase his own status by having himself depicted with Heracles. The hero is immediately recognizable because of his club. Arsameia (Eski Kale), 1st century BCE.

The forum of Pompeii, one of the southern Italian cities supposed to have been founded by Heracles. In 79 CE, Pompeii was buried under ash, rubble, and lava during the eruption of Mount Vesuvius.

Eurystheus) and *Heracles,* in which the hero kills his wife and child in a fit of madness inflicted by Hera. Sophocles' *Trachiniæ (Women of Trachis* or *Heracles' Death)* devotes much attention to the tragic contribution of Deianeira in the developments surrounding the death of Heracles.

The importance of Heracles in Antiquity can be understood most clearly from the behavior of the Roman Emperor Commodus (161-192), who had himself been portrayed and worshiped as Heracles-Hercules. Commodus was a man whose mental health left much to be desired, but the desire for "herculean strength" has continued to exist into modern times.

Hercules, *see* Heracles

Hermaphroditus

Hermaphroditus was the son of Hermes and Aphrodite, goddess of love, who was raised by nymphs on Mount Ida in Phrygia. When, at the age of sixteen, he left his birthplace f and wandered through Asia Minor, he ended up at a particular well. The nymph, Salmacis, who lived by this well, immediately fell madly violently in love with the beautiful boy. Hermaphroditus was not interested in her and was frightened by her advances, but took a cooling bath in her alluring well. Salmacis seized her opportunity. She entered the

143

Hermaphroditus was such a handsome boy that the water nymph Salmacis fell madly in love with him and transformed him into a creature with both male and female sexual characteristics. Torso of a hermaphrodite, marble sculpture, 1st century BCE.

Thanks to his winged headgear and winged sandals, Hermes, the god who often served as messenger for his father Zeus, was able to move through the air very fast.

water, embraced the boy, and begged the gods that she and he be united forever. Her wish was granted and the two were fused into one homogenous creature, a *hermaphrodite*, with both male and female sexual attributes (*see* **Salmacis**). Hermaphroditus, who was not happy with his metamorphosis, now begged his parents to ensure that any man who swam in Salmacis' well, would also be given female attributes, like him. This wish was also granted.

Hermes (Roman=Mercury)

Hermes was a son of Zeus and the nymph Maia, a daughter of Atlas, one of the twelve gods of Olympus, who lived with the supreme god Zeus on Mount Olympus. Hermes had many functions. He served as messenger of his father Zeus, guided the souls of the dead to the underworld, brought prosperity to humans and protected travelers and merchants, as well as thieves. He was a skillful, ingenious, and cunning god, like a young boy with no qualms about playing practical jokes on others, and was never caught out by his own untruths. He had the appearance of an attractive young man and wore a winged hat

with a narrow brim, something like a British army "tin hat," and winged sandals, that gave him the ability to move extremely quickly through the air. In his hand, he held a golden staff that could serve as a magic wand and that he could use to lull people to sleep.

Hermes came into the world in Arcadia, where Zeus visited his mother, Maia, in a cave on Mount Cyllene. Almost immediately after his birth, the precocious child invented the musical instrument, the lyre, by stretching strings across the shell of a tortoise. The same night, in Macedonia, he stole fifteen cows from Apollo, that he took to the Peloponnensus, all the time carefully erasing his tracks. He sacrificed two of the cows to the gods and then returned to the cave in which he was born, and crawled back into his cradle.

Apollo went looking for Hermes and was able to find him thanks to the loquacious shepherd, Battus, who betrayed Hermes and consequently was later turned into a basalt rock by the gods. The still innocent-looking child Hermes initially maintained that he had stolen nothing, but after the issue had been presented to Zeus, an exchange was eventually agreed on. Hermes could keep the cattle and the musical Apollo received the lyre made by Hermes. Thereafter these gods became best friends and Hermes acted as protector of shepherds, flocks, and herds.

As patron of travelers, Hermes, the frequent traveler. was responsible for

Hermes, the messenger of the gods, went everywhere on his travels, even as far as the Netherlands, as shown by this bronze Roman statuette of the 2nd century BCE, found in the River Waal area of Nijmegen.

signposting. In ancient Greece, the *hermaiherm*, a stone pillar topped with the head of Hermes and with a formidable phallus, that was named for the god, served as a signpost and stood beside roads and streets. These had developed from piles of stones which were originally made by travelers to mark certain points along the roads (everyone who passed such a point added a new stone to the pile). Later, in the cities *hermaiherm* were also placed in front of gates and doorways, including gymnasia, as the fast-moving, athletic god was a favorite of athletes.

Hermes had all sorts of amorous adventures. The most important of his offspring was the nature god, Pan, who was born from Hermes' association with a nymph. With Aphrodite, goddess of love, he fathered the handsome Hermaphroditus, who later fused with a nymph into a homogenous creature, and Priapus, who was equipped with a gigantic phallus (according to another version, Priapus was a son of Dionysus). The shepherd, Daphnis, was another of his sons. The mortal women loved by Hermes included Herse, daughter of the Athenian king Cecrops. Her sister, Aglaurus, was terribly jealous and would only allow the god into Herse's bedroom in return for payment. As punishment, Hermes changed her into a statue of black basalt. Another of the god's loves was the nimble Apemosyen, who was initially too fast for him but who was overpowered after he had once let her slip.

As messenger and handyman, Hermes performed errands for other gods and important immortals. He also supported his father Zeus in his extramarital affairs. Whether it was about eliminating the hundred-eyed Argus, guardian of Io, who was desired by Zeus (*see* **Io**), or driving bulls to the beach so that Zeus could seduce the lovely Europa, Hermes was always ready. The Trojan King, Priam, was brought by Hermes to the tent of

The shepherd, Battus, revealing to the god, Apollo, where Hermes lives. He later receives a visit from Hermes, but does not yet know what is in store for him. Hermes was to change him into a block of basalt. Oil painting by Jacob Jordaens, 17th century.

A man brings a sacrifice to a hermaiherm, a stone column with the head of Hermes on it, that served as a signpost. A dog watches in surprise. Painting on Athenian amphora, circe 475 BCE.

Two faces of the three-faced Herme on the Ponte Fabricio, the oldest bridge across the river Tiber in Rome.The Ponte Fabricio was built in 62 BCE and has since been in continuous use.

Achilles, where he begged the hero to hand over the corpse of his son, Hector. Odysseus, himself no less cunning than Hermes, received from him an herb that rendered him immune to the wiles of Circe (*see* **Circe**).

Hermes did much work in his function as guide to the souls of the dead. All of the dead were brought by Hermes Psychopompos ("guide of souls") to the banks of the underworld river, the Styx, where upon payment of an obolus, they boarded the ramshackle rowboat belonging to Charon the ferryman, who took them across to the kingdom of Hades.

Mercury, the Roman counterpart of

Hermes, was originally a god of trade and was often depicted with a purse in his hands.

Hero and Leander

The story of Hero and Leander is one of the saddest love stories in Greek mythology. Hero was a young priestess of Aphrodite in Sestos, by the Hellespont. Leander lived in Abydos, on the other side of the water. Hero and Leander fell passionately in love with each other, but because of her position as a priestess, Hero was not permitted to become Leander's wife. So every night, in secret, Leander swam from Abydos across the narrow strait to Sestos. In the tower in which she lived, Hero would light a lamp for Leander to direct him to the right place. They would lie in each other's arms for a few hours and just before daybreak, Leander would swim back. But one stormy winter's night, the wind blew out the lamp, so that Leander lost his way and drowned. The next morning, his corpse washed up on Sestos. When Hero saw the body of her dead lover lying on the beach, she threw herself from her tower and was dashed against the ground.

Hermes (on the left) with his staff in his left hand and his famous winged hat, opposite the hero Heracles, immediately recognizable by his club and his lion skin. Image on an Ertruscan bronze mirror, 3rd century BCE.

Hesperides, The

The Hesperides ("daughters of the evening") were the seven (or four in some versions) daughters of the Titan. Atlas. Their names were Ægle, Arethusa, Erythea, Hestia, Hespera, Herperusa, and Hespereia. Together with the dragon, Ladon, the Hesperides guarded a tree that bore the golden apples that Gaia had given to Hera as a gift at her wedding to the supreme god, Zeus. This tree stood in a garden at the most westerly point of the world known to the Greeks, close to the Straits of Gibraltar. Near the garden, Atlas bore the vault of the heavens on his shoulders. In the context of the Twelve Labors imposed upon him, Heracles had to bring the golden apples to Eurystheus. Atlas fetched the apples from the garden after Heracles had temporarily taken the vault of the heavens from him. The hero was then able to trick Atlas into keeping the vault while he escaped with the apples (*see* **Atlas** *and* **Heracles**).

Hestia (Roman=*Vesta*)

Hestia, eldest of the three daughters of the Titans, Cronos and Rhea, was the goddess of the hearth and household life. She was one of the twelve gods and goddesses who lived with Zeus on Mount Olympus. Hestia remained unmarried and attached great importance to her virginity, cleanliness, and purity. Her role in mythology is minor, but her function in daily life was not insignificant. The city halls of Greek cities contained a state fire, from which citizens could fetch burning brands to light their own home fires. Hestia was patroness of this hearth. It the city established a colony elsewhere, they took brands from their city hearth with them and lit the new fire from them in the new city.

The Romans were also familiar with the cult of the hearth. The Roman Forum contained a temple dedicated to Vesta, the Roman counterpart of Hestia, in which six priestesses, the Vestal Virgins, kept an eternal fire burning to symbolize the well-being and power of the city of Rome. The Pontifex Maximus, or high priest, selected young girls from patrician families, who had to swear a vow of chastity and serve in the temple of Vesta for thirty years. It was a great honor to be chosen to be a Vestal Virgin, but the codes of behavior were strictly enforced. If a Vestal Virgin was found to be unchaste, she was burned alive.

Hyacinth

Hyacinth was the son of the Spartan King Amyclas. He was a handsome young man with whom the great god Apollo fell passionately in love. Apollo was hardly ever in Delphi and neglected his many duties because he

constantly wanted to be in Sparta with his beloved. Apollo and Hyacinth were inseparable and together hunted in the mountains. But one afternoon, during a discus-throwing contest, fate—or, according to some, the jealous Zephyrus, the west wind—struck. When

Hyacinth rushed forward to pick up the discus after a long throw by the god, he was struck in the face by a disc bouncing upward. All of Apollo's healing powers were of no avail—Hyacinthus was dead. The god had a flower sprout from the boy's blood—probably not the flower we know as a hyacinth, but a type of iris. On the flower petals he wrote the words "*ai, ai,*" the Greek cry of grief. Since then, every year, a Hyacinth festival has been held in Sparta.

Hymen or Hymenæus

The god Hymen or Hymenæus was the personification of marriage. He was regarded as a son of the god Apollo, but according to others, Dionysus was his father. At weddings, the words "O Hymenæus Hymen, O Hymen Hymenæus" were chanted or sung. Virginity is referred to by the word *hymen*, so the wedding song indicated the end of the virginal state of the bride. The hymen is still the scientific name for the maidenhead. Hymenæus is depicted as a handsome young man carrying a wedding torch and other attributes of marriage.

Hypnos (Roman=Somnus)

Hypnos, the personification of sleep, was the son of Nyx, the goddess of night, and brother of Thanatos, god of death. Hypnos lived in a cave on the island of Lemnos or at a place at the edge of the world, close to Oceanus. It was dark and misty there and the waters of Lethe, the stream of forgetfulness, flowed through the cave. Hypnos had many sons, known as the Oneiroi or dreams, who included Ikelos, Phobetor, and Phantasos. The common Oneiroi formed the dreams of the common man while these three visited kings

Hypnos, brother of Thanatos, god of death, could lull men and gods to sleep. The goddess Hera, with her continuous plotting and planning, attempted to use Hypnos' powers to her own advantage.

and chieftains. The chief son was Morpheus, who lives on in the expression "to lie in the arms of Morpheus" (be deeply asleep).

Hera sometimes called on Hypnos whenever she wanted to do something that she did not want her husband, Zeus, to know about. In this way, Hypnos lulled Zeus to sleep at her request, so that Hera could frustrate the hero Heracles whom she detested so much. When Zeus awoke and discovered what had happened, he became furious and wanted to fling Hypnos into the sea. Luckily for the god of sleep, his mother, the night, intervened.

During the Trojan War, when Hera again asked Hypnos to make Zeus fall asleep, Hypnos initially reacted with little enthusiasm, in spite of the fact that Hera had adorned herself with Aphrodite's seductive, colorfully embroidered girdle of love. It was not until Hera offered him one of the Charities or Graces for a wife that Hypnos let himself be persuaded to co-operate with her plan.

Icarus *see* Dædalus

Ino

Ino was a daughter of the Theban king Cadmus and his wife Harmonia. She was the sister of Semele, who was mother of Dionysus, god of wine. After Zeus had rescued Dionysus from the body of Semele, who had been scorched by the supreme god's radiance (*see* **Dionysus** *and* **Semele**), Hermes handed the baby into Ino's charge to be breastfed. But all too soon Zeus' jealous wife Hera, who had engineered the demise of Semele, discovered that she had been duped. Hera enlisted the help of the goddesses of revenge and had Ino and her husband Athamas struck with madness by the goddess Tisiphone. Athamas killed his eldest son and Ino leapt from the rocks into the sea with her youngest son, Melicertes, in her arms. According to some versions of this myth, Ino had already tried to murder the children of Athamas' first marriage, Phrixus and Helle, but they were able to escape on the back of a flying ram with a golden fleece (*see* **the Argonauts**).

149

Io

Io was the daughter of the river-god Inachus, the first King of Argos, and priest in a temple dedicated to Hera. She caught the eye of no less that the supreme god Zeus who overwhelmed her by darkening the sky with thick clouds to hide his activities from the eyes of the other gods. His wife, Hera, immediately grew suspicious, however, but before she could arrive on the scene, Zeus had changed Io into a cow. Hera pretended not to understand what Zeus needed with a cow and Zeus saw no other possibility than to give the beautiful creature to his wife as a gift.

Hera still did not trust Zeus and had Io in her bovine form guarded by Argus, a giant with a hundred eyes. Of these eyes, two would sleep in turn, so that Argus could remain watchful with the other ninety-eight. Io, in the meantime, was successful in writing a message with her hooves in the sand to her father, who grieved deeply for her.

Zeus could not bear the sight of Io and her father's grief. He sent Hermes to Argus, with an order to kill the giant. Hermes disguised himself as a cowherd and was able to close all of Argus' hundred eyes by playing sweet melodies on his flute and telling him stories. As soon as Argus had fallen asleep, Hermes killed him.

Hera was furious. She sent a hornet after Io, that pursued her all over the world. Just as poor Io arrived in Egypt, Zeus got around to begging Hera to cease tormenting her and promised his wife he would behave better in future. Hera yielded to him and Io was returned to her human form. Some time later, she bore a son, Epaphus, who was worshiped in Egypt as the holy bull, Apis.

After Argus, the one hundred-eyed giant who guarded Io, was killed by Hermes, Hera set a hornet onto Io. This insect relentlessly pursued young, undeveloped girls all over the world.

The cunning god, Hermes, about to take the life of Argus—here depicted not as a giant but as an old man—after he has lulled Argus to sleep through his story-telling and lyre-playing. Oil painting by Cornelis Bisschop, 17th century.

Iphigenia

Iphigenia was the eldest daughter of the Mycenean King Agamemnon and his wife Clytemnestra. When Agamemnon, as commander-in-chief of the Greek fleet, wanted to sail from Aulis to Troy, an unfavorable wind blew unremittingly. According to the seer Calchas, Artemis was behind this. The goddess of nature and wild animals had been offended by Agamemnon, probably because he had claimed to be a better hunter than she was. Artemis was only prepared to concede if Iphigenia were sacrificed to her and Agamemnon was prepared to perform this terrible sacrifice. He decided to allow his daughter travel from Mycenæ to Aulis, but did not wish to arouse the suspicions of his wife, Clytemnestra, so he informed her that Iphigenia was to marry the hero, Achilles. Clytemnestra would never forgive him for this deception. When Agamemnon returned from Troy ten years later, he was murdered by her and her lover Ægisthus (*see* **Agamemnon**).

According to some versions, Iphigenia was indeed sacrificed in Aulis. However, in another version, at the eleventh hour, Artemis replaced her body on the altar with that of a doe and transported Iphigenia, wrapped in a mist, to Tauris in the Crimean peninsula. There, Iphigenia became a priestess in the temple of Artemis and had to sacrifice strangers who came to Tauris to the goddess. Much later, Iphigenia's brother, Orestes, and his cousin, Pylades, came to Tauris, to bring the statue of Artemis to Attica, on the orders of Apollo. Orestes was imprisoned by the local king, Thoas, and brought to the sanctuary of Artemis, with the

According to some, including the playwright Euripides, Iphigenia was not actually sacrificed, but was replaced by a doe on the altar, thanks to the goddess, Artemis. Stag on a standard finial from Turkey, circa 2500 BCE.

After her "sacrifice," Iphigenia became a priestess of Artemis, the goddess of the hunt and untamed nature, in a temple in Tauris, Crimea. Reclining Artemis, from the Quattro Fontane in the Quirinale, Rome, late 16th century.

intention of sacrificing him and Pylades to the goddess. There he and Iphigenia recognized each other, at which Iphigenia told the king that the strangers, the statue of the goddess, and she herself had to be washed clean in the sea to remove the impurities that tainted Orestes because he had killed his mother, Clytemnestra. The inhabitants of Tauris had to avert their eyes during this ritual.

Thanks to the ruse, the three were able to escape on board Orestes' ship. The goddess, Athena, stopped Thoas from pursuing them by pointing out to him that the statue had been taken on the divine orders of Apollo and Artemis. The statue of Artemis was placed in a temple in Attica, into the safekeeping of the temple priestess, Iphigenia.

Ixion

The Thessalian King Ixion, a son of Phlegyas, was the first human in Greek mythology to kill a relative. Ixion did not want to pay his father-in-law, Eioneus, a dowry for his daughter Dia. Thus when Eioneus visited him, Ixion caused him to fall into a pit of burning coals, which killed him.

Ixion thus brought terrible disgrace on himself and placed himself outside of human society. Zeus felt compassion and showed himself prepared to hold a purification ritual for Ixion, so he invited the guilty man to a banquet on Mount Olympus. Ixion did not appreciate the value of this extraordinary gesture and even attempted to seduce Zeus' wife, Hera. In order to be sure than Ixion's seduction attempt was serious, Zeus created a

The god Janus was depicted with two faces, with which he looked forward and backward, inside and out, to the future as well as to the past.

cloud that looked exactly like Hera. Ixion did not hesitate and pounced on the cloud, and from this union, Centaurus, the forefather of the centaurs, was born. Zeus caught Ixion in the act and was no longer compassionate. Ixion was locked up in Tartarus, the most inhospitable part of the underworld. There, he was condemned to spend eternity, surrounded by other terrible sinners, tied to a ceaselessly turning, flaming wheel.

Janus

Janus was the Roman god of beginnings, of entrances, doors, and gateways and is always

The impressive Bow of Janus on the Forum Boarium, Rome, was built in the 4th century BCE. Merchants who traded in this forum (the cattle mart) could shelter here from the rain or strong sun.

portrayed as a figure with two faces looking in opposite directions. A temple sacred to Janus, with two doors, stood in the Roman Forum. In times of peace, these doors were always open, but in times of war they were closed. The month of January—during which people look forward to the new year as well as back to the old year—was dedicated to Janus and is named for him.

Janus does not play a very significant role in mythology, but thanks to the eyes in the

Female Janus-type head, possibly based on the face of the goddess Athena, on a silver coin (diobolus) from Lampsakos, 4th century BCE.

back of his head, he once outsmarted the nymph, Carna. She had a habit of making would-be lovers enter a cave, telling them that she would follow them shortly, but instead she would run away. Janus did not fall for this trick, however.

Janus produced offspring who played a role in the legendary early history of the city of Rome and its immediate surroundings.

Jason

The story of Jason is largely that of the Argonauts. Jason was the leader of the heroes who sailed for the land of Colchis on the Black Sea, aboard a ship called the *Argo*, to bring back the golden fleece.

Jason was the son of Æson and Philyra. His father, Æson, was the rightful king of Iolcus in Magnesia, but after the death of his father, Cretheus, Æson's half-brother, Pelias, seized power in Iolcus, though he let Æson live. Jason's mother did not trust Pelias at all and organized a fake funeral for her young son. In reality, she shepherded her baby out of the city and entrusted his upbringing to the centaur Chiron, an excellent teacher who had had various great heroes as his charges (*see* **Chiron**). Meanwhile, Pelias had been told by the Oracle at Delphi that he must beware of a descendent of Æson who wore only one sandal.

The hero Jason enjoyed an illustrious youth full of spectacular adventures, but ended his days as a melancholy old man, spending his time reminiscing about his glorious life on the old ship, the Argo.

Much later, when Jason returned to Iolcus as a young man, he had to ford a river. Just as he was about to enter the water, an old woman asked him if he would bring her across. Jason carried her on his back, but during the difficult crossing, he lost one of his sandals. The old woman was none other that the goddess Hera, who protected Jason and still had a score to settle with Pelias. With one bare foot, Jason presented himself to Pelias. The illegitimate king of Iolcus immediately realized his predicament. He knew that if he killed Jason, this would violate the sacred laws of hospitality and that Jason had much support from the population of Iolcus. Therefore, he promised Jason the throne of the land if he would bring him the golden fleece. This was the skin of the flying ram upon which the royal children, Phrixus and Helle, had flown to the distant land of Colchis. It was considered an impossible task, and Pelias was certain that Jason would not survive it.

However, the Oracle of Delphi judged that, on the contrary, Jason would be able to successfully complete the mission. So Jason commissioned the building of a ship, called the *Argo* and assembled fifty heroes to accompany him on the difficult quest. The

View of part of the ruins of the sanctuary of Delphi, that contained the famous and influential oracle of Antiquity. The oracle had great influence on the decisions that defined the course of Jason's life.

Argo sailed away, and after numerous adventures the Argonauts eventually reached Colchis. Jason was able to capture the golden fleece, largely due to the help of the Colchian princess and sorceress Medea, who fell in love with him. After many adventures, Jason eventually returned home safely to Iolcus (*for details of his adventures during the journey and in Colchis, see* **The Argonauts**).

Pelias, the usurper, did not give up so easily, but due to the intervention of Medea, he was murdered by his own daughters. After this atrocity, Jason and Medea settled in Corinth, as guests of the local King Creon (*see* **Creon** of Corinth) and they had three sons. For a number of years, they lived in peace and harmony, until Creon decided to offer Jason the hand of his daughter, Glauce. If he married her, Jason would become king. It was easy for him to renounce Medea, because, in Corinth, her marriage to Jason was invalid because she was a foreigner. Not surprisingly, the sorceress fell into a terrible rage. She murdered Glauce, Creon, and her own children, after which she fled to Athens (*see* **Medea**).

The unhappy Jason remained in Corinth after Medea's departure. She was obviously a much stronger personality than he was and he had betrayed her in spite of being indebted to her for his most important heroic feats. He remained alone into his old age, still reminiscing about his glory days as an Argonaut. Eventually he was killed by a falling rotten timber from his old ship the *Argo*, on which he used to sit musing over his glorious past deeds. It was perhaps an appropriate end for Jason, who may have been a hero, but not really a strong character. Without the support of the goddess Hera and the sorceress Medea he would not have amounted to much.

Juno, *see* Hera

Jupiter, *see* Zeus

Laius

Laius, son of Labdacus, was king of the city of Thebes and father of Œdipus.

As a young man, Laius had to flee to the court of King Pelops of Pisa. There, he fell in

As a young man, Laius, father of the unlucky Thebian King Œdipus, abducted Chrysippus on his battle chariot. Chrysippus was the son of Pelops, who had extended his hospitality to Laius. This was the preface to a long series of gruesome events in Laius' family. Painting on a Mycenæan cup, 11th century BCE.

love with Pelops' son, Chrysippus, abducting the boy on his chariot and abusing him. Chrysippus hanged himself in shame because of this event and Laius was cursed by Pelops (according to another version, Chrysippus was murdered by his half-brothers, Atreus and Thyestes, (*see* **Atreus**).

When Laius later became king of Thebes, he and his wife Jocasta remained childless, so Laius consulted the Oracle of Delphi. The Oracle advised him against begetting offspring, because he would be murdered by his own son. Nevertheless, in a drunken stupor, Laius impregnated Jocasta. That is how Œdipus was born. The infant was immediately exposed on a distant, inhospitable hillside, and his feet were pierced. Œdipus did not die, however, but was found by a shepherd and brought up by Polybus, King of Corinth.

Much later, Laius visited the Oracle of Delphi again, perhaps because the environs of his city were being ravaged by the Sphinx, a winged lion with a woman's head who presented travelers and citizens with a riddle, and killed them when they could not answer it. Or he may have done so as a penance for Laius' offense with Chrysippus (*see* **The Sphinx**). At a fork in the road near Mount Parnassus, Laius' retinue encountered a young man who did not move aside as quickly as he would have liked. Laius hit the inconvenient passer-by on the head with his staff, as a result of which, the young man beat him and his servants to death with a club.

Only one servant survived to escape to Thebes, where he explained how of the king had been murdered. The murderer, who had acted to some extent in self-defense, was none other than Laius' own son, Œdipus, who had grown up in Corinth, and was just returning from the Oracle of Delphi. The Oracle had warned him that he would murder his father and marry his mother. He had therefore decided not to return to Corinth, to prevent the Oracle's predictions from coming true...

Œdipus traveled on to Thebes, solved the riddle of the Sphinx, married his mother Jocasta, who gave him four children, and did not realize what had really happened for many years. When the true situation came to light, the consequences were dreadful (*for this see* **Œdipus** *and* **Antigone**).

Laocoön

Laocoön was the son of Capys and a brother of Anchises, father of the Trojan hero Æneas. Laocoön was a priest in the temple of the sea-god, Poseidon, in Troy. After the Greeks

The Trojan priest Laocoön had to pay a terrible price for warning his fellow citizens against bringing the wooden horse into the city of Troy. Along with both of his sons he was strangled by two giant sea-serpents.

abruptly abandoned their siege of Troy and left, leaving behind them a huge wooden horse, Lacoön warned his fellow citizens not to bring the horse inside the gates, uttering the famous words, put into his mouth by the Roman poet, Virgil, *"Timeo danaos donna ferentes."* (I fear the Greeks when they bear gifts) The furious priest then drove a spear into the horse's flank.

Sinon, a Greek "deserter," who had remained behind (in reality, a spy), told the Trojans that the horse was intended as a sacrifice to Athena. If the citizens of Troy were to destroy it, it would lead to the downfall of their city, but if they were to bring it into the city, Athena would grant Troy extra protection. The trusting Trojans even removed part of their city walls in order to drag the horse inside, as it was too big enter through the city gates.

Shortly after uttering his warning, Lacoön, and both of his sons were strangled by two enormous sea-serpents that appeared suddenly on the beach and were brought directly to Poseidon's altar. This merely served to strengthen the Trojans' resolve. Was this Laocoön's punishment for daring to distrust the Greeks and trying to have the horse destroyed? The serpents had actually been sent by Athena, in order to remove the obstructive Laocoön and add greater weight lent to Sinon's words.

Once the horse was inside Troy, Sinon signaled to the Greek fleet by flashing a lamp. The Greek ships had not departed at all, but were sheltering at the nearby island of Tenedus and hastily sailed back to the now almost defenseless city. Meanwhile, the Greek warriors who were hidden inside the horse emerged from their concealment, and

The sea-serpents that strangled Laocoön and his sons had been sent by the goddess, Athena, who strove after the valley of Troy. Bronze sea dragon, Roman period.

slaughtered the unsuspecting citizens of Troy.

According to some versions, the death of Laocoön, in fact, had nothing to do with the wooden horse, but was related to an act of vengeance by Apollo, because Laocoön—in this version, a priest of Apollo—had gone against the god's wishes and taken a wife. Whatever the case, the demise of Laocoön and his sons is impressively immortalized in the world-famous group of images that can now be seen in the Vatican Museum in Rome.

Latona, *see* Leto

Leda

Leda was the daughter of the Ætolian king Thestius, and wife of King Tyndareos of the Greek city of Sparta. She was the mother of the Dioscuri (*see* **Dioscuri**), Castor and Polydeuces. Her eldest daughters were Clytemnestra, wife of the Mycenæan king Agamemnon, and Helen, the most beautiful woman in the world. Helen married the Spartan king Menelaus but was abducted by the

The swan—in reality the supreme god Zeus—who has made love to Leda, playfully sucks at her nipple with his beak. Leda's divine children Castor, Polydeuces, and Helen have just hatched from their eggs. Oil painting by Francesco Ubertini, known as Bacchiacca, 16th century.

Trojan prince, Paris, causing the outbreak of the Trojan War. Leda had three other daughters, Timandra, Philonoe, and Phoebe. Just like her even more famous daughter, Leda was a very attractive woman, so much so, that the supreme god, Zeus, transformed himself into a swan in order to make love to her. Leda is supposed to have been given the form of a goose. As a result of their union, Leda laid two eggs, from which hatched Castor, Polydeuces, Helen, and Clytemnestra. However, there are a number of versions of this story. In some of them, Polydeuces and Helen were begotten by Zeus, and Castor and Clytemnestra by Leda's earthly husband, Tyndareos. This meant that Helen and Polydeuces were immortal, while Castor and Clytemnestra were not. There were also stories according to which only Helen hatched from an egg or that Helen and both the Dioscuri all hatched from the same egg. Some people even believed that Helen's egg was not laid by Leda, but by the goddess Nemesis. In that particular version, Nemesis is supposed to have made love to Zeus and Leda merely received the egg resulting from their union (*see* **The Dioscuri**, **Helen**, *and* **Nemesis**).

Leto (**Roman=Latona**)

The Titan, Leto, was the daughter of Cœus and Phœbe. The supreme god, Zeus, made

The Lycian farmers who made it impossible for young mother Leto to drink water from the lake were punished severely by her. They were turned into frogs.

Leto's daughter Artemis, the goddess of the hung and untamed nature, sometimes hunted the animal particularly sacred to her: the deer. Oil painting from Anthony van Dijck, 17th century.

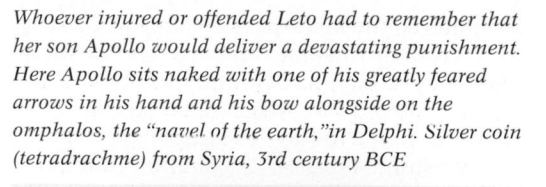

Whoever injured or offended Leto had to remember that her son Apollo would deliver a devastating punishment. Here Apollo sits naked with one of his greatly feared arrows in his hand and his bow alongside on the omphalos, the "navel of the earth," in Delphi. Silver coin (tetradrachme) from Syria, 3rd century BCE

love to her as a result of which, she gave birth to the divine twins Apollo and Artemis. During her pregnancy, Leto experienced many serious difficulties, because Zeus' eternally jealous wife, Hera, had forbidden every country on earth to offer her hospitality. Leto desperately wandered the earth to find shelter. At Delphi, she had to deal with the giant serpent, Python, sent by Hera, who attempted to hinder the birth of Leto's offspring.

Eventually on the orders of Zeus, Leto was brought to the floating island of Delos (according to another version, it was the island of Ortygia, and according to yet another version, Artemis was born on Ortygia and Apollo on Delos). Delos was not yet anchored to the earth, so that the people there did not need to fear Hera's revenge. Leto gave birth to Artemis and Apollo, leaning against a palm tree and an olive tree, or according to another version, on Mount Cynthus. Poseidon then attached Delos to the bottom of the sea, using an enormous pillar. Later, on the island, an important sanctuary was built that was dedicated to Apollo. All of the goddesses attended Leto's delivery, except for Hera and Eileithyia, the goddess of birth. As a result, Leto had a very difficult labor that lasted nine days. Ultimately Eileithyia's help was enlisted, but without Hera's knowledge.

Hera could not leave her rival alone, even after the birth. Leto had to flee to Lycia with her babies, where she was received with great coldness. When she wanted to drink some water from a lake, in order to be able to continue nursing Apollo and Artemis, some local farmers prevented her from doing so, by churning up mud from the bottom of the lake thus making the water undrinkable.

Consequently, Leto turned them into frogs, doomed to forever grub about in the mud.

Others who tried to threaten or insult Leto were immediately punished—some quite harshly. The giant Python was killed by Apollo with a thousand arrows. The giant Tityus, who had tried to rape Leto, was eliminated by Apollo and Artemis with a shower of arrows. In addition, Zeus bombarded him with a bolt of lightning. Tityus was then brought to Tartarus in the underworld, stretched out to his full length, and continuously tortured by vultures who pecked at his liver.

Finally, the Theban Queen Niobe, who bragged that by having given birth to seven sons and seven daughters, she was much more fertile than Leto, had to pay for her arrogance with an terrible attack from Apollo and Artemis. With his arrows Apollo killed her little boys, and Artemis dealt with the little girls (according to some, Niobe's youngest daughter, Chloris, was spared). Niobe herself turned to stone from grief (*see* **Apollo**, **Artemis,** *and* **Niobe**).

Mænads (Roman=Bacchantes)

The Mænads ("mad ones") were female disciples of Dionysus, the wine-god. They indulged in rituals for their god in a wild state of ecstatic intoxication. Dressed in deer and panther skins, they would overindulge in frenzied dancing. They held thyrus staffs in their hands, staffs topped with a pinecone

The Mænads or Bacchantes, the female followers of Dionysus the wine-god, were notorious for their extreme and ecstatic behavior. Here a Mænad dances with a visibly excited satyr. The amphora behind the satyr indicates that the wine will not be consumed sparingly. Painting on Athenian amphora, circa 510 BCE.

A Mænad about to sacrifice a bull. In their state of ecstatic intoxication, the Mænads sometimes devoured wild animals. Fragment of an image on a Roman terracotta beaker, 1st century BCE.

Dionysus, fervently worshiped by the Mænads, has mauled a deer. Fragment from a painting on an Athenian krater, 5th century BCE.

beings were not always safe from their clutches. One of their most famous victims was the Theban king, Pentheus, who was adverse to the worship of Dionysus, but curious about the excessive behavior of the Mænads. When he tried to spy on them from a tree, he fell into their hands, and was torn apart. One of the Mænads who participated in this act was his own mother, Agave (*see* **Dionysus**).

The singer Orpheus, who after the death of his beloved Eurydice was unable to take any interest in women, was killed by the Mænads, who resented the fact that he avoided their company (*see* **Orpheus**). These women came to a bad end, however. Dionysus found them an annoyance, and turned them into trees.

Marsyas, the Phrygian satyr, playing a double flute. The goddess Athena, who made the flute, listens critically to his playing. Marsyas developed into an accomplished flautist, but fell victim to the musical god, Apollo, who sometimes acted unreasonably in artistic matters. Fragment from an Athenian krater, 5th century BCE.

and entwined in ribbons, vines, and ivy tendrils. They also bore clusters of grapes, burning torches, and live snakes.

In their state of intoxication, the Mænads had superhuman power. They were capable of tearing apart wild animals and even human

Mars, *see* Ares

Marsyas

Marsyas was a Phrygian satyr (*see* **satyrs**), who came into possession of a double flute that had been made for the goddess Athena. She had thrown the instrument away when she saw from her reflection in the water how ridiculous she looked whenever she played the flute. Marsyas found the flute and became such a skilful flautist that he aimed to compete with the lyre-playing god Apollo. It came to a musical competition, at which the Muses served as judges. Initially, the competitors were evenly matched, but after a time, the god challenged Marsyas to play his instrument upside-down, the way he was doing. On the lyre that was practicable, on the flute, impossible. So the competition ended in the defeat of the poor satyr, who was then horribly punished by Apollo for his pride. The god skinned him alive, from top to toe. The other satyrs and nymphs cried so much at what was done to Marsyas, that the ground was saturated with their tears causing a new river to be created in Phrygia, the Marsyas (*see* **Apollo**).

Medea was a brilliant sorceress. Using her potions, she had been successful in turning an old ram young again, so that he jumped out of her cauldron as a frisky little lamb. Jason's aged father, Æson, also underwent this treatment.

The goddesses Hera and Athena, who supported the Argonauts, asked Aphrodite if she would make Medea fall in love with Jason. Head of Athena on a silver coin (tetradrachma), Athens, ca. 420 BCE.

Medea

Medea, daughter of king Æetes of Colchis and the sea nymph Idyia was, like her aunt Circe, a formidable sorceress.

When the hero Jason and his Argonauts arrived in Colchis (located on the eastern shore of the Black Sea) to fetch the golden fleece, Medea immediately fell passionately in love with him. This was the work of the goddesses Hera, Athena, and Aphrodite. Hera and Athena protected and supported the Argonauts and asked Aphrodite to ensure that Medea would fall for this most attractive foreigner. Aphrodite found it hard to persuade her recalcitrant young son, Eros, but after she had promised him a lovely ball, he agreed to shoot Medea with a love-arrow.

Æetes allowed Jason to take the golden fleece with him, but only on condition that he would perform some impossible and dangerous tasks (*see* **The Argonauts**). Medea knew that her father's sole aim was to destroy Jason and immediately considered helping him, because she could not bear the thought of his death. She was in two minds, however. Should she betray her father and homeland on behalf of an unknown guest? Should she sacrifice everything for her love?

Deep in the forest, at the sanctuary of Hecate, goddess of witchcraft, Jason and

Medea confessed their love to each other. Jason begged Medea for help and said he wanted to marry her. In tears, Medea promised to guarantee the success of Jason's mission and after Jason had sworn by Hecate and the sun god Helios, Medea's grandfather, that he would take her to Greece as his wife, she gave him a magical herb. Thanks to this herb, Jason became invulnerable to the flaming breath of the bulls with bronze hooves and steel noses with which Æetes had ordered him to plow a field. Jason then sowed dragon's teeth in the furrows which sprouted into heavily armed men, causing even Medea to reel in fright. She uttered a spell, after which Jason threw a stone among the warriors, causing them to fight among themselves.

The ever-wakeful dragon that guarded the tree on which hung the golden fleece was also overcome thanks to Medea's magical arts. She gave Jason an "herb full of slumber-inducing juice," that he had to sprinkle over the beast, and taught him the spell "that induces sweet sleep and even stills the movement of rivers and the sea" (Ovid, *Metamorphoses*, VII,

lines 153-154). The dragon fell into a deep slumber and it was then a simple matter to remove the golden fleece from the tree.

That Medea's character had a dark side is evident from her treatment of her younger brother, Apsyrtus, who accompanied her and Jason on board the *Argo*. To shake off her father, who was in pursuit, she killed her brother and cut him into pieces. The parts of the body were thrown overboard by her, so that Æetes was obliged to retrieve them.

According to another version, Apsyrtus was no longer a child and he set out in pursuit of the Argo. In this variant, Jason was compelled to put Medea overboard in order to be able to put enough distance between himself and his pursuers, but after the furious woman had reminded him of the promises he had made to her and her part in his successes, Jason relented. Together, they thought up a ruse. Apsyrtus was sent wonderful gifts and was invited to talk with Medea in a temple dedicated to the goddess Artemis. While Medea was negotiating with him, Jason suddenly sprung out from his hiding-place and murdered him.

Later, Medea's aunt Circe absolved Jason and Medea of their unspeakable crime but, because of the gruesome nature of their deed, she foresaw a bleak future for both of them. She strongly condemned their behavior and earnestly asked them not to remain in her house any longer.

On Crete, Medea eliminated the bronze man Talos, the guardian of the island, on behalf of the Argonauts when she cast a spell on him so that he struck his ankle on a rock. The bronze man (once given to Europa or Minos by the gods) was then damaged so badly that the divine blood flowed from him and he fell powerless to the ground.

Back in Iolcus, at Jason's request, Medea subjected his aged father, Æson, to a magical rejuvenating treatment. For this, she traveled on a chariot pulled by a winged dragon—a gift from her grandfather Helios—to the mountains in the north and to certain lakes and rivers, where she gathered special herbs and grasses. After nine days, she arranged a site at which to make her magic, sacrificed two sheep, laid Æson on a bed of grass, and brewed a potion containing many mysterious ingredients in her copper cauldron. When a fresh olive suddenly sprouted on the old branch she was using to stir the brew, she knew her mixture was good. Medea cut Æson's artery, let the blood drain out and poured her potion in. Immediately, Æson changed into a vigorous young man.

When the daughters of Jason's malicious

After she had killed Creon, Glauce, and her own children, Medea fled from Corinth to Athens in her chariot pulled by flying dragons. Pen-and-ink drawing by Peter Paul Rubens, 17th century.

uncle Pelias, who refused to relinquish the throne to the rightful heir, Jason, heard this, they wanted to subject their father to the same treatment. Medea was delighted to show them how it was done. She cut an old ram into pieces and cooked the meat and bones in her cauldron, along with ample magical herbs. The animal sprang from the cauldron as a frisky lamb. Under Medea's supervision, Pelias' daughters then killed their father with the sword and cooked him—unfortunately for them and him Medea had neglected to add the necessary herbs.

Because of this crime, Jason and Medea had to flee to Corinth, where they enjoyed the hospitality of King Creon. They spent a number of happy years there and had two sons. Then Jason conceived of a plan to cast aside Medea, to whom his owed his prosperity, in order to marry Creon's daughter, Glauce. Medea flew into a violent rage. She had her sons bring Glauce an enchanted bridal gown, that burned the future bride and her father to death. Then she killed her own children and fled to Athens in her chariot pulled by a flying dragon, where she found protection with king Ægeus. Ægeus was sterile—or rather, he thought he was—but when he married Medea, she gave him a son, Medus.

After a time, however, the hero Theseus, Ægeus' son by Æthra, daughter of King Pittheus of Trœzen, appeared in Athens. He had been raised in Trœzen, without Ægeus' knowledge. Medea immediately realized the identity of the unknown guest, but with Medus' succession in mind, she did not enlighten Ægeus. According to some, she persuaded Ægeus to send Theseus after the dangerous Cretan bull that terrorized the Marathon district after being released by Heracles (*see* **Heracles**). Theseus performed this task, after which Medea reverted to her proven methods, by lacing his wine with a deadly poison. But at the very moment when Theseus went to drink from the cup, Ægeus recognized the insignia on Theseus' sword, that he had left under a rock in Trœzen long ago, and knocked the cup out of his hand (*see* **Ægeus** *and* **Theseus**).

Following these events, Medea fled Athens, escaping Theseus by wrapping herself up in a magical cloud. Together with Medus she returned to Colchis, the land of her birth, where, her father Æetes had been cast from the throne by his brother, Perses. Perses imprisoned Medus, who had traveled on ahead, in spite of his claim to be the son of the Corinthian King Creon. The land was suffering from a terrible drought and Medea, who was posing as a priestess of Artemis, suggested ending it by holding a massive ritual, at which Medus would be killed. During this ritual, she provided Medus with a sword, with which he killed Perses. She may also have been personally involved in ending Perses' life. Medus now became king of Colchis and conquered Media, which was named for him.

Little is known of Medea's end. According to some, she was immortal and lived on forever in the Elysian Fields, the heavenly part of the underworld, as wife of the great hero Achilles.

Medea is one of the most fascinating female figures in Greek mythology. She is often portrayed as a witch, a sorceress with devilish leanings, but different authors have given her character more depth. Ovid and Apollonius of Rhodes wrote beautiful descriptions of her as a young girl in love, torn between feelings of loyalty to her family and country, and her deep longing for Jason. In his tragedy, *Medea,* the great Athenian playwright, Euripides (ca. 480–406 BCE), movingly depicted her as a woman thrown completely off balance by the infidelity of her hypocritical husband, Jason, in the grip of jealousy and bitterness and finally killing her sons in a fit of total despair (*see* **The Argonauts** *and* **Jason**).

Medusa, *see* The Gorgons

Menelaus

Menelaus was the second son of the Mycenæan King Atreus and his wife Ærope whose eldest son was Agamemnon. Agamemnon eventually succeeded Atreus as ruler of the important city of Mycenæ. Menelaus, in his turn, acceded to the throne of this city, thanks to his marriage to Helen, the "faithless" daughter of King Tyndareos of Sparta (*see* **Helen**).

Helen was considered the most beautiful woman in the world and Menelaus was therefore not the only one who wanted her. When Menelaus was finally chosen to marry her, the other Greek nobles who had been her suitors were persuaded by Odysseus to swear an oath that they would always help Menelaus whenever he encountered difficulties because of his wife.

At first, Menelaus and Helen lived in harmony. They had one daughter, Hermione. But after they had been married for ten years, the Trojan Prince Paris visited Sparta. Aphrodite, the goddess of love, had promised him Helen, because he had awarded her the prize in a divine beauty contest (*see* **Aphrodite**, **Helen**, *and* **Paris**). Partly due to the efforts of the goddess of love, Helen quickly fell for the charming guest, who had

Menelaus fought valiantly on the battlefield, but he was not one of the greatest heroes who fought on the Greek side. Portrait of a young warrior on an Athenian dish, 5th century BCE.

Sparta, the city of which Menelaus became king, was known throughout Antiquity for its warlike traditions. Boys received a "spartan" upbringing, which was completely geared toward making them into excellent soldiers. Terra-cotta statuette of a spartan boy on horseback, 4th century BCE

been royally received by her husband. When Menelaus went to Crete for his grandfather's funeral, Paris grabbed his chance. With Menelaus out of the way, Paris grabbed Helen and part of the contents of his host's treasure chest, and sailed back home to Troy.

Menelaus followed the couple to Troy with the eloquent Odysseus, in an attempt to retrieve his wife and possessions, but the Trojans refused to comply with his request. There was nothing else for it, Helen had to be brought back by force. The Greek nobles were reminded of their oath and Menelaus' rich and influential brother, Agamemnon, assembled a massive army that besieged Troy for ten long years, eventually triumphing and destroying the city.

Menelaus did not play a particularly conspicuous role in the battle for Troy. Although he was a brave warrior, he was overshadowed by the great heroes, such as Achilles, Ajax, Diomedes, and Odysseus. Command was in the hands of the rather domineering Agamemnon. The poet Homer describes how, in the last year of the Trojan War, Menelaus and Paris fought a duel, and this should have definitively ended the war. Menelaus appeared to be winning over the vain "womanizing" Paris, but when he threatened to kill his opponent, Aphrodite intervened. She wrapped Paris in a cloud and brought him to

his bedchamber, then called upon Helen to look after him. Helen's love for Paris had by then considerably cooled down.

After Troy had fallen, thanks to Odysseus' trick with the wooden horse, Menelaus' wife was restored to him. Their return journey to Sparta was difficult, because after the destruction of Troy, Menelaus had not offered the gods what they considered to be sufficient sacrifice for their assistance.

He finally arrived home after eight years and many detours, to Cyprus and Libya, among other places. For a while, Menelaus was forced to remain on the islet of Pharos, just off the coast of Egypt. He surprised the old sea-god and seer, Proteus, on the advice of his daughter. After a struggle, during which the god spectacularly changed his shape many times, he explained to Menelaus why the journey home had been so difficult, and advised him to make the required sacrifices in Egypt. Proteus also told Menelaus that after his death he would be taken to Elysium, the heavenly part of the underworld, and told him also of the fate of other Greek heroes of the Trojan War. The report that his brother, Agamemnon, had been murdered soon after arriving home strongly affected Menelaus.

Menelaus turned back to Greece and visited Mycenæ, the city that had been ruled by his murdered brother, shortly after Agamemnon's son, Orestes, had taken his revenge on his father's murderers.

A gathering of Mycenæans condemned Orestes to death for the murder of his mother, Clytemnestra, and Orestes took Helen and Hermione hostage when he failed to receive the support he expected from Menelaus. Thanks to divine intervention, the situation

Pasquino, one of the famous 'speaking statues" which have been decorating Roman street since ancient times. "Pasquino" in fact represents Menelaus, who through the agency of the Trojan hero Hector, tried to protect Patroclus, who was killed in battle.

During his difficult journey home from Troy, Menelaus landed in Egypt. Model of an ancient Egyptian river-craft.

became no worse. Helen and Hermione were released and Orestes was sentenced to banishment instead of death (*see* **Orestes**).

Homer describes how Odysseus' son Telemachus came to obtain information about the fate of his missing father. He was received by an apparently happy and harmoniously reunited couple, who were just celebrating the double wedding of Hermione to Achilles' son, Neoptolemus, and of Megapenthes—a son of Menelaus by a slave-girl—to a daughter of a prominent Spartan. Telemachus was warmly received and there was much reminiscing. Helen told them how she had cared for and assisted Odysseus when he had entered Troy on a secret mission, because she had so longed to be back with Menelaus and her daughter! The reader catches a glimpse of the lingering rancor behind the shining façade of the repaired marriage, however, when Menelaus tells how, shortly afterward, the *femme fatale* Helen playfully and ingeniously tried to lure the Greek heroes of the wooden horse—including Odysseus and Menelaus—from their hiding place.

The question remains as to whether it was truly a blessing for Menelaus to remain forever, after his death, in Elysium with his immortal wife at his side, as Proteus had predicted.

Mercury, see Hermes

Midas

Midas, the son of Gordius and Cybele, was a Phrygian King. In all the known myths about him, he does not appear to be a particularly intelligent person.

After the death of the singer Orpheus, Dionysus, the god of wine, left Thrace. His old guardian, Silenus, who was drunk as usual, "wobbling from wine and years" (Ovid) strayed from the god's retinue and was brought to Midas by Phrygian farmers. Midas, himself initiated into the cult of Dionysus, immediately recognized the old man and prepared a ten-course banquet in his honor. Then he brought Silenus back to Dionysus. Dionysus was delighted to have his old teacher back and wished to reward Midas handsomely. The king was allowed to make a wish. Midas wished that everything he touched would turn to gold. The wish was granted and at first Midas was thrilled with his new powers. In no time at all, gleaming golden objects surrounded him. However, when he sat down at the table, the fun went away, because as soon as he took a bite or tried to chew, the food immediately hardened into the yellow metal. Even wine, Dionysus' other gift, changed into liquid gold in Midas' mouth.

Realizing that he was doomed to die of hunger and thirst, Midas begged the god to deliver him of his "golden hands." Dionysus heard his pleas and charged him to wash

Phrygian king Midas was severely punished for his bad taste in music, by being given donkey's ears.

When Silenus, dead drunk in Phrygia, lost sight of his pupil Dionysus, King Midas received him with pleasure at his court. Small earthenware vase in the shape of Silenus, southern Italy, 4th century BCE.

Midas was a disciple of the god Pan who appreciated the god's flute playing more than the lyre-playing of the rival musician, the god Apollo. Here a satyr plays the double-reed flute. Painting on a vase fragment, Athens, 5th century BCE.

King Minos received a white bull from Poseidon, which he was to sacrifice to the god. Minos thought the animal so beautiful that he kept it. The consequences were horrific.

himself clean in the River Pactolus. In fact, gold has since been found in this river.

Midas no longer had any need for unlimited riches, but that did not stop him from being stupid. He often spent time outdoors and became a dedicated follower of the nature god, Pan. Pan had a high opinion of his own flute-playing and ventured a musical contest with the great god Apollo, just like the unlucky satyr, Marsyas (*see* **Marsyas**). Tmolus, the mountain god, would judge their performances. Midas, who happened to be present, showed himself to be moved by the exotic melodies Pan elicited from his flute. Then Apollo played a superb sample of lyre music. and he played so beautifully that Tmolus immediately awarded him the prize. Everyone agreed heartily, except for Midas, who was not inclined to be shy when giving his opinion. Apollo was so annoyed at his stupidity and his lack of acknowledgement of his musical talent that he turned Midas' ears into donkey's ears.

Midas, who was human in every other way, was extremely embarrassed about this and, after the incident, he always wore a pointed Phrygian cap to hide his deformity. Only his barber knew of it, and he was sworn to secrecy. This vow of silence began to weigh upon him so heavily that he dug a hole in the ground and secretly whispered into it that Midas had donkey's ears. After giving vent to what was on his mind, he closed the hole and went home, liberated. But reeds sprouted at the spot and whenever the wind blew through the reeds, they whispered the secret, so that

everyone who heard it learned that King Midas had donkey's ears.

Minerva *see* Athena

Minos

Minos was born on Crete as a result of a liaison between the supreme god, Zeus, and the Phœnician princess, Europa, who had been abducted by Zeus in the form of a bull (*see*

The supposed throne room of the palace of Cnossos on Crete, second millenium BCE. It is possible that either King Minos, or the monarch who served as a model for him, addressed his subjects here.

The walls of the "throne room" in the palace of Cnossos are decorated with paintings of griffins or gryphons.

Europe). Minos' brothers, Rhadamanthys and Sarpedon, were born of this extraordinary union.

The three brothers were adopted by the Cretan king Asterius, Europa's earthly husband. After Asterius' death, first Minos, then Rhadamanthys, and Sarpedon fought over who should inherit the throne, but Minos became king after clear confirmation of his claim that his prayers had been heard by the gods. The great sea-god, Poseidon, sent a shining white bull that rose up out of the sea, at Minos' request. It was intended that Minos would sacrifice this animal to Poseidon on the altar set up for this purpose, but Minos liked the bull so much that he let it live.

Poseidon never forgave Minos for this selfish act. After Minos married Pasiphæ, daughter of Helios, the sun-god, Poseidon ensured that she fell madly in love with the bull. Dædalus, the Athenian architect, inventor and wizard in the Cretan service, built a

Relief of a bull in the palace of Cnossos, Crete. The diverse decorations with bull motifs in Cnossos match the myths about King Minos, in which the white bull of Poseidon and the half-human, half-bull creature, the Minotaur, played an important role.

hollow, artificial cow. After Pasiphæ had hidden herself inside it, the bull mated with her. Pasiphæ, who had borne Minos many "normal" children, including Andregeos and Ariadne, bore a monster after her unnatural congress with the bull. It was called the Minotaur ("bull of Minos"). The Minotaur looked like a man with a bull's head and it had an irrational, bloodthirsty character. Minos was terribly ashamed of the existence of such a freakish creature and decided that it would have to lead an invisible, shadowy life. For this purpose, he ordered Dædalus to build a giant underground complex, full of dead ends, and with only one entrance. The maze was called the Labyrinth. The Minotaur was locked in this complex.

Meanwhile, Minos had become one of the most powerful monarchs in the Greek world. He ruled over ninety Cretan cities, including Athens, as well as cities outside Crete. He also declared war on Athens after his son Andregeos had died (in some versions he became the victim of the dangerous bull released by Heracles, who terrorized the area of Marathon (*see* **Heracles**)). Minos recruited many allies and fought the monarchs who would not support him. He besieged the city of Megara, located between Corinth and Athens, that was ruled by King Nisus. Nisus'

King Minos became one of the most powerful monarchs in the Greek world of his time. Wooden throne from the palace of Cnossos.

daughter, Scylla, fell in love with Minos and swooning, watched him from a tower beside the royal palace. She decided to hand over the city to him by one night cutting off a lock of her father's unusual purple hair– the symbol of his power—and offering it to Minos. Outraged at her treachery, Minos rejected the lock of hair and Scylla's love. After Minos had conquered Megara and imposed generous conditions of peace on the city, he was cursed by the offended Scylla. As she was no longer welcome in her own city, she demanded that Minos grant her hospitality on Crete. When the Cretans sailed away, she jumped into the sea, seized the bow of Minos' ship, and changed into a sea-bird.

Minos could not bring Athens down by military means, but after sending prayers to his father Zeus, Attica was ravaged by earthquakes, famines, and epidemics. This caused the Athenians to ultimately admit defeat. On the advice of the Oracle of Delphi, the Athenian king, Ægus, accepted Minos' terms for peace, one of which was that once every nine years, seven Athenian boys and seven Athenian girls had to be sacrificed to the Minotaur in the Labyrinth.

The Minotaur was eventually destroyed by the Athenian hero, Theseus, who was assisted in his difficult task by Minos' daughter Ariadne (*see* **Ariadne**, **Dædalus**, **The Minotaur** *and* **Theseus**). Ariadne and Theseus escaped, but Dædalus, who had given Ariadne advice, along with his son Icarus, was imprisoned in his own Labyrinth by the furious Minos The wizard and inventor was able to escape from Crete on wings he made himself, but this action was to prove fatal to his son, Icarus. Dœdalus found refuge on Sicily, where King Cocalus granted him hospitality.

Minos searched for his former protégé, but initially could not find him. He finally located him thanks to an ingenious trick. As Minos had expected, Dædalus was the only person who could run a thread through a complex shell (a convoluted conch shell or Triton's horn). Cocalus did not want to hand over his talented inventor-guest to the Cretan King. Soon after, Minos laid siege to Cocalus' city of Camicus, forcing Cocalus to to concede. He invited Minos to a festive banquet to ratify the peace treaty, but before the meal, Minos was offered a bath, in which he would be pampered by Cocalus' daughters. Dædalus had attached special pipes to the bath, however, through which he allowed boiling water to flow and Minos was scalded to death.

The dead Minos, along with his brother, Rhadamanthys and King Æacus of Ægina, were named judges of the souls of the dead in the underworld (*see* **Hades**).

Some of the mythical tales of Minos are probably based on the actual situation that prevailed at the beginning of Greek civilization (ca. 2000 through 1450 BCE), when Crete was the dominant power in the region. Cretan civilization of this period was at a high level and was characterized by impressive buildings. This is the civilization known as the "Minoan" civilization, for King Minos. The famous palace complex of Cnossos on Crete, excavated from about 1900, originates from the Minoan age and the complexity of the series of rooms may be the inspiration for the myth of the Labyrinth.

The Minotaur

The Minotaur was a monstrous man with a bull's head, the result of a union between the Cretan Queen, Pasiphæ, and a fabulous white bull which had been presented to Pasiphæ's husband, Minos, by the sea-god Poseidon. The intention was to sacrifice the bull on an altar to Poseidon, but King Minos decided to keep the bull, with disastrous consequences. Minos was so ashamed of the existence of the Minotaur (the name means "bull of Minos")

The monstrous Minotaur was the result of a sexual relationship between the white bull of Poseidon and the Cretan Queen Pasiphæ. Minos locked him in the Labyrinth that had been designed by Dædalus.

The Minotaur raises his glass in the company of an attractive young woman. According to the myth, the creature spent his days in the loneliness of the desolate Labyrinth, but Pablo Picasso, who created this image, clearly gave him a more pleasant existence. Etching on paper, 1933.

conception seems to be linked to the bull cult that was said to have existed on Crete between 2000 and 1450 BCE. In excavations in the palace complex of Cnossos, many images have been found of male and female dancers performing acrobatic feats on the back of a bull. There may also have been rituals performed on Crete that involved a form of bullfight (*see* **Ariadne, Dædalus, Europa, Minos, Pasiphæ** *and* **Theseus**).

The three Moiræ or Fates were the personification of destiny. The three of them worked on the threads of human lives. Clotho spun them, Lachesis measured them, and Atropos cut them.

that he had him locked up in a special underground maze, known as the Labyrinth, constructed by the Athenian architect and inventor, Dædalus. There, the bloodthirsty creature was given seven Athenian boys and seven Athenian girls to devour once every nine years. The Athenian hero, Theseus, assisted by Minos' daughter Ariadne, put an end to this practice. Theseus ventured into the Labyrinth, killed the Minotaur, and found his way out of the maze, thanks to the thread that Ariadne had given him which she had tied to the only entrance into the Labyrinth

The story of the Minotaur and its

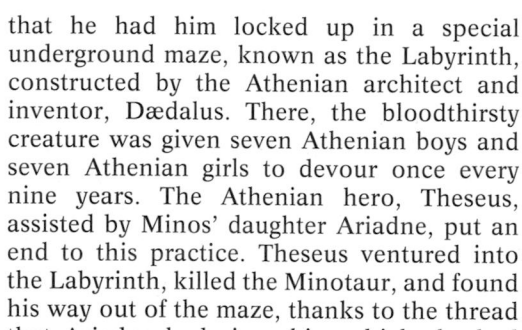

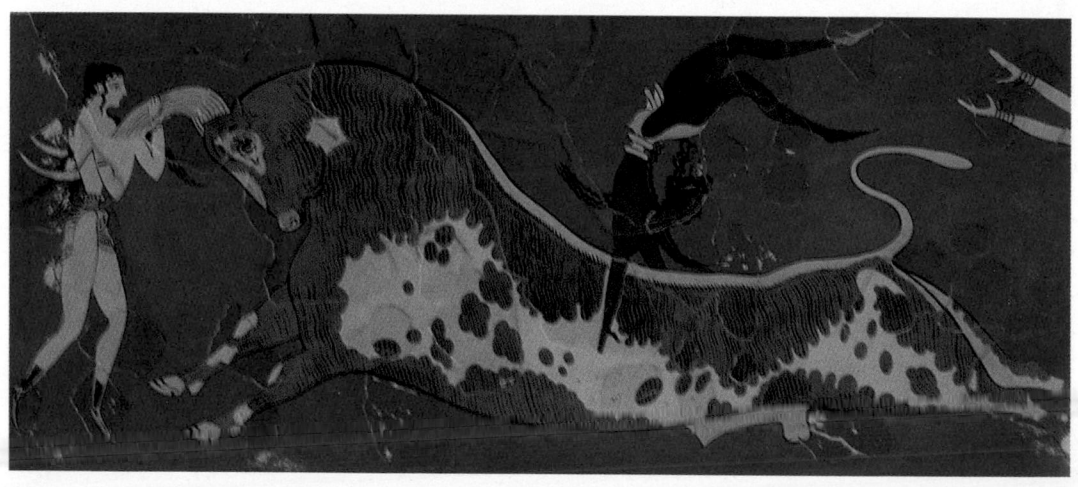

Depiction of the so-called "bull-jumping" on Crete, a ritual from the bull cult that probably existed on the island. Reconstruction from a fresco from Cnossos, second millenium BCE.

Moiræ, The (Roman=Fates)

The Moiræ or Three Fates determined the destiny of mortals. These three goddesses of destiny were considered to be the daughters of the supreme god Zeus and the goddess Themis, the personification of good and orderly. The names of the three Moiræ, who were portrayed as three forbidding old spinsters, were Clotho (the Spinner), Lachesis (the Apportioner), and Atropos (the Inevitable). Clotho spun the web of life of humans, Lachesis decided how long each human was to live, and Atropos cut the thread of life when someone's time had come. According to another version, there was only one goddess of fate, who was a daughter of Nyx, the goddess of night.

Just how power was divided between Zeus, the almighty ruler of the universe, and the Moiræ, the representatives of destiny, was not always clear. The general impression was that Zeus, despite his omnipotence, could not reverse the decisions of fate. Homer describes how Zeus was unable to tolerate the thought that his beloved son, Sarpedon, had to be restrained by fate, manifested in the

Image of a drunken old woman. The Moiræ, irate old spinsters, would not permit themselves to become drunk. It was hard to trick them, even through scheming and deception. The god Apollo managed it, thus preventing the death of his friend Admetus. Earthenware Roman statuette from north Africa, 4th century BCE.

form of the Greek hero, Patroclus. He considered intervening, but his wife Hera pointed out to him that the other gods would not like it. Zeus realized then that he had to reconcile himself to Sarpedon being killed in battle.

Elsewhere in the *Iliad*, however, there are examples of how Zeus himself determined the fate of humans: "(...) then the father of the gods held the golden scales up high and in each scale placed the fate of grievous death, the fate of the horse-taming Trojans, and that of the bronze-armored Greeks. He grasped the scale in the center and lifted it. The fateful day of the Greeks dropped downward."

The god Apollo once reversed a decision of the Moiræ by cleverly tricking them, thus preventing the death of his friend, Admetus. The Moiræ were extremely unhappy about this, and demanded that someone else be sacrificed in Admetus' place. Only Admetus' wife, Alcestis, was prepared to do so (*see* **Alcestis**).

The Moiræ played an important role in the story of the hero, Meleager (*see* **Atalanta**). Shortly after his birth, they threw a branch into the hearth of the delivery room after which his mother, Althæa, heard them say: "You, newborn child, receive from us the same lifespan as this piece of wood." (Ovid, *Metamorphoses* VIII, 454-455). Althæa immediately removed the piece of wood from the hearth, extinguished it, and preserved it carefully. Much later, when Meleager had grown up and killed both of his mother's brothers, Althæa threw the piece of wood into the fire, after having a serious fight with her son, and Meleager did indeed die straight away. In this case, the Moiræ had actually delegated their authority to Althæa.

The Muses

The muses were the daughters of the supreme god, Zeus, and the Titan, Mnemosyne ("memory"). They were the patronesses of the arts and later also of the sciences. The word "music" is named for them.

Originally there was just one muse, who provided poets and singers with inspiration, and who therefore was invoked by them whenever they began their work. Both of Homer's epic poems, the *Iliad* and the *Odyssey*, begin with an invocation to the Muses. The poet, Hesiod, who lived soon after Homer, mentioned nine Muses who lived on the sacred Mount Helicon and who had brought him "delightful singing." He

described the Muses as "charming girls" who danced gracefully and sang with beautiful voices. He believed they were born on Mount Olympus or Mount Pieria, and that they continued to live on these mountains. The Muses and Apollo had given music to humanity so that mortals could forget their sorrows and cares. According to Hesiod, the names of the Muses were Clio, Euterpe, Thalia, Melpomene, Terpsichore, Erato, Polyhymnia, Urania, and Calliope.

Calliope ("with the lovely voice") was the most prominent of the Muses, being the Muse

Homer, the blind poet of the Iliad *and the* Odyssey, *with the Muse he invoked at the start of both these heroic poems. Lower part of the Goethe monument in the Villa Borghese park, Rome.*

of narrative poetry. Clio ("the proclaimed one") was the Muse of stories, Euterpe ("the rejoicer") was the Muse of flute-playing, Thalia ("the blossoming one") was the Muse of farce and comedy, Melpomene ("the singing one") was the Muse of tragedy, Terpsichore ("lover of dance") was the Muse of lyric poetry and song, Erato ("the amiable one") was the Muse of love poetry, Polyhymnia ("with many songs") was the Muse of serious music and hymns, and Urania ("the heavenly one") was the Muse of astronomy. The Muses sang at the banquets of the gods on Mount Olympus, accompanied by the lyre-playing of their mentor, the god Apollo.

In spite of all the gifts bestowed on humanity by the Muses, there were songs that harbored malicious intentions. The brutal Thracian monarch, Pyreneus, once invited the Muses to his home to shelter from a storm, and then tried to assault them. Luckily the Muses had wings which they could buckle on and with which they could easily escape. Pyreneus tried to follow them, but fell to his death from the roof of his own palace.

Just like their leader Apollo, the Muses sometimes let themselves be persuaded to participate in musical contests with mortals. The nine daughters of King Pieros, the Pierides, claimed to be better singers than the Muses and proposed to hold a competition with the goddesses, with a jury of nymphs. The nymphs awarded the prize to the Muses,

Naturally the Muses, for whom music is named, were themselves accomplished musicians. This Muse is playing the kithara, the ancient Greek citern. Red-figured painting on Athenian kylix, 5th century BCE.

but the Pierides turned out to be poor losers. They abused the Muses and wanted to fight them, but were transformed into screaming, quarrelsome magpies. The Thracian singer ,Thamyris, who bragged that he was a better singer than the Muses, was punished by them with blindness and memory loss (*see* **Apollo**).

Naiads, *see* Nymphs

Narcissus

Narcissus was a son of the Boeotian river-god Cephissus and Liriope, the water-nymph. The famous seer Tiresias predicted that he would live for a long time "as long as he did not know himself." Narcissus grew up and at the age of sixteen, he was a beautiful boy who turned the heads of both men and women. He was, however, so arrogant that he was completely indifferent to other people's charms. Then the talkative nymph, Echo, who constantly imitated everyone but could not be the first to speak, fell passionately in love with him. With her noteworthy, parrot-like talent, Echo tended to keep talking whenever Zeus was making love to other nymphs. Narcissus very curtly rejected poor Echo, after which the girl languished completely. Her body faded away, her bones turned to stone, and only her voice, the echo, remained. Narcissus rejected many others after Echo.

Handsome Narcissus is fascinated by his own reflection in the surface of the water. Oil painting by Peter Paul Rubens, 17th century.

One of his rejected suitors wished the boy would himself one day experience unrequited love. This wish was granted. One warm summer's day, when Narcissus was resting from the hunt by a lake with a glassy, smooth surface, he became fascinated by his own reflection in the water. He fell passionately in love with this beautiful reflection which, of course, constantly evaded him. Narcissus stayed close to the water. He was no longer capable of eating or sleeping and suffered greatly because his beloved reflection immediately reacted to his grin and answered his approaches, but then evaporated.

Obsessed by his love for himself, Narcissus pined away, so that even the rejected Echo became sad and tried to imitate his cries of despair. Finally, Narcissus died of a broken heart. Even in the kingdom of the dead, he remained under the spell of his own reflection, which he could admire in the black waters of the Styx, the river of the underworld. Today he lives on in the term "narcissism,"which denotes morbid self-love.

Nemesis

The goddess, Nemesis, was a daughter of Nyx, the goddess of night. She was the goddess of revenge, the personification of

Nemesis, the goddess of vengeful justice, turned on those humans who were not grateful enough to the gods for the prosperity they enjoyed. Bronze statuette from Egypt, Roman period.

Griffin or gryphon, a mythical creature that looked like a winged lion with a predatory bird's head, that was dedicated to Nemesis. Earthenware altar, Tarente, 4th century BCE.

Neoptolemus, son of the great hero Achilles, fought in the very last phase of the Trojan war on the Greek side. He was one of the heroes who hid in the hollow rump of the wooden horse .

vengeful judgment and resentment. The griffin, the mythical creature that resembled a winged lion with an eagle's head, was associated with her. It was believed that Nemesis particularly turned against those who enjoyed easy lives without showing the proper gratitude to the gods, or who refused to share their wealth with others.

In one story, the supreme god, Zeus, is said to have been in love with Nemesis. She tried to escape from him by taking on various guises, but when she transformed herself into a goose, Zeus changed into a swan and made love to her. Nemesis became pregnant and laid an egg that was incubated by Leda. From this egg, the lovely Helen subsequently emerged. According to others, it was actually Leda herself who was loved by Zeus in the form of a swan and laid one or more eggs, from which Helen and possible also the Dioscuri, Castor and Polydeuces, were born (*see* **The Dioscuri**, **Helen** *and* **Leda**).

Neoptolemus

Neoptolemus, who because of his red hair was also called Pyrrhus ("fiery head"), was the son of the great Greek hero, Achilles, and Deidania. Achilles begat Neoptolemus when he himself was very young, after he was brought to the palace of King Lycomedes, where he spent his days dressed as a girl. Achilles' mother, Thetis, was behind this, because she wished to prevent Achilles from

fighting in the Trojan war, where he was doomed to fall in battle (*see* **Achilles**). After Achilles had left for Troy,Neoptolemus remained at Lycomedes' court, thanks to a ruse of Odysseus. Much later, when Achilles had already fallen, Odysseus returned to fetch Neoptolemus. It had become clear from a prophecy that his presence on the battlefield was necessary, and the Greeks were eager for victory.

In spite of the deeds he committed, Neoptolemus was one of the few Greek heroes who was not punished by the gods and could return home safely. He settled in Phtia in Thessaly, the kingdom of his grandfather, Peleus. As spoils of war, he had taken the Trojan seer, Helenus, and Andromache, widow of the great Trojan hero, Hector (*see* **Andromache** *and* **Hector**). Neoptolemus slept with Andromache who conceived a son (three sons in some stories), but his official wife, Hermione, daughter of Menelaus and Helen, produced no offspring. Hermione even tried to kill Andromache out of jealousy but was unsuccessful. In this, Hermione had the support of her father, Menelaus, but Peleus frustrated their plans.

There are many versions of how Neoptolemus met his end. According to some, he was the victim of a conspiracy organized by Orestes at Delphi, where he had gone to consult with the Oracle (Hermione is said to have been promised to Orestes long before

Neoptolemus was faced with the difficult task of killing the courageous Trojan princess, Polyxena, on his father Achilles' grave. Achilles' shade had demanded Polyxena as a sort of posthumous spoil of war. Man with sword, fragment from a vase painting, Tarente, 4th century B.C.

Neoptolemus was faced with the difficult task of killing the courageous Trojan princess, Polyxena, on his father Achilles' grave. Achilles' shade had demanded Polyxena as a sort of posthumous spoil of war. Man with sword, fragment from a vase painting, Tarente, 4th century B.C.

her father decided to marry her off to Neoptolemus for political reasons). Neoptolemus was buried in Delphi.

Neptune, *see* Poseidon

Nereids, *see* Nymphs

Nereus, *see* Nymphs

Nestor

Nestor, the son of Neleus, was the wise King of Pylos, in southwestern Greece. He was the son of Neleus and father of Antilochus. In *The Iliad*, Nestor went with the Greeks to the Trojan War, and although he had lived three generations he was still a vigorous warrior and a respected adviser. In *The Odyssey*, because of his piety and prudence, the gods allowed him to return unharmed to Pylos after the war.

Nestor was by far the oldest of the monarchs to participate in the Trojan war. Because of his age and life experience, he was greatly respected by his fellow warriors. As a young man, Nestor had acquitted himself formidably in various conflicts. He was involved in the fierce battle of the Lapiths against the Centaurs and took part in the hunt for the monstrous Calydonian wild boar. At one point, he was in danger of being gored by the boar, and only just saved himself by climbing a tree (*see* **Atalanta**).

During the Trojan war, he was seen as a wise, diplomatic and articulate man, who nonetheless enjoyed digressions into his own greatest deeds of the past. When during the funeral ceremony of his close friend Patroclus, who had fallen in battle, Achilles handed him a sort of consolation prize, he delivered a long story about his own sport performances as a young man ("when none could match me"), which was patiently heard by Achilles and the others.

Nestor was one of the few Greek monarchs who had no problems returning home after the fall of Troy. He predicted that the gods would take revenge for the atrocities inflicted on Troy by the Greeks and sailed away just in time. Ten years later, when Odysseus" son Telemachus searched him out in Pylos in order to obtain information about his father, Nestor, now very old, still enjoyed outstanding physical and mental health. He enjoyed "a happy old age in his palace, surrounded by sons as excellent in understanding as in the throwing of the spear" (Homer, *Odyssey*, IV, lines 209-211).

Nestor was married to Eurydice (not the same Eurydice as the lover of the great singer, Orpheus). They had seven sons and two daughters. One of their sons, Antilochus, also

Nestor, the oldest Greek participant in the Trojan war, was involved in many legendary conflicts during his long life. His exploits included fighting on the side of the Lapiths against the Centaurs. Mounted rider surrounded by Centaurs, earthenware statuettes from Boeotia, 5th century BCE.

fought in the Trojan War and died when he sacrificed himself for his father.

Nike (Roman=*Victoria*)

Nike was the goddess of victory. In essence, she was little more than a personification of this concept. She was a daughter of the Titans, Pallas and Styx, but in the "war of the Titans" between the Titans and the gods of Olympus, she chose the side of the gods which is why they won.

Nike is depicted as a young winged woman. ("First of all, Nike flies with golden

Nike, the winged goddess of victory, stands by an altar holding a wreath. Painting on Athenian kylix, 6th–5th century BCE.

The goddess of victory on a coin of one of the greatest conquerors of all time, the Macedonian Alexander the Great. Gold coin (stater) from Amphipolis, 4th century BCE.

wings..." Aristophanes *The Birds*, 574). She was frequently portrayed on monuments erected in honor of great victories and was often to be seen on the palm of Zeus or Athena's hand in images of them, to symbolize the fact that these gods had granted victory to the worshippers of these images.

Nike was portrayed with various objects, sometimes carrying a *kithara* (lyre) and a *phiale* (cup), holding a *thymiaterion* (incense burner) and a flower, carrying a sash, or pouring pouring a libation from an *oinichoe* (pitcher) over an altar.

Nymphs

Nymphs were a type of nature goddess, divine creatures in the form of charming young women who lived in the countryside and were often connected with particular places or objects in nature, such as rivers, wells, rocks, mountains, forests, and trees. Most nymphs were benevolent and could grant fertility and prosperity to humans, but they had to be treated with caution. Nymphs could seduce mortals and drive them insane or drag them into wells or rivers, so they would drown. Many nymphs were daughters of the supreme god, Zeus. Gods such as Pan, Dionysus, and Artemis often had nymphs in their retinues.

There were many main groups of nymphs. The dryads, who were associated with trees, were tree-nymphs. The hamadryads, members of a sub-species, lived in specific trees

Nymphs from the retinue of Artemis, goddess of the hunt and untamed nature. Artemis required that her female companions were virginal, just like her. Detail of an oil painting after Titian, 17th century.

One of the Naiads or river-nymphs on the Fontana della Naiadi on the Piazza della Repubblica in Rome. The reptile on which Naiad has settled herself symbolizes the rivers that flow beneath the earth's surface.

Portrait of the nymph, Larissa, on a coin. Silver coin, (drachma) from Larissa in Thessaly, 5th-4th century BCE.

Naiad on the Fontana delle Naiadi in Rome, with a sea-god in the background. When the four naked bronze nymphs created by sculptor Mario Rutelli were unveiled in 1901, they caused a scandal.

easily. Thetis was one of the best-known nymphs. She grew up on Mount Olympus, married the mortal Peleus, and became the mother of the great hero, Achilles (*see* **Achilles** *and* **Thetis**). The Oceanids were the three thousand daughters of the Titans, Oceanus and Tethys (*see* **Oceanus**). They included Doris, wife of Neris and mother of the Nereids, Amphitrite, wife of the great sea-god, Poseidon, and Calypso, who kept the hero Odysseus with her on her island of Ogygia for seven years during his arduous journey home. According to the poet Homer, Calypso was fathered by the Titan, Atlas, whom the gods had forced to carry the vault of the heavens on his shoulders.

Niobe

Niobe was the daughter of Tantalus and Dione and wife of the Theban king Amphion, by whom she had seven sons and seven daughters. Niobe was a proud woman. She was proud of her husband, who with the aid of his superb lyre-playing had ensured that the stones of the city walls of Thebes had adjusted themselves into place, and she was especially proud of herself and her own achievements as a mother. She thought it ridiculous that the goddess Leto was

and died at the same time as these trees. The Melian nymphs were nymphs of the ash trees. They had germinated from the drops of blood that fell to earth when Uranus was castrated (*see* **Cronos** *and* **Uranus**). The Oriads were mountain-nymphs, the Naiads well- and river-nymphs. The Nereids were sea-nymphs who, as their name indicates, were the daughters of the old sea-god Nereus. Nereus could predict the future and change his form very particularly honored in her city. Was she herself not a daughter of Tantalus, who had dined with the gods? Was her mother not the sister of the Pleiades and a daughter of Atlas, and was her father not a son of Zeus? Was she not beautiful and had she not brought seven sons and seven daughters into the world? Leto had only borne two children—Apollo and Artemis—and even if Niobe lost part of her wealth, she would still be richer than Leto. She forbade her subjects to continue to sacrifice to the goddess.

Niobe's pride came before a terrible fall. Leto was deeply insulted that she was no longer honored in a cult and invoked the help of her children, Apollo and Artemis. Niobe's bragging about her fecundity wounded Leto deeply. So Apollo shot Niobe's seven sons dead with his arrows

Together with her brother Apollo, Artemis reprimanded the haughty Niobe. With her arrows, Artemis shot and killed Niobe's daughters, while Apollo dealt with her sons. Artemis with hound, terra-cotta statuette from Boeotia, 3rd–4th century BCE.

while they were riding outside the city walls of Thebes. In his grief, their father, Amphion, ended his own life.

Niobe mourned her sons, but was foolish enough to call out to Leto that she still had more children than the goddess. Artemis then shot Niobe's daughters, who were visiting their dead brothers lying-in-state. When only the youngest daughter, Chloris, was still alive and clinging to her mother's skirts in fear, Niobe begged for her to be spared, but in vain. As Niobe was uttering her pleas, her youngest daughter was fatally wounded (even though in one version, this child survived, *see* **Chloris**). In her sorrow, Niobe herself turned to stone. "But she still weeps. A hard blast of wind took her and brought her to her homeland. She pines away, rooted to a mountaintop. Her marble stone still weeps today," the Roman poet Ovid wrote of her (*Metamorphoses*, VI, lines 310-312).

Notus

Notus, the south wind, was a mild, warm breeze. He is shown here bringing rain, the most welcome gift in the dry Mediterranean world.

Notus was the south wind, a brother of Boreas, the north wind, Zephyr, the west wind, and Eurus, the east wind. Although he was usually mild and warm wind, in the Fall he could sometimes wreak havoc

Oceanids see Nymphs

Oceanus

The Titan, Oceanus, was the son of Uranus and Gaia and the god of the Ocean. This was the ocean that was believed by the Greeks to encircle the—flat—earth. Oceanus and his consort, Tethys, kept out of the Titans' battle against Zeus and the gods of Olympus. They were the parents of the river-gods and the three thousand Oceanids, a significant group of nymphs (*see* **Nymphs**).

The Titan, Oceanus, is the imposing central figure of the Trevi Fountain, the most famous fountain in Rome. In front of him there are two Tritons on seahorses. Pietro Bacci designed the statue of Oceanus in the 18th century.

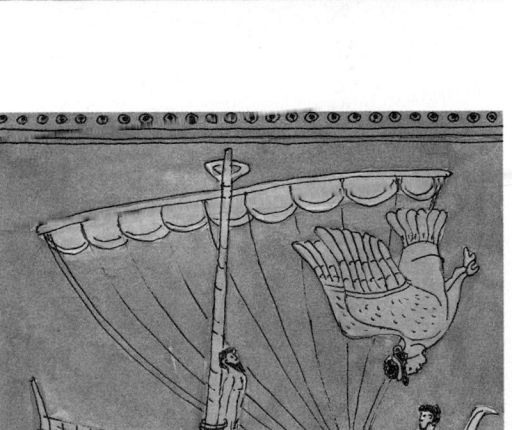

A Siren swoops down to Odysseus' ship, on which he has been bound to the mast. It was no easy matter to pass unscathed by the island of the Sirens and their irresistibly enchanting singing, but Odysseus managed to do so.

Odysseus (Roman=*Ulixes, Ulysses*)

Odysseus, the only son of Laertes and Anti-clea, was king of Ithaca. He was one of the greatest heroes of the Trojan War and one of the most significant figures in Greek mythology, playing a key role in the battle for Troy. Although he was a powerful and highly formidable hero, Odysseus' greatest talent lay not in his weapon-handling skills. The quality in which he surpassed virtually everyone and which enabled him to escape from countless awkward situations was his extraordinary cunning. It was thanks to his craftiness that the wooden horse by means of which Troy was finally conquered was made. And as a result of his cunning, guile, and persistence—not to mention the loyal support he received from the goddess Athena, who had a soft spot for him—he was able to overcome the many terrible setbacks he encountered on his return journey from Troy and finally arrive home safely to the island of Ithaca, where

The goddess Athena supported Odysseus through thick and thin. Without her help and advice there would have been no happy ending to his ten-year wanderings. Statue of Athena from Antalya, Turkey.

practically single-handedly, he went on to defeat the unscrupulous suitors who were courting his wife.

Odysseus is the leading figure of *The Odyssey*, the magical, mythical, epic by the Greek poet Homer, that is entirely devoted to Odysseus' ten-year journey home. Homer's other great epic, *The Iliad*, describes a fifty-one day episode in the ten-year siege of Troy, in which a principal role is also reserved for the "cunning" and "ingenious" Odysseus, two descriptions Homer regularly uses for this extraordinary hero. Around two thousand eight hundred years after Homer, the father of Western literature, wrote his epics, Odysseus remains just as alive and recognizable as he must have appeared to Homer's contemporaries.

Although, as has been said, Odysseus was supposedly the son of Laertes, according to some, the wily scoundrel Sisyphus (*see* **Sisyphus**) was his real father. Odysseus' maternal grandfather, Autolycus, himself a notorious thief and swindler, is said to have ensured that Sisyphus fathered a son by his daughter before she married Laertes.

As a young man, Odysseus was one of the Greek princes who courted the beautiful Helen, the "illegitimate" daughter of King Tyndareos of Sparta. Odysseus quickly realized that as the crown prince of the insignificant island of Ithaca, he had not the shade of a chance against rich and powerful princes such as Menelaus, who ultimately carried off

Decoration in the form of a lion's lower half in the city walls of Troy. Odysseus left for Troy with great reluctance and it was not until twenty years later that he regained his beloved island of Ithaca.

Helen (*see* **Helen** *and* **Menelaus**). Because of the great enmity that prevailed among the suitors, Odysseus suggested to Tyndareos that he have all of them swear to come to Menelaus' aid should he encounter any difficulties on account of Helen. This oath was to have significant consequences, even for Odysseus himself, because he married Tyndareos' niece, Penelope. Ten years after Menelaus and Helen were married, the Trojan Prince Paris abducted Helen, taking her to Troy and making her his wife. Menelaus then reminded his former rivals of their pledge. He and Odysseus made a fruitless trip to Troy to try to secure the return of Helen through negotiation, after which the Greek princes raised a vast army. Menelaus' powerful brother, Agamemnon, King of the wealthy city-state of Mycenae, was in supreme command. This army sailed to Troy and laid siege to the city. The Trojan War, that was to last ten years, had begun.

In spite of his solemn pledge to Menelaus, Odysseus had no desire whatsoever to leave his beloved wife and their little son, Telemachus, and plunge into the turmoil of war. When a delegation including Agamemnon and Menelaus arrived at Ithaca to take him to Troy, Odysseus made what was probably the first attempt in the history of mankind to avoid his military service obligations on the grounds of "mental instability". Wearing a strange item of headgear, he harnessed a horse and an ox to the plow and tilled a beach on his island, sowing in the furrows. However, Palamedes, a member of the delegation, immediately saw through this play-acting. He placed the infant, Telemachus, in front of the plow, whereupon Odysseus, taken by surprise, responded like a sane man, and took evasive action to avoid hurting the child. Odysseus had no choice but to go with them to Troy, although he later wreaked a gruesome revenge on Palamedes. He hid a nugget of gold and a letter apparently written by the Trojan king, Priam, in Palamedes' tent, causing Palamedes to be stoned to death by the other Greeks for alleged treachery.

For the Greeks, Odysseus' cunning was a priceless quality. One of the ways in which he used it was to persuade other "reluctant participants" to enter the fray. It was Odysseus, in fact, who was sent to the court of Lycomedes in the city-state of Sparta to collect Achilles. Achilles was living in the women's quarters there, disguised as a young

girl. However, when Odysseus concealed weapons among the jewelry and raised the alarm, there was one girl who could not conceal his/her real nature. At a much later stage in the war, Odysseus also took Achilles' son, Neoptolemus, and Philoctetes to Troy. The latter had been given Heracles' unfailing bow as a gift when he proved to be the only one prepared to light the funeral pyre of the hero, who was suffering unbearable pain. On the return journey to Troy, at Odysseus' suggestion, Philoctetes, who was suffering from a suppurating wound caused by a snake-bite, was left behind on the island of Lemnos. Odysseus eventually collected him from Lemnos although Heracles, who had since been deified, had to go and visit him to give him the final urging to join in the war.

Odysseus performed a number of heroic deeds in the battle for Troy. Together with Diomedes, he went on a night sortie during what was, for the Greeks, a perilous stage of the war. On the way, they encountered the Trojan, Dolon, who was, in fact, planning to spy on the Greeks. Deceived by Odysseus, he showed them the way to a camp of the Thracian allies of the Trojans outside the city walls and gave them all manner of useful information, after which Diomedes killed him. Odysseus and Diomedes then killed a number of Thracians, including their king, Rhesus, and seized the valuable and magical Thracian horses.

Shortly thereafter, Odysseus was wounded in battle. He recovered quickly though, and performed another special mission. This time, disguised as a beggar, he managed to enter Troy, where he was able to operate unnoticed, although Helen recognized him. However, she did not betray him, and instead provided him with cover. Odysseus told her the Greeks' plans, which delighted Helen, and he killed a number of Trojans. It is possible that at this point he also stole the Palladium, an ancient idol of Athena, from Troy, with or without the help of Diomedes. It had been predicted that the Greeks would only win the final victory once they had captured this idol.

Not long afterward, Achilles was killed by an arrow shot by Paris (or the god Apollo), Odysseus once more found himself at loggerheads with someone. This time it was Ajax, the son of Telamon. Ajax, another hero, (*"great Ajax," see* **Ajax**) had concealed Achilles' body while Odysseus covered his retreat. They both later laid claim to Achilles' magnificent armor, forged by the god Hephæstos himself. The silver-tongued Odysseus prevailed and Ajax later went mad with rage, tried to kill his rivals, and in the end, took his own life.

Odysseus' eloquence and sagacity, to say nothing of his cunning, ultimately settled the Trojan War in favor of the Greeks. Homer gives a magnificent description of the way in which Odysseus was able to captivate others merely through his words. "Odysseus, on the other hand, when he rose to speak, was at first silent and kept his eyes fixed upon the ground. There was no play nor graceful movement of his scepter; he kept it straight and stiff like a man unpracticed in oratory—one might have taken him for a mere churl or simpleton; but when he raised his voice, and the words came driving from his deep chest like winter snow before the wind, then there was no one to touch him." (*Iliad*, III, lines 216-223).

It was Odysseus who took the Trojan visionary, Helenus, prisoner in the final stage of the war. He told him that for the Greeks to triumph they would need Philoctetes with Heracles' bow as well as Achilles' son, Neoptolemus. Some time later, Odysseus hit upon the idea of the wooden horse, which had been made by Epeus, a Greek who had not fought particularly well in battle but proved to be a first-class boxer and formidable discus thrower in Patroclus' games.

Odysseus was among the heroes who concealed themselves in the wooden horse, that had been left on the plain outside Troy, supposedly as an offering of thanks to Athena. In the meantime, the Greeks had broken up their army camp and the fleet had sailed to the nearby island of Tenedos where they awaited a signal to return. When Helen tapped on the flanks of the horse and, imitating the voices of their wives, called the names of the men inside it, it was Odysseus who kept the others in check and in so doing averted the failure of the ruse.

Once Troy had been conquered, Odysseus suffered great misfortunes. The gods who had supported the Trojans during the war felt very embittered toward him. Fortunately for the hero, Athena continued to provide him unflagging support. She did not blame him for "little Ajax" (*see* **Ajax** *and* **Cassandra**) having removed and destroyed her Trojan altar during the capture of the city, because Odysseus had insisted that Ajax would pay for the crime with his life. That was why Odysseus was spared the terrible storm Athena sent to ravage the Greek ships. Even so, Odysseus had plenty of misery to endure. His journey home would ultimately take ten years, longer than those of all the other Greeks who lived to see their homeland again. Of the twelve ships with which he had left Troy not one remained, and all his men had perished.

From Troy, Odysseus traveled to the isle of the Ciconians, off the coast of Thrace, where he and his men destroyed and plundered a city, killing the inhabitants. Other Ciconians took revenge and slaughtered several of Odysseus' unsuspecting comrades while they were celebrating their victory.

Nike, the goddess of victory. The "endlessly cunning" Odysseus could take a lot of credit for the fact that the Greeks finally prevailed in the Trojan War. Earthenware sculpture from Myrina, 2nd century BCE.

Odysseus' voyage from Troy to Ithaca took ten years. He was the only member of his crew to return home unharmed. All his ships had been lost in storms and other calamities, and all his comrades died. Vase painting of Greek ships.

Odysseus had a perilous adventure in the cave of the wicked Cyclops, Polyphemus, who devoured a number of his men. As was so often the case, Odysseus managed to escape by dint of a cunning trick. Polyphemus, Mosaic from the Villa del Casale, Sicily, 3rd–4th century AD.

Odysseus and his comrades escaped from the Cyclops' cave by clinging to the bellies of Polyphemus' sheep. Broadtail sheep on a mosaic fragment from Syria, Roman period, 5th century.

Driven off course by a violent storm, Odysseus' ship reached the Land of the Lotus-eaters. Some of his men sampled the delicious but heavily addictive lotus flowers and forgot all thoughts of continuing their journey. After they had been brought back to the ships by force, the journey was continued, this time to the island of the Cyclopes, brutal one-eyed giants. Odysseus found himself in the cave of the Cyclops, Polyphemus, who ate six men and intended to kill the others as well. Odysseus extricated himself and his six surviving comrades from this perilous situation by plying Polyphemus with liquor, gouging out his one eye while he was sleeping it off, and then escaping from the cave by clinging to the bellies of the Cyclops' sheep. Since Odysseus had deceived Polyphemus into thinking his name was "Nobody," the other Cyclopes did not take Polyphemus' call for help seriously and Odysseus managed to escape from the island in time (*see* **Cyclopes**). Polyphemus' father, the great sea-god Poseidon who, after all, was no friend of Odysseus, blamed the hero entirely for blinding his son, regardless of the provocation that caused Odysseus to commit this act.

Odysseus continued his journey to the island of Æolus, master of the winds. Æolus welcomed Odysseus warmly and gave him a sack containing all the winds needed to send Odysseus on his way home. He then set the west wind free and it blew Odysseus' ships swiftly on toward Ithaca. With land in sight the weary hero fell asleep. His men, who suspected that he was concealing all kinds of treasure in Æolus' mysterious sack, then opened the sack, with disastrous consequences. The winds burst out and swelled into a heavy storm, driving the ships all the way back to Æolus' island. Æolus was so offended that he refused to help Odysseus any further.

The fleet continued to the land of the Læstrygonians, who turned out to be man-eating giants, no less dangerous than the Cyclopes. From the cliffs of their island, they hurled great rocks at the ships, catching their victims like fish and eating them up. Only Odysseus' own ship escaped; the other eleven in the Greek fleet were destroyed

With just one ship, Odysseus reached the island of Ææa, home of the enchantress Circe. She transformed some of the men into pigs but Odysseus, who thanks to a magic potion given to him by Hermes, became immune to her magic, forced her to restore them to human form. He then stayed on Ææa for a year where he shared the bed of the alluring enchantress (*see* **Circe**). She was reluctant to let Odysseus go, but gave him valuable advice, telling him to visit the underworld and consult the shade of the seer Tiresias.

Odysseus was now facing one of the most hazardous adventures of his life, that of

contacting the dead in the Kingdom of Hades. He went to the land of Cimmerians, at the edge of the Ocean, that surrounded the flat world of the Greeks (*see* **Oceanus**) and, at a place specified by Circe, made a special offering to the shades. They appeared immediately, drawn by the blood of the sacrificial beasts. Once they had drunk from the blood, they were released from the state of total oblivion into which they had fallen and returned to their senses.

The first shade to appear was that of Elpenor, a comrade of Odysseus who, unnoticed by the others, had fallen from the roof of Circe's palace. He begged to be buried. The shade of Tiresias gave Odysseus some important warnings and foretold the events of the rest of his life. In particular, the seer urged Odysseus to leave unharmed the cattle of the sun god, Helios, on the island of Thrinacia (possibly Sicily). Odysseus then spoke to the shade of his mother, Anticlea, who told him more about what was happening in Ithaca, and the shades of comrades-in-arms from the Trojan War, including Agamemnon and Achilles. Odysseus also saw the shades of many heroes, the sinners in Tartarus (*see* **Hades**), and the shade of Heracles, who stayed in the underworld while Heracles himself was on Olympus with the gods.

The first move of Odysseus and his men was to return to Æaea to bury Elpenor, after which they finally set sail once more for Ithaca. The island of the Sirens (*see* **The Sirens**) was one of their first obstacles. The Sirens were bird like creatures with girls' faces and exquisite singing voices. This was a great hazard because their singing was so enticing that anyone who heard it experienced an irresistible compulsion to sail up to their island, where he would then run his ship on to the rocks. As a result they were surrounded by skeletons and shrunken corpses. On the advice of Circe, Odysseus stopped the ears of his men with wax. He wanted to hear the Sirens sing and so he had himself lashed to the mast of his ship and ordered his men to tighten his bonds should he become too enthralled by their voices. This enabled his ship to pass the dangerous island safely, although Odysseus was completely spellbound by the unearthly singing of the extraordinary creatures.

Other, no less dangerous obstacles were to follow, including the *Planktai*, the hazardous "wandering rocks," and the sea-monsters, Scylla and Charybdis, who lived under a cliff on either side of a narrow strait. Scylla had twelve legs and six long necks with a hideous head on each (*see* **Scylla**). Charybdis sucked in vast quantities of seawater three times a day, like a whirlpool and later spouted it up again. Odysseus managed to steer his ship just out of Charybdis' clutches, but this enabled Scylla to devour six of his men, one per head.

Against his will, Odysseus and his men then landed on the island of Thrinacia. Unfavorable winds meant they had to stay there for over a month. The men were hungry and although Odysseus had made them swear not to touch any of the herds on the island, they killed some of Helios' cattle. They did so in spite of all the binding oaths they had sworn and the warnings of Tiresias and Circe. Odysseus upbraided the offenders but it was to no avail. For six days, the men feasted on the meat, after which the entire crew left the island. No sooner had they done so than Zeus, at the request of the aggrieved sun-god, raised a terrible storm. Zeus hit the ship with a lightning bolt and thunder and those on board were pitched out into the sea, leaving Odysseus alone on the wrecked ship, which was driven on toward Charybdis, who swallowed up the rest of the ship. Odysseus, the sole survivor, managed to escape onto some floating beams and seven days later drifted

Odysseus implored his men not to touch the magnificent cattle belonging to the sun- god Helios, on the island of Thrinacia, but to no avail. The starving crew slaughtered the cattle. Head of a sea-bull, mosaic from the Hot Baths of Caracalla, Rome, 3rd century CE.

At the request of Helios, who was furious because Odysseus' men had slaughtered his cattle, Zeus destroyed Odysseus' last ship with a thunderbolt. A mass of thunderbolts on a gold coin (stater) from Macedonia, 4th century BCE.

ashore onto the island of Ogygia.

This was the home of the beautiful Calypso who took care of the shipwrecked Odysseus. She kept him with her for seven years in the hope that he would marry her. She even promised him immortality and eternal youth. Odysseus soon tired of the beguiling nymph, however, and yearned to return to Penelope and Telemachus. He spent most of his time in tears on the coast of Ogygia, eaten up with homesickness. In the end, the gods took pity on Odysseus, and Zeus agreed to Athena's request to let him return home. Hermes told Calypso of the gods' decision and, after some protest, she let Odysseus go.

The hero set off for Ithaca in a ship he had built himself, but his old enemy, Poseidon, who had not been present at the meeting of the gods, struck him with a terrible storm. Odysseus would have drowned if the sea-goddess Leucothea—who as a mortal was known as Ino (*see* **Ino**)—had not landed on his ship in the form of a seagull. She advised Odysseus to abandon his ship to the waves and swim for it and she gave him a magic veil which would act as a life-jacket. More dead than alive, Odysseus finally reached the island of Scheria, home of the Phæacians. Naked and exhausted, he fell asleep and was discovered the following morning by Nausicaa, daughter of King Alcinous, who together with her maids had come to wash the clothes of the palace residents in a river.

The girls shrieked in fear when they saw the naked man, but Odysseus won Nausicaa over. She gave him some clothes and showed him the way to Alcinous' palace. She did not accompany him because she could not be seen with him in the city of the Phæacians, as this might have created the wrong impression in some quarters.

Odysseus followed Nausicaa's advice and went to her mother, Queen Arete, begging her for help. King Alcinous and Queen Arete gave their unknown guest a very warm welcome and promised to arrange his passage home. Feasts and games were organized the next day, during which Odysseus impressed his audience with an outstanding discus throw. At the ensuing banquet, Odysseus revealed his identity and explained in detail what had happened to him since he had left Troy. Alcinous and Arete were moved by his tale and gave him valuable gifts to take with him on his journey home to Ithaca. The ship sailed on to Ithaca through the night, and Odysseus fell into a deep sleep. In this condition, he was carried ashore, with his gifts, onto the beach of his own island. The aggrieved Poseidon turned the Phæacians' ship to stone on the way home.

Telemachus was not on Ithaca when Odysseus returned. He had been to Pylos, to visit the aged hero, Nestor, and to Sparta, to see Menelaus, to find out what had happened to his father. Athena had escorted him there in the form of Mentor, an old friend of Odysseus who at the time had taken it upon himself to look after his family—the English term "mentor" is derived from this name. Athena was now preparing to bring Telemachus back to Ithaca, but before she did so, she gave Odysseus the form of an old beggar and advised him to seek temporary shelter with the swineherd, Eumæus, who had remained loyal to his old master for the full twenty years.

Eumæus warmly welcomed the "beggar," not suspecting the true identity of his guest. Odysseus quickly realized that the swineherd had a heart of oak and still had complete faith in him. Telemachus left Sparta under Athena's protection and, thanks to the goddess, avoided an ambush laid by the suitors. He arrived at the swineherd's, whereupon Odysseus revealed himself to Telemachus in his own form. Eumæus was absent at the time, telling Penelope about the safe return of her son.

Odysseus and Telemachus hatched a plan to defeat the suitors and Telemachus left for the palace the next day. Eumæus and Odysseus, back in his beggar's disguise, followed shortly thereafter. On the way there, they were taunted and attacked by the goatherd Melanthius, a supporter of the suitors. No one recognized Odysseus at the palace, apart from his old dog Argos, who had been lying on a dunghill outside the gate and immediately started wagging his tail at the approach of his old master. But the excitement was too much, and the poor old animal suddenly breathed his last breath.

Once inside the palace, the beggar and his friend, Eumæus, were obliged to suffer the obligatory humiliation by the suitors, who were feasting in the great hall. When Odysseus started begging scraps of food from those present, the suitor Antinous, irritated by his comments, even threw a stool at him, hitting him on the shoulder. In the meantime, in the women's quarters, Eumæus had told Penelope about the arrival of the strange beggar, who had some news of Odysseus' fate. Penelope was naturally very keen to speak with him, but before that could happen there was another scuffle between Odysseus and a young "professional beggar" named Irus. He wanted to chase away his rival and threatened him with violence. To the amusement of

Odysseus excelled at discus-throwing in the celebratory games organized by the Phæcians. Discus thrower and flautists on a pitcher (oinochœ) from southern Italy, 5th century BCE.

the suitors, the old beggar knocked his young rival out of action with one blow. Penelope reproached Telemachus for allowing the stranger to be abused and then turned to the suitors, telling them that she would soon be marrying a man who brought his own food and gifts instead of simply feasting at her expense. After Odysseus had dealt with Melantho, an untrustworthy maidservant, and with the suitor, Eurymachos, the suitors went home. Odysseus and Telemachus then quickly removed all the weapons from the great hall of the palace and hid them in the armory.

Penelope later talked with the stranger and told him about the trick she had played with the loom. She misled her suitors, who made so free with her food and drink at her palace, by promising them that she would choose one of them to marry her, once she had woven a shroud for her father-in-law, Laertes. She spent the day weaving this shroud but, by night, she secretly unraveled the work she had done. Despite revealing this secret, she still did not recognize her husband. The "beggar" told her that he had met Odysseus and announced his imminent return, greatly moving Penelope. She made arrangements for the stranger who had given her such encouragement, to be looked after and so it was that Odysseus' old nurse, Euryclea, whose had been summoned to wash his feet, recognized him from a scar caused by a wild boar during a hunt. Odysseus enjoined her to keep her knowledge to herself for a little while longer.

Just before the dramatic showdown with the suitors, Odysseus and Telemachus hid all the weapons in the palace armory. Once Odysseus had shot and killed the two main suitors with his bow and arrow, Telemachus armed his father, himself, and their supporters. Greco-Illyrian bronze helmet, 6th century BCE.

The next day, Penelope organized a competition for the suitors, of which the winner would be allowed to marry her. The victor would first have to string Odysseus' bow and and shoot an arrow straight through the sockets of twelve ax heads lined up in a row. The competition began in a highly charged atmosphere. The suitors had offended Telemachus and the "beggar" again at daybreak. The seer, Theoclymenus, had then predicted a great calamity and straightaway taken to his heels.

Telemachus tried, not as a competitor, of course, to string the bow, and would have succeeded had his father not restrained him. While the suitors vainly tested their powers against the bow, Odysseus was outside revealing his identity to Eumæus and a loyal cowherd. After Antinous and Eurymachus had failed to string the bow as well, the suitors abandoned the contest. That was when the "beggar" asked if he could have a try. The suitors responded resentfully, but Penelope gave him permission at which point, to her surprise, Telemachus hastily sent her away to the women's quarters. To the jeers of the suitors, Eumæus handed the bow over to the "beggar." He examined his arrow, strung it with great ease, and shot an arrow through the sockets in the twelve ax heads. Odysseus then aimed his arrows on the suitors. The first to perish was the arrogant Antinous and straightaway Odysseus made himself known. Eurymachus tried to bargain with him but was the second to die. Telemachus then went to fetch some more weapons and shared them out among his father, Eumæus, and the cowherd. The goatherd, Melanthius, also managed to find his way into the armory, which Telemachus in his haste had forgotten to lock, but Odysseus' two faithful servants hanged him there. With the help of Athena—again in the form of Mentor—Odysseus and his men then killed all the suitors. Only two men, the minstrel Phemius and the herald Medon, were spared. At the conclusion of the bloodbath, Odysseus had Euryclea assemble the maidservants who had not remained loyal to him. They were made to carry away the corpses and then hanged.

Penelope was then woken by Euryclea and told the joyful news. Odysseus' wife, however, remained skeptical. She still could not believe that Odysseus had really returned. It was only when Odysseus told her that one of the bedposts of their marital bed, which he had built himself, was the trunk of an old olive tree still rooted in the ground (a secret known only to his wife and himself), that Penelope was convinced.

The next day, Odysseus went to the country estate to which his father Laertes had withdrawn. The old man was deeply moved upon seeing his son again. In the meantime, relatives of the suitors were preparing for a revenge attack in the city outside Odysseus' palace. Some of them went to Laertes' country estate where a number of Odysseus' faithful followers had now gathered. Laertes, whom Athena had rejuvenated with new power and looks, killed Antinous' father with his spear. After that, however, Athena and Zeus put a stop to any further bloodletting, and peace was made. With Penelope at his side, Odysseus would continue to rule over Ithaca for a long time and die a peaceful death at a very great age.

Immortalized as he is in the Odyssey, Odysseus has, in a way, superseded the status of a mythological hero, and has become one of the great literary figures of Western culture, rivaled only by such characters such as Hamlet, Don Quixote, and Faust. He is the favorite hero of countless readers from many different eras.

The Irish author, James Joyce, drew heavily on his favorite book, *The Odyssey*, for inspiration, when he wrote his groundbreaking novel *Ulysses* (1922), and the rock star Eric Clapton once dedicated a song, *Tales of Brave Ulysses*, to his boyhood hero.

Not everyone is charmed by the cunning, but sometimes downright sneaky and brutal

As a young man, Odysseus had made his marital bed himself. Only he and his wife Penelope knew that one of the bedposts was the trunk of an old olive tree that was still rooted in the ground. Once Odysseus told her this, Penelope knew for certain that he was no impostor.

Odysseus. Around the beginning of the common era (when Homer's epic poem was about eight hundred years old), the Roman poet Virgil described in his *Æneid* a gripping account of the destruction of Troy by "the brutal Ulixes", "instigator of crimes" (*see* **Æneas**). In the late twentieth century a Dutch literary critic described Odysseus, not entirely unjustly, as an immoral, misogynistic predecessor of James Bond.

Œdipus

Œdipus was King of Thebes, the son of Laius and his wife, Jocasta. Œdipus was the central figure in a horrifying family drama that is described in tragedies by the great Athenian playwrights Æschylus, Sophocles, and Euripides. The best known of these plays is *Œdipus Rex*.

When the Theban King Laius and his wife Jocasta found themselves unable to have children, Laius consulted the oracle at Delphi. He was told that on no account must he produce any offspring because his own son would kill him. Laius took this warning very much to heart, but in a moment of drunken abandon, he made love to Jocasta, who then became pregnant. As a precaution, when the baby, Œdipus, was barely three days old, he was given to a herdsman to take far away, and left out on the slopes of Mount Cithæra, with his feet pierced. The child acquired his name from these injuries because Œdipus means "swollen feet." Somehow, the baby survived this brutal treatment because he was found by a shepherd, who took him to the Corinthian King Polybus. The Thebans did not have the slightest suspicion that the baby lived.

Œdipus grew up in Corinth, under the misapprehension that he was Polybus' son. Several years later, though, when Œdipus was an adolescent, a drunken man taunted him, claiming that he was illegitimate. Œdipus was very hurt and, unbeknown to Polybus and his wife, went to the oracle at Delphi where he received no answer to his question concerning his origin, just the horrific prediction that he would kill his father and marry his mother by whom he would even have children.

On his way home from Delphi, at a fork in the road near Mount Parnassus, Œdipus came across the carriage of a wealthy man who was traveling with his retinue at great speed to Delphi. Œdipus did not move to the side quickly enough for the liking of the

Œdipus listens carefully to the Sphinx, who tells him her riddle which thus far no one had managed to solve. A moment later Œdipus would give the right answer and the Sphinx would take her own life.

high-ranking personage, and bore the brunt of the collision. This caused Œdipus to fly into a rage and killed the entire party, apart from one herald who managed to escape.

After this dreadful incident, Œdipus continued on his way and arrived at the city-state of Thebes, which was in angry mood. This was because the citizens had been told that their king, Laius, had been murdered by robbers on his way to the oracle of Delphi. Furthermore, the approaches to the city were plagued by the Sphinx, a winged lion with a female head, who gave unsuspecting travelers

The remains of a stadium in the shrine of Delphi dedicated to the god Apollo. The oracle at Delphi played a key role in the gruesome story of Œdipus .

and Thebans a riddle to solve and then killed them if they gave the wrong answer (*see* **The Sphinx**). The reason why King Laius had been on his way to Delphi is because he was hoping to get information on how to deal with the Sphinx.

The despairing regent, Creon, now promised anyone who could free the city of this monster nothing less than the throne and the hand of the newly-widowed Jocasta. Œdipus solved the riddle of the Sphinx, whereupon the monster fell shrieking into an abyss. He went on to marry Jocasta and became King of Thebes. Without realizing it, he had now completely fulfilled the Delphic prophecy.

The great poet Homer, who referred to Jocasta as "Epicaste," wrote that the gods soon made it clear that the new king had married his mother and that Jocasta subsequently hanged herself, after which the anguished Œdipus ruled Thebes alone. Sophocles, however, gives an entirely different version of this event. According to him, Œdipus and Jocasta were happily married for years and ruled their city without any difficulty. They had two sons, Eteocles and Polynices, and two daughters, Antigone and Ismene.

When Œdipus had been King of Thebes for a good many years, a plague suddenly broke out in the city and the women and the cattle became barren. Creon went to Delphi to find out the cause of this mysterious sickness, where the Oracle told him that the blame lay with the person or persons who had

The Sphinx held the city of Thebes and the surrounding area under a reign of terror. Whoever freed Thebes from the Sphinx would become king of the city and marry the queen, Jocasta. Limestone head of a Sphinx from western Greece.

murdered Laius. The epidemic could only be ended by killing or exiling this man or men. The blind seer, Tiresias, then declared that Œdipus had murdered Laius. Œdipus flew into a rage and even accused the seer of plotting with the former regent, Creon, to depose him and rule in his place.

However, when Œdipus and Jocasta finally told each other their versions of the ill-fated event at the fork in the road near Parnassus, doubts arose for the first time. Nonetheless, Œdipus and Jocasta maintained the fiction that Laius had been killed by more than one man. Further reassurance came in the form of a delegation from Corinth that reported that King Polybus had died and that Œdipus, being his son, was to succeed him. Œdipus refused to do so in order to avoid marrying his mother, Merope, as local custom required. He thus assumed that the Oracle's predictions had been thwarted. At this point, though, the Corinthian messenger, who proved to be one and the same as the shepherd who had found the little Œdipus on the mountain all those years ago, pointed out that Œdipus was not, in fact, Merope's son. Œdipus arranged for the Theban shepherd who had abandoned him to be found and when he questioned him the dreadful truth finally emerged. Horrified at the incest she had committed, Jocasta hanged herself and Œdipus put out his eyes. Creon decreed that he be exiled from Thebes.

Nevertheless, Œdipus did not leave the city straightaway. He was eventually driven out, however, and neither of his sons lifted a finger to help him. Accompanied by his daughter, Antigone, the blind Œdipus wandered through Greece, a repentant sinner. He smuggled himself into the township of Colonus, part of the city of Athens, which was ruled by Theseus at the time. In the meantime, Eteocles and Polynices had fallen out with each other in Thebes and Polynices had been driven from the city by his brother. Œdipus' second daughter, Ismene, came to tell him this. The blind exile was overcome by this news and cursed his sons.

Theseus offered Œdipus asylum in Athens, but shortly thereafter, Antigone and Ismene were taken prisoner by Creon's soldiers. Creon also planned to take Œdipus back to Thebes because it was important for the welfare of the city that Œdipus be buried there. Theseus released the women, who returned to their father in Colonus. His son, Polynices, also went to see Œdipus to persuade him to

take his side, something Œdipus brutally refused to do. In the end, chastened by his lengthy suffering, Œdipus died in Colonus where he was buried. Only Theseus, who had granted him the right to live in Athens, knew the site of his last resting place.

Antigone and Ismene voluntarily returned to Thebes, but it was a long time before there was an end to the misfortunes of this city and those of Œdipus' family were also destined to continue (see **Antigone** *and* **Creon**).

Œdipus, who had had no evil intentions unconsciously committed terrible crimes and is one of the most tragic figures in all of Greek mythology. The Greek plays written about him are still performed and have inspired modern playwrights to create their own works based on his life. Two Dutch authors, Hugo Claus and Harry Mulisch, have written about Œdipus and the unfortunate Theban King has had a modern twist added to his story in the Œdipus complex, the alleged inclination of sons to unconsciously desire their mothers and hate their fathers, observed by the father of psychoanalysis, Sigmund Freud (1856-1939).

Orestes

Orestes was the only son of the Mycenæn King Agamemnon and his wife, Clytemnestra. His sisters were Iphigenia, Electra, and Chrysothemis. When Clytemnestra and her lover Ægisthus murdered Agamemnon (see **Agamemnon** *and* **Electra**) Electra took

A number of moving tragedies were devoted to the terrible events that befell Œdipus. They fascinated the public in ancient Greece and have lost none of their impact today. These very same tragedies are currently performed in the famous Greek amphitheater of Syracuse, Sicily.

Orestes, who at that time was still very young, to safety. She sent him to Phocis, where he grew up at the court of King Strophius. Strophius' son, Pylades, who was raised with Orestes, became his bosom friend. Another version is that Orestes was sent to Phocis a good ten years earlier, at the time his father left for Troy.

Years after Agamemnon's violent death, on the instructions of the god Apollo, Orestes returned to Mycenæ to avenge his father. Various authors (Homer and the three Athenian tragedians Æschylus, Sophocles, and Euripides) give different versions of what happened next. It is agreed that, after consulting with Electra, Orestes killed Clytemnestra and Ægisthus. Some ascribe the initiative to carry out this dreadful act of revenge to Orestes, others to Electra. There are also several versions of the consequences of Orestes' matricide. According to some, Orestes received no punishment for this act. Æschylus, however, who devoted a three-act play, *The Oresteia*, to these events, shows how Orestes had to deal with the Erinyes or Furies (*see* **Erinyes**), the goddesses of vengeance, whose task it was to exact retribution for unspeakable crimes, and who are particularly concerned with crimes committed by one member of a family against another. The Erinyes drove Orestes mad and tirelessly pursued him from country to country. According to some versions, Electra and Orestes were tried and sentenced to death in Mycenæ shortly after the murder. Orestes then captured Helen and Hermione, the wife and daughter of his uncle Menelaus, and held them hostage. They were saved by the intervention of the gods. Orestes was not put to death but exiled.

Orestes, tormented by the Erinyes, visited the Oracle of Delphi, which was dedicated to Apollo. Apollo, who had instructed Orestes to avenge his father, arranged for him to travel to Athens, escorted by Hermes. There, at the court of the Areopagus, the "Hill of Ares" (*see* **Ares**), a special trial was held with an Athenian jury. The Erinyes appeared as the accusers and Apollo as Orestes' attorney. The goddess, Athena, acted as presiding judge, and when the jury's votes turned out to be equally divided, she cast her vote in favor of Orestes. Orestes was acquitted and the gruesome Erinyes allowed themselves to be placated, on the condition that they continued to be worshiped in Athens. From now, on they would no longer be known as Erinyes, but Eumenides, "the well-disposed" or "benevolent" ones.

According to another version, before or after his trial in Athens, on the orders of

The god Apollo ordered Orestes to return to his hometown of Mycenæ and take revenge on the murderers of his father, Agamemnon. Apollo would later defend Orestes at the court of the Areopagus in Athens. Head of Apollo from Nemrut Dagh, Turkey, 1st century BCE.

Many years after his father Agamemnon was murdered by his mother Clytemnestra and her lover Ægisthus, Orestes avenged this terrible crime by killing Clytemnestra and Ægisthus.

Apollo, Orestes was sent to Tauris to fetch a statue of Artemis. King Thoas of Tauris took Orestes prisoner and brought him to the shrine of Artemis to offer him up to the goddess. Unbeknown to Orestes, his sister Iphigenia was priestess of this shrine. She had been living in Tauris since Agamemnon had wanted to sacrifice her in exchange for a favorable wind for the Greek fleet that was intent on sailing to Troy (*see* **Iphigenia**). Brother and sister recognized each other and Iphigenia deceived the king into believing that she, the strangers, and Artemis' statue should be purified in seawater for the sinfulness of the matricide, Orestes. The residents of Tauris were forbidden to watch this ritual, enabling the three to escape in Orestes' ship.

According to some versions, Orestes later had a hand in the death of Neoptolemus, the son of Achilles, who had distinguished himself in the battle for Troy. Neoptolemus was, in fact, married to Orestes' niece, Hermione, whose father, Menelaus, had originally promised her to Orestes.

The most significant element of Orestes' story, however, is his acquittal after the lengthy cycle of murder and revenge, all of which can be traced back to his grandfather Atreus and great-grandfather, Pelops (*see* **Atreus** *and* **Pelops**).

Once Orestes had killed his mother, the goddesses of revenge did not give him a moment's peace. He was ultimately acquitted by a special court convened in Athens. Orestes holding an amphora, weathered limestone relief from Tarente, 4th century BCE.

Orion

Orion, who came from Bœotia in central Greece, was the son of Poseidon and Euryale, and was a mighty hunter. He was an awe-inspiring giant whose passion for the hunt and his libido have been the subject of numerous stories. His first wife, Side, had the temerity to claim that she was no less beautiful than Hera and was consequently banished to Hades for her presumption.

King Œnopion of the island of Chios promised Orion his daughter, Merope, if he could rid the island of wild beasts. When the king failed to keep his promise, Orion, drunk on Œnopion's wine, raped Merope. Œnopion then completely intoxicated Orion, put out his eyes, and abandoned him on the coast of his island. Orion eventually managed to reach the island of Lemnos, where he went to Hephæstos' forge. There he met a young blacksmith, Cedalion, whom he put on his shoulders. Guided by the young man, Orion went to the east coast of the Ocean, the sea encircling the world, where Helios, the sun-god, restored his sight.

An attempt to avenge himself on Œnopion came to naught, however, because the king had gone into hiding in an underground chamber created by Hephæstos.

Orion then traveled to Crete, and went hunting with the goddess Artemis, but Eos, goddess of the dawn, fell in love with the formidable hunter and slept with him. This did not amuse the gods, in particular Artemis, and she killed Orion with an arrow on the island of Ortygia. There are many other versions of Orion's death, however. According to one of them, he was the victim of a giant scorpion sent by Artemis. Yet another account has it that Apollo did not like his twin sister proving susceptible to the charms of the attractive mighty hunter. Once, when Orion was swimming in the sea, Apollo pointed out to Artemis a dot bobbing above the waves far out at sea. It was Orion's head, but Artemis did not recognize it. Apollo goaded Artemis, saying that she would never be able to hit the spot with her arrows. The goddess was having none of this. She shot an arrow and hit Orion in the head, fatally wounding him. Broken-hearted, she placed him in the heavens as a constellation, where he is pursued by her scorpion (Scorpio).

According to another version, as a constellation, Orion hunts the Pleiades, the daughters of the Titan, Atlas. In their earthly

Having accidentally killed the great hunter Orion, Artemis placed him in the sky as a constellation. There he remains, in eternal and fruitless pursuit of the Pleiades, also transformed into a constellation.

existence, Orion hunts them for seven years until the gods, taking pity on them, place them in the heavens, where Orion was doomed to pursue them in vain for eternity.

According to Homer, Orion fared little better in the underworld, spending his time in the asphodel meadow, carrying a bronze club, and hunted down by the wild animals he had killed in his earthly existence.

Orpheus

The master singer and musician, Orpheus, was the son of Apollo, the god of music, and Calliope, the muse of narrative poetry. Others would have it that the Thracian King Œagrus was his father.

Orpheus could sing and play the lute so beautifully that not only mortals but even the animals and trees, rivers, and rocks listened to him, enthralled. Orpheus was one of the Argonauts who, led by Jason, traveled to the distant land of Colchis to fetch the golden fleece (*see* **The Argonauts**). His special talents came in useful to the courageous adventurers. For example, he could smooth over quarrels by bursting into song—the tension would then evaporate immediately. He also neutralized the seductive singing of the perilous Sirens (*see* **Odysseus** and **The Sirens**) who used their irresistible voices to lure mariners to them and drive them to their deaths, simply by drowning out their voices with his lyre-playing.

After the Argonauts' voyage, Orpheus returned to his native land, Thrace, where he fell madly in love with the nymph, Eurydice. The feeling was mutual and Orpheus even went so far as to invite the god of marriage, Hymenæus, to the wedding. However, on the wedding-day itself, Eurydice was bitten on the heel by a venomous snake (according to one version it was as she was fleeing the beekeeper, Aristæus). The bite killed her. The inconsolable Orpheus could not imagine life without her. At his wits' end, he descended to the underworld where he asked Hades and Persephone to return his lover to him. He sang imploring songs to them, providing his own accompaniment on his lyre. His song made a stunning impact in the somber kingdom of death. Even the evildoers in Tartarus, the most inhospitable part of the underworld (*see* **Hades**), were affected. In the words of the poet Ovid: "As he sang these words to the music of his lyre, the bloodless shades were in tears. Tantalus made no effort to reach the

Whenever the brilliant musician Orpheus strummed the strings of his lyre and broke into song, even the wild beasts would listen to him, spellbound.

waters that ever shrank away, Ixion's wheel stood still in wonder, the vultures ceased to gnaw Titys' liver, the daughters of Danaus rested from their pitchers, and Sisyphus sat idle on his rock." (*Metamorphoses*, X. 40-45).

Even the implacable Hades was disconcerted. The singer was allowed to take his bride back to the world of the living on condition that he did not look back at her before she arrived. Rejoicing, Orpheus left, followed by Eurydice's shade. Because of the snake bite on her foot, her progress was slower and, just before he emerged, Œdipus could bear it no longer and threw a quick glance over his shoulder. Eurydice immediately fell back into the "thin mist" of the kingdom of the dead. She bade him farewell, but Orpheus could no longer hear anything.

Orpheus descended once more to the underworld, but the ferryman Charon refused to take him across the the Styx, no matter how beautifully he sang. Realizing that Eurydice was lost to him forever, Orpheus spent seven days grieving on the banks of the Styx, unable to eat anything. After that, he returned to the bleak mountains of Thrace. He wanted nothing more to do with women. Insofar as he was capable of amorous liaisons, men were now his preferred option

This was not at all to the liking of the Mænads with whom, in happier times, Orpheus had happily succumbed to the cult of the wine-god, Dionysus. In a frenzy, they flung themselves on the wretched Orpheus, shrieking so loudly that he was unable to calm them with his singing. The "woman-hater" was torn to shreds while still alive, and only his head was left intact. Together with

his lyre, the head landed in a river, the Hebrus, which carried it on to the sea. The head and lyre, which was still producing weak sounds (according to some, the head continuously called out Eurydice's name), eventually washed ashore on the island of

Eurydice, fatally wounded after having been bitten by a snake, falls into the arms of her dazed lover Orpheus. At the bottom left, the treacherous snake makes a rapid exit. Oil painting by Peter Paul Rubens, 17th century.

Lesbos. The lyre was placed in the heavens as a constellation, and Orpheus' soul eventually found Eurydice in the underworld. From that point onward, he was allowed to dwell with her forever in the Elysian Fields, the paradisiacal realm of the kingdom of the dead.

The veneration of Orpheus in Thrace was closely bound up with that of Dionysus. As is the case with the cult of the great god of wine and vegetation, the *Orphic Mysteries,* named for Orpheus, are dominated by death and resurrection, because according to an old version of the Orpheus myth, the singer eventually managed to release Eurydice from the kingdom of the dead, thanks to the savior, Dionysus. Orphism developed into a sectarian religion in the sixth century BCE, in Greece. Its followers regarded Orpheus as the founder of their creed and probably as a result, believed that the body was a type of jail in which the soul was imprisoned. Only after a cycle of death and rebirth could the soul then free itself from its confines. It is likely that later thinkers, including the great Athenian philosopher, Plato, were influenced by Orphism.

The myth of Orpheus has retained its appeal long after Antiquity, and has inspired numerous artists. These include the composer Claudio Monteverdi (1567–1643), who wrote *L'Orfeo* (1607), Christoph Willibald Gluck (1714-1787) who wrote *Orpheus and Euridice* (1762), and Jacques Offenbach

Orpheus is torn to pieces by a group of angry Mænads who were furious with him for abandoning all interest in women after the death of Eurydice. Fragment of a painting on a vase from Tarente, 4th century BCE.

A satyr and a Nymph or Mænad play a trick on the young Dionysus. The god of wine was angered by the behavior of the Thracian Mænads who had murdered Orpheus that he transformed them into trees and left Thrace for Asia Minor. Bronze statue in the park of the Villa Borghese, Rome.

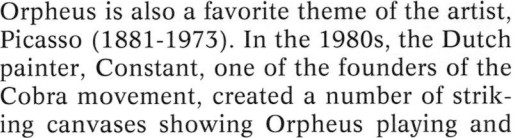

(1819–1880) whose comic opera is known in French as *Orphée aux Enfers*, usually translated as *Orpheus in the Underworld* (1858). Orpheus is also a favorite theme of the artist, Picasso (1881-1973). In the 1980s, the Dutch painter, Constant, one of the founders of the Cobra movement, created a number of striking canvases showing Orpheus playing and singing for the animals.

Pallas Athene, *see* Athena

Pan

The origin of the god of nature Pan is not entirely clear. In some accounts, he was fathered by Hermes, but according to others, he was the son of Zeus, Apollo, or even Cronos. The identity of his mother is equally vague. Her name may have been Dryope, or even Callisto. Whoever she was, there is no doubt that, after the birth, she was so shocked by the appearance of her baby, who was extremely hirsute and had the horns, legs, and tail of a goat, that she immediately took to her heels. Fortunately for the baby, Pan, some nymphs took pity on him and brought him up in Arcadia, a lovely region of mountains and forests.

Pan was a sensual god, who constantly pursued the nymphs around him and

193

produced numerous offspring with them. However, it was not just nymphs who fell prey to him. He managed to seduce the goddess of the moon, Selene, by wrapping himself in a white, woolly fleece. The nymph Syrinx, a fanatical follower of the virginal goddess of the hunt, Artemis, had no intention of being outsmarted by the hot-blooded god and fled to the banks of the River Ladon. Here, the river-nymphs, at her bidding, transformed her into some reed stems. Pan then made the pan pipe or syrinx out of the reed stems. He learned to play this instrument, with its plaintive, whistling sound, very well and even once dared to compete against the great lyre-playing god, Apollo. Apollo won the contest, but the Phrygian King Midas, who was in the audience, thought Pan had played better. The offended Apollo later punished the foolish king by giving him the ears of an ass (*see* **Apollo** and **Midas**).

As the god of woods and fields, Pan kept a watchful eye on the fertility of the herds. In general, he was a benevolent god who in between his courtships enjoyed lazing around in the open air. But anyone who disturbed him soon discovered another side to him, because the god would drive these unfortunates into a blind terror, hence the word "panic." Pan could drive crowds, even entire armies, into the state of panic ascribed to him. According to the Athenians, he caused the Persian soldiers to flee in a panic during the battle of Marathon, in 490 BCE, in which the Greeks were outnumbered. A shrine was later dedicated to Pan in Athens as a sign of gratitude for his help.

The Roman gods, Silvanus and Faunus, have been identified as being one and the same as Pan, although the latter differs from Pan in a number of aspects (*see* **Faunus**).

A comical-looking Pan follows a Mænad who is just visible at the edge of the picture. Painting on a pitcher from Campania, 4th century BCE.

Pan holding the pan pipes named for him, amidst trees and animals. Pan kept a watchful eye on the fertility of the herds and spent most of his time outdoors. Relief from Nysa, Turkey.

Pandora

According to Greek mythology, Pandora was the first woman created. She was made on the orders of the supreme god Zeus as a gift and a plague for mankind. This was because Zeus could not forgive the Titan, Prometheus, for giving fire to man and had resolved to take revenge (*see* **Prometheus**). He set the craftsman god, Hephæstos, to work. Hephæstos fashioned Pandora out of earth and water and gave her the likeness of an attractive woman. Then, according to the Greek poet, Hesiod, other gods also contributed to the creation of the first woman: "Athena was to teach her needlework and the weaving of varied web; and golden Aphrodite to shed grace upon her head, and the cruel longing and cares that weary the limbs. And he charged Hermes, the guide, the slayer of Argus, to put in her a shameless mind and deceitful nature." (Hesiod, *Works and Days,* lines 82-87).

The lovely Pandora with her "shameless" nature was sent to earth where Prometheus' rather dim-witted brother Epimetheus,—who had forgotten that Prometheus had warned him not to accept any gifts from Zeus— accepted her as a gift from the gods and married her. At that time, mankind was still living in a state of paradise, and was free from misery and sickness. However, within Pandora's reach was a sealed gold jar ("*Pandora"s box*"—the word box appears as the result of an early translation error) containing a multitude of disasters, evils, and sicknesses. Pandora could not contain her curiosity and opened the jar whereupon all the misery contained within was scattered among mankind and remained with them forever. Only hope (or premonition) remained in the jar. "But the rest, countless plagues, wander amongst men; for earth is full of evils and the sea is full. Of themselves, diseases come upon men continually by day and by night, bringing mischief to mortals silently; for wise Zeus took away speech from them. Thus is there no way to escape the will of Zeus." (*Works and Days*, lines 127-132)

The tale of Pandora brings to mind the biblical story of the first woman, Eve, who allowed herself to be seduced by the serpent into tasting the forbidden fruit in Paradise. This led to the end of the paradisiacal state of innocence and happiness that she and her husband, Adam, had enjoyed hitherto, and from that point onward, mankind was condemned to a difficult existence full of pain and drudgery.

Although the proverbial term "Pandora's box" is still used, the disasters were actually stored in a jar (the word "box" comes from an old translation error). This jar may have resembled these storage jars from the palace of Cnossos on Crete.

Pandora, the equivalent of Eve in Greek mythology, brought misfortune upon the world by failing to overcome her curiosity and opening the jar containing disasters, evils, and sicknesses.

Paris

Paris (also known as Alexander) was the son of the Trojan King Priam and his wife, Hecabe. His egotistical behavior led to the fall of the city of his birth and of his family.

Shortly before Paris' birth, Queen Hecabe had an ominous dream as a result of which, on the advice of a seer, she abandoned her son far away from Troy. He was raised by a shepherd and later reunited with his family after his clairvoyant sister, Cassandra, had recognized him. The handsome Paris, who was married to the nymph Œnone, nonetheless continued to live as a shepherd on Mount Ida in Asia Minor, where he tended his father's flocks. It was here that he was approached by the goddesses Hera, Athena, and Aphrodite, who needed someone to act as a judge in their "beauty contest." During the wedding of the goddess Thetis and the mortal Peleus, Eris, the goddess of discord, had thrown an apple marked "for the most beautiful" into the crowd of those present. All three goddesses believed that the apple belonged to them, so Zeus decided that Paris must pronounce the final verdict (*see* **Aphrodite**, **Hera**, *and* **Thetis**).

The goddesses tried to bribe Paris with the most extravagant promises. Hera promised him enormous power, and Athena success in battle. Aphrodite, however, promised him the most beautiful woman in the world. It did not take Paris long to decide and he awarded victory to Aphrodite. There was one problem, though. The most beautiful woman in the world, Helen, was already married to the Spartan King Menelaus. However, as goddess of love, Aphrodite knew exactly how to deal with this problem. Paris had been sent by his father to Sparta as part of a delegation and had been warmly received by Menelaus. Under Aphrodite's influence, Helen fell deeply in love with the handsome guest, and when Menelaus left for Crete to attend the funeral of his grandfather, Paris saw his ideal opportunity. Taking Helen and some of Menelaus' treasures with him, he returned to Troy where he married his "conquest." This deed did not meet with universal approval, even in Troy, because there were some who could foresee all the mischief that Paris' evil deed would bring to the city (*see* **Helen** *and* **Menelaus** *as well*).

Nevertheless, the Trojans stood firm when the duped Spartan king, accompanied by the cunning and articulate hero, Odysseus, came to negotiate for the return of his wife and possessions. A war thus became unavoidable because the nobles who had been competing with Menelaus for the hand of Helen had previously sworn to come to his aid should he find himself in difficulties because of Helen. With the backing of his powerful brother, Agamemnon, Menelaus raised a massive army that laid siege to Troy.

During the first part of the ten-year Trojan War, Paris failed to make a favorable impression. Since he was the identifiable cause of the war, both friend and foe "hated him as being dark death." His brother, Hector, in particular, a noble and selfless man and the bravest hero on the Trojan side, took a fairly condescending view of Paris, whom he

As a result of a bad dream experienced by his mother, the Trojan prince Paris was taken far away from Troy and abandoned. He was raised by a herdsman and continued to live as a shepherd even after his family had found him. Flocks of sheep at Milete, almost 200 miles south of Troy.

After Aphrodite had promised him the most beautiful woman in the world, Paris had no problem deciding the winner of the goddesses' beauty contest. This striking, whimsical family portrait painted by Ferdinand Bol in 1656 shows a couple portrayed as Paris and Aphrodite. Their child is presented as Eros, although the "apple of discord" is absent.

regarded as an idle "womanizer." At some point during the tenth year of the war, it was decided that Menelaus and Paris should fight a duel, in the hope that this would finally settle the war. The effete Paris turned out to be hopelessly outclassed. After Menelaus had thrust his lance through Paris' breastplate and brought his sword down on Paris' helmet ridge, smashing the blade to pieces, he grabbed him by the plume of his helmet and started dragging him toward the Greek lines. He would certainly have succeeded had not Aphrodite, who could see her favorite was on the point of being strangled by the chin-strap of his helmet, intervened. She snapped the chin-strap just in time, leaving Menelaus holding an empty helmet. The goddess wrapped Paris in a cloud and took him to his bedchamber in Troy. Aphrodite then ordered Helen to go and tend to her husband. Helen obeyed the order with great reluctance, having long tired of Paris and being keen to return to Sparta.

Ironically, a short time later, it was precisely the weak and spineless Paris who managed to kill the most formidable Greek hero, the virtually invincible Achilles. Paris struck Achilles with an arrow in the only vulnerable part of his body, his heel (the "Achilles heel.") But this was not really of Paris' doing, because the god Apollo, himself an unerring shot, had carefully guided the arrow released by Paris to its target. Paris did not live for much longer after Achilles' death. He was also the victim

of an arrow. The man who killed him was Philoctetes, who as a youth had been given an arrow by the dying hero Heracles (*see* **Heracles**). For a long time, Philoctetes had been unable to take part in the war as the Greeks had left him behind on the island of Lemnos because of his suppurating wound.

The fatally wounded Paris asked to be taken to his first wife, Œnone, who had once promised that she would heal all his wounds. However, she refused to keep to her promise because he had abandoned her for Helen, and Paris was doomed to die. He therefore played no further part in the fall of his father's city, Troy, for which he was responsible.

Pasiphæ

Pasiphæ, a daughter of the sun-god Helios and the Oceanid Perseis, married the Cretan King Minos. She gave Minos numerous children, but fell deeply in love with the white bull that Poseidon had given to Minos as a gift. It had been intended that Minos should offer the animal back to Poseidon, as a sacrifice, but the king was so fond of the bull that he preferred to keep it for himself. This was why Poseidon caused Pasiphæ to develop her unnatural passion.

Dædalus, the master craftsman and artist at Minos' court, made an artificial cow for Pasiphæ in which Pasiphæ hid and coupled with the bull. This bizarre liaison resulted in the birth of the Minotaur, a monstrous and

Achilles collapses, fatally wounded by an arrow shot by Paris, who has been lying in wait. Paris' arrow is guided by the god Apollo, who is standing or floating behind him. Oil painting by Peter Paul Rubens, 17th century.

Pasiphæ, the wife of king Minos of Crete, fell hopelessly in love with the white bull that the sea god Poseidon had presented to her husband.

bloodthirsty creature with a human body and a bull's head. Minos was so ashamed of the existence of this freak that he made Dædalus build a vast underground maze, the Labyrinth, in which the Minotaur was locked up (*see* **Minos**, **Minotaur,** *and* **Theseus**).

Patroclus

Patroclus was the son of King Menœtius of Opus, brother-in-arms of the great hero, Achilles. As a young man, he killed Clitonymus, the son of Amphidamas, after a quarrel. Menœtius took his son to the court of Peleus, Achilles' father, to protect him from retaliation. The young men formed a close friendship and Patroclus went into battle with Achilles in the Trojan War.

When Achilles clashed with the Greek supreme commander Agamemnon in the tenth year of the war and lost his appetite for fighting, Patroclus stood by his friend (*see* **Achilles**). However, when Achilles, the most powerful of all the Greek heroes, lay down his weapons, it left the Greeks in a difficult position. The Trojans advanced up to the Grecian encampment and wounded a number of significant Greek heroes. In a roundabout way, the old hero, Nestor, made an urgent appeal to Patroclus to change the mind of his friend Achilles. Patroclus was impressed by what Nestor had to say, and tended one of the wounded fighters. Later, when the Trojans had pushed even further forward and were threatening to set fire to the Greek ships, Patroclus could stand idly by no longer. After a sharp exchange of words with Achilles, his friend gave him permission to join the battle, wearing his armor. As the first Greek ship went up in flames, Patroclus entered the battle on Achilles' chariot, leading Achilles' men. The impact was huge. The Trojans had thought the feared Achilles had rejoined the battle, suffered heavy losses, and

fled in their masses. To his distress, the king of the gods, Zeus saw Patroclus kill his son, Sarpedon, although he had considered saving his son from death (*see* **Sarpedon**).

Patroclus was dazzled by his success and forgot Achilles' warnings not to venture too far after the Trojans. He followed them to the walls of their city and there, the god Apollo, who had supported the Trojans through thick and thin, stopped him four times, but Patroclus would still not see reason. He threw a stone, killing Hector's charioteer, whom he then mocked. While he was fighting Hector beside the body of the charioteer, the overconfident Patroclus suddenly experienced a dizzy spell. He lost his helmet and shield, and his lance snapped. Another Trojan stabbed him in the back with a spear and Hector finished him off. With his last breath, Patroclus told Hector that he would soon be killed by Achilles (*see* **Hector**). After that, there was a tremendous fight over Patroclus' body and armor. Hector took the weapons, but "great Ajax" (*see* **Ajax**) removed the body to safety.

Achilles was beside himself when he heard of his friend's death. He swore he would not bury Patroclus until he had had his revenge on the Trojans. His reluctance to fight was at an end. The furious Achilles killed Hector—as Patroclus had predicted in his last

When the Greeks found themselves in a very tight spot, Patroclus joined the fray wearing the armor of his comrade-in-arms Achilles. This Nereid, possibly Achilles' mother, Thetis, is carrying a helmet whilst riding a seahorse. This is very likely the new helmet Hephæstos forged for Achilles after Patroclus' death. Fragment of a comb from Arezzo by Tigranus, 1st century CE.

moments—dragged his corpse to where his friend's body was laid out, and only then allowed Patroclus (whom Achilles' mother Thetis had embalmed in ambrosia, food of the gods, and nectar, the drink of the gods) to be cremated and his bones buried. There was a barbaric and gruesome adjunct to the funeral. Achilles killed twelve Trojan prisoners of war and burned them on Patroclus' funeral pyre.

After the death of Achilles, the mortal remains of the brothers-in-arms were buried in the same golden urn, wrought by Hephæstos.

Pegasus, *see* Bellerophon

Peleus, *see* Thetis

Pelops

Pelops was a son of the Lydian King Tantalus and a brother of Niobe. The Greek peninsula called the Peloponnese (literally, "island of Pelops") is named for him.

When Pelops was still a small boy, his father invited the Olympian gods to dine with him. To find out whether they really were omniscient, Tantalus slaughtered his son and

The "speaking statue" Pasquino which stands on a street corner close to the Piazza Navona in Rome. The weathered and battered statue is of Menelaus, who tried to protect Patroclus' corpse from the Trojans.

served him to his guests. All the gods saw through Tantalus' gruesome deed and turned away from the table in disgust, apart from Demeter, goddess of the grain and crops. She tucked into a piece of Pelops' shoulder. The gods then restored Pelops to life and Demeter gave him an ivory shoulder. All his descendants could be identified by a white birthmark on the shoulder (*see* **Tantalus**). After Tantalus' death, Pelops inherited his father's

Pelops was slaughtered by his father Tantalus and served up to the gods. Demeter, the absent-minded goddess of agriculture, ate his shoulder.

throne, but the Trojan King Ilus drove him out and he fled to the part of Greece that would later bear his name.

In the district of Elis, in the northwest of the Peloponnese, Pelops courted Hippodamia, the daughter of King Œnomaus of Pisa. According to some versions, it was predicted to Œnomaus that his future son-in-law would kill him. According to another tale, Œnomaus was in love with his own daughter and therefore wanted to prevent her marrying Pelops. In any event, he challenged her future husband to a chariot race. The race was held on a vast track that extended from Pisa to the Isthmus of Corinth, on the other side of Peloponnese. The suitor had to start first, taking Hippodamia with him in his chariot. Œnomaus first made an offering to Ares, the god of war, and then set off in pursuit a little later. If he overtook Pelops, he would be allowed to kill him, but if Œnomaus did not win, not only would he lose his daughter but his son-in-law would be allowed to kill him as well. This last eventuality was extremely unlikely since Ares had given Œnomaus some special weaponry and two immortal horses. Moreover, he had an excellent charioteer, Myrtilus, son of Hermes, who was himself in love with Hippodamia but did not dare compete against his master.

Pelops, who was about as unscrupulous as his criminal father, bribed Myrtilus by offering him a night with Hippodamia and half of Œnomaus' kingdom if he would sabotage his master's chariot. And indeed, thanks to Myrtilus' sabotage, the wheels of Œnomaus' chariot flew off. The king died as a result of the accident, or, as some say, he was killed by Pelops. He cursed his charioteer with his last breath, realizing he had been betrayed by him, and predicted that Pelops would kill Myrtilus as well.

Pelops married Hippodamia and became King of Pisa. He did not, however, honor his promises to the charioteer Myrtilus. On the contrary—during a trip along the coast he tipped him out of Myrtilus out of his chariot, where he fell over the high cliffs. Just as he had been cursed by Œnomaus, the drowning Myrtilus now cursed Pelops—and not just Pelops but all of his descendants.

Pelops regretted his crimes and dedicated a monument to Myrtilus in Olympia. He was a powerful ruler, eventually expanding his kingdom over the entire Peloponnese. However, Myrtilus' curse still held good. Pelops' sons, Atreus and Tyestes, in turn, committed

Pelops won his wife Hippodamia by beating her father Œnomaus in a chariot race. It was not a clean victory, because he arranged to sabotage his opponent's chariot and this resulted in Œnomaus having a fatal accident. Picture on an Etruscan amphora, 6th century BCE.

the most terrible crimes, which lead to a cycle of murder and revenge that did not end until Pelops' great-grandson Orestes was tried at the court of Areopagus in Athens (*see* **Agamemnon**, **Atreus** *and* **Orestes**) and was acquitted. Long before this, Pelops had been deeply affected by the death of his sister Niobe, who had turned to stone after Apollo and Artemis shot and killed all her children because she had been boasting that she was more fertile than the goddess.

Penelope

Penelope was the daughter of the Spartan King Icarius and the nymph, Periboea. She was the wife of Odysseus, King of the island of Ithaca and the wisest of all the Greek heroes of the Trojan War (*see* **Odysseus**). Odysseus and Penelope had one son named Telemachus. During Odysseus' twenty-year absence (after the ten-year Trojan War it took him another ten years to reach home again) Penelope proved herself to be an extraordinarily faithful wife. She remained constant in the belief that her husband would eventually return and resisted the pressure of the nobles of Ithaca to marry one of them.

She misled these "suitors," who made free with her food and drink at her palace, by promising them that she would make her choice once she had woven a shroud for her father-in-law, Laertes. She spent the day weaving this shroud but, by night, she secretly unraveled the work she had done. That Penelope was on a par with her smarter husband in terms of intelligence was further borne out when he finally returned to Ithaca and killed the suitors. Penelope would not believe that he really was Odysseus until he had revealed a secret known only to the couple, namely that one of the bed posts of their marital bed, which Odysseus himself had made, was the trunk of an old olive tree that was still rooted in the ground. After their reunion Odysseus and Penelope lived a long and happy life.

Persephone (Roman= Proserpina)

Persephone was the only daughter of the goddess of agriculture, Demeter. Her father was the king of the gods, Zeus. Persephone, sometimes called Core (the maiden) for short.

She was originally goddess of agriculture, just like her mother, but later became the wife of the god of the underworld, Hades, and mistress of the kingdom of the dead.

Demeter was very much against her daughter marrying Hades. Without her knowledge, Zeus had promised the beautiful Persephone as a bride to his sinister brother. One day, when the girl was gathering flowers in a wood in Sicily, the gloomy god of death suddenly appeared in his two-horse chariot. In the words of the poet Ovid: "While Proserpina (Persephone's Latin name) was playing in this glade, and gathering violets or radiant lilies, while with girlish fondness she filled the folds of her gown, and her basket, trying to outdo her companions in her picking, Hades, almost in a moment, saw her, prized her, took her: so swift as this, is love. The frightened goddess cried out to her mother, to her friends, most of all to her mother, with piteous mouth. Since she had torn her dress at the opening, the flowers she had collected fell from her loosened tunic, and even their scattering caused her virgin tears." (*Metamorphoses*, V., lines 391-401)

The broken-hearted Demeter did everything in her power to recover her daughter, but in the end, she had to resign herself to Persephone spending part of the year (four to six months) in the underworld and the other part of the year with her (*see* **Demeter**). This was because, whilst in the kingdom of the dead, Persephone had eaten some pomegranate seeds and an ancient rule stipulated that only those who had eaten and drunk nothing in the underworld could ever be allowed to leave it for good.

It appeared that Persephone found it easier to accept her fate than her mother, who grieved so much during her absence that the earth became arid and barren at this time. Persephone behaved as if she were a herself a goddess of death. Homer calls her "the dreaded Persephone," and in his epic poem, *The Odyssey*, Odysseus ascribes to her an active role as ruler of the dead in his report of his visit to the underworld. It is she who decides which shades may approach him (*see* **Hades**). Persephone's death and return to earth feature prominently in the Eleusinian Mysteries, the ceremonies that were held annually at Eleusis, near Athens, and which only initiates could attend (*see* **Demeter**).

Perseus

Perseus was the son of the supreme god, Zeus, and the mortal, Danæ. He was one of the heroic demigods of Greek mythology who, just like Heracles and Theseus, performed a number of super-human heroic deeds.

Danæ's father, Acrisius, King of Argos, had locked her up in a bronze tower because an oracle had predicted that the son she would bear would kill his grandfather, Acrisius. Zeus, who coveted Danæ, refused to let

this severe punishment stand in his way. He visited Danæ in the form of a shower of gold and Perseus was born as a result of this liaison (see **Danæ**). The shocked Acrisius put mother and son in a chest and put them to sea in it. However, thanks to Zeus' protection, the chest landed safely on the island of Seriphos, where Danæ and her little son received a warm welcome from the fisherman Dictys, brother of King Polydectes of

Demeter had to reconcile herself to the ruling that her daughter would be forced to spend part of the year in the underworld and the rest of the year with her. Earthenware bust from Tarente, 4th century BCE.

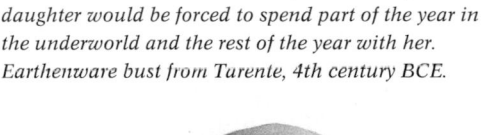

Seriphos. Perseus was raised by his mother and Dictys, but Polydectes developed a strong passion for Danæ and decided to rid himself of the young hero, who was keeping a watchful eye on his mother. That was why he gave Perseus the task of bringing him the head of the gorgon, Medusa. By normal mortal standards this was an impossible task because Medusa's appearance was so dreadful that no living thing could look at her without being turned to stone (*see the* **Gorgons**).

Fortunately, Perseus was helped by the goddess Athena who bore a grudge against Medusa because she had had relations with Poseidon (or, according to some, been raped by Poseidon) at a shrine dedicated to Athena. Athena gave Perseus a bronze, reflective shield and told him what he should do. First of all he was to go to see the gorgons, sisters who lived in North Africa. There were three of them (two, according to another version), ancient crones who shared one eye between them which they took turns to use. Perseus stole this eye from them as they were passing it round, forcing them to show him the way to the gorgons. Once they had reluctantly given him the information he required, he threw their eye into the water so they could not warn the gorgons of his impending arrival. Some nymphs later gave Perseus a cap that made him invisible, a pair of winged shoes, and a sack in which to carry Medusa's head. Hermes gave him a magic saber.

With the aid of his winged shoes, Perseus flew to the home of the gorgons beside the

Equipped with winged shœs, a cap that made him invisible, a saber, and the petrified head of Medusa as a weapon, the hero Perseus was able to perform the most spectacular feats.

Ocean, the sea that encircled the world. The three hideous sisters had fallen fast asleep and Perseus backed cautiously past them, keeping a careful eye on Medusa using his reflective shield, thus enabling him to watch her without being turned to stone. Unflinchingly, he cut off her monstrous snake-covered head with Hermes' magic saber, and placed it in his sack. Medusa's blood produced the monster Chrysaor and the winged horse Pegasus (*see* **Bellerophon**).

According to the poet Ovid, Perseus' first

With the support of Athena, Perseus managed to carry out his impossible task, without suffering any injury himself. He secured the hideous head of the Gorgon, Medusa. Medusa's head, relief from Aphrodisias.

encounter on his return journey was with the Titan, Atlas, to whom he introduced himself as a son of Zeus. He did not find Perseus a welcome visitor because an oracle had told Atlas that a son of Zeus would rob him of the golden apples of the garden of the Hesperides. When the giant adopted a threatening attitude, the hero showed him Medusa's head, whereupon Atlas turned to stone, becoming the mountain range that still bears his name (*see* **Atlas**). Perseus then continued westward on his journey across Africa. As he flew over Ethiopia, he spied a beautiful girl chained to a rock beside the sea. This was Andromeda, the daughter of King Cepheus, who was being offered as a sacrifice to a sea-monster as an act of appeasement for the arrogant words of her mother, Cassiopeia (*see* **Andromeda**). Perseus watched in horror as the sea-monster rose from the depths to devour Andromeda. He told her despairing parents, who were watching from the shore, that he would save her on the condition that Andromeda would then become his wife. Cepheus and Cassiopeia agreed immediately and even offered him their kingdom as a dowry as well. Like a bird of prey, Perseus dived down onto the sea-monster and stabbed

Andromeda watches anxiously from her perilous position as Perseus executes a daredevil dive onto the sea monster that is planning to devour her. Oil painting by Peter Paul Rubens, 17th century.

it in the side with his saber. His winged shoes enabled him to avoid the monster's counterattacks, and after suffering further stab wounds from the saber, the monster died.

The subsequent wedding of Perseus and Andromeda was not as happy an occasion as it might have been. This was because Cepheus had previously promised Andromeda to his brother, Phineus, who was not to be fobbed off. With a large party of supporters, Phineus burst into the wedding party which then turned into a massive and bloody free-for-all. There were countless victims and Perseus faced fearful odds, leaving him with no alternative but to use his weapon of destruction, Medusa's head. He employed it to turn Phineus and his supporters to stone.

Years later, after Andromeda had given Perseus a son, the couple traveled to Seriphos. Perseus arrived just in time to rescue his mother and Dictys who had been beleaguered by Polydectes and forced to seek sanctuary in a temple. Polydectes refused to believe that Perseus really had returned with Medusa's head and treated the hero contemptuously. Perseus then showed him Medusa's

head and Polydectes was turned into "bloodless stone."

Perseus made Dictys, King of Seriphos, and himself continued his journey to Argos, the kingdom of his grandfather. Acrisius feared that his predicted end was near and fled to Thessaly, but he was unable to avoid his fate. Perseus followed him to Thessaly and both he and Acrisius competed in the games before the father of the local king. During one event, Acrisius was accidentally struck by a discus thrown by Perseus, with fatal consequences.

Back in Argos, Perseus turned the usurper Prœtus to stone and then ascended the throne of Argos or, according to some, that of the city-state of Tiryns. Whatever the case, he went on to live a long and happy life with Andromeda, who gave him another five sons and one daughter.

After Perseus' death, his former protectress, Athena, placed him in the heavens as a constellation. The same honor was accorded to Andromeda and her parents. Long before this, Athena had taken Medusa's head from Perseus and fixed it on the shield or the *ægis*

Perseus as a constellation. He is holding the head of Medusa that he has just sliced off her body with his raised sword.

Coin of a historical namesake of the hero Perseus, King Perseus of Macedonia. The reverse of the coin shows an eagle perched on a thunderbolt, symbolizing the power of the king. Silver coin (tetradrachma), 2nd century BCE.

that she wore over her shoulders.

Phædra, *see* Theseus

Phæthon

Phæton was a son of Helios, the god of the sun, and the Oceanid (sea-nymph) Clymene. He grew up in Egypt, looked after by his mother. When Phæton was a young man, his friend Epaphus claimed that he was not Helios' son at all and that his mother had lied to him about his origins. Clymene swore to her son that Helios really was his father and told him where he could find the sun-god.

Phæton set off on his quest and visited his father in his glittering palace, decorated with gold, silver, and ivory, that lay at the eastern edge of the world. The sun-god gave him a warm welcome whereupon Phæton asked him for indisputable proof that Helios really was his father. Helios swore by the underworld river, the Styx, that he was prepared to give his son anything he needed to put an end to his doubts. This was a mistake because the young man immediately asked to be allowed to drive the chariot of the sun through the heavens for one day (*see* **Helios**). Straightaway, Helios deeply regretted his promise, but could not go back on it. He warned Phæton of the grave dangers to which he was exposing himself and the world. This was because only Helios, and no-one else, not even Zeus, the king of the gods, was allowed to drive the sun-chariot and the wild horses of the sun. Phæton, however, refused to change his mind so, full of trepidation, Helios led him to the chariot.

The four fire-breathing horses were harnessed and after Helios had warned his son not to let the horses run too fast, not to fly too high and, above all, not to fly too low, Phæton leapt into the magnificent chariot. In raptures, he set off but almost immediately lost control of his steeds. The chariot of the sun veered off course, causing panic among the constellations in the firmament and then hurtled along far too low over the earth. Entire cities, countries, and mountains were scorched by the heat of the sun and terrible fires broke out all over. Phæton caused rivers to dry up, deserts to form, and the skin of the Ethiopians to turn black. Gaia, mother earth, suffered dreadful anguish and called upon

Zeus for help. The king of the gods realized that rapid intervention was needed and knocked the unfortunate charioteer from his post with a well-aimed lightning bolt. The young man landed in the River Eridanus (later, the Po), but the fall killed him. He was buried by the nymphs and the following words were inscribed on his grave:

> *Here lies Phæton who the sun's journey made,*
> *Dared all, though he by weakness was betrayed.*

(Ovid, *Metamorphoses*, II., lines 237-238).

Helios was so distraught at his son's death that the earth had to endure a day without sunlight. Clymene roamed the world, crazed with grief, Phæton's sisters turned into amber-producing trees and Phæton's friend and relative Cycnus, (not to be confused with Cycnus, son of Poseidon, *see* **Poseidon**) turned into a swan out of grief. Cycnus then cried aloud in lamentation. This is where the term "swan song" originates.

Phœbe

A number of mythological figures bear the name Phœbe. The most important Phœbe was a Titan, a daughter of Uranus and Gaia. Leto, mother of the remarkable divine twins Apollo and Artemis, and of Asteria resulted from Phœbe's union with Crœus. Leucippus also had a daughter called Phœbe as did Tyn-

Phæton's mother, Clymene, was so distraught at his death that she roamed the world, crazed with grief. Wailing woman, fragment of a painting on an Athenian vase, 5th century BCE.

The Titan, Phœbe, "the shining one," was the grandmother of Apollo and Artemis.

dareos and Leda. This latter Phœbe was a half-sister of Helen, the most beautiful woman in Greek mythology, and of the Dioscuri, Castor and Polydeuces. Finally, Artemis, the goddess of the hunt, unspoiled nature, and grain, was sometimes called Phœbe, as the female counterpart of her brother Phœbus ("the shining one") Apollo, god of the sun.

Pluto, *see* Hades

Polyphemus

Polyphemus, son of the sea-god, Poseidon, was the Cyclops who extended the hero Odysseus and his followers a gruesome welcome in his cave on their return journey from Troy. He devoured several of Odysseus' men, but the quick-witted hero made Polyphemus drunk and put out his one eye. He and his men hung under the bellies of the Cyclops' sheep, and thus managed to escape from the cave (*for details of this tale see* **The Cyclopes** *and* **Odysseus**).

Just before these grisly events, Polyphemus had fallen madly in love with the Nereid, Galatea. The sea-nymph, however, was already in love with Acis, a son of the god of nature, Pan, and was frightened by the brutal Cyclops who, to win her over, had even tried to trim his hair and beard. Polyphemus

ignored the warnings of the seer, Telemus, that Odysseus would one day blind him, and set about composing a serenade to the charms of Galatea. This love-song, in which he complained of Galatea's callousness, simply made Polyphemus a laughing-stock. He also extolled his own virtues with a bizarre list of everything he would give her (including a "hairy she-bear" by way of a soft toy) and praised his own manly looks, saying that a real man should have a heavy beard and a lot of body hair and likened his one eye to the disk of the sun.

When, not surprisingly, Galatea remained

The hero, Odysseus, gouges out the one eye in the forehead of the Cyclops Polyphemus who is drunk.

unmoved by this serenade, Polyphemus abandoned all his good intentions of behaving like a civilized human being and reverted to the coarse brute that was his true nature. He flew into a jealous rage and murdered Galatea's lover Acis by hurling a rock at him. Acis was later changed into a river.

Polyxena

Polyxena was a daughter of the Trojan king, Priam, and his wife, Hecabe. After the fall of Troy, the Trojan women were distributed among the Greek commanders as part of the spoils of war. Around that time, the shade of the great hero, Achilles, arose from his grave to demand his own share of the booty. He insisted that Polyxena be offered to him and the Greeks decided to honor their greatest hero and grant his wish. Polyxena's mother, Hecabe, was beside herself, but the girl climbed onto Achilles' tomb calmly and with dignity and voluntarily removed her upper clothing to enable Achilles' son, Neoptolemus, to run her through with his sword. The Athenian playwright, Euripides, describes what the young princess said to her executioner during this shocking event: "'Young prince, if it is my breast you would strike, lo, here it is, strike home, or if at my neck thy sword thou would aim, behold, that neck is bared.' Then he, half-glad, half-sorry in his pity for the maid, cleft with the steel the channels of her breath and streams of blood gushed forth; but she, even in death's agony, took good heed to fall with maiden grace, hiding from gaze of man what modest maiden must." (Euripides, *Collected Works I*, p. 329).

According to some versions, there was a deeper reason behind Achilles' shade specifically choosing Polyxena. The hero was thought to have been in love with her when he was alive. Polyxena's brother, Hector, apparently prevented them from marrying, but after Achilles killed Hector, Polyxena and Achilles are said to have met up again. It was during this encounter that Paris, who had concealed himself, killed Achilles with an arrow guided by Apollo.

Pomona, *see* Vertumnus

Poseidon (Roman=Neptune)

Poseidon, the great sea-god who ruled all the seas and water elements on earth, was the son of Cronos and Rhea, and an elder brother of the king of the gods, Zeus. He was one of the twelve Olympian gods who lived with Zeus on Mount Olympus, although he was usually to be found in his glittering undersea palace, mainly visiting Mount Olympus to meet with the other gods.

Cronos and the other Titans (*see* **Cronos** *and* **Titans**) ruled supreme until Zeus waged war against them. Following the victory of the

The lumbering Polyphemus falls passionately in love with the Nereid, Galatea, and makes a complete fool of himself by composing a love-song to her. Nereid on Neptune's Fountain in the Piazza Navona, in Rome, 16th century.

The shade of the great hero, Achilles, rises from his grave and demands that the Trojan princess, Polyxena, be sacrificed to him. Achilles' son, Neoptolemus, has to kill Polyxena on Achilles' tomb, using Achilles' sword. She goes to her death fearlessly. Achilles, painting on a fragment of an amphora, 6th century BCE.

younger gods, the brothers Zeus, Hades, and Poseidon divided the world between them. Hades was allotted the underworld, Zeus dominion of the sky, and Poseidon, the sea. Being king of the gods, Zeus ruled the earth, but it remained "neutral territory" as well. That is why the ruler of the seas regularly made his presence known, usually through earthquakes. The short-tempered Poseidon was feared as an "earth-shaker"—one of the nicknames that Homer frequently used to describe him—and the instigator of devastating tidal waves and terrible storms at sea.

Poseidon did not wholeheartedly accept the sovereignty of his brother Zeus. Once he even joined in a conspiracy with Zeus' wife, Hera, and daughter, Athena, in an attempt to depose him. The three of them were planning to put Zeus in chains, but the Nereid Thetis came to the rescue of the king of the gods. She quickly summoned the exceptionally strong, hundred-armed giant, Briareus, to Olympus. He took up a menacing position next to Zeus' throne and, in so doing, quelled the rebellion.

The fearsome and capricious sea-god, with whom mariners certainly needed to remain on good terms, was worshiped throughout the Greek and Roman world. There are numerous images of him, portraying him as an imposing figure with a full beard and carrying a trident. This weapon, intended to be used to spear fish, had been made for him by the Cyclopes who had also made Zeus' lightning bolts and Hades' helmet which rendered

When the three sons of Cronos and Rhea divided the world between them, Poseidon was given dominion of the seas and the waters. Statue of Poseidon from Milete, Classical period.

him invisible. According to some, Poseidon had originally been an earth-god (his name is actually said to mean "husband of the earth") who later took over from older, more benevolent sea-deities such as Nereus and Proteus. It was also supposed that he was once worshiped in the form of a horse (just as Hera once assumed the form of a heifer and Athena the form of an owl). In any event, he was credited with creating the horse, the bull, and the dolphin.

Poseidon would occasionally give special horses to a few favorite mortals. For example, he gave Pelops the horses with which he won

Poseidon did not wholeheartedly accept the sovereignty of his brother Zeus. He even once tried to depose Zeus in a conspiracy with the latter's wife Hera and daughter Athena. Head of Zeus from Nemrut Dagh, Turkey, 1st century BCE.

The mighty Poseidon, ruler of the waters, with his permanent adjunct, the trident.

the races that gave him his wife Hippodamia (see **Pelops**), and, together with the other gods, he gave the immortal, talking horses, Xanthus and Balius, to Peleus upon his marriage to the goddess, Thetis. Poseidon himself had a chariot pulled by seahorses that enabled him to travel over the waves at breathtaking speed. His wife, Amphritrite, a daughter of the old sea-deity Nereus, lived by his side in his golden palace under the sea. They were surrounded by an extensive retinue of sea-nymphs and unusual sea creatures. Their son, Triton, who had the appearance of a merman (see **Triton** for further details), and their daughters, Rhode and Benthesicyme, were also part of the sea-god's entourage.

In common with his brother Zeus, Poseidon was anything but a faithful husband. He seduced and raped numerous goddesses, nymphs, and mortal women who produced countless descendants for him. Before his marriage to Amphritrite, he had had romantic liaisons with his sister, Demeter, and even fathered the giant, Antæus, with his grandmother, Gaia. The infamous Cyclops, Polyphemus, was also a son of Poseidon (see **Polyphemus**), and even the paternity of the great hero, Theseus, is sometimes attributed to him. Poseidon made his son Cycnus invulnerable to the effects of weapons, but this did not prevent the great Greek hero Achilles from killing Cycnus. He did so by strangling the demigod with the chin-strap of his own helmet. Poseidon later transformed Cycnus

It is possible that Poseidon was not originally a sea god. He was once worshiped in the form of a horse. His special seahorses enabled him to travel over the waters at high speed. Seahorse on Neptune's Fountain, Piazza Navona, Rome, 16th century.

The retinue of Poseidon, king of the seas, included numerous sea nymphs or Nereids, as well as the sea god Triton. There was frequent mention of several "Tritons." A Nereid astride a Triton, terra-cotta sculpture from Tarente, 2nd–1st century BCE.

into a swan.

One victim of Poseidon's lechery was the gorgon, Medusa (see **Gorgons**). Although the gorgons were known for their repellent and frightening appearance, according to some, Medusa had once been a beauty. So beautiful was she that Poseidon could not control himself and raped her at a shrine to Athena, who was so enraged by this that she punished Medusa—and curiously not Poseidon!—by transforming her beautiful hair into writhing snakes. When Perseus killed Medusa shortly thereafter, with the help of the still wrathful Athena, Medusa was pregnant as a result of her encounter with Poseidon. No sooner had she been beheaded, than Poseidon's sons, Chrysaor and Pegasus (a winged horse, see **Bellerophon**), sprouted from her blood.

Other victims of Poseidon's lust included the beautiful princess, Cornix, who escaped being raped by the sea-god at the last minute when Athena transformed her into a crow, and the Thessalonian king's daughter, Cænis. At Cænis' request, Poseidon changed her into a man after raping her.

In common with all the other sea-gods, Poseidon could transform himself into different shapes with great ease and exploited this ability during his amorous escapades. For example, he variously "disguised" himself, among other things, as a horse, bull, bird, ram, and dolphin.

Poseidon's relationship with mortals was by no means of an exclusively erotic nature. Together with Apollo he built the walls of the

Poseidon was surrounded by a host of special sea creatures, including dolphins, of course, as they were sacred to him. He is clearly displeased to see a winged god on the backs of these dolphins. Relief on terra-cotta plaque from Tunisia, 4th century CE.

Poseidon presented the Cretan King Minos with a magnificent bull,. The plan was that Minos would offer the animal to him as a sacrifice., but Minos loved the bull so much that he wanted to keep him for himself. Rhyton in the form of a bull's head, Asia Minor (Turkey).

city of Troy for King Laomedon. Laomedon, however, refused to pay the sea-god his agreed fee in gold. Poseidon took his revenge by producing a terrible flood and went on to demand that Laomedon's daughter be offered as a sacrifice to a sea-monster. Heracles rescued her, and he too was cheated of the reward promised by her dishonest father (*see* **Heracles**). Poseidon's resentment spilled over to Laomedon's descendants and—apart from his co-builder Apollo—Poseidon was one of the most fanatical Olympian supporters of the Greek besiegers of the city during the Trojan War. However, after the fall of Troy, the Greeks were no longer safe from him either. For example, he killed "little Ajax" (the son of Oileus), who had desecrated Athena's Trojan shrine by raping the Princess Cassandra there (*see* **Ajax**). Odysseus himself later incurred Poseidon's wrath when he blinded Poseidon's son, Polyphemus.

A separate conflict arose between Poseidon and Minos, King of Crete. Minos asked Poseidon for a bull that he could offer to him as a sacrifice and the sea-god then produced a glittering white bull which surfaced from the waves. Minos was so delighted with this bull that he wanted to keep it for himself, instead of returning it to Poseidon. The outraged Poseidon then caused Minos' wife Pasiphæ to fall in love with the bull and even mate with it. This liaison resulted in the birth of the Minotaur, a monstrous creature with a human body and the head of a bull (*see* **Minos**, **Minotaur**, and **Pasiphæ**), which led to numerous gruesome sequels.

Poseidon's problems with the residents of the city of Athens were a different matter altogether. He had competed against Athena for domination of the region of Attica in which Athens was located. They had to wager which of the two could offer the Athenians the most useful gift. Poseidon used his trident to tap the rocky bottom of the Acropolis causing a source of brackish water to form there. Athena went one better. She caused an olive tree to sprout up and was then declared the winner and goddess–protector of the city. Poseidon proved a sore loser and caused a great flood in Attica. Zeus later reconciled Poseidon and the Athenians. From that point on, they worshiped him in a manner of which he approved, Athens being largely dependent on shipping and sea-trade

After two thousand years of Christianity, Poseidon, certainly under his Roman name of Neptune, has remained one of the best-known and most recognizable Greek gods. At best, Zeus has enjoyed a shadowy existence since the spread of Christianity, and Hades has passed completely into oblivion. Since the Renaissance, Poseidon/Neptune has regained a solid position in general Western ideography. He features in countless monumental fountains of the neo-classical period. In the early modern period, a new rite devoted to this god appeared. Mariners and passengers crossing the equator for the first time by sea would undergo the "baptism of Neptune, "a sort of hazing ceremony in which a crew member dressed as Neptune would pour salt water over the victim, or dunk them in it.

Priam

Priam was the son of the Trojan King Laomedon, who ruled the city of Troy during the Trojan War.

When Heracles destroyed Troy, as revenge for Laomedon failing to give him the promised reward for saving his daughter Hesione (*see* **Heracles**), Hesione begged that Priam be allowed to live and Heracles granted this request. Under Priam's rule, Troy grew into a mighty and prosperous city governing an extensive hinterland. Priam produced fifty sons, nineteen of whom were by his wife Hecabe. His eldest and favorite son was Hector, who proved to be an extraordinarily brave and noble hero in the Trojan War (*see* **Hector**). According to some versions, however, Paris was Priam's eldest son.

Paris was a much less distinguished figure than Hector and his indolent and egotistical

Poseidon, or Neptune, on the point of killing a monstrous octopus. The fearsome and violent sea-god has remained one of the most famous mythological figures. Neptune's Fountain, Piazza Navona, Rome, 16th century.

Incited by a personification of envy (the old woman at the top left), a number of sea-gods are involved in a battle. The rich mythological tradition concerning Poseidon and his entourage was a source of inspiration for Renaissance artists. Engraving by Andrea Martegna, 15th century.

behavior was the downfall of his father's city (*see* **Paris**). Priam's other sons included Deiphobus, Troilus—who was ambushed and murdered by the great Greek hero Achilles—the clairvoyant Helenus, and Polydorus. Priam also had fifty daughters, the best known of whom are Cassandra, the clairvoyant whose predictions were never believed (*see* **Cassandra**), and Polyxena.

As a young man, Priam acquired experience of warfare when he fought alongside the Phrygians as an ally in the battle against the Amazons. By the time of the outbreak of the

The aged Trojan king, Priam, views the battles taking place on the plain between Troy and the Grecian encampment and fleet from the walls of his city.

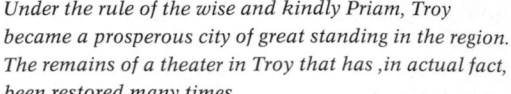

Trojan War, Priam was very old and no longer able to play an active part in the fighting. He appeared only once more on the battlefield when he concluded a treaty with the supreme commander of the Greeks, Agamemnon, concerning the duel to be fought between Menelaus and Paris, that was intended to put an end to the war. Shortly thereafter, the old king, escorted by the god Hermes, went to the Grecian encampment to beg Achilles to relinquish the body of his son Hector, whom Achilles had killed. The poet, Homer, movingly describes the meeting between the youthful, tempestuous hero and the grieving old king. Although at first Achilles was disinclined to return Hector to his father, he was won over by the old man's grief and changed his mind (Priam also paid him a considerable ransom). "Achilles (...) rose from his seat, raised the old man by the hand and, filled with pity now for his gray head and gray beard, he said: 'Poor man, how much you have borne—pain to break the spirit.'" (*The Iliad*, XXIV, lines 513-517). A form of friendship between the enemies began to emerge and when Achilles took his leave of Priam, he promised the King a safe return to Troy with Hector's body. "With that he clasped the old king by the wrist, by the right hand, to free his heart from fear."

The image of Priam as a warm, kind-hearted man is also confirmed by Helen, the woman abducted by Paris and on whose account the war was started. Not everyone in Troy was fond of her, but Priam treated her as a benevolent father-in-law would, and regarded her as innocent of any involvement in the dreadful events.

Priam's end was no less dreadful. When the Greek warriors who had been concealed in the wooden horse forced their way into his palace, the elderly man donned, with some difficulty, the armor he had not worn for a very long time. He had to watch Achilles' son, Neoptolemus, murder his son, Polites, before the Trojan palace altar, and he feebly threw his spear at the merciless young hero, reminding him that his father had behaved more worthily. With a sarcastic remark, Neoptolemus then dragged the trembling Priam to the altar and killed him.

Priam's wife, Hecabe (Roman=Hecuba), who witnessed her husband's death, survived but went on to endure much misery. She became a slave of the Greek commander-in-chief Agamemnon and was told that her daughter, Polyxena, would be offered as a sacrifice to the shade of Achilles (*see* **Polyxena**). Furthermore, the body of her youngest son, Polydorus, was found on the beach, having been murdered by the Thracian King Polymester, who had offered him asylum, in return for a large quantity of gold. Agamemnon gave Hecabe the opportunity to avenge this crime. Under false pretences, he invited Polymestor to the Grecian army encampment where Hecabe and her maidservants killed Polymestor's children and put out his eyes. According to some versions, Hecabe then changed into a bitch before dying.

Prometheus

The Titan, Prometheus, was the son of Iapetus and Themis. Some believed that he was the creator of man, whom he is said to have molded out of the earth into the image of the immortal gods after which the goddess, Athena, apparently blew life into the first human. As a tireless champion of the rights of mankind in respect of the gods, Prometheus occupied a unique position among the immortals. His name meant "forethought" and, to a certain extent, that described Prometheus exactly. He was someone who was too quick and too smart for others. The most prominent dupe of his cunning was the king of the gods, Zeus, who nonetheless punished Prometheus cruelly for his tricks.

In the war of the Titans, the battle in which Zeus and the other Olympian gods fought against these giant monsters, Prometheus did not fight alongside his fellow Titans. He later tried to improve the living conditions of the then still backward and primitive humans and hoped he could count on Zeus' support. When this was not forthcoming, Prometheus tried other means. An ox was slaughtered to celebrate an agreement establishing the relationship between the gods and man. Prometheus ensured that the best parts of the sacrificial beast were distributed to man rather than the gods. Zeus pretended not to notice Prometheus' trick, and chose the worst bit, but he then flew into a rage—not without an ulterior motive, because he now had a reason to withhold from mankind the gift of fire. Prometheus then brought fire down from the sky, where Zeus had hidden it. The cunning Titan put the fire into a hollow fennel stalk and gave it to man. Fire would underpin all of civilization, and Prometheus brought mankind many other blessings as well.

First of all, Zeus punished man. He instructed his son, Hephæstos, the craftsman among the gods, to create Pandora, the first woman. Pandora was presented as a wife to Prometheus' less intelligent brother, Epimetheus, ("afterthought"), who ignored

Zeus imposed a terrible punishment on the Titan Prometheus for the services he rendered mankind. Zeus had him chained to a cliff face and throughout the day an eagle came to peck at his liver.

Prometheus' warnings never to accept a gift from Zeus. Unable to contain her curiosity, Pandora, despite strict instructions to the contrary, opened a golden jar containing sicknesses, disasters, and calamities ("Pandora's box."). These have plagued mankind ever since (*see* **Pandora**).

On Zeus' instructions, Hephæstos chained Prometheus to a rock (probably in the Cauca-

According to some, Athena, the goddess of wisdom and the arts and crafts, having been fashioned out of clay by Prometheus, was the first mortal to draw breath. Athena and her owlet, drawing on an Athenian funeral urn, 5th century BCE.

sus). By way of additional torture, an eagle would appear every two days to peck out a piece of his liver—which renewed itself as fast as it was eaten. Prometheus, however, held the trump cards all the time. On learning that Zeus was in love with Io, the jealous Hera had been chasing her all over the world. Prometheus told Io that she would end up in Egypt and that a distant descendant of hers (Heracles) would rescue him from his perilous position (*see* **Io**). He also knew that the son of the beautiful Nereid, Thetis, whom Zeus had passionately desired, would produce a son who would dethrone his father. He kept this last piece of information to himself, and when Hermes went to see him to persuade him to reveal his secret he maintained his silence. At that point, Zeus struck the rock to which Prometheus was chained with a lightning bolt, leaving the stricken Titan covered with rocks.

Zeus and Prometheus later came to an agreement. Prometheus revealed his secret to Zeus whereupon the king of the gods wisely arranged for Thetis to marry the mortal Peleus (the awesome hero, Achilles, was the result of this union), thus avoiding being dethroned by his own son, something Zeus himself had done to his own father, Cronos.

In exchange for revealing his secret, Prometheus regained his freedom. Heracles killed the eagle with an arrow and released the Titan from his chains. Prometheus later told Heracles how to deal with his brother, Atlas, in order to obtain the apples of the

Hesperides (*see* **Heracles** *and* **Atlas**).

Prometheus also played a role in the story of the Greek Flood, in which his son, Deucalion, and wife, Pyrrha, were the only mortals to survive the floods caused by the gods (*see* **Deucalion**).

The figure of Prometheus, who had to pay for his good deeds on behalf of mankind with lengthy and dreadful suffering, inspired the Athenian playwright, Æschylus (ca. 525–456 BCE), to write a dramatic trilogy, *Prometheus Unbound*, of which only one part, the *Prometheus in Chains* section, has been preserved. Later artists, including the eighteenth and nineteenth century poets Johann Wolfgang von Goethe and Percy Bysshe Shelley, and the composer Beethoven, dedicated works to the well-meaning but unlucky Prometheus.

Proserpina, *see* Persephone

Psyche

Psyche, the personification of the soul (her name means "soul" in Greek), was the youngest of the King of Sicily's three beautiful daughters. Psyche was said to be so extra-

A terrifying eagle inflicted unbearable pain on the chained Prometheus by pecking out pieces of his liver which constantly renewed itself. The hero, Heracles, finally eliminated the beast. Eagle and thunderbolt dedicated to Zeus, bronze coin from Alexandria, 3rd century BCE.

After Prometheus had presented man with fire, Zeus punished both mankind and its benefactor. Thanks to Pandora, the first woman, mankind was saddled with every conceivable misfortune. Prometheus was captured and chained to a cliff face. Here, Hermes and an eagle carry the Titan away. Max Klinger, German artist, 1894.

ordinarily beautiful that she outshone even Venus/Aphrodite, the goddess of beauty and love. Men flocked from far and wide to come and gaze at her and Aphrodite's altars were completely abandoned, since men now worshiped the irresistible princess, instead of the goddess, bringing offerings to her and strewing the streets with flowers whenever she went out.

The abruptly discarded Aphrodite was furious with Psyche, even though the girl could not help what was happening. She called her son Amor or Eros—presented as a handsome young man in this myth (*see* **Eros**)—to her and directed him to make Psyche fall in love with the lowest and most despicable man he could find.

In the meantime, Psyche was suffering dreadfully as a result of the devotion heaped upon her. She was worshiped and praised but no one dare ask for her hand in marriage. Whereas her elder sisters were happily married to handsome princes, poor Psyche sat alone at home, privately cursing her beauty. Her father consulted an oracle of the god Apollo who instructed him to take Psyche, dressed in a bridal gown, to a high mountain where she should await the arrival of her bridegroom. According to the oracle, this would be a fire-breathing dragon who filled even the gods with terror.

Dismayed, Psyche's father obeyed the advice of the oracle, and in a mood of general mourning, the girl was led away from

Zephyr, the gentle West wind, picked up the defeated Psyche and carried her to a lovely valley, where she discovered a magnificent palace.

her home. Psyche tried to comfort her parents, but they remained in their gloomy palace, broken-hearted. Psyche herself waited on the high mountain, weeping, but Zephyr, the gentle west wind, picked her up and carried her to a lovely valley where she fell into a deep sleep on the fresh grass. When she awoke, she discovered a pleasant forest, a fountain producing clear waters, and a glittering palace built by the gods, the walls of which were decorated with carvings of all kinds of wild animals. The floors were covered with magnificent mosaics, and other walls were of solid gold, which meant that even when the sun wasn't shining, the palace was bathed in a golden light.

Psyche entered the palace hesitantly and was tended by invisible maidservants. She had a nap, took a bath, and enjoyed a delicious meal and delightful music. That night, an unknown man visited her and joined her in her bed. Psyche was frightened to death, but the unknown man treated her tenderly, although he disappeared before morning

Psyche, the personification of the soul, inspired the envy of Aphrodite, the goddess of love and beauty, who could not bear the fact that Psyche attracted greater admiration than she did. Vase in the form of Psyche with butterfly wings from Egypt, 2nd–1st century BCE.

light. He returned every night and Psyche fell deeper and deeper under the spell of his lovemaking.

In the meantime, Psyche's sisters were feeling so sorry for their parents that they set out to look for her. Psyche's husband alerted her to the fact that they were approaching the cliffs and urged her to ignore them. If she did not she would hurt him and bring about her own downfall.

At first, Psyche agreed to obey his wishes, but she was deeply distressed at the thought of treating her sisters so hard-heartedly. Her husband took pity on her and allowed her to receive her sisters, speak to them, and present them with gifts. He told her, however, that if her sisters asked who he was, she must not discuss this and should not try to discover his identity herself either. This would be a disastrous move for her and would mean the end of their love. Psyche thanked him, told him there was no way she wanted to lose him and asked him to arrange for Zephyr to bring her sisters to the palace.

Eros—for he was Psyche's secret lover— granted her request and kept his promise. Psyche rapturously received her sisters at her palace, and when one of them persisted in questioning her as to the identity of her husband, she simply replied that he was a handsome young man who always spent the day hunting. Laden with magnificent jewelry, the sisters went home where they became consumed with terrible envy. Their youngest sister had suddenly become immensely wealthy, and had also found herself an unbelievably handsome man, whereas they were saddled with unattractive, old, and sickly husbands. And Psyche thought she could palm them off with a few items of jewelry!

The sisters resolved to teach Psyche a hard lesson. Eros (Psyche still hadn't realized he was her lover) repeated his warning about her sisters and then told her she was pregnant. If she said nothing to her sisters, she would bear a divine child, otherwise the child would be an ordinary mortal. Psyche was in raptures over this news, but did not take seriously the warning that her sisters were up to no good.

Gradually, using deceitful ploys, the sisters managed to win Psyche over, and she declared—forgetting the white lie she had told earlier—that her husband was a well-to-do, albeit fairly elderly salesman. The sisters became even more envious and fooled Psyche into believing that an oracle had told them that her husband was actually a dragon who would devour her upon the birth of her child. The naïve Psyche was completely unnerved by this, admitted that she did not know who her husband was, and begged her sisters for help. They advised her to have a sharp knife

The walls of the mysterious palace that Psyche entered were decorated with reliefs of wild animals. Ceiling relief from the 18th century ornamental temple to Diana (Artemis) in the park of the Villa Borghese in Rome.

ready beside her bed and to hide a lamp there as well. Once her husband had fallen asleep she was to hold up the lamp and see if what they said was true. If this was the case, she should stab him with the knife. The sisters would then take her home and arrange for her to marry a mortal.

Psyche decided to put this to the test, but when, with the knife at the ready, she looked at her husband in the lamplight, she received a terrible shock: there was no hideous dragon before her, but the winged Eros himself! His bow and arrows lay beside the bed. Inquisitively, Psyche touched the tip of one of the arrows and wounded herself, causing her to fall deeply in love with Eros. However, a drop of hot oil from the lamp fell onto the sleeping Eros' shoulder, so that he woke up with a start and he flew off, furious at Psyche for failing to keep her word. Psyche was just able to grab hold of his leg and was borne up into the air with him. When exhaustion forced her to let go, Eros admitted that he had not carried out his mother's instructions to the letter, had wounded himself with his own arrows, and therefore fell hopelessly in love with Psyche. He realized she had been misled by her sisters and resolved to punish them.

He then flew off, leaving Psyche alone in the wilderness. Pan, the god of nature, took pity on her and advised her to try to win her way back into Eros' favor. Psyche set off on a lengthy trail, ending up in a city ruled by the husband of one of her sisters. She told her sister what had happened, but ended her story by saying that Eros now wanted to marry this sister. The sister became crazed with lust, concocted an excuse to her husband, and rushed to the top of the mountain where Psyche had been left at the start. She threw herself down to the bottom in the hope

that Eros would catch her, but she was dashed to pieces and the birds and carrion-eaters devoured her corpse. Psyche then set off to visit her other sister and told her the same story, whereupon the second sister threw herself from the mountain top as well.

In the meantime, Eros was languishing in in his mother's bed, suffering dreadful pain from the oil burn. A seagull told Aphrodite, who was playing in the sea, what had happened to her son. The seagull pointed out that there was little likelihood of people returning to worship Eros and Aphrodite and that ugliness and lovelessness were now governing the world.

When Aphrodite heard that Eros had taken Psyche as his sweetheart, she went to him in a fury and gave him a roasting. Firmly resolved to let her son suffer a great deal more, she left her house again. Demeter and

217

Hera, who came across her by chance, pointed out to her that her son was a fully-grown man and had the right to lead his own lovelife, but the goddess of love would not be reasoned with. Psyche, meanwhile, was still wandering despairingly from place to place in pursuit of her husband. She begged Demeter and Hera to help her, but the two goddesses refused to do anything for her. That was when Psyche decided to approach Aphrodite herself to try to assuage her fury. The goddess of love had not been sitting idle either. In the chariot made for her by Hephæstos, she drove to see Zeus and asked him for Hermes'

Whilst Eros lay wounded in bed, Psyche roamed the world in despair, looking for her lover. No one could or would help her. Illustration of a winged female figure, fresco from Boscoreale, 1st century CE.

help to enable her to track down Psyche. Hermes called upon the people to state if and where they had seen Psyche. Almost immediately, a maidservant of Aphrodite recognized Psyche, and she was dragged into the goddess' palace by her hair. Aphrodite had the unfortunate Psyche thrashed, completely unaware that the girl was pregnant. She tore Psyche's clothes into shreds and ordered her to grade and sort a vast quantity of all kinds of grains and beans. Psyche had no idea where to start, but some friendly ants offered to help and sorted all the grains for her.

Aphrodite suspected somebody had helped Psyche and immediately commanded her to fetch a sample of wool from some vicious, golden-fleeced wild sheep. This time, it was a reed that grew on the riverbank the came to the aid of the desperate girl. It advised her to avoid the sheep during the hottest part of the day and later, when they were resting in the shade, to pick some of the wool that had stuck to the branches. Again, however, Aphrodite was not satisfied. Psyche now had to go to the top of a mountain and fill a crystal vase with black water from a spring fed by the underworld river, the Styx. Psyche's heart sank as she climbed the mountain. Dragons crept out of their holes and even the waters raised their voices to discourage her. At that point an eagle, who was a friend of Eros, rushed to help her.

He advised Psyche against going to fetch the dangerous water herself and filled the vase for her. Once again, Aphrodite was not satisfied. She gave Psyche a small box and told her to go down to the underworld. There she had to fill the box with the beauty salve used by Hades' wife, Persephone. Psyche was beside herself and contemplated jumping from a tower. The tower, however, took pity on her and explained to her how she could ensure her safe return from the underworld. Psyche was told to take some coins with her for the ferryman, Charon (who conveyed the dead across the Styx, *see* **Charon**), and special cakes to offer to Hades' bloodthirsty, three-headed guard-dog, Cerberus (*see* **Cerberus**). Psyche also needed to be on her guard against a lame mule-driver whom she might encounter on her way, and an old man who would be gliding down the Styx and might ask her to take him on Charon's boat, since these were both traps set by Aphrodite. If Persephone were to invite Psyche to make herself at home and offer her a meal, she should refuse it and only accept a crust of bread from her.

Psyche carefully followed the tower's instructions and received a warm welcome from Persephone. The goddess straightaway filled the box with the salve and Psyche returned safely from the kingdom of the dead. At that point she was overcome with curiosity and opened the box. There appeared to be nothing in it, but Psyche immediately fell into a deep sleep.

Eros had since recovered from his burn. Filled with a passionate desire for Psyche, he escaped from the room in which his mother had imprisoned him, found his lover, and returned the coma-inducing sleep to the box, enabling Psyche to perform her task in full. He then flew to Zeus to beg him to approve his marriage to Psyche. Zeus agreed to Eros' request and convened the gods to a meeting to make his decision known. He declared that Eros must now finally start behaving like a true husband instead of a frivolous young man, and made it clear to Aphrodite that Eros had not made a bad marriage because Psyche would be turned into a goddess. He arranged

The heartless Aphrodite subjected Psyche to a number of dreadful tests. Psyche even had to go down into the underworld to fill a box with Persephone's beauty salve. Bronze Psyche from Naucratis, 1st/2nd century AD.

for Hermes to bring the girl to Olympus where the wedding was celebrated joyfully. Eros and Psyche remained man and wife and had one son, Voluptas ("voluptuousness.")

The story, as retold here, a world-famous tale, is related by the Roman author Apuleius (ca.123–c.170 CE), who includes it in his anthology, *The Golden Ass.* In addition to being a writer, Apuleius was a philosopher and injected his tale with much symbolic meaning. Psyche stood for the soul, Amor/Eros stood for divine love. Only by overcoming divine love could the soul find its true fulfilment. this was the message of Apuleius' tale. Fortunately, in this case, the philosopher was carried away by the pleasure of telling the tale and does not indulge in too much philosophizing.

Pygmalion

Two characters are called Pygmalion in Greco-Roman mythology. The first was a brother of the Carthaginian or Phœnician Queen Dido (*see* **Dido**).

The second Pygmalion was a sculptor who lived on Cyprus and had no time for women and therefore remained a bachelor. He did, however, make a beautiful sculpture of a

After his marriage to Psyche, Eros changed from a frivolous young man into a faithful husband who was fully aware of his responsibilities. At least that's how the story goes. Bronze Eros from Egypt, Roman period, 2nd/3rd century AD.

woman from of white ivory. It was so lifelike that Pygmalion fell in love with his own creation and treated it as if it were a living being. In the words of the poet Ovid: "He kisses it and his kisses are returned; and speaks to it; and holds it, and imagines that his fingers press into the limbs, and is afraid lest bruises appear from the pressure." (*Metamorphoses*, X., lines 256-258). Pygmalion gave his ivory lover gifts, dressed her in beautiful clothes, and laid her beside him in his bed. His behavior was so moving that Aphrodite took pity on him. During the celebrations held annually on Cyprus in her honor, she changed the sculpture into a real woman of flesh and blood. Pygmalion married his dream-woman whom had been brought to life and she had a daughter by him, named Paphos.

Pyramus and Thisbe

It may surprise those who are familiar with the play about Pyramus and Thisbe as acted by Bottom, the Weaver, and his fellow amateur thespians in Shakespeare's *A Midsummer Night's Dream*, to learn that the story of Pyramus and Thisbe is well-known in Greek mythology. Far from being farcical, as depicted in Shakespeare's comedy, it is a rather poignant one.

Pyramus and Thisbe grew up together in the Mesopotamian city of Babylon and lived in adjoining houses. They were in love with each other but their fathers would not allow them to marry and forbade any contact between them. However, there was a gap in the wall between their houses through which Pyramus and Thisbe would secretly whisper words of love to each other.

One day, though, their passion for each other overcame them and they arranged to meet at night beneath a mulberry tree, next to a tomb just outside the city walls. Unnoticed in the dark, the veiled Thisbe was first to slip out of the city gates. However, as she waited beside the mulberry tree for Pyramus, she noticed a lioness approaching who had just devoured an ox and wanted to drink from the nearby spring. Thisbe fled into a cave, dropping her veil. The lioness found the veil and smeared it with the ox's blood. A little later, Pyramus discovered the lioness' footprints and the bloodied veil, and was overcome with despair. He couldn't bear the thought that Thisbe had been eaten and that it was his fault. He stabbed himself with his own sword under the mulberry tree and in so doing pierced an artery, drenching the ground and

A lion caught Thisbe unawares outside the city walls of Babylon. She took refuge in a cave but lost her veil, which the lion smeared with blood. Lion from Nemrut Dagh, Turkey, 1st century BCE.

The brilliant but shy sculptor, Pygmalion, fell passionately in love with the statue of a woman he himself had created.

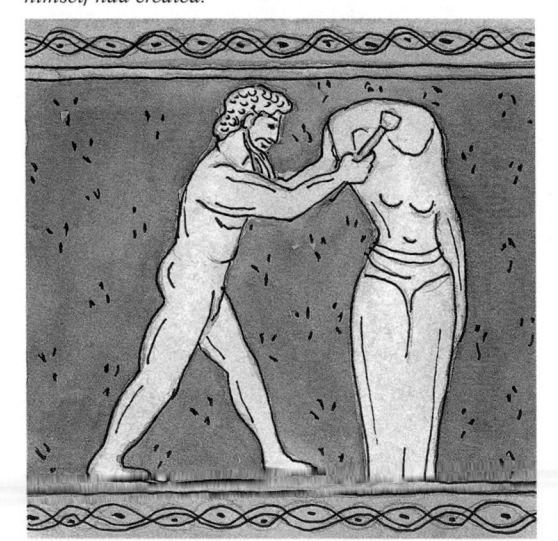

the roots of the mulberry tree with his blood. The mulberry fruits, that had previously been white, now turned red.

Not longer after, Thisbe returned to the tree. She found the body of her lover next to her veil and realized what had happened. Distraught, she stabbed herself with Pyramus' sword and at the same time called out, asking to be laid to rest in the same grave as Pyramus and for the fruit of the mulberry tree to be turned black as a form of memorial. The gods heard her last wish—ripe mulberries would from now on be black—and the parents of Pyramus and Thisbe burned their ashes in the same urn.

Python, *see* Apollo

Remus, *see* Romulus

Rhadamanthus

Rhadamanthus, or Rhadamanthys, was a son of the king of the gods, Zeus, and the Phœnician princess Europa, who was seduced by Zeus in the form of a bull (*see* **Europa**). Rhadamanthus' brothers were Minos, king of Crete (*see* **Minos**), and Sarpedon. According to some versions, Rhadamanthus ruled Crete before Minos and proved to be an outstanding legislator. After a quarrel, Minos drove Rhadamanthus and Sarpedon out of Crete.

After his death, Rhadamanthus, together with Minos and Æacus, became judges of the shades in the kingdom of the dead. Opinions vary as to exactly what his role was in the underworld. The prevailing view is that he

Thisbe found the dead Pyramus and turned his sword upon herself. Oil painting by Abraham Hondius, 17th century.

governed the Elysium, where Alcmene, the mother of the great hero Heracles, acted as

his spouse. However, in *The Æneid*, the great epic by the Roman poet Virgil,

After his death, Rhadamanthus, brother of the Cretan King Minos, became a judge in the underworld.

Rhadamanthus appears as a strict ruler of the sinners in Tartarus, the "hellish" part of the underworld.

Rhea

The Titan Rhea was a daughter of Uranus and Gaia and wife of the fearsome Titan Cronos, who deposed his father in order to become supreme ruler of the world. Rhea bore Cronos six children, the gods and goddesses Hestia, Demeter, Hera, Hades, Poseidon, and Zeus. Since Cronos' mother, Gaia, had told him that he too would be dethroned by one of his children, he ate them as soon as they were born. Only Zeus, his youngest son, escaped this sorry fate, because Rhea handed Cronos a stone wrapped in cloth instead of the newly-born child (*see* **Cronos**).

Rhea took Zeus to Crete where the nymph—or nanny-goat—Amalthea looked after him (*see* **Amalthea**). As soon as he reached adulthood, Zeus forced his father to regurgitate his brothers and sisters. After that, there was a terrible power struggle between the younger gods and the Titans (the "War of the Titans,") that was ultimately settled in favor of Zeus and his side.

Rhea was primarily worshiped on Crete, in Arcadia, and Phrygia, where she was regarded as one and the same as Cybele.

Rhea hands over a stone wrapped in a cloth to her husband Cronos, who up to now has swallowed all their children immediately after they were born. Cronos will swallow the stone straight away, believing that in so doing, he is eliminating his youngest son Zeus.

Romulus

Legend has it that Romulus founded Rome, the city named for him, in the year 753 BCE.

Romulus and his twin brother, Remus, were sons of Princess Rhea Silvia, a descendant of Æneas, the Trojan hero who traveled to Italy after Troy was destroyed and founded a new kingdom there (*see* **Æneas**).

Æneas' son, Ascanius, founded the city of Alba Longa where, a few centuries later, his descendant Numitor became king. Numitor was dethroned by his brother Amulius, who, in order to prevent Numitor acquiring a legitimate male successor, forced his daughter, Rhea Silvia, to become a Vestal Virgin (*see* **Hestia**). As such, Rhea Silvia was forbidden to have sexual relations, but Mars (the Roman counterpart of Ares), the god of war, ignored this prohibition and raped the virgin princess in a forest dedicated to him.

When Amulius discovered that Rhea Silvia was pregnant, he imprisoned her and ordered her twin sons to be drowned in the Tiber. His underlings, however, could not bring themselves to kill the babies and left the cradle in a flooded section of the river. When the water level dropped, the cradle landed on dry land,

The twin brothers Romulus and Remus were distant descendants of the Trojan hero Æneas. They were regarded as the founders of the city of Rome. Here the two youths are caressing the head of a she-wolf, who had suckled them. Sculpture at the Piazza del Campidoglio, Rome.

where it was found by a she-wolf who suckled the starving little boys.

A short time later, the shepherd Faustulus found Romulus and Remus and he and his wife, Larentia, raised them in their hut. The boys grew up to become tough herdsmen who defended their flocks against wild beasts. Occasionally, they would be attacked by robbers, but they would capture their booty and distribute it among the herdsmen. One day, some robbers took Remus prisoner and handed him over to Amulius. Amulius instructed Numitor to try him and that is when the true

The remains of the House of the Vestal Virgins in the Roman Forum. Rhea Silvia, the mother of Romulus and Remus, was condemned to live as a Vestal Virgin, so as to prevent her having children. However, she became pregnant by the god Mars (Ares), who raped her.

identity of the twin brothers emerged. Amulius was himself dethroned in a rebellion led by Romulus and Remus, and Numitor regained control of his city.

After that, Romulus and Remus decided to found a city for themselves and selected as a site, the point on the Tiber at which they had been abandoned and where the she-wolf had later looked after them. Straightaway, however, they quarreled over whose name the city should bear and who should rule it first. Being twins, they were identical in age which meant that neither of them could invoke primogeniture. That is why they decided to wait for a sign from the gods. Romulus climbed the Palatine Hill and Remus the Aventine Hill. Remus was first to spot a sign from the gods. He saw six vultures in the sky, but immediately afterward, Romulus reported that he had seen twelve vultures. Once again, they failed to reach an agreement. Remus had been first, but Romulus had seen the most birds. A fight broke out between the two brothers and their supporters, during which Remus was killed.

In another version of the story, to provoke his brother, Remus jumped over a wall that was being built around the new city, at which point Romulus hit him, and killed him, warning that anyone else who jumped over his walls would meet the same fate. In any event, Romulus became the sole ruler of the city, which was also named for him.

Rome became a thriving city, thanks to Romulus' offer to allow men without land the opportunity to set themselves up in his city. The only disadvantage was that the city very quickly acquired a significant surplus of men. Furthermore, the neighboring tribes were disinclined to marry their daughters to the Romans, who were not particularly well thought-of.

Romulus dreamed up a solution to the

The she-wolf who suckled Romulus and Remus is constantly quenching the thirst of the inhabitants of Rome. Small faucet from a Roman public garden.

problem. He arranged the Consualia, a huge feast including games dedicated to the sea-god Neptune (Poseidon), and invited all the neighboring tribes to attend. Large numbers came, including women and children, in particular the Sabines. They were warmly received, but when the games began, the Roman men sprang into action in response to an agreed signal, raped the Sabine women and drove out their menfolk. Needless to say, the victims of the "Rape of the Sabine Women" did not hesitate to protest against what had been done to them, but Romulus managed to convince them that the Romans would treat them well and make them excellent husbands. Some of the neighboring peoples then attacked the Romans in an attempt to win back their women, but they were defeated. At some point, the Sabines managed to drive the Romans into a tight corner. An act of treason enabled them to take control of the Capitoline Hill, whereupon a great battle began on the site of what would later become the Roman Forum.

Romulus invoked the king of the gods Jupiter (Zeus) asking him to put an end to the fighting, and a short time later the Sabine women ran onto the battlefield, their hair flowing free and clothes torn. Their plan was

The banks of the Tiber at the Tiber Island in central Rome. Romulus and Remus founded their city at this spot.

to prevent their fathers and husbands from killing each other over them. Deeply affected, the men stopped fighting, peace was declared, and eventually, the Romans and Sabines merged to form one nation.

Four years later Romulus' existence as a mortal came to an end. Whilst he was inspecting his troops on the Campus Martius (the Field of Mars) in Rome, there was a sudden thunderstorm. Romulus was enveloped in a dense mist and, after the storm had abated, appeared to have vanished from his throne. In no time at all, he was turned into a god and, shortly afterward, Julius Proculus claimed that Romulus had appeared before him and declared that it was the will of the

gods that Rome should become the most powerful city in the world.

Romulus' tale is probably a good example of an historical story being given a mythical gloss to make the truth appear more palatable than it really was. It is more than likely that early Rome was little more than a den of robbers, led by a bandit who would stop at nothing. Ascribing his uncertain origin to the mythical Trojan heroes and turning him into a god after his death, lends an aura of greatness to a less than charming reality. Augustus, the first Roman emperor (27 BCE—14 CE), would later deliberately use mythology as a political propaganda tool and make out that his family, the Julii, were direct descendants of Iulus or Ascanius, son of the Trojan hero Æneas, himself a son of Aphrodite.

Salmacis

Salmacis was a Naiad or fountain nymph who lived in Asia Minor next to a glittering fountain that produced crystal-clear water and was surrounded by very little vegetation. Salmacis was an idle, indolent nymph who never went hunting with Artemis and the other nymphs, but devoted most of her time to improving her appearance. One day, the handsome sixteen-year old Hermaphroditus, son of Hermes and Aphrodite, appeared at her fountain. Salmacis was immediately smitten with him and tried

At the site upon which the Forum Romanum would later be established, Romulus and his Romans defeated the Sabines, who were trying to recover their stolen wives. Capriccio with motifs of the Forum Romanum, oil painting by Giovanni Paolo Pannini, 18th century.

to seduce him. Hermaphroditus started blushing and brushed off her advances. Later, however, he undressed and dived into the refreshing water of the fountain. Salmacis, by now unable to control her lust, jumped in as well, seized the irresistible boy, and started kissing him. His struggles were to no avail. Salmacis would not let go now. She begged the gods not to let them ever be separated and her wish was granted, because nymph and boy were merged into a hermaphrodite, a transexual being (*see* **Hermaphroditus**).

Sarpedon

Three figures called Sarpedon appear in Greek mythology. The first was the son of Zeus and Europa, the Phœnician princess who was visited by the king of the gods in the form of a bull. Sarpedon's brothers were Minos and Rhadamanthus (Rhadamanthys) (*see* **Rhadamanthus**). The three boys grew up on Crete, but eventually, Minos drove Rhadamanthus and Sarpedon from the island (*see* **Minos**). Sarpedon later settled in Lycia, in Asia Minor. His son Evander married

The fountain nymph Salmacis was passionately in love with the handsome Hermaphroditus. She merged with him to form a hermaphrodite being after he had bathed in her fountain. Oil painting by Jan Gossært, 16th century.

a daughter of the hero Bellerophon and became king of Lycia.

The second Sarpedon was a Lycean king and an important ally of the Trojans during the Trojan War. Some have it that he was one and the same as the first Sarpedon, who had clearly reached a much greater age. According to others, he was the grandson of the first Sarpedon and, according to Homer, he was son of the king of the gods, Zeus.

Sarpedon fought on one of the front lines during a Trojan attack on the Greek ships. Then he was attacked by Achilles' comrade-in-arms, Patroclus, and was on the point of being strangled but Zeus could not bear the thought of his son dying. He managed to intervene, although Hera pointed out to him that this would not go down well with the other gods.

Sarpedon, then, was killed against the wishes of the king of the gods. Zeus later commanded the god, Apollo, to bathe Sarpedon's body in ambrosia and wrap it in a shroud of the gods. Finally, the twin brothers Sleep and Death (Hypnos and Thanatos) took Sarpedon's body back to Lycia (*see* **Thanatos**).

Saturn

Saturn was an ancient Italian god of the countryside, who is identified with the Greek

The Lycian king Sarpedon was a son of Zeus. The king of the gods was greatly affected by his death during the Trojan War. After Apollo had tended to his body, the twin brothers Sleep and Death carried it back to Lycia.

Titan Cronos (see Cronos). Saturn, however, was a slightly less gruesome character than the downright brutal and barbaric Cronos. After his son Jupiter (Zeus) had driven him into Tartarus at the end of the War of the Titans, Saturn is said to have settled in Italy. He was married to his sister Ops (equated with the Greek goddess, Rhea) and taught man how to cultivate the fields. The Saturnalia, a joyful public feast at which which gifts were exchanged and masters and servants temporarily changed places, was held annually in Rome, from December 17 through 23 in his honor (see **Cronos**).

Satyr

A satyr was a wild creature of the forests who, together with the Mænads, formed part of the retinue of Dionysus, god of wine and vegetation. The satyrs were sensual creatures, who were not entirely trustworthy and frequently misbehaved. They were small, hairy figures, often portrayed with the characteristics of animals. Sometimes they had horse's legs and hooves, something they had in common with the Centaurs, and frequently had pointed horns and goat's legs, causing them to resemble the god of nature Pan, who was just as hot-blooded as they were.

The satyr's favorite occupation was to pursue attractive nymphs in the paradisiacal outdoors. Some satyrs, however, harbored other ambitions. For example, the satyr, Marsyas, was a creditable flautist. He decided to

Some impressive columns at the temple of the ancient god Saturn are still a dominant feature of the Roman Forum in Rome.

compete against the god Apollo, but this turned out to be a step too far, and proved to

Satyrs were not conspicuous for their decency and generally allowed themselves to be governed by their carnal desires. As followers of the god of wine, Dionysus, they rarely declined the chance to imbibe.

be poor Marsyas' undoing (see **Marsyas**).

The great Dionysia, the major festival dedicated to Dionysus in Athens, was the occasion for visiting the theater. The satyrs

A satyr leading a donkey. The satyrs were portrayed as comical figures in the Greek theater. "satyr plays" (satires) provided a light-hearted conclusion to a program that contained three serious tragedies. Painting on an Athenian vase., 5th century BCE.

A satyr abandons himself to solitary physical pleasure. Picture on an Athenian kylix, 6th century BCE.

Scylla (below) accompanied by a monstrous crab. The dog's heads around Scylla's middle are clearly visible. Silver coin (tetradrachm) from Sicily, 5th century BCE.

appeared in the theater as clowns, the "satyr plays" or "satires," burlesque-type events, being interspersed with the heavy tragedies. It was customary to end three serious dramas with a light-hearted satyr play in which fun was poked at all manner of subjects.

Scylla

Scylla is known, above all, from Homer's epic poem, *The Odyssey*, in which she appears as a terrifying sea-monster which, together with the whirlpool, Charybdis, made a narrow strait (probably the Strait of Messina) completely unnavigable. Before this, she had been a charming sea-nymph who had turned many a head and rejected countless suitors as well.

Among those who pursued her was the sea-god Glaucus, who had originally had a mortal form. Glaucis had been changed into a merman, someone with the head and torso of a man and the tail of a fish when, as a fisherman, he set foot on a virgin meadow beside a beach. He emptied his net onto the grass there so that he could count the fish he had caught, but the fish then came back to life and returned to the sea. In amazement, Glaucus tasted some of the clearly magical grass in the meadow and experienced an irresistible urge for the water. He dived into the waves, was received by the sea-gods, and was given immortality and a new, fishlike form.

Scylla, to whom he related this tale, showed no interest in him, so Glaucus turned to the enchantress Circe (*see* **Circe**). He asked her for some magic herbs with which to win over Scylla. The fiery enchantress advised him against this and intimated that she herself had some feelings for him. When Glaucus rejected her, Circe was so insulted that she prepared a poisonous spell and poured it into a bay in which Scylla frequently went swimming. The water polluted by Circe's brew changed Scylla into a monster. She acquired twelve legs and six long necks with a hideous head on each. According to the poet, Ovid, her belly and haunches were covered with the heads of barking dogs resembling the head of Cerberus, the terrible guard dog of the underworld.

Upon seeing his loved one in this condition, Glaucus burst into tears and left Circe's palace, frightened that the sorceress would force him into marriage. Scylla remained in the Strait of Messina and, according to Ovid, avenged herself on Circe by devouring a number of the crew of the Odyssey when they passed through the strait, since she knew that Odysseus had been Circe's lover. In the end, Scylla was turned into a rock. The expression "between Scylla and Charibdys" lives on and means "between a rock and a hard place."

The dog's heads around Scylla's middle have seized a mariner and are enjoying their prey. Fragment of a limestone sculpture on a memorial temple from Tarente, 4th–3rd century BCE.

that she could not bear the thought of him

Semele is visited by her lover Zeus, who at her request has assumed his true form. A moment later Semele will be scorched by Zeus lightning bolts and his unbearable glow.

ever dying. She therefore showered him with moonbeams and put him into a state of eternal sleep (*see* **Endymion**).

Selene (Roman=Luna)

Selene was the goddess of the moon, the daughter of the Titans, Hyperion and Theia, and a sister of the sun-god Helios. She had a pale, white face and traveled on a silver chariot drawn by two horses. She is also often shown riding a horse or a bull. She wears flowing drapery, carries a torch, and has a half-moon or crescent-moon on her head. After her brother Helios completed his journey across the sky, it was time for Selene to begin hers, but before she started, she would bathe in the sea. Pan once seduced her by wrapping himself in the fleece of a white sheep.

Other love affairs of Selene's included involvement with Zeus by whom she had three daughters, and Pan who gave her a herd of white oxen. Some sources report that the Nemean lion (*see* **Nemean lion**), that fell to the earth from the moon, was the result of an affair between Zeus and Selene. Although Selene had many lovers, she had fewer than her sister, Eos, the dawn.

The myth for which Selene is best known involves her relationship with Endymion, a young man whom she loved so passionately

Semele

Semele was the daughter of Cadmus and Harmonia, and the mother of the wine and vegetation god, Dionysus. The king of the gods, Zeus, visited her in the form of a mortal and Semele became pregnant by him. When rumors of this reached Zeus' wife, Hera, she was overcome by a terrible jealousy. She decided to destroy Semele and devised a cunning trick in order to achieve this. She adopted the form of Semele's elderly nurse, Beroe, and sowed doubts in the girl's mind. How could she be certain that her lover really was Zeus? He would have to come up with some proof of his identity.

So, when Zeus next visited Semele asked him if she could make a wish. Zeus agreed without a second thought and swore on the underworld river, the Styx, that he would grant her request. Thereupon Semele asked him if he would reveal himself to her in his true form, the form in which he made love to Hera. Zeus immediately realized the consequences of this request, but he had given his word and couldn't take it back. In despair, he

The young Dionysus is bathed by his female attendants. Dionysus grew up without a mother because Semele died just before his birth. Relief from Nysa, Turkey.

returned to the sky and gathered clouds, thunderstorms, and lightning bolts, the elements that characterized his appearance.

Although he did his best to minimize the effect, the consequences were terrible. Semele was scorched by the heavenly radiance of the king of the gods. Just in time, Zeus managed to rescue the unborn fruit of her womb and implanted him in his own thigh (*see* **Dionysus**).

The possible import or concealed meaning of the myth of Semele is that man is far too insignificant to withstand the magnitude of the divine.

Silenus

Silenus has settled down to sleep using a wineskin as a pillow. Vase in the form of Silenus, southern Italy, 4th century BCE.

The aged Silenus was part of the retinue of the god of wine and vegetation, Dionysus.

The extremely drunk Silenus can barely stand and needs help. Relief from Nysa (Turkey).

Silenus, the son of Pan or Hermes and a nymph, was a corpulent, pug-nosed creature. He is sometimes portrayed with a horse's tail and horse's ears and is often shown riding a donkey, or carried around on the shoulders of a group of satyrs, who support him in his more-or-less constant state of intoxication.

Despite his fondness for liquor, Silenus is supposed to have been a wise figure, and could also predict the future. He made him-

Head of Silenus, the constantly inebriated but nonetheless extraordinarily wise teacher and comrade of the god of wine, Dionysus. Terracotta antefix from Etruria, 500-475 BCE.

Silenus was often represented as a comical figure, but probably also played a role in the Dionysian Mysteries, which were intended to be anything but amusing and were secret rituals in which Dionysus was worshiped as a savior and conqueror of death. In this picture Silenus is playing the lyre. Fresco from the Villa of Mysteries, Pompeii, 1st century BCE.

self useful as a tutor and guru to the young Dionysus. Once, in Phrygia, he became separated from the rest of Dionysus' companions. Some Phrygian peasants took him back to their king Midas, who gave him a hospitable welcome and later returned him to the wine-god. The reward the grateful Dionysus later bestowed on Midas had unhappy consequences for the Lydian sovereign, however (*see* **Midas**).

Despite his great age, Silenus sired many sons with a wide variety of nymphs. These Silenians, who bore a close resemblance to their father, behaved just as sensually and comically as the satyrs and often appeared in the satirical plays of Athenian playwrights, the farces which concluded a trilogy of profound tragedies (*see* **Dionysus** *and* **Satyrs**).

The Sirens

The sirens were creatures with bird-like bodies, girl's faces, and exquisite singing voices, so exquisite that almost every mariner who passed the island they inhabited (it lay between Circe's island, Æææ, and the sea strait ruled by the monsters, Scylla and Charybdis, probably the Strait of Messina) fell completely under the spell of their seduc-

According to the pœt Ovid, the Sirens were once ordinary girls or nymphs. After Hades abducted Persephone in their presence, they acquired wings to make it easier for them to search for her. Earthenware Siren from Athens, 5th century BCE.

tive voices and stayed there listening to them for ever more, or else smashed their ships to smithereens on the rocky coast of the island. It was littered with the shipwrecks bleached bones and of their countless victims.

No one could agree on the number and origin of the sirens. According to Homer, there were two sirens, others had it that there were three or four. They were called Hemeropa and Thelxiepeia, or Leucosia, Ligeia, and Parthenope, or Thelxiepeia, Aglaopheme, Peisinoe, and Molpe. According to some, their father was Phorcys and their mother was one of the muses, but the poet Ovid believed the sirens were daughters of the river-god, Achelous. He relates that the sirens were at one time friends of Demeter's daughter Persephone and that they were the companions with whom she was gathering flowers when the god of the underworld, Hades, abducted her (see **Persephone**). The sirens really desired wings to enable them to fly over the sea looking for their missing friend, but because of their exceptional talent for singing, they retained their female heads.

Although almost all the ships which passed the islands of the sirens went down, mythology reports two successful attempts to pass the sirens unscathed. On his lengthy return journey from Troy to Ithaca, the hero Odysseus heeded the advice of the enchantress Circe and stopped the ears of his men with wax to prevent them from hearing the enticing singing. Since he was keen to hear the sirens himself, he left his own ears unprotected. He took took the precaution, however, of having himself strapped to the mast of his ship and ordered his men to bind him even tighter if he appeared to be too carried away by the singing.

The Argonauts, the heroes who had set sail on the ship, the *Argo*, led by Jason, chose a simpler but no less effective solution. One of those on board the *Argo* was the great singer Orpheus. With his own lovely voice, he effortlessly drowned out the voices of the sirens (see **Orpheus**).

Sisyphus

Sisyphus is known mainly on account of the terrible punishment inflicted upon him in the underworld. He was the son of Æolus and Enarete and founded the city-state of Corinth. Sisyphus was renowned for his cunning. According to some, he was the real

No matter how cunning he may have been in life, Sisyphus was unable to avoid the dreadful punishment to which he was subjected in the underworld. There was never any end to "the task of Sisyphus."

father of Odysseus, the hero famed for his quick-wittedness (who in most versions is thought to be the son of Laertes).

On several occasions Sisyphus succeeded in fooling the gods. One day, while standing on the ramparts of his city, he spied the king of the gods, Zeus, abducting the river-nymph, Ægina. He reported this to her father, the river god Asopus, who caused a fountain to spring up on the acropolis of Corinth in return for this information. Zeus was less impressed with Sisyphus' communicativeness and ordered Thanatos, the god of death, to take him off to the kingdom of the dead. The wicked Sisyphus was too sharp for Thanatos, however, and shackled him. For as long as he remained in chains, no mortal would die. Zeus was forced to send the god of war, Ares, to rescue Thanatos.

When Thanatos returned to fetch Sisyphus the latter already had another trick up his sleeve. He told his wife, Merope, not to bury him when he died. Later, when he arrived in the underworld after his demise, he would ask Persephone, the wife of Hades and female ruler of the kingdom of the dead, to let him go back to the land of the living so that he could punish his wife for her misbehavior (the Greeks considered that failure to bury the dead was utterly beyond the pale).

Sisyphus managed to persuade Persephone to allow him to come back to life. Naturally, he had no intention of returning voluntarily to the underworld and lived on earth to a very great age. In the end, the god Hermes had to bring him back to the kingdom of the dead, where a terrible punishment awaited him in Tartarus for all his cunning tricks. He was forced to expend every ounce of energy pushing a gigantic boulder up a hill. When the stone had almost reached the top, it would suddenly roll back down again and Sisyphus had to start again—over and over again. This is the origin of the expression "Sisyphean task, "describing a never-ending, futile task (*see* **Hades**).

Sphinx, The

The Sphinx, a winged creature with the body of a lion and the head and shoulders of a woman, was the daughter of Echidna and the monster Typhon. The goddess, Hera, sent her to the city of Thebes because the Theban King Laius had broken the laws of nature and run off with the youth, Chrysippus, the son of King Pelops (*see* **Laius**). Others have it that the Sphinx appeared on the instructions of Apollo or Dionysus.

The Sphinx would stop travelers at deserted spots just outside the city or fly to the citadel of Thebes to launch attacks upon it. She put the following riddle, that she had learned from the Muses, to her victims: "What animal is it that in the morning goes on four feet, at noon on two, and in the

It needed a man as intelligent as Œdipus to solve the ingenious riddle of the Sphinx. After Œdipus gave the right answer, the Sphinx hurled herself into an abyss. Sphinx and body in two parts on an earthenware altar from Tarente, 4th century BCE.

A mythical creature closely related to the Sphinx was the griffin or gryphon, which had a head similar to that of a bird of prey atop its winged lion's body. Head of a griffin on a silver coin (tetradrachm) from Phokaia, 5th/4th century BCE.

evening on three?"

The Sphinx (her name means "strangler") immediately killed and devoured anyone who failed to solve the riddle. Many were fated to meet this dreadful end, including one of the sons of the Theban, Creon, who served as regent, after the death of his brother, Laius. This caused Creon to promise the throne of Thebes and the hand of Queen Jocasta as a reward to anyone who could rid the city of the monster. Œdipus, the abandoned son of Laius, had no problem solving the riddle. The creature in question was man, he replied. Man, after all, crawls on his hands and feet as a baby, goes on to walk on two legs, and when he is old and bent needs a stick to serve as a "third leg." Upon hearing his reply, the Sphinx hurled herself off a cliff and was smashed to pieces.

Œdipus became king of the grateful Thebans, married Jocasta (who was, in fact, was his mother though neither mother nor son had the slightest suspicion of this) and embarked on a prosperous family life that would last for many years. It wasn't until much later that fate struck with redoubled force when the true identities of Œdipus and Jocasta became known (*see* **Œdipus**).

Stentor

Tantalus, who fed his son Pelops to the gods, had to endure eternal hunger and thirst in Tartarus after his death. The delectable fruit he could see before him drew back as soon as he stretched his hand out to it.

Stentor was a Greek hero who fought in the Trojan War. He was mainly known for his extraordinarily powerful voice, which was as loud as fifty others. That is why the adjective "stentorian" is used to describe a person with a very loud voice.

Styx, *see* Hades

Syrinx, *see* Pan

Tantalus

Tantalus, the son of Zeus and the Titan, Pluto (not to be confused with Hades, who was also called Pluto by the Romans) was one of the long-term sinners who was forced to dwell in Tartarus, the most forbidding part of the underworld.

Tantalus ruled a kingdom in Asia Minor. Pelops and Niobe were two of his children. At first, Tantalus was a favorite of his father, Zeus, the king of the gods. He was even allowed to sit at the table of the gods and taste ambrosia, the food of the gods, and nectar, the drink of the gods. However, he betrayed some

of the gods' secrets to man, and stole nectar and ambrosia, which he shared out among his friends. These were minor misdemeanors, however, compared to his greatest crime.

One day, when the gods came to dine with him, he slaughtered his son, Pelops, and offered the meat to his guests to find out if they really were omniscient. Almost all the gods passed this "test" and refused to eat even a morsel of Tantalus' main dish. Only Demeter, who was distracted on account of her grief over her daughter Persephone (*see* **Demeter**), failed to realize what was happening and ate Pelops' shoulder. The outraged gods brought Pelops back to life. He was given a new shoulder of ivory, but grew up to be almost as villainous a figure as his father (*see* **Pelops**)!

Tantalus' crime was regarded as so heinous that he was given an eternal punishment in the underworld, as were the Danaides, Ixion, Sisyphus, and Tityus. During his brief visit to the kingdom of the dead, the hero Odysseus witnessed what the punishment entailed: "He stood erect in a pool as the water lapped his chin—parched, he tried to drink, but he could not reach the surface, no, time and again the old man stooped, craving a sip, time and again the water vanished, swallowed down, laying bare the caked black earth at his feet—some spirit drank it dry. And over his head leafy trees dangled their fruit from high aloft, pomegranates and pears, and apples glowing red, succulent figs and olives swelling sleek and dark, but as soon as

As a young man, Telemachus finally met his father Odysseus, who had left for Troy shortly after his birth and did not return until twenty years later.

the old man would strain to clutch them fast a gust would toss them up to the lowering dark clouds." (Homer, *The Odyssey*, Book 11, lines 583-592). So that is why the adjective "tantalizing" used to describe a greatly coveted item that remains just out of reach. A tantalus is a set of decanters that are clearly visible but secured by a locking device.

Telemachus

Telemachus was the son of Penelope and of Odysseus, King of the island of Ithaca and the man who, thanks to a brilliant ruse, brought down Troy.

Telemachus was still a baby when his father left for Troy. Odysseus tried to avoid going to war by pretending to be mad. Bizarrely dressed, he plowed the beach of his island and scattered salt in the furrows. Palamedes, however, saw through this trick and put the tiny Telemachus in front of the plow, whereupon Odysseus reacted entirely normally and swerved to avoid the child, thus having to abandon his play-acting.

Telemachus was therefore raised without his father, who was unable to return home for twenty years. During this period, Telemachus had to watch his mother being pursued by the so-called "suitors," scions of the noble families of Ithaca who insisted that she marry one of them—Odysseus, after all, would not be coming back. Telemachus was too young to

fight them off, but not long before Odysseus' return, inspired by the (disguised) goddess Athena, he set off to discover his father's fate. He went to Pylos, ruled by the aged King Nestor, and to Sparta, where Menelaus and Helen gave him some valuable information (*see* **Menelaus** and **Helen**).

Odysseus returned to Ithaca while his son was still away looking for him. Athena made sure that Telemachus avoided an ambush laid for him by one of the suitors, and father and son were reunited at the home of the swineherd, Eumæus, who had remained unconditionally loyal to Odysseus. All Eumæus knew was that the man he had welcomed into his modest dwelling was a Cretan who had been roaming the world for years. When the householder briefly went outside, Odysseus made himself known to his son. Telemachus wouldn't believe him at first, but Odysseus soon managed to convince him. "At that, Odysseus sat down again, and Telemachus threw his arms around his great father, sobbing uncontrollably as the deep desire for tears welled up in both. They cried out, shrill cries, pulsing sharper than birds of prey—eagles, vultures with hooked claws—when farmers plunder their nest of fledglings that are too young to fly." (Homer, *The Odyssey*, 16, lines 213-219).

In the battle against the suitors, which broke out shortly afterward, Telemachus proved to be a fervent, courageous, and indispensable helper to his father. He was more than just a callow youth, he had it in him to

When Odysseus returned to Ithaca, Telemachus stayed on the Greek mainland, trying to find out what had happened to his father. The goddess Athena prevented Telemachus' ship falling into an ambush laid by the "suitors."

follow in the footsteps of his formidable father, as could be seen from the archery competition the suitors had organized at Odysseus' palace. Whilst none of the suitors had the strength to string Odysseus' old bow, Telemachus could do so easily, but he had to restrain himself (*see* **Odysseus**).

There are various accounts of what happened to Telemachus later in life. According to some, he married a daughter of Nestor, others say that he married the captivating Nausicaa, the young princess who was responsible for finding Odysseus when he was washed ashore on the island of the Phæacians. There is also a version which claims that Telemachus married the enchantress Circe after Odysseus' death.

Thanatos

Thanatos, the personification of death, was a son of the goddess Nyx ("Night") and a brother of Hypnos ("Sleep.") When someone was due to die, Thanatos would appear and use his sword to cut off a lock of the person's hair, and this would be used to dedicate the unfortunate mortal to Hades. Thanatos was portrayed as a winged youth carrying a torch that he held upside down.

Thanatos does not feature prominently in myths. Homer describes how he and his brother brought the body of the fallen Sarpedon back to Lycia. The Athenian playwright Euripides allocates him a minor role in the play *Alcestis*, in which Thanatos comes to collect the eponymous Alcestis, who is prepared to die instead of her husband Admetus (*see* **Alcestis**). Thanatos has a brief exchange of words with the god Apollo, who wants to prevent the wife of his favorite, Admetus, from being taken away. Thanatos proves to be an uncompromising figure on this occasion whom no words can move. As far as is known, the only human who ever managed to escape his attentions was the villain, Sisyphus. He chained Thanatos up for a time with the result that while Thanatos was held prisoner, no mortal could die. In the end, the war god Ares released Thanatos.

Theseus

The Athenian hero, Theseus, was one of the most distinguished heroes in Greek mythology. He was a son of Ægeus and Æthra, but some believe the mighty sea-god Poseidon was really his father.

In this version, the Athenian King Ægeus

Roman sarcophagi were often decorated with images relating to death and the hereafter. Hermes, who led the victims of Thanatos to the underworld, can be seen second from the right on this sarcophagus from Aphrodisias, Turkey.

failed to produce any children even though he married twice. When he went to consult the oracle at Delphi, he was told that he must not open his wineskin until he was back in Athens. Ægeus was baffled by this advice and related it to his friend, King Pittheus of Troezen. Pittheus knew that the oracle had also predicted the birth of a great hero and immediately saw a connection. He made Ægeus drunk and had him sleep with his daughter, Æthra, so that the future hero would be his grandson. When Ægeus realized what had happened, he placed a sword and a pair of sandals under a huge boulder. If his son were one day to come to Athens, Ægeus would acknowledge him and name him heir to the throne.

Theseus grew up in Troezen and on his sixteenth birthday, his mother revealed to him the identity of his father. He then raised the boulder, removed the sword and sandals, and set off for Athens. At that time, the land between the two cities of Troezen and Athens was plagued by robbers and wild beasts. Following the example of the hero, Heracles, whom he revered, Theseus resolved to conquer them. His first victim was Periphetes, a son of Hephæstos. This robber attacked hapless travelers in the Epidaurus area, beating out their brains with a gigantic club. Theseus disarmed him of his weapon and killed him with it. The club has remained a hallmark of Theseus ever since.

The Isthmus of Corinth was ruled by the extremely strong warlord, Sinis, the "pine-bender." Sinis was so strong that he could bend two pine-trees to the ground and tie a victim between the trees. He would then release the trees, causing the unfortunate tortured sufferers to be torn apart. Theseus overpowered Siris and killed him, using the villain's own tried and tested method. He later had a son, Melanippus by Sinis' comely daughter, Perigune.

At Cromyon, Theseus went on to kill a wild sow, the offspring of the monsters Echidna and Typhon, that was relentlessly

destroying the fields of the local population.

The rocky coastal road to Megara was the hunting ground of the outlaw Sciron, who would stop travelers and force them to wash his feet. When they knelt down in front of him, he would push them off the cliff into the sea, where a giant turtle would devour them. Theseus knelt down in front of Sciron, grabbed his legs, and flung him into the sea. In some versions, Sciron fell victim to the turtle and in others he turned into some cliffs that have borne his name since then.

Cercyon, King of Eleusis, near Athens, forced passers-by to wrestle with him and killed them if they lost the bout. Theseus beat the king, killed him, and himself became ruler of Eleusis, which he later annexed to Athens.

Before reaching his home town, Theseus had one more obstacle to face. At Erineus, he encountered the innkeeper, Procrustes ("the stretcher,") who was keen to offer his guests a bed. He was most concerned that the bed was the right fit for the guests, or rather, that the guests were the right fit for the bed. He stretched short guests until they were long enough to fit the bed and taller guests were cut down to size until they were the right fit. Theseus questioned whether Procrustes himself actually fitted his own bed. He did not. The innkeeper was in fact, literally, a head too tall. Theseus didn't find this an insurmountable problem. Since then, the term "Procrustean bed" has been used to describe a tricky, embarrassing predicament in which a person unwillingly finds themself.

When Theseus finally arrived in Athens, Ægeus was King although the Pallantides, the fifty sons of his brother Pallas, were trying to seize the throne. Ægeus' wife was the dangerous sorceress, Medea, who had received asylum in Athens after her flight from Corinth (*see* **Medea**). Medea was determined that her son should succeed Ægeus. And even though she realized straightaway that the young hero who had made the area around the city considerably safer was Theseus, she didn't tell Ægeus. On the contrary, she told him that Theseus was an ally of Pallantides and proposed poisoning him. At a subsequent banquet, however, when Theseus was cutting some meat Ægeus recognized the sword he had placed under the boulder in Troezen all those years ago and, just in time, he managed to knock the goblet containing Medea's poison out of his son's hands. Medea fled from Athens and Ægeus named Theseus as heir to the throne.

Theseus went on to defeat the Pallantides, who had launched an attack, and went to Marathon, which was a good thirty miles from Athens (the marathon race is named for it—the first "marathon runner" was an Athenian soldier who carried news of a Greek victory over the Persians in 490 BC to Athens—and then dropped dead from exhaustion). The area surrounding this place was plagued by the Cretan bull that Heracles had once captured (*see* **Heracles**, *Seventh Labor*) and was later released again. Theseus eliminated the evil beast once and for all (according to some versions, he did this on Medea's instructions before Ægeus recognized him), and offered it as a sacrifice to the god Apollo.

The killing of the bull was the precursor to Theseus' most hazardous and best-known heroic deed. Androgeous, a son of the Cretan King Minos, had been killed by the Athenians (or by the bull). This caused the mighty monarch to declare war on Ægeus and force the Athenians to send seven young men and

After he had defeated the Pallantides who had challenged his father for the Athenian throne, Theseus killed the Cretan bull that had been plaguing the Marathon area. Rhyton in the form of a bull's head from the palace of Cnossos on Crete, 16th century BCE.

seven young women to Crete every nine years (*see Ægeus*) where they were sacrificed to the Minotaur, a monstrous creature with the body of a man and a bull's head. It lived in the Labyrinth, an underground maze that King Minos had commissioned the Athenian

Theseus kills the monstrous Minotaur in the Labyrinth, under the watchful eye of a young man and a girl. Black-figure painting on an Athenian kylix, approx. 535 BCE.

master craftsman Dædalus (*see* **Dædalus, Minos,** *and* **Minotaur**) to build, so that the hideous beast would be out of sight. The third sacrifice was imminent and, according to some, Minos expressly demanded that Theseus be thrown to the Minotaur as well. Others have it that Theseus went voluntarily, all the more since the population of Athens did not approve of the king's son being exempted from the drawing of lots to decide who would be sent. Before leaving, Theseus arranged with his father that if he returned safe and sound he would raise a white sail on his ship.

When Theseus landed on Crete, Minos' daughter Ariadne fell deeply in love with him. Her help proved invaluable to the hero. She consulted the master-builder, Dædalus, who confirmed that there was just one way in and out of the Labyrinth. Then, after Theseus had promised to marry her, Ariadne gave the hero a ball of thread. The thread was tied to the entrance so that, having unwound it, Theseus would always be able to find his way back.

Theseus left the young Athenians behind at the entrance and made his way through to the heart of the Labyrinth where he came across the monstrous creature. He killed the Minotaur with his sword or with his bare hands and, thanks to the thread, found his

According to some versions of the myth, the god of wine, Dionysus (left), took pity on Ariadne on the island of Naxos after Theseus had inexplicably abandoned her there. Oil painting by Peter Paul Rubens, 17th century.

Parade of the followers of Dionysus. As bride of the god of wine, Ariadne was, of course, part of his entourage. Fragment of a relief on a memorial temple from Tarente, 4th–3rd century BCE.

adne as his bride and made off with her. According to Homer, however, the goddess Artemis killed Ariadne on the island at Dionysus' request.

Having called at the island of Delos, Theseus continued his journey to Athens. His father saw him approach from the acropolis and to his horror the ship was sailing under a black sail. In his misery over the loss of Ariadne, or joy at the successful outcome of his mission, Theseus had forgotten to raise the white sail as arranged. It didn't occur to Ægeus that Theseus might still be alive, and he hurled himself into the sea.

Theseus succeeded his father as King of Athens and Attica. He brought law and order to Attica and, in honor of Athena, introduced the Panathenæan festival, one of the major religious festivals in ancient Greece. He also extended his territory to include Megara and Troezen.

Theseus was not the type of man who, just because he was now king, would embark upon a peaceful and retiring life. He went on on to enjoy countless more adventures. According to some, Theseus became one of the Argonauts, the heroes who, led by Jason, sailed to the distant land of Colchis to fetch the golden fleece (*see* **The Argonauts**). He was also said to be one of the heroes who took part in the hunt for the wild boar sent by Artemis that terrorized the Calydon area. The Calydon Boar was eventually killed by the local hero, Meleager.

Theseus participated in a campaign against the Amazons, during which he abducted a leading Amazon. According to some, this was Antiope, others believe it was her sister, Hippolyta. The Amazon either fell in love with Theseus or was simply abducted. In any

way back to the entrance and then escaped to his ship with Ariadne and the young Athenians. In the dead of night, the escapees drilled holes in the bottoms of the Cretan ships to make pursuit impossible.

Theseus, Ariadne, and their companions managed to flee from Crete and landed on the island of Naxos. There are widely divergent versions as to what exactly happened there. According to some, Theseus was bewitched and forgot Ariadne completely. Others have it that he was happy to leave her because he had fallen in love with someone else. Dionysus, the god of wine and vegetation, is then said to have taken pity on her. Yet another version claims that Dionysus demanded Ari-

Dionysus (right) beside his tutor Silenus (center). The figure on the left might be Dionysus' bride, Ariadne. The precise meaning of this scene from the Dionysian Mystery cult is unclear. Fresco from the Villa of Mysteries, Pompeii, 1st century BCE.

event, the other Amazons pursued Theseus to Attica where they besieged the Athenian acropolis and, after heavy fighting, were defeated by Theseus. Antiope or Hippolyta, became Theseus' wife and bore him a son, who was named Hippolytus.

Theseus granted asylum in Athens to the blind Œdipus and his daughter Antigone, who had been driven out of Thebes, and when the Theban regent, Creon, tried to force Œdipus back to Thebes and kidnapped Œdipus' daughters, Theseus intervened. The tormented Œdipus died on Athenian soil and was buried there, but only Theseus knew the location of his grave (*see* Œdipus). According to the playwright Euripides, Theseus is also thought to have intervened in the fratricidal struggle between Œdipus' sons, Polynices and Eteocles, and forced Creon to give Polynices and his fellow fighters (the "Seven against Thebes") a decent burial.

Theseus became a close friend of king Pirithous of the Lapiths and was naturally one of the guests when Pirithous married Hippodamia. It goes without saying that he also took part in the terrible fight that broke out during this wedding when the centaurs tried to steal Pirithous' bride and other Lapithian women (*see* **The Centaurs**).

Given the strange way in which his relationship with Ariadne turned out, it is noteworthy that, when Theseus was much older, he married Phædra, who was another daugh

ter of the Cretan King Minos. At the time of the wedding, Theseus' son Hippolytus was in Troezen—with his great grandfather Pittheus—but when he visited Athens, Phædra fell deeply in love with her stepson, who was around her age, as a result of the goddess Aphrodite's intervention. Not long afterward, Theseus and his young wife were sent in temporary exile to Troezen because Theseus had spilled a lot of blood in a new conflict with his uncle Pallas and his sons. When Theseus left Troezen for Delphi to consult the oracle,

Theseus fought on the side of the Lapiths against the Centaurs in the shocking battle that broke out during the wedding of Pirithous and Hippodamia. Painting of a Centaur on an Athenian kylix, approx. 500 BCE.

Phædra instructed her nurse to tell Hippolytus that she loved him. Hippolytus, a devoted follower of Artemis, the virginal goddess of the hunt, was deeply shocked. He was revolted by his stepmother but swore to keep the matter secret. When Phædra learned of Hippolytus' reaction, she killed herself. Before doing so, however, she wrote a letter to Theseus in which she accused Hippolytus of trying to assault her. When Theseus returned, he was deeply upset by the suicide of his wife and believed her version of events. He cursed his son and told him he hoped he would die in exile. Hippolytus felt honor-bound to keep the secret and was therefore unable to say what had really happened. A little later, Poseidon (possibly Theseus' father!) heard the terrible news. One day, when Hippolytus was driving his chariot along the shore, the sea-god unleashed a monstrous bull from the sea. Hippolytus' horses bolted and he perished when his chariot smashed into a cliff. Artemis eventually revealed to Theseus the true nature of Phædra's involvement with Hippolytus.

As a widower, it was not long before Theseus once more started looking for a new wife. And who was more fitting for a hero of his standing than the most beautiful woman in the world, the Spartan princess Helen? He and Pirithous went to Sparta and abducted the beauty, who was just twelve years old. Back in Attica, he entrusted her to the care of his mother, Æthra, until she was old enough to marry. Pirithous also wanted a new wife and he wasn't prepared to settle for any old wife either. Persephone, the beautiful mistress of the kingdom of the dead, seemed a good match to him. He and Theseus went to the underworld, but Hades knew what to do with people like them. He invited them to sit on the chairs of forgetfulness. They promptly lost their memories and were unable to stand up again. The poet Virgil has his hero, Æneas, report that he had seen Theseus during his visit to the underworld and that he was doomed to remain on his chair for eternity. According to other versions, however, Theseus was freed by Heracles when he went to the underworld to fetch the monstrous dog Cerberus (*see* **Heracles, Twelfth Labor**). Pirithous had to pay for his desire for Persephone by remaining in the underworld forever.

After his return to Athens, Theseus was waylaid by the Dioscuri, Castor and Polydeuces, who had come to retrieve their abducted sister Helen. Theseus had to take refuge on the island of Scyros, but the ruler, King Lycomedes, was not best pleased by his arrival. He took Theseus up to a high cliff and, in a surprise attack, pushed him over it, putting an end to the life of the great Athenian hero.

The Dioscuri, Castor and Polydeuces, have Theseus in a very tight corner at the end of his life. One of the Dioscuri, bronze statue from Turkey, 2nd century BCE.

The Nereid Thetis inspects the new armor Hephæstos has forged for her son Achilles at her request.

Thetis

Thetis was a sea nymph—a Nereid, or a daughter of the sea-god Nereus (*see* **Nymphs**). Despite her origin, the comely Thetis was raised by Hera on Mount Olympus, the home and meeting-place of the twelve Olympian gods. She later returned to her home at the bottom of the sea.

When Hera slung the newly-born Hephæstos off Olympus, furious because she had brought a deformed child into the world, Thetis and her sister Eurynome took pity on him. For nine years, they looked after the blacksmith and artist of the gods who thereafter cherished a special affection for them, and never refused to help Thetis when she approached him. Zeus, the king of the gods , was particularly fond of Thetis as well—and with good reason. Once, when Hera, Athena, and Poseidon joined in a conspiracy against Zeus and were planning to him in chains, Thetis summoned the exceptionally strong, hundred-armed giant, Briareus, to Olympus and for a time he acted as Zeus' bodyguard. A third god whom Thetis rescued and cared for was the god of wine and vegetation, Dionysus. She had taken pity on him when, as a young man, he had had to leap into the sea to escape from Lycurgus, King of Edones (*see* **Dionysus**).

Thetis' beauty also caused Zeus and Poseidon to lust after her. However, the Titan Prometheus knew that a son born to Thetis would overthrow his father. Prometheus was not prepared to reveal this secret until he was freed from the rocks to which Zeus had had him chained for giving fire to mankind (*see* **Prometheus**).When the tormented Titan finally told Zeus, he realized how fortunate he had been. Had he given in to his lecherous impulses he would have met the same fate as his father Cronos, whom he had dethroned (*see* **Cronos**). That is why Zeus decided that Thetis should marry a mortal instead of a god.

Peleus, King of Phthia, who has a favorite

Peleus, who has received permission from the gods to make Thetis his own, and is trying to overpower her, but Thetis will not surrender without a struggle. Black-figure painting on an Athenian alabastron, ca. 470 BCE.

Thetis was a Nereid, a beautiful sea-nymph. This Nereid is taking a ride on the tail of a Triton who is enthusiastically blowing his shell. Oil painting by Peter Paul Rubens, 17th century.

of the gods, was the lucky man. First of all, however, he had to win Thetis over, using his own resources. This would be no easy matter, however, because Thetis, in common with all of the sea-gods and sea-goddesses, could change her shape at lightning speed. Peleus went to visit his future wife on a rocky shore in Thrace, where she lay asleep in a cave. After she had rejected his advances, Peleus attempted to rape her, but Thetis transformed herself first into a bird, then a tree trunk, and then a tigress. On the advice of the sea-god Proteus, he then tied her up while she was sleeping and withstood several more of her changes of form. At that point, Thetis finally surrendered. Peleus went on to have intercourse with her and this is how Achilles was conceived. He would later become the greatest hero of the Trojan War (*see* **Achilles**).

The seeds of this war were sown during the wedding of Peleus and Thetis. All the gods attended the celebrations, bringing magnificent gifts with them. All that is, apart from the one goddess, who was not invited. Her name was Eris, and she was the goddess of discord. Full of spite at having been excluded, she tossed a golden apple (the proverbial "apple of discord") among the guests that bore the inscription "For the fairest." Hera, Aphrodite, and Athena each assumed the apple was theirs. In the end, the Trojan prince-regent, Paris, had to decide, and he chose Aphrodite because she promised him the most beautiful woman in the world. This was Helen, but Helen was already married to Menelaus, King of Sparta. No sooner had Paris abducted her and taken her home to Troy, than a war broke out between the Trojans and the Greeks who were allies of Menelaus (*see* **Aphrodite, Helen,** *and* **Paris**).

Thetis knew her son Achilles was not immortal and that he would be cut down in battle. That is why she did everything in her

Thetis felt deeply for her son, Achilles, during the Trojan War and did as much for him as much as she could. Here Hephæstos presents her with the glittering new armor the god has forged for Achilles at her request. Oil painting by Peter Paul Rubens, 17th century.

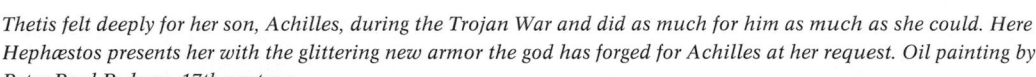

power to make him invincible. For example, just after he was born, she dipped him into the black waters of the underworld river, the Styx, but because she had to keep hold of his heel while doing, so this part of his body remained vulnerable. In fact, Paris' arrow would later fatally wound the hero on his "Achilles' heel." According to another tale, Thetis placed her little son upon a fire overnight to make him immortal and protect him from the aging process. To make sure he could endure such treatment, she would smear him with ambrosia, the food of the gods. One night, Peleus found Achilles in the fire and he flew into a raging panic, after which Thetis left him.

The anxious Thetis continued to do all she could to keep Achilles far away from war and combat. She even went so far as to send him to the island of Scyros, where, dressed as a girl, he had to live among the daughters of Lycomedes. However, a simple trick played by Odysseus was enough to separate the man from the girls (*see* **Achilles**). During the Trojan War, Thetis supported her son in a manner befitting a loving mother. When he found himself at odds with the supreme commander, Agamemnon, who had stolen him his conquered mistress, Briseis, as war booty, she pleaded his case with Zeus and asked the king of the gods to give the Trojans temporary ascendancy in the war, so that Agamemnon would be forced to eat humble pie. Zeus foresaw problems with his wife—Hera was a fanatical supporter of the Greeks—but was unable to refuse Thetis anything.

When, a short time later, Achilles was distraught at the death of his comrade-in-arms Patroclus at the hands of the Trojan hero Hector, she mourned with him. She also commissioned Hephæstos to make a magnificent new suit of armor for Achilles (he had lent his last suit to Patroclus, and Hector had seized for himself upon Patroclus' death).

When Achilles' inevitable end finally arrived, Thetis and her sisters' mourning was so great that the Greeks flew into a panic and fled to their ships. The ancient hero, Nestor, brought them back to their senses. Thetis and the other Nereids wept for Achilles for seventeen days. Even the Muses appeared to sing a lament. Once Achilles had been cremated, Thetis put his bones into a golden urn that also contained the bones of Patroclus.

Thetis was one of the most good natured and kindly goddesses in Greek mythology.

Her concern and grief over the mortality of her beloved son gave her a human dimension rarely seen in the other gods and goddesses.

The blind seer, Tiresias, predicts the future. Not everyone was pleased with Tiresias' prophecies.

Thisbe, *see* Pyramus

Tiresias

The blind Theban, Tiresias, son of Everes and the nymph Chariclo, and Calchas, were the two most famous seers in Greek mythology.

There are two different accounts of the cause of Tiresias' blindness and of his paranormal powers. According to the first version, he once saw the virgin goddess, Athena, naked when she and her mother were bathing. After that, Athena deprived him of his sight but gave him the power to understand the language of birds and predict the future. She also presented him with a special staff and granted him an exceedingly long life.

According to the second version, Tiresias once came across two snakes mating on a mountain. He hit the female snake with his stick and promptly changed into a woman himself. Eight years later, Tiresias, still a woman, saw the same snakes again. On this occasion, he hit both the snakes and changed back into a man. One day, when the king of

the gods Zeus and his wife Hera were discussing which of the two sexes most enjoyed lovemaking, Tiresias was the person chosen to provide a decisive answer. Tiresias replied that the woman experienced much more pleasure during sex than the man. This answer, however, did not suit Hera and that is why she deprived Tiresias of his sight. There was nothing Zeus could do to rectify Hera's cruel action, but he compensated Tiresias by giving him the gift of clairvoyance. Tiresias made his predictions by observing the behavior of the birds. He studied the sounds they made and, where necessary, substantiated his findings with the results of certain sacrificial offerings.

The first person to have his—doomed—future predicted by Tiresias was Narcissus. When his mother asked the seer if he would be granted a long life, she was told that Narcissus would continue to live so long as he never set eyes on his own image. The meaning of this pronouncement only became clear to her later on (*see* **Narcissus**).

Tiresias made many pronouncements and predictions which the people concerned did not initially take seriously. The Theban king Pentheus, who did not understand why Tiresias worshiped the god of wine and vegeta-

tion, Dionysus, rejected his advice to take the worship of this god seriously and ultimately had to pay for this attitude with his life (*see* **Dionysus** and **Mænads**).

Tiresias forecast an important role in the tragic developments in Thebes during and after the rule of Œdipus, the prince who, without realizing it, murdered his father and married his mother (*see* **Œdipus**).It was he who pointed out to Œdipus that the plague had broken out in Thebes as a result of his wrongdoing. Œdipus was far from grateful to him for this information and even accused Tiresias of bad faith. King Creon, who ruled Thebes before and after Œdipus, also received extremely unwelcome advice from Tiresias. When the seer instructed him to give the corpse of Œdipus' son Polynices, who had been killed in a duel with his brother Eteocles, who also died as a result, a decent burial (a sacred obligation in ancient Greece), Creon accused him of being untrustworthy and simply out for money (*see* **Antigone** and **Creon**).

Tiresias died after Thebes had been conquered by the sons of Polynices' allies—an event which he, naturally, had foreseen. In the underworld, Tiresias' shade took up a highly exceptional position. Other shades were denied all consciousness, but Tiresias was even allowed to continue making predictions. After the hero Odysseus had given him some sheep's blood to drink during his brief visit to the kingdom of the dead, Tiresias warned him that he must on no account kill the cattle of the sun-god Helios on the island of Thrinacia. If he followed this advice, he would return safely to his island home of Ithaca, slay the suitors who were besieging his wife, Penelope, and live to a great age. Tiresias' predictions came true. A striking detail in this story related by Homer is that the shade of Tiresias recognized Odysseus straightaway. So clearly, he had regained his sight after death.

Titans, The

The Titans were deities who resulted from the union of Uranus (the sky) and Gaia (the earth). They were of gigantic proportions and ruled the world at the beginning of creation. The foremost Titans were Cronos, who castrated his father Uranus and remained king of

The Titan, Cronos, emasculated his father Uranus and devoured his children. He ruled the world until his son, Zeus, deposed him.

the gods until he was overthrown by his son Zeus, Rhea, his wife, Oceanus, the ruler of the ocean that surrounded the earth, Tethys, Iapetus, Hyperion, Cœus, Crius, Phœbe,

According to the pœt Hesiod, men lived in great harmony with the universe under the rule of the Titans. It is not clear whether they had to placate the Titans by offering them sacrifices, as was the case with later gods. Sacrificial scene at the Arco degli Argentari, 3rd century BCE.

Themis, Mnemosyne, and Theia. A number of their descendants were also considered Titans. These included the sun-god Helios (son of Hyperion), Prometheus, who championed the rights of mankind, Epimetheus and Atlas (all three sons of Iapetus). The children of Cronos and Rhea, however, were not Titans. Their youngest son, Zeus, who thanks to a trick played by his mother was the only one not to be swallowed by his father (*see* **Cronos**), began an uprising which resulted in him taking control of the universe, together with his brothers, Poseidon and Hades, who had by now been regurgitated by Cronos.

The War of the Titans lasted ten years. Most of the Titans (Prometheus, Oceanus, Helios, and the female Titans had stayed out of the fight) were based at Mount Othrys and Zeus and his supporters remained on Mount Olympus—the mountain that would later be their permanent home and meeting-place. The war continued, with no sign of a break through until Zeus, on the advice of his mother Rhea, freed the hundred-armed giants Briareus, Cottos, and Gyes from Tartarus—the most inhospitable part of the underworld. They pelted the Titans relentlessly with rocks while Zeus fired lightning bolts at them. Unsurprisingly, the Titans were unable to hold their own against this double bombardment. After their defeat, they were imprisoned in the bowels of Tartarus, with the hundred-armed giants acting as their guards. An alternative punishment was imposed on Atlas, who was forced to support the heavens on his shoulders for eternity (*see* **Atlas**).

It is not entirely clear exactly how life was ordered when the Titans ruled the world. The Titans were primitive beings, but according to the poet Hesiod, there was a golden race of mortal men who lived on earth "in the time of Cronos when he was reigning in heaven." They lived like gods, did not need to struggle to survive, and did not suffer painful old age. "When they died, it was as though they were overcome with sleep, and they had all the good things; for the fruitful earth, unforced, bare them fruit abundantly and unstintingly. They dwelt with ease and peace upon their lands with many good things, rich in flocks and loved by the blessed gods." (Hesiod, *Works and Days*, lines 146-150)

Triton

The sea god, Triton, was a son of Poseidon,

The sea-god, Triton, had the appearance of a '"merman" with a long fishtail. Relief on a Roman earthenware lamp, 1st century AD.

the divine ruler of the seas, and Amphritrite. He was usually portrayed as a "merman," a creature with the upper body of a man on top of a one, or even two, long fishtails. His attributes included a trident and a large, convoluted conch shell, a member of the family of triton shells named for him. Triton could calm the turbulent waters by blowing through this shell. According to some, there were several Tritons, and they formed part of Poseidon's retinue.

Triton was a great help to the Argonauts, the heroes who, led by Jason, went to fetch the golden fleece (*see* **The Argonauts**), in the form of a young man. Their ship, the *Argo*, had a short time earlier sailed into Lake Tritonis in Libya, from which they could find no way out back to the sea. Apollonius Rhodius (fl. third century BCE) tells the story in his *Argonautica*.

"Orpheus suggested that they should bring out the great tripod that Apollo had given Jason and offer it to the gods of the land... no sooner had they set up the tripod than the great god Triton appeared before them, taking the form of a young man. He picked up a

This Triton is blowing two shells simultaneously. He has two scaly legs instead of one fishtail. Sculpture on the Fontana del Moro, Piazza Navona, Rome, 16th century.

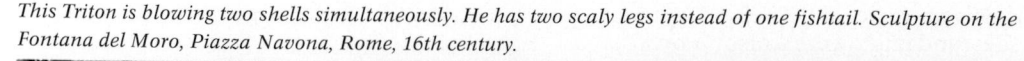

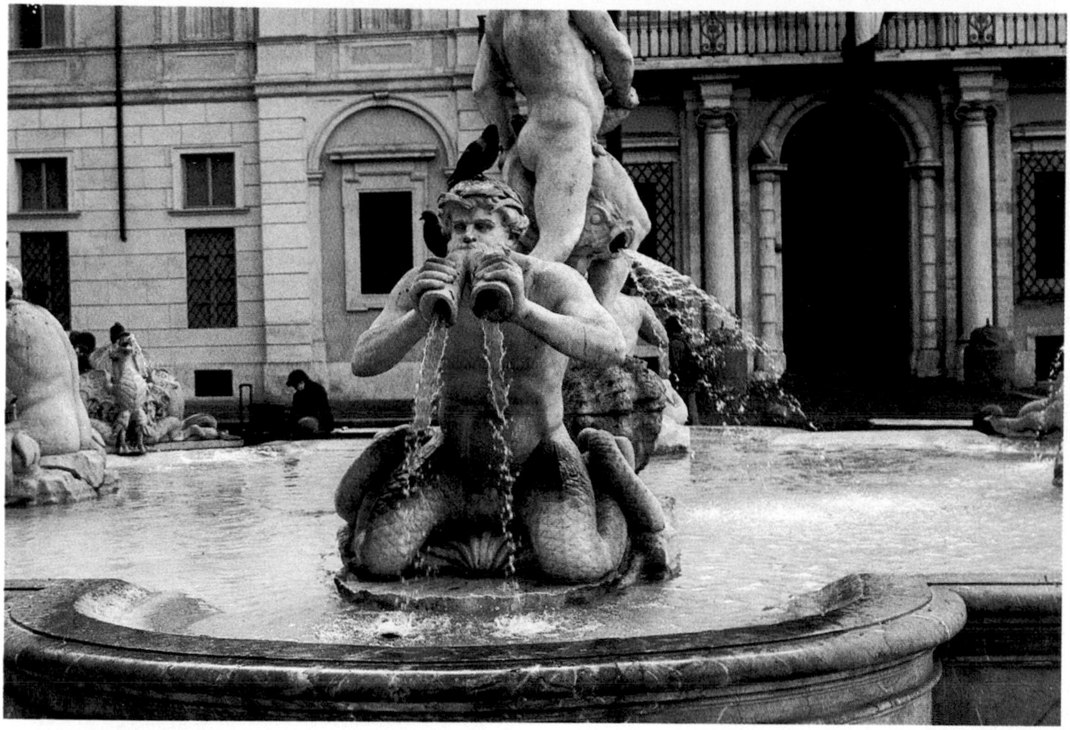

The Titan Cronos emasculated his father Uranus and devoured his children. He ruled the world until his son Zeus deposed him. During the Renaissance period Tritons once again became fashionable decorations on fountains and other water features. Triton by the sculptor Moratti on the Fontana dei Tritoni on the Piazza Santa Maria in Cosmedin, Rome.

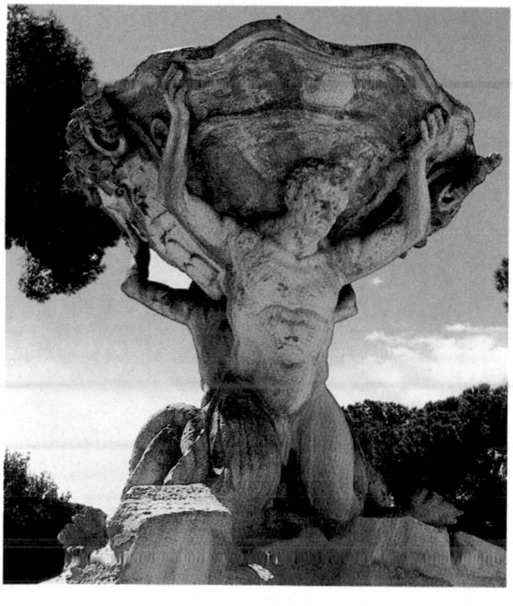

clod of earth and held it out to them by way of welcome, saying: 'Accept this gift, my friends. Here and now, I have no better one with which to welcome strangers such as you. But if you have lost your bearings, like many a traveler in foreign parts, and wish to cross the Libyan Sea, I will be your guide. My father, Poseidon, has taught me all its secrets, and I am the king of this seaboard. You may have heard of me though you live so far away.' Euphemos gladly held his hand out for the clod and said: 'My lord, if you know anything of the Minoan Sea and the Peloponnese, we beg you to tell us. Far from meaning to come here, we were driven ashore on the borders of your land by a heavy gale. Then we hoisted our ship, and for all her weight, carried her across country till we came to this lagoon. And no we have no idea how to get out of it and reach the land of Pelops.'

"Triton, stretching out his hand, pointed to the distant sea and the deep mouth of the lagoon. At the same time he explained: 'That is the outlet to the sea; the smooth, dark water marks the deepest spot, but on either side of it are beaches where the rollers break – you can see the foam from here – and the fairway in between them is a narrow one ...

Typhon's one hundred heads could produce a number of sounds. One head could roar like a lion, and another bellowed like a bull. Lion and bull on a silver coin (stater) from Lydia, 6th century BCE.

Once you are out in the open, keep the land on your right and hug the coast as long as it runs north. But when it gathers toward you and then falls away, you may safely leave it at the point where it projects and sail straight on.' Thus encouraged by the friendly god, the Argonauts embarked at once... Meanwhile Triton picked up the heavy tripod and walked into the water. They saw him stepping in; yet in a moment he had disappeared, quite close to them, tripod and all. Jason killed a sheep over the stern, praying in these words: 'God of the sea, you that appeared to us on the shores of these waters...be gracious and grant us the happy return we desire.'

"As he prayed, he slit the victim's throat and threw it into the water from the stern. Whereupon the god emerged from the depths, no longer in disguise but in his own true form, and grasping the stem of their hollow ship drew her on toward the open sea...The body of the god, front and back, from the crown of his head to his waist and belly, was exactly like that of the other immortals; but from the hips down he was a monster of the deep, with two long tails, each ending in a pair of curved flukes shaped like the crescent moon. With the spins of these two tails he lashed the surface of the water, and so brought Argo to the open sea, where he launched her on her way. Then he sank into the abyss, and the Arg-

onauts cried out in wonder at the awe-inspiring sight." (*Argonautica*, Book IV).

In some accounts, Triton—or the Tritons—also had another, less benevolent side. Rather like "satyrs of the sea," the Tritons were in the habit of molesting bathing women and young men. Once, when Triton cornered some female followers of the god of wine and vegetation, Dionysus, in Bœotia, there was a fight between the two gods that ended in a defeat for the sea-god. The great hero Heracles is also said to have once wrestled

After he had fled Typhon for Egypt, Zeus changed himself into a ram. The Egyptian variant of Zeus, Zeus-Amon, was depicted with ram's horns. Head of Zeus-Amon on a bronze coin, Alexandria, 3rd century BCE.

with a sea monster called Triton.

Typhon

Typhon (or Typhœus) was a terrifying monster, the result of a liaison between Gaia (Mother Earth) and Tartarus, the deepest and most inhospitable part of the underworld. Typhon was as strong as an ox and had a hundred terrible snake heads with black tongues and flaming eyes that sprouted from his shoulders. All these heads had their own voices producing indescribable sounds. One head could speak the language of the gods, whilst other heads bellowed like a bull, roared like a lion, bayed like a pack of bloodhounds, or made hideous hissing sounds. Typhon was intent upon world domination.

When he set eyes upon Typhon, Zeus, the king of the gods, caused Olympus shake to its foundations. His thunder and lightning and the monster's fire caused such turmoil on earth, in the seas, and in the sky that even Hades and the Titans locked up in Tartarus sat quaking with fear. Zeus gathered all his lightning flashes and thunderbolts, leapt down from Olympus and struck Typhon and all his one hundred heads. Ablaze, the monster fled and collapsed, causing fires to break out all over the earth. Zeus flung the defeated Typhon into Tartarus, where he brought forth fierce gales that would endanger mankind. That is why the typhoon is named for him.

In other versions of the tale, it cost Zeus a great deal more effort to eliminate Typhon. For example, at some point Typhon managed to purloin Zeus' sickle and used it to slice Zeus' tendons leaving him permanently lame. Typhon then took control of Zeus' lightning bolts and arranged for another monster to guard him and his tendons. Hermes later

Aphrodite, the goddess of love and beauty, emerged from the foam that formed in the seawater around Uranus' amputated member. Although Aphrodite was not as powerful as Uranus once was, she was worshiped fervently throughout Antiquity. The temple of Venus and Rome dedicated to her (2nd century AD) was one of the major shrines of ancient Rome.

managed to trick the monster and mobilize Zeus again, whereupon Zeus went back to Olympus to collect more lightning bolts and drove Typhon to Mount Nysa. There, Typhon became the victim of a trick played by the Fates (*see* **The Fates**). They advised him to eat some human flesh to make him even stronger, but this meal seriously weakened him. A confrontation between the king of the gods and the monster then took place on a mountain in Thrace, culminating in Zeus pursuing Typhon to the southern coast of Italy and burying the monster under the island of Sicily, where to this day, the volcano, Mount Ætna, emits the hot, poisonous breath of the monster.

According to yet another version, after Typhon appeared, the gods fled in a panic to Egypt where they disguised themselves as animals, thus explaining why the Egyptians worshiped their gods in the form of animals. Apollo became a raven, Dionysus a buck, Artemis a cat, Hera a white cow, Aphrodite a fish, and Hermes, an ibis. Even Zeus assumed a new form, changing himself into a ram. That is why Amon, the god with whom Zeus is identified,

is portrayed with ram's horns. According to the historian, Herodotus, Typhon was eventually killed in Egypt by Apollo, who, in Egypt, is identified with Horus, son of the god of death and resurrection, Osiris.

Before he was finally defeated, Typhon is said to have fathered a host of other monsters by the serpent, Echidna, including the Chimæra, the dragon Ladon, the Sphinx, the Cromyon sow, the Nemean lion, and the eagle that pecked out Prometheus' liver.

Ulixes or Ulysses, *see* Odysseus

Uranus

Without the intervention of a male creature, Gaia, the earth, who herself was created from Chaos, the primitive world, produced Uranus, the sky. The Titans, the giants who ruled the world before the Olympian gods led by Zeus successfully seized power, were the results of

In the all-or-nothing attempt to conquer the fruit-grower Pomona, the despairing Vertumnus successfully disguises himself as an old woman. Oil painting by Emmanuel de Witte, 17th century.

the union of Uranus and his mother. The Cyclopes and the hundred-armed giants were also descendants of Uranus and Gaia. Uranus, however, proved to be a brutal father and husband. Immediately after they were born, he pushed the Cyclopes and hundred-armed giants back into their mother's womb, causing Gaia considerable distress. Gaia did not put up with this abuse. She made a sharp sickle out of flint and asked her children to help her teach their cruel father a lesson. Cronos, the youngest and craftiest Titan, was the only one who dared help her. He set up an ambush, lying in wait with the sickle until Uranus went to lie with Gaia. He then rushed forward and cut off Uranus' sexual organs, hurling them into the sea. The Erinyes, the Gigantes, and the nymphs of Melos sprung up where drops of Uranus' blood fell onto Gaia. Uranus' sexual organs drifted to Cythera or Cyprus and Aphrodite, the goddess of love (*see* **Aphrodite, Cronos** *and* **Gaia**) emerged from the mist enshrouding them.

Venus, *see* Aphrodite

Vertumnus

Vertumnus was the Roman or Italian god of change and the seasons. In common with the Greek sea gods, he had an almost limitless capacity to change his form. He deployed this gift to win over Pomona, a tree-nymph whose

Xanthus and Balius, the immortal horses of Achilles, were exceptionally intelligent and sensitive animals. A youth giving a horse water to drink, painting on a fragment of a vase from Tarente, ca. 380 BCE.

entire life was dedicated to cultivating fruit-trees and was not in the slightest bit interested in love. Vertumnus was besotted with her and revealed himself to her in the form of a peasant, cattle-drover, vegetable-grower, vine-grower, apple-picker, soldier, and fisherman, but it was to no avail. Pomona was only interested in her apples.

Vertumnus then approached her in the guise of an old woman. He heaped praise on her apples and beautiful orchard and went to advise her on how to find a man. Did Vertumnus, who shared her interests and loved her deeply, mean absolutely nothing to her? As a warning of the consequences of adopting too hard-hearted an attitude, he related to her the story of Iphis, a young man hopelessly in love, who hanged himself after the object of his passion, Anaxerete, constantly rejected him. Anaxerete turned to stone when she realized what she had done.

This would not happen to Pomona. When the "old woman," Vertumnus, had finished his tale and regained his own dazzling and youthful form, Pomona immediately fell in love with him.

Vesta, *see* Hestia

Victoria, *see* Nike

Zephyr was a gentle, benevolent wind—although he also had a vicious and grudging side to his character.

Zephyr fathered the immortal horses, Xanthus and Balius, by the Harpy, Podagre. Greek bronze horse, 9th–8th century BCE.

The almighty king of the gods, Zeus, with his scepter in one hand and one of his feared thunderbolts in the other, enthroned on Mount Olympus.

Vulcan, *see* Hephæstos

Xanthus and Balius

Xanthus and Balius were the immortal talking horses of Achilles, the most formidable Greek hero of the Trojan War (see Achilles). These extraordinary beasts were sons of Zephyr the west wind, and the harpy, Podarge, who had one day been grazing in the form of a horse on the banks of the Ocean, the sea that encircled the world. Hera presented the two horses with the gift of speech. The gods gave Xanthus and Balius to Achilles' father Peleus as a wedding gift (*see* **Peleus** and **Thetis**).

When Patroclus, was killed in Achilles chariot drawn by the two horses (*see* **Patroclus**), Xanthus and Balios burst into tears and stopped responding to the commands of Achilles' charioteer, Automedon. Zeus, the king of the gods, took pity on them and blamed himself for the fact that he and the other gods had given the sensitive, immortal horses to Peleus. He made sure that they managed to return to the Greek camp.

When, a short time later, Achilles was preparing for battle, he reproached Xanthus and Balius

for failing to bring back his friend alive from the battlefield. At this Xanthus replied that on this occasion they would bring Achilles back alive, but that he would perish soon afterward and there would be nothing they could do about it. These were the last words he spoke because after that the Erinyes (Fates) silenced the horse.

Zeus once adopted the form of the creature associated with him, the eagle, in order to abduct Ganymede, a handsome youth. These eagles have caught a hare. Silver coin (tetradrachma). Sicily, 5th century BCE.

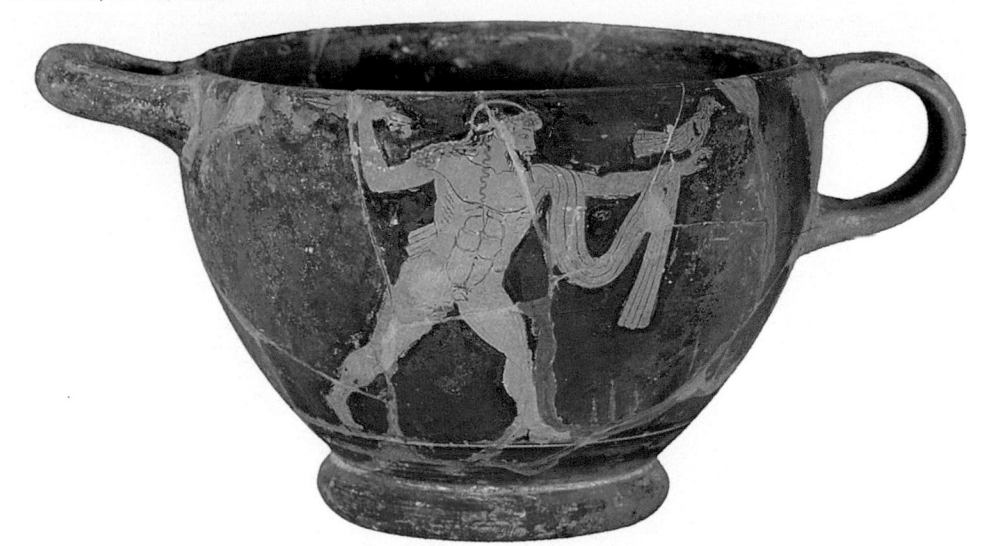

Zephyr

Zephyr, the west-wind, was the son of the Titan Astræus and Eos, the goddess of the dawn. As a gentle and pleasant wind, he countered the venomous Boreas, the North-wind. He fathered Achilles' immortal horses Xanthus and Balius by the harpy Podagre, and, according to some versions, was in love with Hyacinthus. When the god Apollo began a relationship with this handsome youth, Zephyr was apparently so jealous that he blew a discus thrown by Apollo off course so that it hit Hyacinthus' head with fatal consequences (*see* **Hyacinthus**). Zephyr played a more benevolent role in the story of Psyche. When the unfortunate princess was forced to sit on a mountain ridge awaiting the dragon whom an oracle had predicted she must marry, Zephyr picked her up and carried her to Eros. This god would turn out to be her true love (*see* **Psyche**).

Zeus (Roman=Jupiter)

Zeus was the son of the Titans Cronos and Rhea, and he was the king of the Greek gods or the supreme god. He lived on the summit of Mount Olympus, a real mountain around ten thousand feet high, in northeastern Greece. There he dwelt with his sister-wife, Hera, and ten of the other gods.

Zeus is often referred to by the poet, Homer, as the "cloud-gatherer." He ruled and exploited all the forces of the skies, from rain to snow, hail, and thunderstorms. The creature associated with him was the eagle, the bird of prey that rules the skies (Zeus once adopted the form of an eagle to abduct the youth Ganymede with whom he was in love). Zeus' sacred tree was the oak. His weapons were the thunderbolts that he used to strike his adversaries. He also had the ægis, a tasseled or fringed goatskin that he could wear over his shoulders and use as a shield (his daughter Athena also wore the ægis, *see* **Athena**). Zeus would announce his arrival by flourishing the ægis, whereupon the sky would darken, and thunderbolts fly.

Zeus was regarded not just as god of the skies, but also as "the father of gods and man" (an honorary title because although he produced a vast number of divine and mortal descendants, many of the gods were not his children, nor was he was not the creator of mankind). In this role, he granted kingship to nobles, was the protector of family life. and ensured that humans and gods adhered to "standards and values," the unwritten divine laws that could not be broken.

For example, there was the sacred law that hospitality had to be offered to strangers and travelers. Anyone who violated the law of hospitality could count on being severely

Zeus was presented as an imposing, majestic figure with luxuriant hair and a full beard. Silver statue from Egypt, Roman period.

The stalactite cave in Mount Dicte on Crete where Zeus is said to have been raised by the goat or nymph, Amalthea. According to some, this cave was also the birthplace of the king of the gods.

punished by Zeus. Anyone who swore a false oath, or attacked or killed a supplicant at an altar in a temple, would fall into disfavor with the king of the gods.

Zeus could inflict severe punishment on serious transgressors. Tantalus, who offered the gods his son Pelops to eat by way of an experiment, had to endure eternal torment in Tartarus, the most inhospitable part of the underworld (*see* **Tantalus**). The Danaides, who violated the sacred laws of marriage by murdering their husbands on their wedding night, and the villain Sisyphus, who managed to trick death, met a similar fate (*see* **The Danaides** and **Sisyphus**). Not even the gods were allowed to meddle with the basic principles of life and death. When Asclepius, the god of medicine, succeeded in bringing the dead back to life, Zeus punished him with death. The Titan, Prometheus, the tireless champion of the rights of mankind, was exposed to horrific torture on the instructions of an enraged Zeus because he had brought a divine secret—fire—to mankind.

Zeus is portrayed as an imposing, majestic figure with luxuriant locks and a full beard, who kept a watchful eye on the Olympian gods, acting the part of *paterfamilias*, a strict—albeit, sometimes fickle—father figure. The other gods often pursued their own interests, but in the final analysis, Zeus' will was law. The purpose of the meetings Zeus convened on Mount Olympus was therefore not so much to hold discussions but more to enable the king of the gods to announce his most recent decisions. If Zeus wanted to inform mortals of his decisions he would usually do so via omens, such as the flight of the eagle or specific lightning strikes. He would sometimes send the Olympian messengers, Iris or Hermes, to earth to issue detailed instructions.

Zeus was the youngest (according to Homer, the eldest) son of Cronos and Rhea, who had already brought Hestia, Demeter,

Hera, Hades, and Poseidon into the world. Shortly after they were born, their father, knowing that one of his descendants would dethrone him, had taken the precaution of swallowing them. Zeus was spared this grisly fate because Rhea gave her husband a stone wrapped in cloth, instead of the baby. He swallowed it without even looking at it. Zeus was taken to the island of Crete where the nymph or goat, Amalthea, secretly raised him on Mount Ida or Mount Dicte (*see* **Amalthea**). The residents of Arcadia also believed that Zeus was born in their part of the world, but the Cretans steadfastly maintained that his birthplace was a cave on their island. When Zeus was fully grown, he forced Cronos to regurgitate his brothers and sisters, probably

One of Zeus' earthly loves was Leda, whom he seduced in the form of a swan. Sitting on the pillar next to this representation of Leda is a small swan nestling lovingly against her hip. Earthenware statue from Bœotia, 4th century BCE.

with the help of the Oceanid, Metis (the personification of wisdom and intelligence). A power struggle, The War of the Titans, then ensued among the gods over supreme rule (*see* **The Titans**), that ended in victory for Zeus and his brothers, who divided the world between them. Hades was allotted dominion of the underworld, Poseidon, the waters, and Zeus, the sky. As leader of the revolt against the Titans, Zeus was proclaimed king of the gods.

In common with numerous subsequent rulers, be they pharaohs, sultans or American presidents, Zeus was far from monogamous. His official consort was his sister, Hera, the goddess and protector of marriage. Their children were the god of war, Ares, Eileithyia, the goddess of birth, and Hebe, the goddess of youth. Hephæstos, god of the blacksmith's forge and patron of craftsmen, was also regarded as a son of Zeus and Hera, although according to the poet, Hesiod, he was only a son of Hera. Zeus fathered countless other descendants with goddesses, nymphs, and mortal women.

According to Hesiod, Hera was actually Zeus' seventh wife. His first wife was the Oceanid, Metis (the personification of wisdom and intelligence), who became pregnant by him but never gave birth to a child of his. This was because Gaia and Uranus had told Zeus that this child would overthrow him. As a precaution, Zeus swallowed Metis and a short time later their child was born out of the head of the king of the gods himself. This was the goddess Athena (*see* **Athena**).

According to Hesiod, Zeus' second wife was the Titan, Themis, the personification of law. The Fates, the goddesses of human destiny (*see* **the Fates**) were among the children she bore him. Zeus' third wife was the comely Oceanid, Eurynome, by whom he fathered, among others, the Charities or Graces. With his sister, Demeter, he went on to father Persephone, who was later abducted by his brother Hades (*see* **Persephone**). Zeus' next wife was Mnemosyne ("memory") who bore him the Muses. After this, Zeus fathered the twins, Apollo and Artemis, with Leto, and only then, according to Hesiod, did Hera become his consort.

Irrespective of whether she was Zeus' first or seventh wife, Hera was exceedingly jealous, and not without justification. Zeus' lust made him very inventive. For example, he seduced the beautiful princess Danæ, who had been locked up in a bronze tower by her father, in the form of a shower of gold (*see*

Zeus was worshiped throughout the Greek world and beyond. These are the ruins of the altar to Zeus in Pergamon (Asia Minor).

Danæ and **Perseus**), abducted the Phœnician princess Europa by taking the form of a bull (*see* **Europa**) and visited Leda, by whom he fathered Helen and one of the Dioscuri, in the guise of a swan (*see* **Leda**). Hera inflicted terrible punishments on some of Zeus' mistresses and "illegitimate" offspring. Semele, mother of the god of wine and of vegetation, Dionysus, to whom Zeus revealed himself as an "ordinary" mortal, was tricked by Hera into asking him to show himself to her in his true form. This proved fatal for her, since she was unable to withstand the scorching brilliance emanating from the god of the sky (*see* **Semele**). Alcmene, mother of the great hero Heracles, and the hero himself, both had to endure Hera's persecutions from his birth (*see* **Alcmene** *and* **Heracles**). At one point, Zeus became so enraged by her tormenting of Heracles that he suspended her by her wrists with two anvils tied to her feet.

Hera's attempt, assisted by Athena and Poseidon, to chain Zeus and depose him is an illustration of the sorry state of their relationship. This plan failed as a result of the intervention of the Nereid, Thetis, and the hundred-armed giant, Briareus (*see* **Thetis**).

During the Trojan War, Hera had no scruples about deliberately wronging her husband to enable the Greeks, whom she favored, to make headway in the battle. To this end, she once called on Hypnos, the god of sleep, for assistance. She bribed him by promising him the hand of one of the Charities or Fates (*see* **Hypnos**).

Tales such as these indicate that Zeus' omnipotence was not absolute and unshakeable. This notion was reinforced by the belief that Zeus was at the mercy of the whims of the Fates, the three goddesses who acted as personifications of fate. That is why the king of the gods sometimes had to resign himself to events he found dreadful, such as the death of a mortal he loved. Other accounts, however, create the impression that it was actually Zeus, and Zeus alone, who decided what happened in the world (*see* **The Fates**).

The worship of Zeus began very early on throughout the Greek world. There was a major shrine to Zeus in Dodona, in Epirus. From a sacred oak tree, that functioned as an oracle, he revealed his views to men and predicted their future by rustling the tree's leaves. Zeus' opinion or intentions could also be inferred from thunderbolts and the flight of birds, in particular the eagle.

Olympia (not to be confused with Mount Olympus) was one of the centers of the worship of Zeus, and it is here that the Olympic Games were held every four years in his honor. A magnificent temple dedicated to Zeus stood here, which held the famous, statue of the king of gods, sculpted by Phidias that stood forty feet high and was hailed as one of the seven wonders of the world.

Zeus' Roman counterpart was Jupiter, the god of the sky and the weather. The best-known temple dedicated to Jupiter stands on the Capitoline Hill, overlooking the Roman Forum .

Bibliography

Æschylus	David Green (Editor), Richmond Lattimore (Editor), *The Complete Greek Tragedies: Æschylus*, University of Chicago Press: Chicago, June 1992.
Apollonius of Rhodes	R. L. Hunter (Editor), *Apollonius of Rhodes: Argonautica*, Cambridge University Press: Cambridge, June 1989.
Apuleius	Robert Graves (translator), *The Golden Ass: The Transformations of Lucius*, Noonday Press: New York, August 1998
Bonnefoy, Yves	Wendy Doniger (Translator), *Greek and Egyptian Mythologies,* University of Chicago Press; Chicago, June 1991
Bourbon, Fabio	Fabio Bourbon (Editor), *Lost Civilizations: Rediscovering the Great Cultures of the Past*, White Star Editions, USA, November 2001.
Braakhuis, H.E.M.	Braakhuis, H.E.M., "The Way of All Flesh, Sexual Implications of the Mayan Hunt," in *Anthropos* 96.2001: 391-409, Friburg, Switzerland, 2001
Catullus	Guy Lee (Translator), *The Poems of Catullus* (Oxford World's Classics), Reprint edition, Oxford University Press; Oxford, September 1998
Cotterell, Arthur	Arthur Cotterell, *Encyclopedia Of Mythology*, Lorenz Books: Bath & London 2000.
D'Aulaire, Edgar	Edgar Parin D'Aulaire, *D'Aulaire's Book of Greek Myths*, Doubleday; New York, October 1962
Euripides	David Green and Richmond Lattimore (Eds.), *The Complete Greek Tragedies: Euripides*. University of Chicago Press: Chicago, June 1992.
Euripides	James Morwood (Translator), *The Trojan Women and Other Plays*, Oxford University Press: Oxford, November 2001.
Euripides	Paul Roche (Translator), *Ten Plays by Euripides*, Signet Classic, Penguin Putnam Inc.: New York, October 1998
Evslin, Bernard	Bernard Evslin, *Gods and Monsters of Greek Myths*, MacMillan Publishing Company: New York, June 1967.
Grant, Michael and John Hazel	Michael Grant and John Hazel, *Who's Who in Classical Mythology*, Routledge, London and New York, 2002.
Graves, Robert	*The Greek Myths*, parts 1 and 2, Penguin Books: Harmondsworth Middlesex, 1990.

Gibbon, Edward
Gibbon's The Decline and Fall of the Roman Empire, Fawcett Books, New York, June 1994.

Harries, Jill Dana
"Resolving Disputes: The Frontiers of Law in Late Antiquity," in R.E.Mathisen (ed.) *Law, Society and Authority in Late Antiquity*, Oxford University Press: Oxford 2001.

Herodotus
John M. Marincola, Aubrey De Selincourt (Introduction), *Herodotus: The Histories* (Penguin Classics), Penguin USA, New York, September 1996.

Hesiod
M.L. West (translator), *Theogony* and *Works and Days*; Oxford University Press: Oxford, 1999.

Homer
Hugh G. Evelyn-White (Translator), *Homeric Hymns. Epic Cycle. Homerica*, Harvard University Press: Harvard, July 1936.

Homer
Robert Fagles (Translator), *The Iliad/The Odyssey*, Penguin USA: New York, November 1999.

Horace
David Mankin (Editor), *Horace: Epodes*, Cambridge University Press: Cambridge, UK, November 1995.

Ions, Veronica
Egyptian Mythology, Paul Hamlyn, Feltham, UK, 1968.

Kerényi, C.
The Gods of the Greeks, Thames & Hudson: London & New York, 2000.

Kerényi, C.
The Heroes of the Greeks, Thames & Hudson: London & New York, 2000.

Kirk, G.S.
The Nature of Greek Myths, Penguin Books: Harmondsworth Middlesex, UK, 1990.

Leick, Gwendolyn
A Dictionary of Ancient Near Eastern Mythology, Routledge:London & New York, 1998.

Ovid
A. D. Melville (Translator), E. J. Kenney (Introduction), *Metamorphoses*, Oxford University Press: Oxford, June 1998.

Plato
John M. Cooper (Editor), D. S. Hutchinson (Editor), *Plato: Complete Works,* Hackett Publishing Company: Indianapolis, May 1997.

Sophocles
Dudley Fitts (Translator), Robert Fitzgerald (Translator), *Sophocles, The Œdipus Cycle: Œdipus Rex, Œdipus at Colonus, Antigone,* Harcourt, Inc.: Orlando, Florida, November 2002.

Strassler, Robert B.
Victor Davis Hanson (Introduction), *Thucydides: A Comprehensive Guide to the Peloponnesian War,* Touchstone Books: Carmichael, USA. September 1998.

Storm, Rachel
The Ultimate Encyclopedia of Mythology, Anness Publishing: London, 2000.

Virgil   Charles J. Billson, *The Æneid*, Dover Publications: Mineola, USA, October 1995.

Virgil   R. G. G. Coleman (Editor), *Virgil: Eclogues*, Cambridge University Press: Cambridge, UK. April 1977.

Woodford, Susan   Susan Woodford, *Images of Myths in Classical Antiquity*, Cambridge University Press: Cambridge, UK. December 2002.

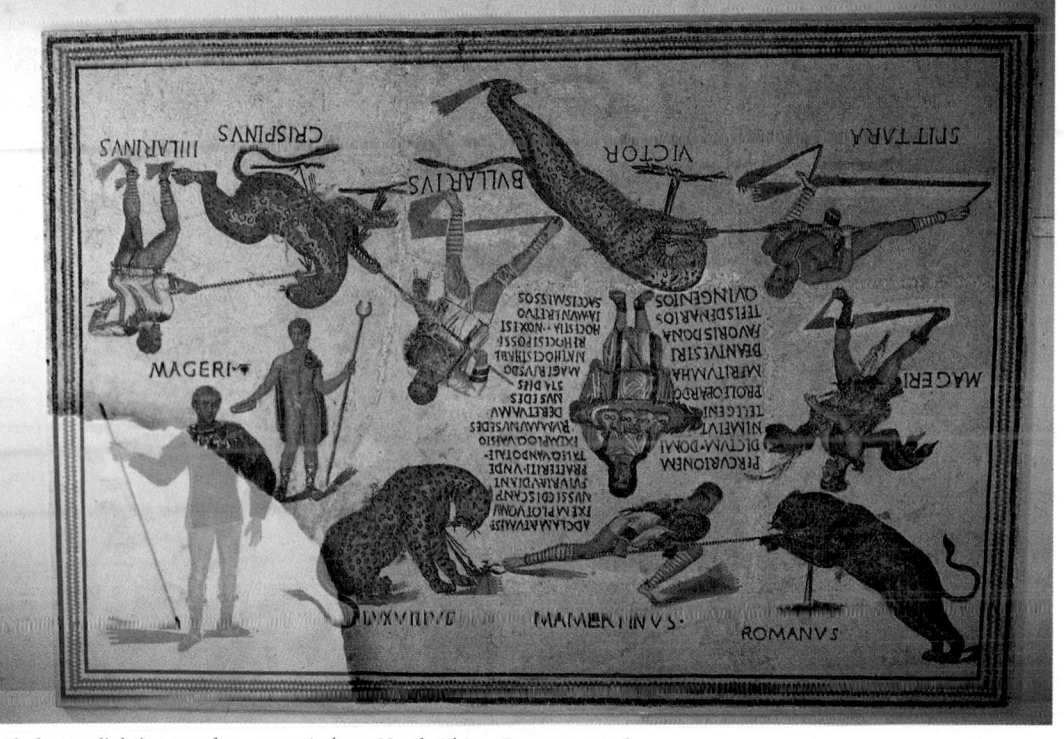

Gladiators fighting panthers, mosaic from North Africa, Roman period.

Index

Cecrops 68, 77, 145
centaurs 63, 64, 78, 81, 133, 152, 173, 228, 241
Centaurus 152
Cerberus 79, 139, 219, 229, 242
Ceryneian hind 133
Chaos 108, 112, 251
chariots 46, 79, 149, 257
Charon 80, 118, 139, 146, 192, 219
Charybdis 58, 83, 182, 228, 231
Chimæra 72, 79, 80, 251
Chiron 24, 29, 54, 63, 78, 81, 133, 153
Chloris 51, 82, 157, 176
Circe 57, 82, 125, 146, 159, 181, 228, 231, 232, 236
Clio 48
Clymene 205
Clytemnestra 26, 36, 68, 77, 102, 104, 107, 123, 151, 156, 189
Cœus 247
Colossus of Rhodes 125
Cos 63
Creon 45, 83, 154, 161, 187, 233, 241, 246
Crete 59, 74, 88, 120, 129
Cretan bull 135, 238
Crius 247
Cronos 15, 46, 58, 81, 84, 86, 92, 106, 110, 112, 114, 117, 127, 147, 193, 208, 214, 222, 227, 243, 247, 251, 254
Cybele 65, 71, 85, 92, 164, 222
Cyclops 84, 112, 119, 125, 181, 206, 251
Cycnus 26, 141, 206, 209
Corinth 58, 60, 72, 84, 131, 154, 155, 161, 166, 200, 232, 237, 238

D
Dædalus 31, 59, 87, 166, 167, 198, 238
Danæ 89, 202, 257
Danaids 89, 119, 234, 255
Daphne 20, 51, 90, 109
Daphnis 91, 145
Deianeira 79, 100, 139
Delphi 31, 49, 54, 74, 102, 107, 113, 131, 140, 148, 153, 154, 156, 167, 173, 186, 190, 236, 241, 248
Demeter 74, 84, 85, 92, 97, 112, 119, 124, 139, 199, 201, 209, 218, 222, 232, 234, 255, 257
Deucalion 94, 215
Dido 19, 34, 48, 109, 220
Diomedes 33, 49, 54, 96, 135, 163, 179
Dionysia 100
Dionysus 47, 59, 74, 79, 91, 115, 126, 133, 141, 145, 148, 149, 157, 164, 174, 193, 227, 229, 230, 233, 240, 243, 246, 249, 250, 257
Dioscuri 55, 102, 123, 131, 156, 172, 206, 242, 257

Dolon 97

E
Echo 171
Electra 36, 104, 189
Eleusian Mysteries 92, 139
Elysium 40, 74, 119, 162, 163, 193, 222
Endymion 105, 229
Eos 73, 105, 113, 114, 190, 253
Epidaurus 63
Epimetheus 247
Erichthonius 68, 77
Erinyes 34, 68, 105, 106, 112, 114, 189, 252, 253
Eris 24, 48, 107, 129, 196, 244
Eros 46, 47, 90, 108, 159, 215, 254
Erymanthian boar 79, 133
Eteocles 45, 83, 188, 241, 246
Etruscans 34
Eumenides 107
Euphrosyne 79
Euripides 19, 39, 43, 72, 77, 105, 124, 143, 162, 186, 189, 207, 236, 241
Europa 73, 109, 146, 165, 222, 226, 257
Eurus 110, 176
Eurydice 12, 119, 157, 191
Eurynome 126, 257
Eurystheus 40, 70, 79, 147

F
Fates 39, 115, 168, 250, 257
Faunus 110, 195
Flora 82
Fortuna 111

G
Gaia 15, 49, 67, 69, 84, 86, 107, 108, 112, 114, 138, 147, 177, 205, 206, 209, 222, 247, 249, 251
Ganymede 113, 254
Geryones 136
Gigantes 40, 94, 112, 114, 130, 140, 252
Glaucus 228
golden fleece 54, 153, 159, 191, 240, 248
Gorgon 44, 67, 72, 79, 89, 136, 202, 209
gorgons 116
griffons 117, 171
gryphons 117, 171

H
Hades 14, 39, 79, 80, 84, 86, 92, 93, 112, 117, 124, 139, 146, 181, 192, 201, 208, 219, 222, 232, 234, 236, 242, 248, 250, 255, 257
Harmonia 47, 74, 100, 149, 229
Harpies 33, 55, 73, 120, 253
Hebe 127, 142, 256
Hecabe 26, 121, 207, 212

Acknowledgements

The author would like to thank the following individuals and agencies without whose help or helpful collaboration this book would not have been written.

Allard Pierson Museum, Amsterdam, Artis Planetarium, Amsterdam, Fokke van Balen, Maarten van Balen, B. te Boekhorst, Museum Boijmans Van Beuningen, Rotterdam, Michiel Bootsman, Dick Coert, Kitty Coert, Dordrechts Museum, Dordrecht, Renate Hagenouw, Peter Homan, Frans de Jong, Geralda Jurriaans-Helle, H. Knol, Janneke Maas, Phœbe Maas, Surhuisterveen Coins and Medals, Christine Waslander, Mieke Zilverberg.

Gold coin (⅙ stater) from Cyzicus, 5th century BCE.

Picture Credits

Janneke Maas drew the illustrations especially for this book. The photographs were taken and/or provided by:

rb, 177 m, 182 lb, 183 t, 193 b, 199 t, 207 lt, 209 t, 211 lt, 216, 223 b, 223 0, 224 b, 224 0, 225 b, 227 lt, 246, 247 t, 249 b, 249 t, 251, 261.
Mieke Zilverberg, **art dealer**
pages 99 rt, 116 rb, 120, 162 lt, 185, 231 m.

Coins and Medals, Surhuisterveen:
pages 10 rb, 39 t, 66 rt, 80 m, 94 lb, 94 rb, 105 rt, 114 lb, 132 lt, 135 lb, 142 rt, 152 rt, 159 b, 174 lt, 183 b, 214 rt, 233 b, 250 rb, 250 rt, 267.